Tony Hillerman's Navajoland

Tony Hillerman's Navajoland

Hideouts, Haunts, and Havens in the
Joe Leaphorn and Jim Chee
Mysteries

Laurance D. Linford

THE UNIVERSITY OF UTAH PRESS

Salt Lake City

06 05 04 03 02 01
5 4 3 2 1

Library of Congress Cataloging-in-Publication Data

Linford, Laurance D.
Tony Hillerman's Navajoland : hideouts, haunts, and havens in the Joe
Leaphorn and Jim Chee mysteries / Laurance D. Linford.
p.   cm.
Includes bibliographical references and index.
ISBN 0-87480-698-4 (pbk. : alk. paper)
1. Hillerman, Tony—Settings—Dictionaries. 2. Leaphorn, Joe, Lt.
(Fictitious character) Dictionaries. 3. Detective and mystery stories,
American—Dictionaries. 4. Southwestern States—In literature—
Dictionaries 5. Four Corners Region—In literature—Dictionaries.
6. Chee, Jim (Fictitious character)—Dictionaries. 7. Navajo
Indians in literature—Dictionaries. 8. Police in
literature—Dictionaries. I. Title.
PS3558.I45 Z76 2001
813'.54—dc21
2001002731

To my sons,
Justin and Micah
What they've taught me of life
has made mine a better one.

Contents

Illustrations

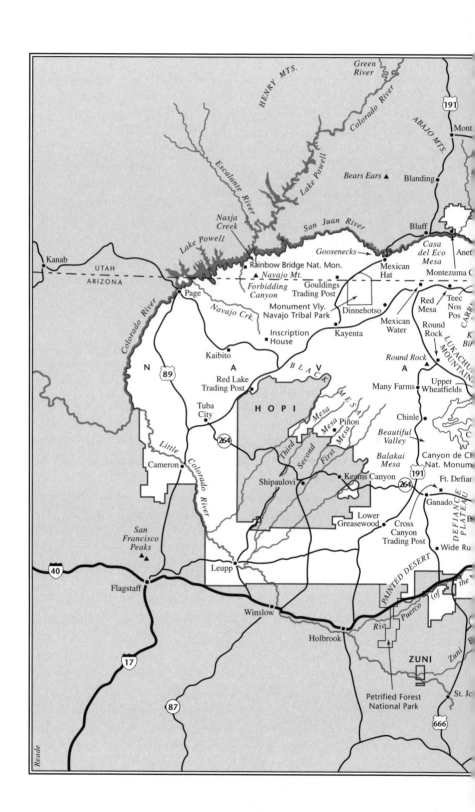

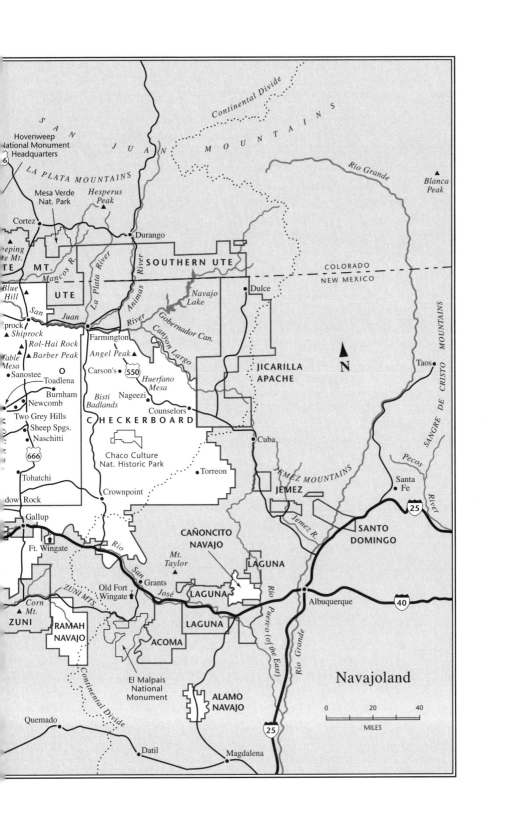

Hovenweep
National Monument
Headquarters

S A N

J U A N

M O U N T A I N S

Continental Divide

Rio Grande

▲ *Blanca Peak*

LA PLATA MOUNTAINS

Mesa Verde
Nat. Park

Hesperus Peak

Cortez

Durango

eping Mt.

MT.

SOUTHERN UTE

Mancos R.

COLORADO
NEW MEXICO

UTE

UTE

La Plata River

Animas River

Navajo Lake

Dulce

Blue Hill ▲

San Juan

River

Gobernador Can.

Canyon Largo

JICARILLA
APACHE

Taos ▲

prock ▲ *Shiprock*

Farmington

Angel Peak ▲ ▲

N

SANGRE DE CRISTO MOUNTAINS

▲ *Rol-Hai Rock*
▲ *Barber Peak*

Carson's • 550

Huerfano Mesa

able Mesa

• Sanostee

Toadlena

Bisti Badlands

Nageezi •

Counselors •

Burnham

Newcomb

Two Grey Hills

Pecos River

Cuba •

Santa
Fe •

Sheep Spgs.

Naschitti

C H E C K E R B O A R D

666

Chaco Culture
Nat. Historic Park

JEMEZ MOUNTAINS

Tohatchi

Torreon •

JEMEZ

25

dow Rock

Crownpoint •

SANTO
DOMINGO

Gallup

CAÑONCITO
NAVAJO

Ft. Wingate •

Rio

Mt. Taylor ▲

LAGUNA

San

Grants •

LAGUNA

José

Old Fort
Wingate ⌂

LAGUNA

Albuquerque •

40

ZUNI MTS

Corn ▲ *Mt.*

ZUNI

RAMAH
NAVAJO

Rio Puerco (of the East)

Rio Grande

LAGUNA

ACOMA

Continental Divide

El Malpais
National
Monument

ALAMO
NAVAJO

Navajoland

Quemado •

25

0   20   40

MILES

Datil •

Magdalena •

Foreword

This book is more a digression from, rather than a continuation of, a decade-long project of Laurance D. Linford to sort out the mysteries of places and place names in Diné Bikéyah (Navajo Land). Mr. Linford served as an archaeologist for the Navajo Nation and as Executive Director of the Inter-Tribal Indian Ceremonial Association and is an acknowledged authority on the naming of places throughout the Four Corners Indian Country. Thus the reader must wonder how a fiction writer such as myself became involved in his project. I will try to explain.

The root cause is that Linford and I share a deep respect for both the Navajo culture and the dramatic landscape of the Four Corners country they share with other tribes. Most of my stories involve two fictional members of the Navajo Tribal Police, Lieutenant Joe Leaphorn and Sergeant Jim Chee. While I don't claim the sort of certified knowledge of Southwestern tribes that would be recognized in academia, I do claim a long and active interest in Native America. In Navajos, that dates back to 1945, when I witnessed part of an Enemyway ceremonial on the Checkerboard Reservation. My interest in general, however, goes back to 1931, when I was a six-year-old first-grader in an Indian school in Oklahoma.

The Indians of my childhood were mostly Citizen Band Potawatomies and Seminoles. They were farmers like us, fully assimilated and no more interesting to me than my other friends. But the Navajo curing ceremonial I happened upon was fascinating. I was just back from the war in Europe, sans any special welcome, and here were two Navajo Marines back from the war in the Pacific, surrounded by friends and family and being formally and ritually cleansed of their exposure to death and hatred and restored to the wonderful harmony of the Navajos. I was given a glimpse of people who had kept their religion and cultural values strong, welcoming home two of their warriors with a ceremony of love and healing. I liked that idea a lot.

That memory was strong twenty years later when I decided to try to write a novel. I'd base it on the Navajo Reservation. I'd devise a plot that would make the Diné culture and landscape of the reservation germane to the plot. In this first effort, I spent a lot of pages acquainting the readers with the canyons draining the Chuska Mountain Range, and the mystery is solved by what Leaphorn learns at an Enemyway ceremony. I've followed pretty much the same idea ever since, causing my Navajo policemen to travel back and forth across the Four Corners country, as far south as Corn Mountain in Zuni Land, as far northwest as the badlands beyond Tuba City, as far east as Mount Taylor, and as far north as Montezuma Creek.

Thus, while our methods were totally different, Mr. Linford and I were writing about the same people and the same territory. We encountered each other's work. I was immensely impressed by his *Navajo Places,* and recommend it to all who want to learn about the history and culture of the Navajo people, and the role Navajos played in the history of the the American Southwest. I welcomed the opportunity to work with Mr. Linford when he suggested we apply his special knowledge of the history, legends, and mythology to the places where my plots are set to give readers a sort of informed and enlightened tour of the scenes where my fictional Lieutenant Joe Leaphorn and Sergeant Jim Chee are solving their fictional mysteries.

To explain why, I will recall a westward flight from Albuquerque. The pilot was on the public address system identifying what we were flying over. The mountain to the right, he said, was Mount Taylor, an extinct volcano over 11,000 feet high with its dried lava flow forming El Malpais monument. Had he known, he might also have told us that before we Whites re-named it after a deceased president, it was Dootł'izhii Dziil, the sacred Turquoise Mountain of Navajo mythology. It was built by the supernatural First Man, decorated with mist and turquoise beads. It is one of the four Navajo sacred boundary-marker mountains. It is one of the sacred mountains brought up from a previous world.

Here the spirit of Blue Bead Girl lives and here the sons of Changing Woman began their campaign to free the Glittering World from the monsters created by human evils. Here they killed Ye'iitsoh, the leader of the Enemy Gods, and it is his dried blood that forms the black ocean of malpais (Spanish for "badlands") below. The pilot might also have mentioned that this is Dark Mountain to some of the Rio Grande Pueblo peoples, where their own War Gods stand guard against evil, and a sacred place as well as for the Zunis to the south.

I'm sure the pilot's omissions weren't caused by disrespect for earlier American cultures. It was the product of universal ignorance on the part of the great American public of Indian religions, tribal value systems, all things foreign to our dominant system.

Mr. Linford and I agree that this is a case in which ignorance is not bliss. We agree that the beauty of the Four Corners Country is enhanced when one sees the history, legends, and mythology that hang over it all.

—Tony Hillerman

Preface

In the spring of 2000, the University of Utah Press published my book *Navajo Places: History, Legend, Landscape.* This compendium of geographical places important to Navajo history, ceremonialism, and commerce was going to press when the publisher took the daring step of asking Tony Hillerman to review the manuscript in light of his considerable fame as the author of 14 mysteries taking place in Navajo country.

Mr. Hillerman consented to the review, and his comments were so favorable that, tongue in cheek, I asked the University of Utah Press if we might not move a few more copies of my book if we changed the title to *Tony Hillerman's Navajo Places* as a marketing ploy.

We all chuckled over the audacity of that notion, but it actually planted the seeds for a more realistic one, for I recalled that my enjoyment of the Hillerman novels was enriched by my familiarity with the places as I read. As I observed the way in which Tony infuses into his stories the Navajo affinity for—and sense of stewardship of—the land, the logic of the project became even more apparent.

About the time *Navajo Places* was released, I suggested a new project to the Press: a melding of the previous book with all 14 of Hillerman's Navajoland novels. This project would combine the cultural-historical elements of my book with descriptions of how the places fit into Hillerman's stories.

The Press liked the idea, but only if I could get Mr. Hillerman to consent to the use of his name in the title, and if he would contribute to the project. I sent Tony a proposal, and the rest is, as they say, history.

I re-read all of Tony's 14 Joe Leaphorn–Jim Chee mysteries, taking copious notes on places as their role in the stories became apparent. The resulting list of places included about one-third of those discussed in *Navajo Places,* plus a few that had not been included in that tome.

The goal of this book is to present the reader with verbal portraits of the haunts and hideouts that serve as backdrop to Hillerman's yarns. Elaborations on the necessarily brief snapshots Tony serves up in the stories are embellished with notes on history and Navajo cultural significance attributed to the places. The places are listed alphabetically, and each is accompanied by a novel-by-novel discussion of how it fits into Mr. Hillerman's plots.

In the first draft of this book, I included page numbers from the Hillerman novels in my possession for my own reference and to make it easier for readers to find the same information. This would have created something of a dilemma for dedicated bibliographers, I realized, due to the number of editions published for each book and differences in pagination from one edition to the next. In purely scholarly works, it is best to reference first editions (unless, of course, revisions have rendered earlier editions obsolete—rarely the case in a work of fiction). I intend this book, however, as much for enjoyment as for academic pursuits. Moreover the average reader of Hillerman's novels is more likely to be carrying around a well-worn, mass-market paperback edition than a first edition. But in the end the country itself decided the issue: it proved impossible to acquire a complete set of the 14 Hillerman books in any single edition in the small, reservation border town of Gallup, New Mexico, where I live and write. Deadline constraints also prohibited me from spending additional time seeking specific editions elsewhere. In agreement with the publisher, I deleted the page numbers prior to publication but kept references to the chapter numbers in each book. I give my apologies to any readers who are inconvenienced.

I hope that this book will serve as both a visitor's guide to the land of Tony Hillerman's mysteries and an album for those who cannot make the trip themselves. Toward this end, I have included my own photographs of some 50 of the places listed. It was my initial intent to include pictures of the most "important" places, but then I decided that most of those have been photographed ad nauseam and chose to focus on some of the lesser-known places. Few of the pictures were taken expressly for this book, as most come from my personal collection, taken during extensive travels and labors in Navajoland over the past twenty-three years for the dual purposes of preserving memories and documenting change in region.

Acknowledgments

I would be remiss if I did not recognize a few people who played important roles in the successful completion of this volume. First, I must thank Tony Hillerman for taking time from his relentlessly demanding schedule to assist me in this endeavor. He was always ready to answer questions, despite being under the deadline gun himself.

Jeff Grathwohl, Director of the University of Utah Press, was ever encouraging and enthusiastic about the project, and without the initial efforts by Marcelyn Ritchie in contacting Mr. Hillerman about my previous book *(Navajo Places),* the project might never have been conceived.

And, as always, I must thank my wife, Karen, for her endless patience, her abundant encouragement, and her assistance.

The Places

ABAJO MOUNTAINS: San Juan County, UT. Also Blue Mountains. Navajos call this range Dził Ditł'ooí, or "Fuzzy Mountain." These high, steep mountains rising five miles east of Monticello include Abajo Peak (11,360 ft), Mount Linaeus (10,959 ft), and Blue Mountain (11,209 ft). Mount Linaeus is called Nát'ohdziil, "Tobacco Mountain," by the Navajos.

First surveyed in 1873, these mountains were badly overgrazed by Mormon stock throughout the 1870s. Ute Indians from this region were considered a bad influence on northern Navajos, and by the mid-1880s a company of soldiers was stationed in the area. In June and July 1884, Utes were blamed for the loss of 150 horses and 750 cattle in the region.

The Abajos are important to the Navajo Ghostway tradition of the Male Shootingway ceremony, and both Navajos and Zunis traditionally hunted in these mountains.

✤ Role in Hillerman Fiction:

Coyote Waits: These mountains are visible to the northwest as Janet Pete and Jim Chee approach Red Rock, New Mexico (chap. 6).

ACOMA PUEBLO: (7000 ft) (Population: 2,590) Cibola County, NM. Navajos call this Keresan village Haak'oh, "Acoma," from the native Keresan name of the pueblo, meaning "People of the White Rock." It is perhaps best known as "Sky City." Old Spanish documents refer to the community as "the Kingdom of Hacus," "Acus," and "San Estevan de Acoma." The pueblo is located 14 miles south of Interstate 40, some 56 miles west of Albuquerque. According to Van Valkenburgh, the community had a population of 1,210 in 1940.

Sitting atop a 357-ft-high mesa, the pueblo was reached by a single trail before the road was constructed. Captain Alvarado of the Coronado Expedition described the pueblo in 1540 as having two hundred houses. Three miles east of this mesa is the famed Enchanted Mesa, of traditional importance to the Acomas, and with sheer walls that have been ascended by very few Whites. Some anthropologists believe its people to be related to those of the pueblo of Zia.

Historically, the pueblo was well known for its stalwart unfriendliness to Whites, a condition brought about by the January 22, 1599, attack on the pueblo by Vicente de Zaldívar. Approximately 800 Acomas were killed in the attack, and all male captives over 25 years of age were sentenced to have one hand and one foot cut off, and to 20 years "personal service" (slavery). All males between the ages of 12 and 25 were sentenced to 20 years of servitude, as were all females above the age of 12.

During the time of the seventeenth-century Spanish explorer Espejo, the Acoma people farmed fields to the north of the village, but no permanent settlements were built until the 1863–64 Navajo deportation to Fort Sumner ended Diné raiding.

The village has been continuously occupied, except for very short intervals, and competes with the Hopi village of Oraibi for the title of the oldest continually occupied settlement in North America. Acomita, San Fidel, and McCarty's are all Acoma colonies.

✦ Role in Hillerman Fiction:

The Ghostway: When Jim Chee discovers that the medicine man at Two Story (who can conduct the five-day Ghostway) is in Cañoncito performing the ceremony on a girl named Sosi, he is at once elated at finding Margaret Billy Sosi once again, but dismayed at the distance he will have to travel—to the region near Acoma and Laguna Pueblos (chap. 24).

AGUA SAL CREEK: Apache County, AZ. Also Agua Sal Wash. Navajos refer to this stream as Tó Dík'óózh, meaning "Saline Water" or "Bitter Water," which approximates the Spanish "Aqua Sal," which means "Salt Water." This 25-mile-long, often-dry creek runs northwest from the vicinity of Tsaile (about 7000 ft). It flows into Lukachukai Wash just north of Navajo Route 12, 10 miles southeast of that wash's confluence with Chinle Wash.

✦ Role in Hillerman Fiction:

The Blessing Way: Joe Leaphorn drives past here while trying to figure out what the Big Navajo was doing on Ceniza Mesa (chap. 15).

ALBUQUERQUE: (5000 ft) (Population: 419,311) Bernalillo County, NM. In Navajo, this city is Bee'eldííldahsinil, "At the Place of the (Bell) Peals." New Mexico's largest city, Albuquerque is located near the geographic center of the state, straddling the Rio Grande at the western foot of the 10,678-ft Sandia Mountains. Interstate 25 and Interstate 40 intersect near the city's center.

Roughly the same elevation as Denver (5000 ft), Albuquerque was founded by Spaniards in 1706 in an effort to colonize and promote protection from Indian attacks along the lower Rio Grande Valley.

The city was named by its founder for Don Francisco Fernandez de la Cueva Enriques, Duke de Alburquerque, the 34th Viceroy of New Spain. (The

first "r" was later dropped.) The origin of the word itself is commonly attributed to the Latin *albus quercus,* meaning "white oak." However, an alternative
is that the word derives from the Arabic *al-barquq,* meaning "plum." (Spain
was occupied by the Arabs from the eighth century until 1492, and remains
today rich in Arabic influence.)

Ranchos in this vicinity were raided by Navajos as early as March 1786.
Many military expeditions against the Navajos were launched from or
marched through Albuquerque—with varying levels of success. (Colonel Andrew W. Doniphan led a column from the city on October 26, 1846, intending
to impress and contain the Navajos, only to have the Navajos attack the city
later the same day.)

Today Albuquerque houses the Indian Pueblo Cultural Center, the University of New Mexico, the Southwest Indian Polytechnic Institute, the Maxwell
Museum of Anthropology, the Atomic Museum, the Museum of Albuquerque, and the New Mexico Museum of Natural History. Many eastern
Navajos conduct business there, and a sizable community of Navajos resides
in the city.

❖ Role in Hillerman Fiction:

Albuquerque is Hillerman's most commonly mentioned metropolitan
city, and figures into ten of the Leaphorn/Chee novels. Though the city is normally a background to the plot, primary action takes place here in two of the
stories.

The Blessing Way: The home of anthropologist Bergen McKee is located
here (chap. 2).

Listening Woman: Leaphorn visits FBI agent George Witover here about
the Buffalo Society's Santa Fe armored truck robbery, and the capture of John
Tull (chap. 11).

People of Darkness: A bomb explodes in the back of a pickup truck in the
parking lot of the Cancer Treatment Center on the University of New Mexico
north campus (chap. 1). Jim Chee attended the University of New Mexico
here (chap. 11). Chee is hospitalized at Bernalillo County Medical Center
(now called UNM Hospital) here after being wounded in an ambush in El
Malpais (chap. 15).

The Dark Wind: It is surmised that the jewelry stolen in the burglary of
Burnt Water Trading Post would turn up in Albuquerque, Durango, Phoenix,
or Farmington (chap. 3).

The Ghostway: Jim Chee had not often thought of himself by his secret
war name, Long Thinker, since his years at the University of New Mexico in
Albuquerque (chap. 8). Chee considered the housing in Gorman's Los Angeles neighborhood a little worse than the neighborhood he had lived in while

attending the University of New Mexico in Albuquerque, but a little better than the average housing in Shiprock (chap. 12). Chee had seen prostitutes in Gallup and in Albuquerque at state fair time, but not like the children plying the trade in Los Angeles (chap. 14). From Jimmy Yellow's place on Mesa Gigante, the view is extraordinary, taking in the valley of the Rio Puerco, the Sandia Mountains and the lights of Albuquerque to the east, and the Sangre de Cristos to the north (chap. 25).

A Thief of Time: Eleanor Friedman-Bernal was unable to find ammunition for her odd-caliber pistol in Albuquerque (chap. 1). Joe Leaphorn flies into and out of here on a trip to Washington, D.C., to visit Nelson's (and ultimately Richard Dumond) (chap. 12). Friedman-Bernal's project supervisor, Lehman, is in Albuquerque (chap. 10).

Coyote Waits: Ashie Pinto once traveled to Albuquerque with Dr. Bourebonette to listen to tapes of interviews on Navajo ceremonialism (chap. 3). Jim Chee visits UNM Hospital's Burns and Trauma Unit here for treatment on his burned hand (chap. 4). Chee's erstwhile love interest, Janet Pete, is a Public Defender in Albuquerque. At the University of New Mexico (UNM) library, Chee listens to tapes of Ashie Pinto that were last checked out by William Redd (chap. 7). Chee visits the UNM History Department in search of Dr. Tagert, and instead meets Tagert's assistant, Jean Jacobs (chap. 8). Chee then visits William Redd's home, noticing that Redd is a pack rat and collector of stamps and coins. It is here Chee learns of Tagert's theory that the famous outlaw Butch Cassidy died on the Navajo Reservation (chap. 9).

Sacred Clowns: Sergeant Harold Blizzard is stationed at the BIA police office in Albuquerque (chap. 3). The FBI maintains an office here as well (chap. 3). The body of murdered clown Frances Sayesva is sent to Albuquerque for autopsy (chap. 3). Joe Leaphorn remembers that his wife, Emma, would get nervous when she was away from home, even if it was only to Albuquerque (chap. 7). BIA Law Enforcement Sergeant Harold Blizzard is telling the Feds in Albuquerque he has caught Delmar Kanitewa, when Kanitewa takes off from Blizzard's car, where he had been left unattended (chap. 10). The FBI office here blames BIA Police Sergeant Harold Blizzard for Kanitewa's escape from Blizzard's car (chap. 12). The FBI and the BIA set up a cross-jurisdictional arrangement for Joe Leaphorn (chap. 14). Frances Sayesva had driven to Tano Pueblo from here the day of his murder at Tano (chap. 14).

The Fallen Man: Just out of law school, Janet Pete worked for "Granger-hyphen-Smith's" Albuquerque office (chap. 6). John McDermott calls Joe Leaphorn from Albuquerque to ask him to help the Breedlove family investigate the death of Hal Breedlove and any connection with the Fallen Man's skeleton on Shiprock (chap. 10). Years ago, McDermott had taken advantage of the professor/student relationship when he seduced Janet Pete and took her to Albuquerque as a live-in intern prior to taking her to Washington, D.C., where he broke her heart (chap. 15). Hosteen Sam's log notes the arrival at Shiprock of three climbers in a "funny, green van" on a day when his daughter Lucy is in Albuquerque, about the time Hal Breedlove disappeared (chap. 18).

The First Eagle: FBI Agent Jay Kennedy calls Leaphorn from here about Jim Chee's unauthorized recording of an FBI agent telling him to destroy evidence (chap. 26).

AMBROSIA LAKE: (6971 ft) McKinley County, NM. Navajos call the lake Bits'ádi, translation uncertain. The full Spanish name is La Laguna del Difunta Ambrosio, named for a man killed by arrows, whose body was found in the seasonal lake bed. Three miles southeast of the dry lake bed is a uranium processing plant located on New Mexico Highway 509 five miles northeast of its junction with New Mexico Highway 53.

❖ Role in Hillerman Fiction:

People of Darkness: Jim Chee and his pursuer, Colton Wolf, pass the uranium mills here on their way to the Bisti country (chap. 29).

ANETH: (4550 ft) San Juan County, UT. The Navajo name is T'áá Bíích'įįdii, meaning "One Who Barely Gets Along" (apparently referring to an early trader who was so feeble he appeared barely able to take another step). This community is located in extreme southeastern Utah on Utah Highway 262, at the juncture of McElmo Creek and the San Juan River. Founded in the early 1880s, Aneth Trading Post was first called Riverview. It was established on the north bank of the San Juan River, near the mouth of McElmo Creek, by Owen Edgar Noland in 1885. By 1886, the community was called Holyoak (after another early settler).

Although the region known as the Aneth Strip had been a part of the Navajo habitat since prior to the Long Walk to Fort Sumner, it was not affixed to the reservation until the first half of this century (by a presidential Executive Order of 1905 and by an Act of Congress in March 1933).

Henry L. Mitchell and his partner, named Daugherty, were traders in the region in the 1860s, when the area was the scene of many difficulties between the incoming White settlers and the Paiutes, Navajos, and Utes who were already there. Mitchell (father of Ernest Mitchell, for whom Mitchell Butte and Mitchell Mesa in Monument Valley are named) was issuing passes to Navajos to graze on Mormon-controlled range in this area in 1883.

Sometime after 1889, the post was run by Pete and Herman Guillet. Purchased by Englishman Dick Simpson in 1921, it was sold five years later to Bob Smith, formerly of Toadlena Trading Post in New Mexico. Although the name

Aneth is purported to commemorate a trader, it is uncertain when one by this name (or Anseth, as suggested by at least one historian) ran the post. Historian Robert McPherson notes that the name Aneth was bestowed by Howard Antes (see below) who claimed it is a Hebrew term meaning "The Answer." The post was at one time part of the Foutz and Sons trading empire.

On October 29, 1907, Superintendent Shelton dispatched Captain H. O. Willard and two troops of the 5th U.S. Cavalry from Fort Wingate, New Mexico, to arrest Be'álílii near here. Be'álílii and a number of followers, in a near re-enactment of the 1893 Black Horse incident at Round Rock, were resisting the forced relocation of Indian children into government boarding schools. Following a brief encounter near Aneth, in which two Navajos were apparently killed, Be'álílii and eight of his followers were arrested. These men were sentenced—without trial—to two to 10 years hard labor. However, the Indian Rights Association protested the affair and the men were released from Fort Huachuca, Arizona, in March 1909.

In a highly unusual turn of events, Superintendent William T. Shipley invoked a little-used point of the Indian Trade Act in evicting Reverend Howard R. Antes and his wife from the reservation in 1911, when Antes (of a small Methodist mission in the region) took over the trading post temporarily for the trader, who was to travel for several months. Shipley also confiscated 116 sheep and other goods that had been obtained in "illegal trade."

In 1956, oil was struck near Aneth, boosting the Navajo tribal treasury by a remarkable $34.5 million that year alone. In 1978, operations of Texaco, Superior, Continental, and Phillips oil companies (and the tribal government) were closed for 17 days by a protest led by the Council for Navajo Liberation (CNL), which sought renegotiation of oil leases and more emphasis on local needs. The oil companies agreed to many improvements for the Navajos, including reclamation of the areas damaged by oil activities and preservation of cultural resources.

In addition to Aneth Trading Post, the community has seen a number of mercantiles come and go, including Spencer's (early 1880s to early 1890s), Ames and Scott's (late 1890s), and Hayes's (opened 1904). Aneth still hosts a day school.

✤ Role in Hillerman Fiction:

Hunting Badger: A Utah Highway Patrolman tries to stop a speeding truck near Aneth, but occupants shoot a hole in his radiator (chap. 4). Joe Leaphorn crosses the Aneth Oil Field approaching Casa del Eco Mesa, as per Oliver Potts's map, on his way to Desert Creek in search of Everett Jorie (chap. 7). Joe Leaphorn discovers an open file on Everett Jorie's computer that identifies Alexander "Buddy" Baker as the man who shot at a policeman near

Aneth (chap. 7). Leaphorn realizes George Ironhand came home from war when they were drilling new wells in the Aneth Oil Field, meaning he served in Vietnam (chap. 13). A BIA cop sent from the Jicarilla Reservation spotted the truck stolen from the gas station assault in the Aneth Oil Field—within walking distance of Gothic Creek Canyon (chap. 15).

ANGEL PEAK: (6880 ft) San Juan County, NM. Also called "Angel's Peak." Navajos call this feature Tsélgizhíí, "Rock Pass," or Ma̧'ii Dah Siké, "Two Coyotes Seated at an Elevation." This is the chief landmark in the "Garden of Angels," 80 square miles of tortured landscape with formations resembling a group of angels.

✤ Role in Hillerman Fiction:

Sacred Clowns: Badlands of this formation extend north of Jim Chee's drive in search of the anonymous confessor to the hit-and-run death of Victor Todachenee (chap. 19).

AZTEC: (5650 ft) (Population: 6,134) San Juan County, NM. Navajos call this agricultural town Kinteel, "Wide House," a reference to the Anasazi ruin (now a national monument). It sits at the crossroads of U.S. Highway 550 and New Mexico Highways 173, 544, and 574, on the south bank of Animas River, some 13 miles northeast of Farmington. In 1940, the population was only 1200, and the town was served by the Denver & Rio Grande Railroad, which moved largely livestock. It is the home of Aztec National Monument, a partially excavated (in 1916 and 1924) and reconstructed Chacoan Anasazi great-house community. The ruins figure heavily in Navajo folklore.

The first White settlers were wheat farmers Frank and George Coe in the 1880s, following the reopening of portions of the Jicarilla Apache Reservation in 1876. Aztec became the seat of San Juan County when, due to political upheaval, that body was carved out of Rio Arriba County in 1887.

✤ Role in Hillerman Fiction:

A Thief of Time: Chee ascertains that Joe B. Nails, renter of the U-Haul truck leaving tracks of newly installed Dayton tires, is from Aztec (chap. 5).

Coyote Waits: Jim Chee remembers first meeting Janet Pete at the San Juan County Jail here (chap. 4).

Sacred Clowns: Joe Leaphorn reaches Jim Chee at the San Juan Motel at 6 a.m.; Leaphorn is pleased and Chee is very happy after a night with Janet Pete, who drove up here with him from Gallup. Leaphorn tells Chee to meet him at St. Bonaventure Mission in Thoreau (chap. 27).

The Fallen Man: A pair of cattle-stealing brothers are jailed here by New Mexico Brand Inspector Dick Finch (chap. 16).

The First Eagle: Jim Chee remembers the first time he met Janet Pete at the San Juan County Jail in Aztec, when she was defending a man Chee had arrested (chap. 7).

Hunting Badger: Vacationing Jim Chee gets information on the Ute Casino and Teddy Bai from a friend (chap. 5).

BABY ROCKS: (5500 ft) Navajo County, AZ. Called by the Navajos Tsé 'Awéé, "Baby Rocks." This low mesa of fragmented sandstone sits south of U.S. Highway 160, 11 miles east of Kayenta. The name derives from the unusual character of the fractious sandstone, which appears to be comprised of countless small stones rather than continuous layers of sediment. Baby Rocks Trading Post opened in the early 1960s.

Navajo settlers came here from Kayenta to farm, but the floods of 1912 destroyed the natural earth dams in Upper Laguna Creek and released tremendous heads of water, which cut the channel of lower Laguna Creek down to bedrock and rendered diversion of water for irrigation impossible.

Old Crank, who had been the leader of the Baby Rocks colony, then led a movement to establish Dinnehotso about 10 miles upstream, where there was a shallower channel and a natural dam site. Old Crank's earthen dam, reinforced with brush and tree branches, was replaced prior to 1941 with a modern reinforced concrete diversion dam, which irrigated 793 acres of excellent agricultural land.

✤ Role in Hillerman Fiction:

Talking God: This is a favorite lurking spot for Officer Jim Chee, where he waited for the endless miles of U.S. Highway 160 to provoke drivers into speeding (chap. 4).

BACAVI: (6583 ft) Navajo County, AZ. Also Bacabi, Bakabi, Bacobi. Navajos refer to this Hopi community as Tł'ohchintó Biyáázh, "Offspring of Wild Onion Spring" (which apparently refers more to Hotevilla). Hopis call it Baakavii, "Place of the Jointed Reed." Located on Arizona Highway 264, this Hopi village on the eastern flank of Third Mesa was founded in 1907. In 1941, Navajo historian Richard Van Valkenburgh described this community of 184 people as the "newest Hopi village."

This village was populated originally by "Conservatives" or "Hostiles" forcibly evicted from Oraibi by "Progressives" in 1906. Under the leadership of Lomahongyoma, they helped found the village of Hotevilla, but shortly after, Lomahongyoma led a more moderate contingent back to Oraibi. Finding they were not welcome, they left once again to found Bacavi in 1907.

The town was laid out by Hopi agent Lee Crane, with houses built separately to allow for filling in as the population increased. A school was constructed here in 1910.

✤ Role in Hillerman Fiction:

The Dark Wind: This Third Mesa village is visited by Jim Chee and Deputy Sheriff Cowboy Dashee investigating rumors that witchcraft killed the "John Doe" found on Black Mesa. They are sent to Mishongnovi (chap. 10). Jim Chee passes through the villages of Oraibi, Hotevilla, and Bacavi on his way to see if Ben Gaines and Gail Pauling are still residing at the motel in the Hopi Cultural Center on Second Mesa (chap. 18).

BACOBI: See Bacavi.

BADWATER CLINIC: In *Skinwalkers,* this fictitious location is set in the flats between Dinnehotso (on U.S. Highway 160) and Chilchinbito (on Navajo Route 59).

✤ Role in Hillerman Fiction:

Skinwalkers: This clinic is the scene of much catalytic and direct action throughout the book. A clinic here was founded by Bahe Yellowhorse, who is half Oglala Sioux (chap. 2).

BALAKAI MESA and **BALAKAI POINT:** (7000–7460 ft) Apache and Navajo Counties, AZ. Also Salahkai, Balukai. Navajos call the mesa Báálók'aa'í, meaning "Reeds Under the Rim," or Tsélgai, "White Rock." Located off the southeastern corner of Black Mesa, Balakai is associated with the Navajo Blessingway tradition, and is considered to be the feet of Pollen Mountain, a gigantic female anthropomorphic figure that incorporates Navajo Mountain, Black Mesa, Comb Ridge, Tuba Butte, and Agathla Peak. The extreme southeastern projection of the mesa, looming some 900 ft above the valley of Chinle Wash, is called Balakai Point.

✤ Role in Hillerman Fiction:

The Dark Wind: Pauling checks his chronometer as he reaches the rim of Balakai Mesa, which he knows is protecting him from Salt Lake City and Albuquerque radar (chap. 2). The home of Fannie Musket, mother of Joseph Musket, is near here, on the edge of Black Mesa (chap. 135).

BARBER PEAK: (5600 ft) San Juan County, NM. To Navajos it is Tsé Naajin, "Black Downward Rock." This sandstone butte in the San Juan Basin sits on the east side of U.S. Highway 666, directly opposite the much larger Table Mesa, about 13 miles south of the town of Shiprock.

Figure 1. Barber Peak hardly rises to the lofty heights normally associated with the label "peak," as demonstrated by this photo taken from U.S. Highway 666, about a mile west of the feature.

✦ Role in Hillerman Fiction:

Coyote Waits: This feature is visible along U.S. Highway 666 as Jim Chee and Janet Pete drive to the Red Rock vicinity (chap. 6). In studying rock formation photos in the darkroom of murdered Huan Ji, Joe Leaphorn and Louisa Bourebonette conjecture the formations Ji photographed could be, among other places, near Barber Peak (chap. 17).

BEAUTIFUL MOUNTAIN: (9400 ft) San Juan County, NM. Navajos refer to this feature as Dził́k'i Hózhónii, "Mountain Beautiful on Top." This large mountain spur runs northeast from the Tunicha Range along the Arizona–New Mexico state line 24 miles southwest of Shiprock. It was known in the 1800s as Mesa Cayatano and Corona de Geganta, and the region is most likely the Navajo stronghold referred to as "Casafuerte" ("Fortification") in Spanish documents as early as 1673. The tallest peak, reached by only two horse trails, is sacred to the Navajos.

Governor Antonio Perez visited the region in 1836, and Colonel Edward E. B. Newby led 150 men of the 3rd Missouri Mounted Volunteers and 50th Illinois Infantry in May 1848. This latter incursion led to a treaty signed by Navajo headmen José Largo, Narbona, Zarcillos Largos, and five others. A year later, Colonel Washington's expedition camped in this vicinity, his jittery men shooting at one another in the dark.

White expeditions attacked the region in 1858 (led by Lieutenant Cogswell under Colonel Dixon Stansbury Miles), in May 1859 (Major John Smith Simonson), and in October 1859 (Major Oliver L. Shepherd). A civilian militia expedition marched on the vicinity in 1861.

Beautiful Mountain was the home of Navajo medicine man Hastiin

Figure 2. Beautiful Mountain, from the south, on Navajo Route 34.

Bizhóshí. In September 1913, Bizhóshí's son, Hataałii Yázhí ("Little Singer") was sought by Shiprock Navajo Agent W. T. Shelton for bigamy. When his three wives were taken into custody at Shiprock, Hataałii Yázhí, Hastiin Bizhóshí, and nine other men rode into Shiprock and freed the women by force—and then went into hiding.

Shelton intended to make examples of these Navajos, and issued warrants charging 13 men with everything from horse-theft to deadly assault. Hastiin Bizhóshí announced he would not surrender without a fight. Fr. Anselm Weber, Chee Dodge, and the Fort Defiance Agency superintendent negotiated with the "renegades," who remained encamped for three months on Beautiful Mountain, visiting Frank Noel's Sanostee Trading Post almost daily.

On November 18, Troops A, B, C, and D of the U.S. 12th Cavalry (261 men with 300 rounds per man, 256 horses, 40 mules, and a "jackass battery" of Gatling guns) were dispatched from Fort Robinson, Nebraska, to Gallup. General Hugh L. Scott ordered Shelton to stay away and arrived at Sanostee Trading Post on November 27 (Thanksgiving Day). He conferred with Bizhóshí and his men, who agreed to surrender, thus bringing to an end the last use of U.S. Army troops against American Indians.

In Gallup, nearly all charges were dropped. Bizhóshí and two of his sons were sentenced to 10 days in jail; Hataałii Yázhí and another man were sentenced to 39 days. All sentences were served in the McKinley County Jail in Gallup.

In Navajo mythology, this mountain is the feet of Goods of Value Mountain, a male anthropomorphic figure, the head of which is Chuska Peak, the body the Chuska Mountains, and the feet the Carrizo Mountains. Shiprock is a medicine pouch or bow that he carries. (This figure is balanced by a female figure known as Pollen Mountain, comprised of Navajo Mountain, Black Mesa, and other features.)

❖ Role in Hillerman Fiction:

Listening Woman: Leaphorn's maternal grandmother was a renowned hand-trembler here and at Toadlena (chap. 18).

Coyote Waits: Officer Delbert Nez is killed south of Navajo Route 33, between Beautiful Mountain and Shiprock (chap. 10). According to Ashie Pinto's grandfather's story from the late 1880s, Delbito Willie saw two White men riding between Rol Hai Rock and Little Water Wash, apparently traveling toward Beautiful Mountain (chap. 11).

Sacred Clowns: Joe Leaphorn's family home is here, where his parents buried his umbilical cord, tying him forever to the place (chap. 27).

The Fallen Man: The sun sets behind Beautiful Mountain as Jim Chee leaves Lucy Sam's home near Shiprock (chap. 19).

BEAUTIFUL VALLEY: (5500–5800 ft) Apache County, AZ. The Navajo name is uncertain, but it likely means "Beautiful Valley." This lowland area stretches some 20 miles south from Chinle, and in fact comprises the southern end of the Chinle Valley. The southern end lies in the watershed of Nazlini and Bis'ii Ah Washes near Ganado.

❖ Role in Hillerman Fiction:

The Blessing Way: Between Chinle and Ganado, Leaphorn drives past this "lifeless depression," which falls away from the highway into the region of Nazlini and Biz-E-Ahi (Bis'ii Ah) washes (chap. 4).

BECLABITO: (5802 ft) San Juan County, NM. Also Biklabito, Beklabito, Behclahbeto. In Navajo, the name is Bitł'ááh Bit'o, meaning "Spring Underneath," though the U.S. Geological Survey of 1915 listed the translation as "Spring Under a Rock." This day-school, chapter, and trading-post community is located on the rolling and rocky northeastern slopes of the Carrizo Mountains of extreme northwestern New Mexico, on U.S. Highway 504, 10 miles east of the Arizona state line.

This was one of the five regions explored for uranium in the late 1970s. (The others are Shiprock, Red Rock, Sanostee, and Two Grey Hills.)

❖ Role in Hillerman Fiction:

Skinwalkers: Shaken by the ambush on his trailer, Jim Chee, leaving Shiprock, stops just outside of Beclabito to see if anyone is following him (chap. 1).

Coyote Waits: Officer Chee drives south from here on a dirt road in order to meet up with soon-to-be-murdered Officer Delbert Nez (chap. 1).

The Fallen Man: Acting Lieutenant Jim Chee parks here waiting to intercept officer Teddy Begayaye on his way to work from Teec Nos Pos, so he can talk to Begayaye about his vacation request in private (chap. 13).

Figure 3. Beclabito Trading Post, like so many other contemporary "trading posts," is primarily a convenience store.

Hunting Badger: Professor Louisa Bourebonette, with Joe Leaphorn in tow, interviews an old woman at the day school here, who speaks briefly of Ironhand before being admonished by a younger woman (chaps. 13, 14).

BEKIHATSO WASH: (6050–3000 ft) Coconino County, AZ. The wash is named for an ephemeral lake in its vicinity, known to Navajos as Be'ek'id Hatsoh (meaning "Big Water Place") or Be'ek'id Di'níní ("Groaning Lake"). This 15-mile-long tributary of the Little Colorado River enters the latter from the north through Salt Trail Canyon.

✤ Role in Hillerman Fiction:
The First Eagle: Tommy Tsi, who tried to sell a Jeep radio-tape player at Cedar Ridge, lives across Blue Moon Bench, along Bekihatso Wash (chap. 17).

BIDAHOCHI: (5500 ft) Navajo County, AZ. Also Bitahoii, Bita Hochee. The Navajo name is actually Bidahóóchii' (meaning "Red Streaks Going Up" or possibly "Red Rock Slide"), referring to a nearby sandstone cliff face. This trading community sits on Arizona Highway 77, 15 miles south of White Cone. The trading post was established by Julius Wetzler in 1880.

✤ Role in Hillerman Fiction:
Talking God: Lieutenant Leaphorn has to pass through a highway intersection two miles north of here to reach Agnes Tsosie's place. This is where Lower Greasewood residents get mail (chap. 3).

BIG MOUNTAIN and **BIG MOUNTAIN TRADING POST:** (7000–7100 ft) Navajo County, AZ. The Navajo name is Dził Ntsaaí (meaning "Extensive Mountain"), and refers to a rugged, rolling uplift atop central Black Mesa, about 20 miles northwest of Piñon and 15 miles southeast of Klethla Valley. In the literature it has been referred to as Ziltahjini Mesa, but that name (actually Dziłłátahzhiní, or "Black Mountain Peak") applies to Little Black Spot (or Speck) Mountain, 15 miles to the southwest.

This locale was the scene of considerable civil unrest in the late 1970s and early 1980s when the region, part of the heretofore Navajo-Hopi Joint Use Area, was divided and fenced, the land split between the two tribes. Many families—mostly Navajo—were forcibly relocated from lands occupied for generations because they suddenly were on the "wrong" side of the new fences. Such removal has proven highly emotional among people so firmly attached to their land.

Big Mountain Trading Post was once owned by Lorenzo Hubbell.

✤ Role in Hillerman Fiction:

The Dark Wind: Chee inspected tributaries of Wepo Wash draining Big Mountain in search of the missing cargo from Pauling's crashed plane, as well as for the phantom car or truck Chee heard the night of the crash (chap. 14).

Skinwalkers: Three of the unsolved homicides marked on Joe Leaphorn's infamous map took place near here, along the Utah-Arizona state line, and near Window Rock (chap. 2)—all possibly related.

BIRD SPRINGS: (4900 ft) Navajo County, AZ. Navajos refer to this watering hole as Tsídiito'í, meaning "Bird Spring." A small community and chapter seat has grown on Navajo Route 15 in the vicinity of the spring, some 15 miles east of Leupp. Before the development of water wells by the U.S. Indian Service, Bird Springs was one of the most important watering places for the Navajos between the Hopi (Moqui) Buttes country and Leupp.

✤ Role in Hillerman Fiction:

Coyote Waits: The home of Officer Delbert Nez is between here and Jadito Wash (chap. 10).

BIS-E-AHI WASH: See Bis'ii Ah Wash.

BIS'II AH WASH: (6800–5800 ft) Apache County, AZ. The Navajo name is Bis'Íí'á ("Adobe Spire"). This tributary of Nazlini Wash rises on the west foot of the Defiance Plateau, five miles south of the community of Nazlini. It flows southwest to the north edge of Ganado Mesa, then turns north along the perimeter of Beautiful Valley before merging with Nazlini Wash some 20 miles north of Arizona Highway 264.

✤ Role in Hillerman Fiction:

The Blessing Way: Between Chinle and Ganado, Leaphorn drives past the "lifeless depression" known as Beautiful Valley, which falls away from the highway into this wash and Nazlini wash (chap. 4).

BISTI (BADLANDS and TRADING POST): (5750 ft) San Juan County, NM. The Navajo name is Bistahí, "Among the Adobe Formations," referring to striking, rock-hard formations of sand and silt that abound in this region of the San Juan Basin west of Chaco Canyon. Once an ancient lake bed, this area is now characterized by broken badlands, steep-sided gullies, and low hills. It is found some 30 miles south of Farmington, where New Mexico Highway 371 crosses Hunter Wash.

The trading post here was established in the early 1900s, possibly by Billy Hunter, who established Beclabito Trading Post in 1911, and who is most likely the namesake of Hunter Wash.

✦ Role in Hillerman Fiction:

People of Darkness: Windy Tsossie (survivor of the oil rig explosion) moved to this region to join his wife's family (chap. 28). Jim Chee and Mary Landon are ambushed near the trading post (chap. 30).

A Thief of Time: Jim Chee is driving through Bisti on his way to Farmington when he hears about Harrison Houk's sudden demise (chap. 13).

Coyote Waits: In studying rock formation photos in the darkroom of murdered Huan Ji, Joe Leaphorn and Louisa Bourebonette conjecture the formations photographed could be in the Bisti Badlands, El Malpais, the Zuni Mountains, on Black Mesa, in Monument Valley, the Hopi Buttes region, near Shiprock, Little Water, Sanostee Mount Taylor, or Barber Peak (chap. 17).

Sacred Clowns: Jim Chee can see the discoloration of this feature from the summer camp of Frank Sam Nakai, high in the Chuska Mountains (chap. 12). Jim Chee and Janet Pete drive past this location on their trip from Gallup to Aztec (chap. 26).

BITANI TSOSI WASH: (7200–6300 ft) San Juan, Sandoval, and Rio Arriba Counties, NM. Also Betonnie Tsosie Wash. This is an anglicized pronunciation of Bit'ahniits'ósí ("Slim Bitani," which, according to Richard Van Valkenburgh, was the name of a wealthy Navajo). Navajos call the wash K'aí' Naashchii' Bikooh, or "Wending Red Willow Wash." It is shown as Eduardo Wash on the U.S. Geographical Survey map of 1884. This 20-mile-long wash drains an area rich in paleontological remains. Beginning in badlands a couple of miles southwest of Lybrook, it flows southwest to merge with Escavada Wash some two miles east of the mouth of Kimbeto Wash. Like nearly all washes in Navajo country, this one is normally dry, carrying water only after heavy rain storms.

✦ Role in Hillerman Fiction:

A Thief of Time: Near here, Jim Chee finds tracks of the U-Haul truck rented by Joe B. Nails, assumed to be the Backhoe Bandit (chap. 5).

Sacred Clowns: Jim Chee and Janet Pete drive past this location on their trip from Gallup to Aztec (chap. 26).

BLACK CREEK VALLEY: (7200–6862 ft) Apache County, AZ. The Navajo name is uncertain, but possibly the same as that applied to Black Creek Canyon: Tsétł'áán Ndíshchí'í ("Ponderosa Rock Rim Crescent"). This 12-mile stretch of the Black Creek drainage lies between Red Lake (north) and Fort Defiance (south). Captain James H. Simpson noted the striking features of this valley in 1849–50.

✣ Role in Hillerman Fiction:

Hunting Badger: Hillerman has Joe Leaphorn and Professor Louisa Bourebonette head south from here heading toward the Painted Cliffs (chap. 24), but this would actually take them north.

BLACK MESA: (6000–8000 ft) Navajo and Apache Counties, AZ. Also Black Mountain or "Black Streak Mountain." The Navajos call it Dził íjiin, "Mountain which Appears Black," or "Mountain that Extends Black." This immense upland west of Chinle and south of Kayenta resembles a raised, shallow bowl tilting to the south. It measures 75 miles east-west and 50 miles north-south. It is the heart of the Navajo Reservation, and it includes much of the Hopi Reservation.

The terrain is a mix of broad, gently sloping valleys and steep canyons, rolling hills, and abrupt mesas and buttes. It is drained by Moenkopi, Dinnebito, Oraibi, Wepo, and Polacca washes, all of which are tributary to the Little Colorado River (though Polacca Wash merges with Jadito Wash to form Corn Creek Wash just before merging with the Little Colorado), and comprises the largest watershed in Navajo Country.

Along the southern perimeter, several "finger mesas" extend to the southwest, forming the Hopi Mesas along Polacca, Wepo, Oraibi, and Dinnebito drainages. Springs fed by seepage in porous sandstones provided early Hopi villages here with a permanent water supply.

Most of this region was inaccessible to automobiles as late as the 1960s. Until 1982, Navajo Route 4 was the only all-weather road into the region, connecting Piñon to U.S. Highway 191 (in the vicinity of Chinle).

Navajos used to say that bears crossing over to this mesa from the Chuska-Tunicha-Lukachukai range on the east would bring bad luck, and people would go to considerable effort to stop any bears traveling westward in the intervening Chinle Valley. Black Mesa is associated with Blessing Way traditions as the body of female anthropomorphic Pollen Range. (See also Navajo

Mountain, Balakai Mesa, Agathla Peak, and Comb Ridge.) Black Mesa has also been the site of much suspected witchcraft.

The mesa was first traversed by Whites when Vizcarra visited in 1823. It was referred to as Mesa de las Vacas by Ramon Luna in 1850. Captain John Walker used the same name in a report to the War Department in 1858, as did J. F. Mc-Comb on his map of 1860. A single Navajo was killed on the mesa by a U.S. Army detachment under Captain George McLane in October 1858 (McLane was later killed by Navajos at Black Pinnacle), and other expeditions crossed the mesa in 1859 and 1860.

During the Navajo Wars of 1863–65, remote reaches of the mesa served as a refuge for many Navajos fleeing Kit Carson's invading army. Among these was Old Man Hat, the father of the subject of Walter Dyk's famous 1938 study, *Son of Old Man Hat*. Ute Indians raided Caballado Mucho's band of Navajos on the mesa in January 1866, causing Caballado Mucho to surrender at Fort Wingate for subsequent transfer to the Bosque Redondo.

There are many coal beds on Black Mesa, and several small mines (some dating back to prehistoric times) predate the massive strip-mines opened by Peabody Coal in the region south of Marsh Pass during the late 1960s and early 1970s. A special electric railroad was constructed to haul Black Mesa coal to the Navajo Power Plant at Page, 50 miles to the northwest.

The mining has been the source of considerable controversy. In 1964 the Navajo Tribe was told that their fossil fuel reserves would soon be worthless, so they sold the rights to the coal atop Black Mesa to Peabody Coal for a mere two million dollars per year royalties. (This was not renegotiated until the 1990s.) Many Navajos oppose the mining, calling it the rape of the Earth Mother. The boundaries of the lucrative coal leases also became a focal issue in the Navajo-Hopi Land Dispute in the Joint Use Area.

Regulations of the National Environmental Policy Act and other laws governing the disturbance of federally owned or overseen lands have made Black Mesa one of the best studied regions of the Navajo Nation archaeologically and historically.

Black Mesa Trading Post opened at the foot of the north slope of the mesa in the early 1970s and is still operating.

❖ **Role in Hillerman Fiction:**

The Dark Wind: Pauling could see Black Mesa to the south, hiding his plane from the probing radar at Phoenix (chap. 2). The body of "John Doe," shot in the head and with fingers, palms, toes, and soles skinned off, is found on Black Mesa (chap. 3). Navajos from this region are considered more isolated and conservative than most (chap. 7).

The Ghostway: After failing to reach Frank Sam Nakai's winter place via Greasewood Flats, Jim Chee circles back and drives through Round Rock, Many Farms, and Chinle, to the south side of Black Mesa, past Cottonwood and Blue Gap, before attempting to mount Carson Mesa again from the south (chap. 24).

Skinwalkers: On his way to Badwater Clinic, Jim Chee sees lightning-laced clouds forming over Black Mesa, offering a false promise of rain (chap. 6).

Coyote Waits: In studying rock formation photos in the darkroom of murdered Huan Ji, Joe Leaphorn and Louisa Bourebonette conjecture that Black Mesa is one of many possible locations for the formations photographed by Ji (chap. 17).

The First Eagle: Hillerman places the fictional Yells Back Butte on the west side of Black Mesa (chap. 2). Officer Benny Kinsman harbors an anti-Hopi sentiment due to his Navajo grandmother being relocated from her home near here to Flagstaff when the lands in the Joint Use Area were split between the Hopis and Navajos (chap. 2). The cluster of black pins at Black Mesa on Joe Leaphorn's notorious map denoted reports of skinwalkers (chap. 6).

BLANCA PEAK: (14,345 ft) Costilla, Alamosa, and Huerfano Counties, CO. Also Sierra Blanca, Sierra Blanco. To Navajos, this peak is Sisnaajiní, "Descending Black Belt (or Mountain)." Its ceremonial name is Yoołgaii Dziil, "White Shell Mountain." This peak lies in the Sangre de Cristo Mountains, about 10 miles north of the community of Blanco, Colorado (some 20 miles east of Alamosa, on U.S. Highway 160).

This is one of several mountains hypothesized to be the Navajo sacred mountain of the east. (Wheeler Peak, Pelado Peak, and Pedernal Mesa, all in New Mexico, have also been suggested as the sacred mountain of the east, but those sources deemed most reliable agree that Blanca Peak is Sisnaajiní.)

Descriptions of the mountain in Navajo mythology suggest the colors of Sisnaajiní shift according to the position of the sun, and that it has an encircling black band. This may be due to its glistening snowfields and clearly visible timber line.

Generally speaking, there are six Navajo sacred mountains, though other landmarks are also mentioned in the mythology. The four primary sacred mountains mark the four cardinal directions and were once considered boundaries of Navajo range. Colorado's Hesperus Peak (Díbé Ntsaa, "Big Sheep") is the sacred mountain of the north; New Mexico's Mount Taylor (Tsoodził, "Tongue Mountain" or, ceremonially, Dootł'izhii Dziil, "Turquoise Mountain") is the sacred mountain of the south, and Arizona's San Francisco Peaks (Dook'o'słííd, "Never Thaws on Top") form the sacred mountain of the west. Navajos consider Blanca Peak and Hesperus Peak as female, and Mount Taylor and the San Francisco peaks as male.

Gobernador Knob (Ch'óol'į́'í, "Spruce Hill," or, ceremonially, Ntł'iz Dziil, "Hard Goods Mountain") and Huerfano Mountain (Dził Ná'oodiłichííł, "People Encircling Mountain"), are two New Mexico promontories internal to Navajoland that are also sacred, having their own places in Navajo mythology.

Each sacred mountain houses gods, and upon these four mountains sit "sky pillars" (Yá Yíyah Niizíinii, "Those Who Stand Under the Sky"), which hold up the sky.

According to the Navajo creation myth, Sisnaajiní was the first sacred mountain created by First Man and First Woman in the upper world. It was made from mud brought up from the Yellow World by Hashch'é'éłti'í (Talking God) and another being called Hozdziłkhe Naat'aanii, "the Crane." It was then decorated with white shell, the source of the mountain's ceremonial name. It belongs to Hashch'é'éłti'í, who placed animals, plants, and other things upon it.

Sisnaajiní also figures in Navajo traditions relating to the separation of Athapaskan-speaking peoples. According to legend, when the Diné lived between the four sacred mountains, the different factions of the Diné were always quarreling about what territory they should occupy. At this time, there was a mountain near Sisnaajiní called "Flat Topped Mountain." It was covered with fine stands of flora, including berries and nuts, while Sisnaajiní was barren but covered with grass, upon which thrived deer, horses, and other animals. The Navajos told other Diné that they could take their choice between the two mountains. The other Diné could think of nothing except to get food easily and chose Flat Topped Mountain for theirs. As soon as the Diné moved up on the mountain, Naayéé' Neizghání ("Monster Slayer") blew on Flat Topped Mountain and moved it far into the south. This is now the home of the Apaches in the White Mountains of Arizona, and it is now called Mount Thomas or Baldy.

✤ Role in Hillerman Fiction:

The Ghostway: After returning from Los Angeles, Chee returns for the third time to Ashie Begay's hogan in the Chuskas to see if he can verify Bentwoman's assertion that Begay must be dead. In the chinde hogan, Chee finds Ashie Begay's Four Mountains Bundle, containing herbs and minerals from the four sacred mountains: the San Francisco Peaks in Arizona (sacred mountain of the west), Hesperus Peak in the La Plata Mountains of Colorado (sacred mountain of the north), Blanca Peak in the Sangre de Cristo Mountains of Colorado (sacred mountain of the east), and Mount Taylor in New Mexico (sacred mountain of the south) (chap. 22).

BLANCO: (5600 ft) San Juan County, NM. Navajos refer to this community as Taahóóteel, or "A Broad Strip of Land (Valley) Extends to the River." This largely Hispanic farming village on U.S. Highway 64 is strung along the north bank of the upper San Juan River at its confluence with Largo Canyon, some 11 miles east of Bloomfield. A school and Franciscan mission operated here in the 1940s, when Blanco Trading Co. was the main mercantile.

U.S. Army Captain J. F. McComb listed this site as Station 44 in his survey of 1859, the same year Major John Simonson also led a column through here.

The mouth of the Largo forms a large fan-shaped muddy delta nearly half a mile wide, which Navajos call Tsííd Bii' Tó, meaning "Spring in the Coals." According to Navajo traditions, this region of broad alluvial flats sloping upward to cobbled river terraces was one of the places where the early clans lived for some years, and where they learned agriculture and the manufacture of pottery from incoming Puebloan clans. This is a part of the Dinétah—the "homeland," or old habitat of the Navajos. The ruins of many Anasazi and Navajo sites are found in the vicinity. Across the river and to the south stands Dził Ntsaa, "Big Mountain" (Mesa Quartado), important in Navajo clan traditions.

✤ Role in Hillerman Fiction:

A Thief of Time: Mechanic Bernie Tso, while working on the Buick Riviera Janet Pete intended to buy (now wrecked by Jim Chee) tells Chee that the Backhoe Bandit works out in the Blanco gas field (chap. 3).

BLANCO CANYON and **BLANCO PLATEAU:** San Juan County, NM. The most prominent feature of this broad, barren highland to the south of the San Juan River is the network of canyons formed by Blanco Canyon and Blanco Wash. The Navajo people have a variety of names for this feature. The upper canyon is T'iistah Diiteelí ("Spread Among the Cottonwoods"), while the lower portion is called Tó Diłhił Bikooh ("Dark Water"). Other names include Tsííd Bii' Tó, meaning "Coal Spring Canyon," and Tsébááłigai, translating as "White Rock-Edge."

This wide, sandy canyon dotted with clusters of cottonwood trees runs some 40 miles south to north between Lybrooks and Blanco. Blanco Wash stretches beyond the length of the canyon, which is bounded abruptly on the east by Cibola Mesa and on the west by gently rising plains.

This region has long been an important Navajo agricultural area, with water in seepages and shallow wells. Some White ranchers also live in the canyon, as this is "checkerboard" land, where every other quarter-section of land can have different ownership.

In 1941, Van Valkenburgh noted a somewhat isolated group of Navajos living along the lower courses of the Blanco, having entered the region in the late 1800s from the vicinity of present-day Carson's Store. The headman of those Navajos living in the upper reaches of the canyon was named Comanche. These people were linked with the people in the Counselor region.

Archaeologists have identified Navajo "constellation" glyphs in this canyon, giving rise to theories of ancient Navajo archaeoastronomy.

✤ Role in Hillerman Fiction:

A Thief of Time: Jim Chee concentrates his search for Joe B. Nails, tentatively identified as the Backhoe Bandit, in features of this upland, including Blanco Canyon (chap. 5).

BLANCO TRADING POST: (5600 ft) San Juan County, NM. Founded about 1920, by Wilfred "Tabby" Brimhall and Jim Brimhall. The trading post is still in operation, located at the junction of U.S. Highway 550 (formerly New Mexico Highway 44) and New Mexico Highway 57 (the latter serving as the northern entry to Chaco Canyon National Historical Cultural Park). New housing developments are plentiful, and the community is home to a major Indian Health Service facility and a modern school.

✤ Role in Hillerman Fiction:

A Thief of Time: Dr. Eleanor Friedman-Bernal drops outgoing mail from Chaco at Blanco Trading Post on her way to disappearing (chap. 1).

BLANDING: (5865 ft) (Population: 3,516) San Juan County, UT. The Navajo name remains uncertain. This community is located on Utah Highway 47, 22 miles southwest of Monticello, at the north end of White Mesa. Blanding is an important commercial center for Navajos of southern Utah.

Settled in 1905, by 1915 this was the largest town between Moab and Arizona. It was first named Grayson, but in 1915 an eastern tycoon named Thomas W. Bicknell offered a thousand-volume library to any town in Utah named after him. The towns of Grayson and Thurber competed for this jackpot, and ended up compromising. Thurber became Bicknell and Grayson became Blanding, after Grayson's wife. They split the library.

✤ Role in Hillerman Fiction:

A Thief of Time: Harrison Houk's LDS stake high counselor from Blanding had to warn Houk about his "deals" (chap. 11).

Coyote Waits: William Redd tells Chee that Dr. Tagert found a Blanding newspaper article about a train robbery in the late 1800s, in which one robber was identified by some passengers as Butch Cassidy (chap. 9). One of the robbers—named Wagonstaff—was shot and died in the Blanding hospital (chap. 11).

Hunting Badger: Before the Ute Casino robbery, old man Timms was going to Blanding to get his plane inspected (chap. 5). Buddy Baker is thought to have possibly moved here (chap. 6). Rancher Eldon Timms has gone to see his insurance agent at Blanding when Jim Chee and Deputy Sheriff Cowboy Dashee arrive at this ranch to question him some more; the widow Eleanor Ashby tells them that Timms was supposed to bring her some stuff from Blanding the day the robbers came through (chap. 8). An ambulance has to be summoned from Blanding to Bluff to assist the injured gas station attendant apparently attacked by fugitive Ironhand (chap. 17).

BLOOMFIELD: (5500 ft) (Population: 6,260) San Juan County, NM. Navajo: 'Ahihodiiteel ("Where Two Wide Valleys Come Together"); also 'Anabi'ání or Naabi'ání, "Enemy's Cave." This community sits on the north bank of the upper San Juan River, eight miles south of Aztec, at the junction of New Mexico Highway 64 and U.S. Highway 550 (formerly New Mexico Highway 44). Oil and gas wells abound in the badlands some 10 miles to the south, in the vicinity of Kutz Wash. In 1941, a trading post here was operated by R. L. Tanner.

Bloomfield was originally settled in 1881 by William B. Haines, an Englishman. In its early days, it was a wild cow town, home of the Stockton Gang, led by Port Stockton (a cattle rustler and stagecoach robber).

✤ Role in Hillerman Fiction:

A Thief of Time: Jim Chee drives through here on his trip to find Joe B. Nails, tentatively identified as the Backhoe Bandit (chap. 5).

Sacred Clowns: Jim Chee observes a Bloomfield School District bus drop a retarded boy at the home Chee has identified as the home of the anonymous radio confessor to the hit-and-run death of Victor Todachenee (chap. 19).

The Fallen Man: New Mexico Brand Inspector Dick Finch has been trailing a rustler who "picks up a load" in this vicinity every six months or so, using the same MO as was used at Shiprock (chap. 13).

BLUE GAP: (6500 ft) Apache County, AZ. Navajos call this community Bis Dootł'izh Ndeeshgiizh, meaning "Blue Adobe Gap." This small mission and school community is situated in the Polacca Wash Valley on Aspen Wash, on the southeast margin of Black Mesa. It sits on Navajo Route 29, halfway between Navajo Route 4 and Tachee.

✤ Role in Hillerman Fiction:

The Ghostway: After failing to reach Frank Sam Nakai's winter place via Greasewood Flats, Jim Chee circles back and drives through Round Rock, Many Farms, and Chinle, to the south side of Black Mesa, past Cottonwood and Blue Gap, before attempting to mount Carson Mesa again from the south (chap. 24).

Skinwalkers: Joe Leaphorn races past the turnoff to Blue Gap on his way to join the wounded Jim Chee at Badwater Clinic (chap. 22).

A Thief of Time: Emma Leaphorn's brothers had taken her body from Gallup to her mother's place at Blue Gap, where they concealed it nearby; Leaphorn was supposed to stay with her family here for four days, but—to the family's displeasure—he could manage only two days (chap. 4).

BLUE HILL: (5800 ft) San Juan County, NM. The Navajo name is uncertain. This small, conical sandstone mesa sits two miles east of U.S. Highway 666, roughly 12 miles north of the community of Shiprock.

Figure 4. Blue Hill, as viewed from the southwest, on U.S. Highway 666.

✤ Role in Hillerman Fiction:

The Dark Wind: As a boy, Jim Chee accompanied Hosteen Nakai here to collect herbs and minerals (chap. 17).

Coyote Waits: According to one of Dr. Tagert's translations of Pinto's stories, Utes passed Thieving Rock and Blue Hill on their way to raid in the vicinity of Ceniza Mesa (chap. 11).

BLUE MOON BENCH: (6000 ft) Coconino County, AZ. The Navajo name for this region is uncertain. The name applies to a broad, flat bench between Marble Canyon (on the west) and the Yon Dot Mountains and Bodaway Mesa. Most scholars agree that the Navajos entered this region fairly late in their occupation of the Southwest.

Much of this westerly-sloping valley is visible from the North Rim of the Grand Canyon, which is approximately 2000 feet higher in elevation than the Bench.

❖ Role in Hillerman Fiction:

Coyote Waits: Murder victim Ashie Pinto's home is situated on Blue Moon Bench (chap. 5).

The First Eagle: Tommy Tsi, who tried to sell a Jeep radio-tape player at Cedar Ridge, lives across across Blue Moon Bench, along Bekihatso Wash (chap. 20).

BLUE POINT: (6300 ft.) Coconino County, AZ. The Navajo name remains uncertain. This point is on the southeast rim of Padilla Mesa, 15 miles southwest of the Hopi Mesas.

❖ Role in Hillerman Fiction:

The Dark Wind: Jim Chee drives past Blue Point, Newberry Mesa, Garces Mesa, and Padilla Mesa on his way to the Hopi cultural center to see if Ben Gaines and Gail Pauling are still in residence (chap. 18).

BLUFF: (4465 ft) San Juan County, UT. Navajos call this community, at the convergence of Cottonwood Wash with the San Juan River, Tséłgaii Deez'á, meaning "White Rock Point." It is situated on Utah Highway 47, at the south end of Tank Mesa.

A rock formation called "the Navajo Twins," once sacred to the Navajos, lies in Cow Canyon (now within the town). The rock formation is inundated by a restaurant-lodge complex. Prehistoric roads—differing from the straight-line roads associated with the Chacoan system—have been identified in this vicinity. The area was a refuge for Navajos during the Bosque Redondo Period (1864–68) when most tribal members were incarcerated at the Fort Sumner reservation.

The community was founded in April 1880. Amasa Barton, a trader at Rincon, outside Bluff, was killed on June 9, 1887, by Navajos who plundered the post. A week later, 60 Navajos threatened the 15 Mormon families at Bluff, but they were apparently dissuaded by threats of bringing in the cavalry.

Benjamin Albert Wetherill noted that in 1895 a flash flood of Cottonwood Creek buried the entire town under a four-foot layer of sand and debris.

❖ Role in Hillerman Fiction:

A Thief of Time: Dr. Eleanor Friedman-Bernal drives through Bluff, making sure no one sees her (chap. 1). Joe Leaphorn discovers that Friedman-Bernal's calendar refers to H. Houk at Bluff on the San Juan River (chap. 2). Pottery that interested missing anthropologist Eleanor Friedman-Bernal was supposedly taken from a private ranch between Bluff and Mexican Hat (chap. 4). Maxie Davis remembers a happy Friedman-Bernal returning from Bluff on earlier occasions; Randall Elliot tells Leaphorn that Friedman-Bernal went

Figure 5. U.S. Highway 191 is the main street of Bluff. This shot faces west from the approximate center of town.

to Bluff to look for pothunters (chap. 6). Leaphorn goes to Bluff to question Houk about Friedman-Bernal's disappearance (chap. 8). Jimmy Etcitty had told Friedman-Bernal that a pot he sold to a collector was from Bluff; Jim Chee drives to Bluff to see Etcitty (chap. 9). Joe Leaphorn puts a kayak into the San Juan River at Bluff in hopes of finding the ruins in Many Ruins Canyon downstream (chap. 16).

Hunting Badger: A banged-up pickup truck fitting the description of the casino robbery getaway vehicle is found abandoned near here (chap. 4). This community was evacuated during the great 1998 manhunt (chap. 10). Hosteen Frank Sam Nakai tells Jim Chee that Utes and Mormon miners from Bluff once dug coal in the wall of Gothic Canyon (chap. 11). Chee and Officer Jackson Nez stay at a motel in Bluff while searching Gothic Creek for the Ute Casino robbers (chap. 15).

BLUFF BENCH: (5226 ft) San Juan County, UT. The Navajo name is uncertain. This upland, measuring approximately three miles square, is the flat, mesa-topped bench immediately west of the community of Bluff, Utah, and north of Utah Highway 163.

✤ Role in Hillerman Fiction:

Hunting Badger: Joe Leaphorn visits Oliver Potts at his ranch on Recapture Creek, five miles northwest of Bluff, which would put it on Bluff Bench (chap. 7). Leaphorn discovers Everett Jorie's computer file, which suggests looking for Ironhand and Baker near Recapture Creek, below the Bluff Bench and south of White Mesa Ute Reservation (chap. 9).

BORREGO PASS (TRADING POST): (7000 ft) McKinley County, NM. To Navajos this is Dibé Yázhí Habitiin, "Ascending Lamb Trail." The trading post and tiny community are located on Navajo Route 48 some 15 miles southeast of Crownpoint. The post was opened in the early 1930s by Don and Fern Smouse, and has been operated since 1990 by Merle and Rosella Moore.

❖ Role in Hillerman Fiction:

People of Darkness: Jim Chee and Mary Landon visit Fannie Kinlichee-nie (sister of Woody Begay, survivor of the oil rig explosions) at Borrego Pass (chap. 22).

The Ghostway: One of Ashie Begay's daughters stayed behind, living at Borrego Pass, when the rest of his family was relocated to Los Angeles in the 1940s (chap. 3). This turns out to be Emma Begay Sosi (deceased), mother of Margaret Billy Sosi (who runs away from St. Catherine Indian School in Santa Fe) (chap. 6).

Skinwalkers: Joe Leaphorn can see the red sandstone cliffs stretching all the way to Borrego Pass from the fifth-floor windows of the Public Health Service Hospital in Gallup (chap. 22).

Sacred Clowns: Hillerman has Joe Leaphorn and FBI Agent Streib pass through Borrego Pass on their way to Thoreau, after meeting with Lieutenant Toddy in Crownpoint (chap. 5). (However, this would make for a long, round-about trip from Crownpoint to Thoreau; Mr. Hillerman probably meant Satan Pass as the pass traversed in this instance, as this pass is on New Mexico Highway 371 connecting the two communities.)

BOSQUE REDONDO: (4025 ft) De Baca County, NM. This infamous location is to the Navajo people what the Nazi concentration camps are to Jews. The Navajos simply call it Hwéeldi, a corruption of the Spanish "fuerte," or "fort," though some older Navajos called it T'iis Názbąs, meaning "Cotton-wood Circle" (the same as Teec Nos Pos, Arizona).

This now-deserted site is four miles south of U.S. Highway 60, three miles east of the present town of Fort Sumner in southeastern New Mexico. The old fort was built in the Bosque Redondo (Spanish meaning "Round Grove") on the Pecos River in 1863 to house Army units guarding the Indian residents of a newly established reservation. The fort was situated just north of the con-fluence of the Pecos River with Alamogordo Creek. This locale was visited by Captain Arellano of Coronado's 1541 Quivira expedition, de Sosa in 1590, the Rodriguez-Chamuscado expedition in 1581, and by Espejo in 1583.

In 1863–64, roughly 8,500 Navajos were removed from their homeland in the Four Corners region and were force-marched on the infamous "Long Walk" to the Bosque Redondo—a trek of some 300 miles for the under-clothed, under-fed, and oft-abused Indians. Here they were settled on a reser-vation 40 miles square, which they were to share with the Mescalero Apaches, under the hostile eyes of the troops at Fort Sumner. (The Apaches stayed only until 1865 and decamped in one night.)

The Long Walk was devastating to the Navajos, and tales of cruelty on the part of their White guards persist today. It has been said that the trail to the Bosque Redondo reservation could be identified by the bodies strewn along the way. While many were the victims of brutality, even more were the unfortunate casualties of stupid oversights. For instance, the Army issued wheat flour to the Navajos, but did not give any instructions for cooking a substance so alien to the Indians, and many died of dysentery after eating flour mixed with water.

While at the Bosque, Navajos lived a rigidly controlled life. Article 6 of the treaty sending them to the Bosque read: "Any adult Indian who shall be found absent from his or her village between the hours of 7 o'clock pm and 5 o'clock am in winter, and between 8 o'clock pm and 4 o'clock am in summer, shall be imprisoned."

The Navajos tried to farm the alkaline soil from the irrigation system laid out by Army officers, but each year brought greater failure and a mounting death rate. Desertions (escapes) were numerous, and graft by military and civil agents robbed the Navajos of government supplies.

Conditions became so deplorable that in the spring of 1868, General William T. Sherman ("The only good Indian is a dead Indian") and Colonel Francis Tappan, Indian Peace Commissioners, were sent to Fort Sumner and there drafted the Navajo Treaty of June 1, 1868. Within one month, the Navajos were on their way home. Many old Navajos calculated their age from the date of return.

The home of Lucien B. Maxwell, in which famed bandit Billy the Kid was killed on July 18, 1881, served as the Army officers' billet during the Navajo incarceration. Deluvina Maxwell, the woman who first entered the dark room where the dead or dying Billy lay, was an Indian slave girl who claimed to be a Navajo from Canyon de Chelly, sold to Lucien Maxwell by Apache captors.

On June 6, 1868, the Navajo return to their homeland was nearly cancelled when renegades fled the reservation and killed six Whites on Twelve Mile Creek (12 miles from the post). The Army pursued these fugitives with the help of the Navajo headmen from the reservation, and all were killed or captured near Apache Springs. The planned Navajo release of June 18 took place as scheduled.

The location today is a New Mexico State Monument, though visitors will find only a few visible remnants of the original fort. At this writing, a movement has begun to construct a Navajo monument at the site of the old reservation.

✤ Role in Hillerman Fiction:

Sacred Clowns: Jim Chee's singer mentor Frank Sam Nakai reminds Chee of hardships of the tribal imprisonment at the Bosque from 1863 to 1868, leading to a mixing of clans through marriage (chap. 12).

BRIDGE TIMBER MOUNTAIN: (8385 ft) La Plata County, CO. The Navajo name is uncertain. This mountain is located on the Southern Ute Indian Reservation, approximately five miles east of Colorado Highway 140 and the community of Breen.

✤ Role in Hillerman Fiction:

The Fallen Man: Mesa Verde throws shadows on nearby Bridge Timber Mountain, as Jim Chee and New Mexico Brand Inspector Dick Finch drive to Mancos to visit the widow Mrs. Breedlove (chap. 5).

BURNHAM: (5450 ft) San Juan County, NM. Navajos call this tiny community (trading post and chapter house) T'iistsoh Sikaad Tséta', which means "Big Cottonwood Tree Sitting Between the Two Walls of the Canyon." Located in the barren, treeless country of Brimhall Wash, 12 miles east of U.S. Highway 666 on Navajo Route 5, the trading post was founded about 1927 by Roy Burnham, and a U.S. Indian Service day school was operated here in the 1940s. Surface coal deposits are found near the community.

✤ Role in Hillerman Fiction:

The Ghostway: Captain Largo surmises that Albert Gorman, after the shooting in the Shiprock Economy Wash-O-Mat parking lot, must have gone into the Chuska Mountains, because he would not have turned onto the Burnham road, which is a dead end (chap. 2).

Figure 6. The hollow remains of the old Indian Service day school dating to the 1940s, standing in the middle of nowhere.

The Fallen Man: When Officer Bernadette Manuelito discovered loose fence posts near Shiprock, she was supposed to be searching the Burnham area for the Roanhorse couple, who had witnessed a shooting at a dance near Lukachukai (chap. 9). New Mexico Brand Inspector Dick Finch trails a rustler who "picks up a load" in this vicinity every six months or so, using the same MO as was used at Shiprock (chap. 13).

BURNT WATER: (6000 ft) Apache County, AZ. The Navajo name for this location is Tó Díílidí ("Burnt Water"). The name derives from a burned ramada (pole shade) that collapsed into the well of the trading post established by Burris N. Barnes sometime between 1915 and 1920. Ashes in the water gave the post its Navajo name.

Stanley Smith operated this post in the 1930s. Don Jacobs, Sr., ran it from 1957 to 1974, and E. Brady ran it until 1983. The post closed in 1983.

✤ Role in Hillerman Fiction:

The Dark Wind: After the Burnt Water Trading Post was burglarized, 20-year owner Jake West accuses former employee Joseph Musket (chap. 3). The post is out of Navajo jurisdiction, but the first report of the "John Doe" body (with the skinned fingers, palms, toes, and soles) comes from someone at the post, bringing Jim Chee to the scene (chap. 3). During one of Jim Chee's visits to the trading post, owner Jake West discusses the Hopi shrine in a tributary of Wepo Wash near vandalized Windmill No. 6 and the site of Pauling's plane crash (chap. 9).

Skinwalkers: Looking out his Window Rock office window, Joe Leaphorn knows from the clouds that it's raining here while Chee is visiting the Dinnebito Wash country (chap. 19).

A Thief of Time: Jim Chee learns that the Backhoe Bandit must have known the trailer he stole was used to haul equipment to Burnt Water for repairs (chap. 5).

Talking God: Lieutenant Leaphorn discovers a Yeibeichai ceremony is planned here for someone in the Gorman family (chap. 3).

The First Eagle: Shirley Ahkeah was born here (chap. 1). Joe Leaphorn listens to KNDN on the limousine radio as he is driven to Santa Fe to meet Millicent Vanders; Billy Etcitty announces on the open mike that his roan mare is missing from north of Burnt Water (chap. 3). Officer Bernadette Manuelito invites Jim Chee to a Kinaalda at Burnt Water (chap. 17).

BUTLER WASH: (5400–4400 ft) San Juan County, UT. Also called Butler Creek. The Navajo name is uncertain. Rising some five miles northwest of Black Mesa Butte, this water course parallels the east face of Comb Ridge for some 25 miles until it flows into the San Juan River two miles south of Utah Highway 47, three miles east of the mouth of Comb Wash. Benjamin Albert Wetherill noted the presence of an abandoned stone cabin on the south bank of the San Juan River opposite the mouth of Butler Creek, said to have been the home of "a trader named Smith," killed by Indians some years prior to his seeing the cabin in 1895.

❖ Role in Hillerman Fiction:

A Thief of Time: Joe Leaphorn searches the mouth of this creek while floating down the San Juan River in a kayak, looking for missing anthropologist Eleanor Friedman-Bernal (chap. 8).

CAMERON and **CAMERON TRADING POST:** (4200 ft) (Population: 493) Coconino County, AZ. The Navajo name, Na'ní'á Hayázhí, means "Little Span Across." This community straddles U.S. Highway 89, where it crosses the Little Colorado River.

Bill Kona Sani (actually Bilagáana Sani, "Old Anglo") conducted the first trading here by pack train as early as 1850. The community began when S. S. Preston, a Navajo, erected the first trading post during the construction of "Government Bridge" (the suspension bridge across the Little Colorado River Gorge) in 1910–11. A longer-lived post was built in 1914 by Hubert Richardson (previously operator of the Blue Canyon Trading Post).

The community was named for Senator Ralph H. Cameron, the last territorial delegate from Arizona to the U.S. Congress, formerly sheriff of Coconino County in the 1880s and 1890s, and noted entrepreneur of the Grand Canyon's resources. Prior to the construction of the first bridge, the main crossing of the Little Colorado River had been Tanner's Crossing, three miles upstream from the bridge site. However, the crossing was treacherous with quicksand, and the bridge was built at Senator Cameron's urging, with moneys taken from the Navajo Tribe's Trust Funds (without tribal consent). It was replaced with a wider bridge in 1958.

Tourism was the main impetus for construction of the bridges and is the mainstay of the community. An early auto camp and the Klo-A-Chee-Kin Hotel catered to the tourists as well as to Navajos.

Arizona Highway 64, originally constructed in 1923–24 by the Fred Harvey Company (for the benefit of the company's world-renowned "Indian Detours") connects Cameron with the South Rim of the Grand Canyon. This steep road climbs (or drops) three thousand feet in 35 miles. Cameron received a post office in 1917; today it is a Navajo chapter seat and hosts a large trading concern—complete with motel, restaurant, trailer park, and RV campground.

✤ Role in Hillerman Fiction:

The Dark Wind: Largewhiskers Begay, accused of trespassing on Mary Joe Natonabah's grazing rights near Twentynine Mile Wash, is at Cameron when Chee arrives at his Cedar Ridge camp to question him (chap. 18). At Cameron Jim Chee buys a bag of cement, a tub, and a funnel for Sawkatewa, as payment for information the old man divulged at Piutki (chap. 24).

A Thief of Time: Slick Nakai had conducted a revival here before meeting the missing anthropologist Eleanor Friedman-Bernal for the first time (chap. 4).

The First Eagle: Joe Leaphorn stops here on his way from Flagstaff to Tuba City to visit with Deputy Sheriff Cowboy Dashee, who tells him that Jim Chee has arrested the wrong man in the murder of Officer Benny Kinsman (chap. 11).

CAÑONCITO: (6200–5250 ft) (Population: 1,189) Cibola and Bernalillo counties, NM. Navajo: Tó Hajiileehé, "Where Water is Drawn Up Out." An island of Navajo Indian Reservation in rolling country west of the Rio Puerco of the East, 28 miles east of Albuquerque and four miles north of Interstate 40. At the instigation of the residents of this community, highway signs on Interstate 40 now identify it as "Tohajeeli."

A small band of Navajos lives here on allotted land, separated by 75 miles from the main body of the tribe, who call this isolated group Diné 'Ana'í ("Enemy Navajos"). The Diné 'Ana'í lived in the Cebolleta and Mount Taylor country under headman Sandoval as early as 1858, having remained there when the main tribe pushed westward to Canyon de Chelly. Especially vulnerable to reprisal attacks by the Mexicans and Pueblos, they early allied themselves with these neighbors and acted as spies and guides against the larger body of Navajos. Later, when the rest of the Navajos began to retaliate, the Diné 'Ana'í moved to Cañoncito in order to benefit from the proximity of the Mexicans for protection.

According to historian Richard Van Valkenburgh, some informants believe Cañoncito Navajos are descended from Navajos who escaped the Long Walk to Fort Sumner, while still others consider them a band who stopped there on the way back from the Bosque Redondo in 1868. Historically, at least 19 Navajos wandered into the rugged Cañoncito region (west of the Laguna Paguate tract) between 1869 and 1881. They settled (and later homesteaded, under the Indian Homestead Act of July 4, 1884) lands over which the Lagunas had grazed for many years.

There are no cultural differences between the Cañoncito Navajos and the main body of Navajos, though some among the main body say their witches come from the Cañoncito people.

✤ Role in Hillerman Fiction:

People of Darkness: A distant cousin of Joseph Sam (survivor of the oil rig explosion) tells Jim Chee that Joseph Sam may have moved here some time ago (chap. 22).

The Ghostway: Jim Chee wonders if the missing Margaret Billy Sosi, granddaughter of the missing Ashie Begay, could have gone to Cañoncito trying to track down members of her clan who moved there (chap. 11). When Jim Chee discovers that the medicine man at Two Story (who can conduct the five-day Ghostway) is in Cañoncito performing the ceremony on a girl named Sosi, he is at once elated at finding Margaret Billy Sosi once again, but dismayed at the distance he will have to travel—to the region near Acoma and Laguna Pueblos (chap. 24).

Skinwalkers: The Tribal Councilwoman from Cañoncito drives all the way to Window Rock (after a chapter meeting the night before) to visit Joe Leaphorn (chap. 2). She tells Leaphorn that the Cañoncito band has not been happy with the main tribal government since 1868 for many shortcomings—like no Navajo cops on Cañoncito reservation (chap. 2). Leaphorn's infamous map had only two kinds of pins on Cañoncito, denoting either alcohol-related or witchcraft-related disruptions of the peace (chap. 2).

CANYON DE CHELLY (NATIONAL MONUMENT): (Rim: 7000–6000 ft; Floor: 6400–5800 ft) Apache County, AZ. De Chelly is pronounced "de-shay," apparently the closest early Spaniards could come to pronouncing the Navajo "Tséyi." This is the Navajo name most commonly used for the de Chelly system. Another name is Tséyi' Etso, meaning "Big Canyon" or "Big Canyon among the Rocks."

This extensive, deep canyon system drains the northwest portion of the Defiance Plateau, emptying into Chinle Wash at Chinle. Headwaters for the system begin in the Lukachukai, Tunicha, and Chuska Mountains, 40 miles to the east.

Canyon de Chelly appears on the Dominguez-Escalante map of 1776–77, at which time Navajos were already present. Spanish expeditions probed the canyon by 1805, but it was not extensively surveyed until the Wheeler Expedition in 1873. The canyon became a national monument encompassing 83,000 acres on February 14, 1931.

The first Anglo settlers in the vicinity were Don Lorenzo Hubbell and C. S. Cotton, who set up trading concerns in Chinle in 1886. The numerous prehistoric ruins in the canyon system have been subjected to extensive and intensive scientific excavations, beginning with Mummy Cave, Sliding Rock, White House, and Antelope House from 1923 to 1929.

Geologically, the canyon cuts through or into four massive layers of sandstone. The Supai Formation lies at the bottom—exposed only here and there beneath the sandy river beds—and dates to the Permian age (about 250 to 280 million years old). Above this is the immense, 200-million-year-old layer of De Chelly sandstone, which comprises the bulk of the canyon walls. Between this layer and the next higher one, the Shinarump Conglomerate, is the "Unconformity," a gap of about 30 million years. The Shinarump Conglomerate was laid down about 170 million years ago, during the Triassic period. This sediment yielded the first uranium strikes in the region (though not in the canyon). The topmost and youngest layer is the Chinle Formation, which has been eroded away from most of the rim, but is visible near the National Park Service Visitor Center.

Early Spanish explorers regarded this vast canyon system as an impregnable stronghold of the Navajos. Few Spanish expeditions dared to enter the upper canyons with their sheer walls 1000 ft high or more. Antonio de Narbona traversed the northern branch (Canyon del Muerto), but the first full exploration by non-Indians did not occur until the winter of 1863–64, when Captains A. F. Pfeiffer and Asa B. Carey of the 1st New Mexico Volunteers swept the entire canyon system of its Navajo occupants, killing 22 in their ruthless campaign.

Since the early Navajo lifestyle did not leave behind the kinds of tangible evidence left by the ancestors of the pueblos, determining their time of arrival in the canyon is conjectural. Spanish documentation suggests that they were in the canyons by the 1720s, in villages of up to 10 conical "forked-stick hogans" on the north rim of Canyon del Muerto. Anasazi remains, on the other hand, suggest human occupation in the canyons by the Basketmaker II era, or between 200 B.C. and A.D. 400. Considered progenitors of the Pueblo Indians, the Anasazi remained until the later decades of the thirteenth century.

In the early 1700s, residents of the Hopi Mesas to the west and Jemez Pueblo (near the Rio Grande) in the east fled the Spanish reconquest of New Spain (following the Pueblo Revolt of 1680) and came to the de Chelly region for its permanent water. They brought peach trees to the Navajos and merged with the Navajo population to become Mą'ii Deeshgizhnii, "Jemez Clan."

Valuable crops of corn, melons, squash, and peaches grow in the many alluvial flats and small rincons of the canyons, where in 1941 nearly 400 people farmed in Canyon de Chelly proper and in its tributary Canyon del Muerto. During the winter, people traditionally camped on the wooded canyon rim owing to a lack of fuel in the canyon bottoms, but this has changed with the availability of propane.

Much of the history of the Nightway Chant centers in the Canyon de Chelly area (along with the lower Chama River and San Juan drainage regions of New Mexico), and a great many of the individual geological and archaeo-

logical features within the canyon have considerable historical and/or ceremonial significance to the Navajos.

✤ **Role in Hillerman Fiction:**

Listening Woman: The Boy Scouts hold a regional encampment here
(chap. 22). This is the scene of the hostage kidnapping (chap. 15).

The Fallen Man: Harold Breedlove and his wife had been visiting the
monument when Mrs. Breedlove reported Harold's sudden disappearance
(chap. 3). Amos Nez, who guided Hal Breedlove and his wife on a tour of the
canyon just before Breedlove disappeared 11 years ago, is shot here just after
Breedlove's remains are discovered atop Shiprock (chap. 3). On his way to
Flagstaff, retired Joe Leaphorn stops at the Canyon de Chelly National Monument to visit the old guide, Amos Nez (chap. 7).

CANYON DEL MUERTO: Apache County, AZ. Navajos call this major tributary of Canyon de Chelly 'Ane'étséyi' meaning "Back Of In Between The
Rocks" or, more simply, "Back Canyon." The name del Muerto is Spanish for
"the Dead Man." Del Muerto enters de Chelly from the northeast some four
miles upstream from Chinle. At this point, del Muerto rims are roughly 6000
ft in elevation, climbing to 7200 ft at the headwaters of the canyon some 20
miles upstream. The canyon was created by the erosion of the Rio del Muerto,
which emanates now from Tsaile Lake, a man-made reservoir on Tsaile Creek
(formerly called Spruce Creek).

Del Muerto has three significant tributaries: Black Rock and Twin Trail
Canyons, branching off to the east, and Middle Trail Canyon, branching to
the north where del Muerto turns sharply to the east.

Captain John G. Walker, in his 1858 exploration of the canyon system, referred to del Muerto as "Cañon Trigo," or "Wheat Canyon," probably a reference to Wheatfields near its headwaters.

Some say Canyon del Muerto took its Spanish name (Canyon of the Dead
Man) from the massacre of Navajos by Lieutenant Chacon's Spanish soldiers
and Zunis in 1805. However, it is also said that the name was bestowed in the
1880s by Colonel Stephenson, following his excavation of mummy burials at
Mummy Cave.

Like de Chelly, del Muerto is characterized by towering, sheer, red sandstone cliffs. The peninsula of land separating the two canyons is appropriately
named Ata'adeez'á ("Point Between the Canyons").

✤ **Role in Hillerman Fiction:**

The Fallen Man: Guide Amos Nez took the Breedloves up this canyon
the day before Hal Breedlove disappeared 11 years ago; they were going to tour
Canyon de Chelly proper the day he disappeared (chap. 3). Joe Leaphorn

confronts the sniper who was hunting Amos Nez, and who is driving the "funny green van" described by Hosteen Sam at Shiprock 11 years earlier (chaps. 25–26).

CANYON LARGO or **LARGO CANYON** (and **LARGO CREEK**): (6600–5550 ft) Rio Arriba County, NM. Also Cañon Largo, Cañada Largo. This extensive drainage system in northwestern New Mexico is known to the Navajos by several names. The Franciscan Fathers list Taahóóteel Ńlíní, meaning "Stream in a Broad Strip that Extends to the River," as a name for the whole canyon system. The upper canyon (shown on at least one map as Cañada Larga) is known to Navajos as 'Ahidazdiigaii, meaning "Where Treeless Vales Come Together." The lower canyon is called Tsííd Bii' Tó, or "Spring in the Coals." The mouth of the canyon, at Blanco, is called Taahóóteel, which translates as "Broad Strip Extends to Water." Early Spanish documents refer to this canyon as Cañada Grande Larga.

Largo Canyon is one of the main silt feeders of the San Juan River, with headwaters of the system near the continental divide just east of U.S. Highway 550 (formerly New Mexico Highway 44), close to the southern Jicarilla Apache boundary. Fed by several substantial arroyos (including Blanco Creek), Largo Creek joins the San Juan River at Blanco, 10 miles east of Bloomfield.

This rugged canyon system of Largo Creek played a central role in early Navajo/White contact. Roque Madrid's expedition passed through a portion of the canyon, and, on August 14, 1705, fought their third and final battle with Navajos near its junction with Tapacito Creek. As with the earlier battle at Los Peñoles, the Navajos held the high ground and fended off Spanish attacks until Madrid, while pretending to parley for peace, sent his Pueblo auxiliaries up Tapacito Creek to attack the Navajos from behind. The ruse was successful, and the Navajos were driven from the field. An unknown number of Navajos died, while Madrid lost one Indian auxiliary.

Cañon Largo later became the most important route for Indians and Whites from the Rio Grande to the upper San Juan River. Captain J. F. Mc-Comb passed through the canyon in 1859.

In 1941, Van Valkenburgh described the wagon road as impassable in bad weather. Today it is graded and graveled, but still treacherous when wet. There are a number of White ranches in the rincons of the Largo, and many prehistoric and historic Indian sites—some of them watchtowers—line the canyon rims. Some in the section of the canyon between Trubey's and Haynes Canyon are Navajo in origin, dating from the eighteenth century, when the Navajos were joined by Jemez and other Pueblo Indians fleeing the Spanish Reconquest (following the Pueblo Revolt of 1680).

At least one Navajo pueblito ruin (known as LA 2298), located on a bench above the north bank of Largo Canyon (just north of the mouth of Tapicito Creek), has provided tree-ring dates clustering around 1690 and 1694, among the earliest for Navajo sites. Some historians doubt this date, however, insisting that the structure was almost certainly not present during the battle fought there by Madrid's force in 1705.

✤ Role in Hillerman Fiction:

A Thief of Time: This feature is scouted by Jim Chee in his search for Joe B. Nails, whom he believes to be the Backhoe Bandit (chap. 5).

CANYON WHERE WATERSPRINKLER PLAYS HIS FLUTE: A fictional location.

✤ Role in Hillerman Fiction:

A Thief of Time: Amos Whiskers tells Jim Chee that the pots in which missing anthropologist Eleanor Friedman-Bernal is interested were excavated from this canyon before they reached Slick Nakai (chap. 13).

CARRIZO MOUNTAINS: Apache County, AZ. Navajos call these mountains Dził Náhoozilii, casually interpreted as "Circular Mountains" by Van Valkenburgh in 1941, but acually meaning "Mountain that Gropes Around." The Spanish "Carrizo" means "Reed Grass." The large, detached, pine- and spruce-covered mountain is located at the extreme northern end of the Chuska-Tunicha-Lukachukai-Carrizo chain. Pastora Peak is the highest point, at 9412 ft. The Carrizos lie south of U.S. Highway 160 and Teec Nos Pos, with the eastern slope touching the New Mexico state line. According to Navajo historian J. Lee Correll, these mountains were also known as the Polonta Mountains—presumably Spanish, but translation unknown.

The Carrizos are separated from the Lukachukais by the Red Rock country, and were labeled "Sierra de Chegui" on the Dominguez-Escalante map of 1776 (though historian Dave Brugge believes that this designation referred to the entire Chuska-Tunicha-Lukachukai-Carrizo range), and as the Sierra de Carriso on the J. F. McComb map of 1850. Major J. S. Simpson passed over a trail along the southern flank in 1858.

Many Navajo traditions refer to these mountains, which constitute the lower extremities of the mythological Yódídziil, Goods of Value Range, of which Chuska Peak is the head. Beautiful Mountain is his feet and Shiprock is a bow or medicine pouch he carries. (This figure is the male counterpart of the female anthropomorphic figure, Pollen Mountain, made up of Black Mesa, Navajo Mountain, Balakai Mesa, and other features.)

Some medicine men state that certain Navajo clans took their names from

Figure 7. The Carrizo Mountains as seen from New Mexico Highway 504, about four miles west of Shiprock.

places in this range. In the Navajo creation myth, Shásh Na'ałkaahí ("Tracking Bear") was killed by the Twin War Gods in these mountains, and this may be the range alluded to as "Dziłyi'" in John Wesley Powell's 1887 discourse on the Navajo Mountain Chant. Anasazi ruins dot the lower slopes.

Until the 1920s and 1930s, the Carrizos are said to have sheltered a small number of grizzly bears. Beaver and muskrat still inhabit the upper elevations. Rumors of silver and other ore deposits in the Carrizos resulted in repeated encroachments by White prospectors from the 1880s until the 1940s; some left great holes visible on the slopes.

In the 1880s a prospector named Swift was killed in the Carrizos by Niche, a Navajo. Niche was caught, tried, and convicted, and was sent to the penitentiary two years later. One rush lasting from 1889 to 1892 led to a confrontation with the Diné that was dispelled only by cavalry intervention. In March 1890, Agent C. E. Vandever (called Bináá Dootł'izhí, meaning "Blue Eyes") learned that a party of 50 prospectors had illegally entered the Carrizos. Accompanied by Chee Dodge, Ben Whittick (well-known photographer of the 1880s and 1890s), and two troops of cavalry from Fort Wingate, he rescued 15 miners holding out against infuriated Navajos, and promptly escorted them off the reservation.

Despite fantastic stories, no appreciable amounts of any minerals have been taken from this area. The Navajo Commission examined the mountains in 1892, but found no minerals (and so allowed the Navajos to keep their mountain). More rumors led to 640 acres of land being leased to George F. Hull at the turn of the century. He employed six Navajos at five dollars per day in a mining enterprise, but came up dry. In the 1940s, however, vanadium was discovered and mined.

❖ Role in Hillerman Fiction:

The Blessing Way: From Shoemaker's Trading Post, anthroplogist Bergen McKee watched a thunderhead build over the Carrizos as he listened to the banter of Leaphorn, Old Man Shoemaker, and "the Big Navajo" (chap. 4).

The Ghostway: Captain Largo surmises that Albert Gorman, after leaving the shooting at the Shiprock Economy Wash-O-Mat, must have laid up in the region bounded by the Shiprock pinnacle and the Chuska, Carrizo, and Lukachukai Mountains (chap. 2).

Skinwalkers: Jim Chee sees thunderheads growing over the Carrizos as he approaches Badwater Clinic (to the west), where he hopes to acquire the list of names Irma Onesalt had been seeking when she was killed (chap. 18).

A Thief of Time: The dim outline of the Carrizos is visible beyond Shiprock from the site of the pothunter murders (chap. 9).

Coyote Waits: The community of Red Rock is located in a triangle formed by the Carrizos, the Chuska Mountains, and Shiprock (chap. 1). Officer Chee remembers performing a Blessing Way on Joe Leaphorn at a hogan west of these mountains (chap. 3). Ashie Pinto's grandfather had told him of two White men killed by Navajos between the Chuskas and the San Juan River many years ago (chap. 7).

The Fallen Man: A November sunset colors the clouds above the Carrizos as Jim Chee pursues the Porsche that passed him doing 95 mph (chap. 2). From partway up Shiprock, Elisa Breedlove could see the Carrizo Mountains, Ute Mountain, Casa del Eco Mesa, and Mount Taylor (chap. 5). West of Red Rock, the Carrizos could be seen from the Sam home between Little Shiprock and Red Washes (chap. 11).

CARSON MESA: (5889 ft) Apache County, AZ. The Navajo name of this feature is uncertain. The English name almost certainly commemorates the American Colonel Christopher "Kit" Carson, whose scorched-earth policy subdued the Navajos in 1863–64.

This mesa rises some 300 ft off the floodplain of Chinle Wash. From a point roughly adjacent to the juncture of Lukachukai and Chinle Washes, it runs southward about 20 miles, to Black Mountain Wash. From the Chinle Wash floodplain, it gently slopes downward in a westerly direction, to the foothills of Black Mesa.

❖ Role in Hillerman Fiction:

The Ghostway: Jim Chee tries to approach Frank Sam Nakai's winter place by driving across Greasewood Flats, Tyende Creek Canyon, and Carson Mesa in the deep snow, before turning back to Dinnehotso to try another approach (chap. 24).

Figure 8. U.S. Highway 191 follows the western cliffs of huge, sprawling Casa del Eco Mesa for about 10 miles in southern Utah.

CASA DEL ECO MESA: (5218 ft) San Juan County, UT. Also (occasionally) Casa del Echo Mesa. The Navajo name is uncertain. The Spanish Casa del Eco means "Echo House." This feature is a broad, low-relief highland on the south back of the San Juan River, opposite the community of Bluff. It extends roughly seven miles north-south, by five miles east-west, though the highest elevation and most distinctive section, with its 218-foot crown, is about four miles on a side.

✤ Role in Hillerman Fiction:

Skinwalkers: Badwater Clinic is a rare oasis in these immense, dry badlands (chap. 6).

The Fallen Man: From partway up Shiprock Pinnacle, Elisa Breedlove could see Ute Mountain to the north, Casa del Eco Mesa and the Carrizo Mountains to the west, and Mount Taylor to the east (chap. 5).

Hunting Badger: Joe Leaphorn and Louisa Bourebonette drive across this mesa on their way to Red Mesa (chap. 6). Jim Chee is not too familiar with this territory, because he's worked mostly out of Shiprock and Tuba City (chap. 12). Chee believes that Casa del Eco Mesa does not fit into the carefully planned robbery (chap. 12). He believes that the robbers could have dropped into Gothic Creek Canyon, then gone down the creek to the San Juan River, maybe up Butler Wash or Chinle Canyon—but Casa del Eco is an awkward place to start walking (chap. 12).

CEBOLLETA MESA: Here, Mr. Hillerman is apparently referring to that feature shown on most modern maps as Horace Mesa, the southern foot of the San Mateo Mountains (Mount Taylor [7992 ft], Cibola County, NM). The mesa rises some 1125 ft above the north end of the lava-laden floor of El Malpais.

❖ Role in Hillerman Fiction:

People of Darkness: This is described by Hillerman as forming the northern boundary of El Malpais (chap. 13).

CEDAR RIDGE TRADING POST: (5900 ft) Coconino County, AZ. To the Navajos, this concern is K'iishzhinii, meaning "Black Alder." This trading post is situated on U.S. Highway 89, about seven miles north of the Gap; it is named for a geologic feature two miles to the southwest. The post was established in a partnership between John P. Kerley and the Babbitt Brothers prior to 1920. According to Elizabeth Compton Hegemann, the original post was east of the highway, and later moved to its present location adjacent to the road.

❖ Role in Hillerman Fiction:

The Dark Wind: Jim Chee stops here on his way to visit Largewhiskers Begay (in the Yon Dot Mountains) concerning Begay's trespassing on Mary Joe Natonabah's grazing rights (chap. 18).

Coyote Waits: Mary Keeyani's youngest daughter saw a dust trail from a car apparently carrying Pinto traveling the road that went toward Twentynine Mile Canyon before it connects with the road to Cedar Ridge Trading Post (chap. 3).

The First Eagle: Jim Chee finds out someone tried to sell a Jeep radio-tape player here, possibly from the missing Catherine Ann Pollard's Cherokee (chap. 17).

CENIZA MESA: (6400 ft) Apache County, AZ. The feature shown as Ceniza Mesa on the Southern California Automobile Association's Indian Country Guide seems to coincide with a feature labeled Toh Chin Lini Mesa on the USGS Shiprock 1:250,000 map. This mesa is actually a western peninsula of the Carrizo Mountains, directly south of Black Rock Point. It measures approximately four miles east to west, and is bounded on the south by Toh Chin Lini Canyon. (Tó Ch'ínlíní is Navajo, meaning "Water Flowing Out.")

❖ Role in Hillerman Fiction:

The Blessing Way: Joe Leaphorn, on horseback, discovers on this mesa the final piece of the puzzle of why Luis Horseman was murdered (chap. 15).

Coyote Waits: According to one of Dr. Tagert's translations of Pinto's stories, Utes passing Thieving Rock and Blue Hill would raid in the vicinity of Ceniza Mesa (chap. 11).

CHACO CANYON: (6100 ft) McKinley and San Juan counties, NM. The Navajo name for this feature is highly conjectural. Some historians suggest it is Tségai, meaning "White Rock," and supposedly Hispanicized to "Chaca."

According to historian Dave Brugge, "Tségai" can mean "Home" to many Navajos, particularly those who trace their ancestry to the Chaco region. Or, Chaco may derive from a Navajo phrase, "tséyaa chahałeeł Ńlíní," which is interpreted as "Stream in the Dark Under Rock" or "Darkness Under the Rock Stream."

Chaco is located 70 miles north of Thoreau, and 61 miles south of Aztec. A community at Pueblo Bonito, with a post office operating from 1936 to 1942, consisted of a trading post, National Park Service personnel, and the surrounding Navajos. A Civilian Conservation Corps camp operated here as well, housing at various times young men from the eastern states and Sioux Indians from the Dakotas. During this period, Chaco was also the focus for the University of New Mexico Summer Field School, which excavated Pueblo Bonito and other sites.

Approximately 21,000 acres in and around the canyon became a National Monument on March 11, 1907. This was expanded to 33,989 acres on December 19, 1980, with the establishment of Chaco Culture National Historical Park in 1981.

The 12-mile-long "canyon" proper is generally broader than it is deep, so it hardly resembles a canyon in the traditional sense of the word. It is bounded on the south by Chacra Mesa (also called Chaco Mesa), South Mesa, and West Mesa, and on the north by North Mesa; its topography rarely varies more than 400 ft from mesa to tops to canyon bottom, stair-stepped in increments of 50 to 100 ft. In contrast, the canyon floor varies roughly a quarter-mile to a half-mile across.

The source or meaning of the name "Chaco" remains a mystery, despite considerable study on the topic. The name appears on the Dominguez-Escalante Map of 1776, and is shown as a Navajo habitat. In 1796, Lieutenant Colonel Don Antonio Cordero identified Navajo "domiciles of which there are ten, namely Sevolleta, Chacoli, Guadalupe, Cerro-Cabezon, Agua Salada, Cerro Chato, Chusca, Tunicha, Chelle and Carrizo." At least two of these, "Chacoli" and "Cerro Chato," sound suspiciously like "Chaco," and in fact are seemingly equated with Chaco Canyon and Chacra Mesa by Frank McNitt in his book *Navajo Wars* as "one of four regions of contiguous Navajo occupation."

However, on the slightly later Miera y Pacheco map of 1779, Chacoli was shown as the name of a minor tributary of the Jemez River, and Vizcarra's journal records "El Chacolin" as a camp nine leagues from Jemez Pueblo and two leagues from the Rio Puerco of the East—not far enough to be Chaco Canyon. Furthermore, Cerro Chato referred to a hill near the Rio Puerco of the East, just south of Salado Creek, about a half mile west of the east boundary of the Cebolleta Grant.

In 1804–5, Lieutenant Vicente Lopez "defeated the foe at Chacra," which McNitt equated with either Chaco Canyon or Chacra Mesa. (The meaning and origins of the word Chacra are not explained in the historic record, though New Mexico toponomist Pearce suggests it is regional dialect Spanish for "desert.")

At any rate, the literature next refers to the area as "Mesa Azul" (Spanish for "Blue Mesa") in an 1824 report by Colonel Jose Antonio Vizcarra. He also calls the river through the canyon "La Agua de San Carlos." Apparently, however, the name Chaco was in vogue by 1849, when the region was traversed by Colonel John M. Washington's force of two companies of the Second Artillery (complete with 12 mountain howitzers), four companies of the Third Infantry, and 197 militia. The journal of Lieutenant James H. Simpson of this command provided the first written accounting of the assemblage of massive prehistoric ruins in the canyon.

The half-mile-wide, 10-mile-long main body of the canyon contains 18 major Anasazi ruins and thousands of smaller units, the earliest dating back to about A.D. 800. During the next five centuries, the region served as a focal point of religious and/or economic activity. The latter half of this period is marked by the intense building activity that resulted in the "Chacoan Great Houses" and "Chacoan Roads" (which may or may not have been roads), both characteristics that quickly spread throughout and beyond the Four Corners region. The term "Chaco Phenomenon" refers to an integrated system of co-operating towns and villages that produced and assembled goods for local consumption and for widespread distribution.

Prehistorically, the canyon may have been a turquoise distribution center. Large quantities of finished items and raw turquoise have been found at Pueblo Alto and several small sites excavated by the Chaco Center, as well as in earlier excavations at Pueblo del Arroyo, Una Vida, Kin Kletso, Pueblo Bonito, and other sites. But the canyon was largely (almost abruptly) abandoned by A.D. 1275, with the next occupation being left to the Navajos, who appear to have arrived about A.D. 1720.

A Spanish force under Lieutenant Vicente Lopez attacked Navajos in the vicinity of the canyon in 1804, and Colonel (Governor) Jose Antonio Vizcarra visited the region in 1823. On September 5 or 6, 1849 (shortly after Colonel Washington's incursion into the region), mail carrier Charles Malone and his guide were killed by Navajos at the canyon in retaliation for the killing of Navajo headman Narbona by Washington's troops near today's Narbona Pass (formerly Washington Pass). The Navajos were excluded from the canyon in the 1855 Treaty of Laguna Negra, a treaty that inexplicably—but luckily for the Navajos—was never ratified by Congress.

Lieutenant James H. Simpson's first substantive reports on Chaco Canyon recorded many of the larger ruins in 1849. The U.S. Geological and Geographical Survey examined the area in 1877.

Research in Chaco Canyon began in 1888 with a visit by Charles Lummis. Shortly thereafter, the first excavations were conducted by the Hyde Expedition for Explorations in the Southwest, under the guidance of Richard Wetherill, who homesteaded in the canyon in 1896. Since that time a number of expeditions have carried on the work of excavation, including the National Geographic Society (1921), the Smithsonian Institution (1929), the Museum of New Mexico and the School of American Research (1930s), the University of New Mexico Field Schools (1930s and 1940s), and the Chaco Center, a joint National Park Service–University of New Mexico research facility (1970s). Intensive stabilization began in 1933. A hundred thousand trees were planted along the Chaco River for erosion control. The Chaco Center surveyed 435 square miles, recording over 2000 sites and identifying roads, irrigation systems, and other features.

A trading post at Pueblo Bonito was operated by Richard Wetherill until he was shot dead by a Navajo on June 22, 1910. In 1936, the traders were Colonel Springstead and his wife, who was a member of the Kirk trading family.

Lately, astronomers and archaeologists have become increasingly interested in the possibility of archaeoastronomical observations by the Chacoans. The canyon is one of 12 U.S. sites on the international list of World Heritage Sites.

The ruin names used by the Park Service are those found in early exploration records. Most of the names were applied by Rafael Carraval, a Jemez guide from San Ysidro with Washington's 1849 expedition.

✤ **Role in Hillerman Fiction:**

A Thief of Time: Unobserved, Dr. Eleanor Friedman-Bernal drives away from Chaco and disappears (chap. 1).

CHACO MESA: (7400–6550 ft) McKinley County, NM. Shown on most maps as Chacra Mesa; also Mesa Azul. Navajos refer to this landform as Tségai, "White Rocks." This 31-mile-long sandstone mesa runs southeast to northwest and forms the southeast terminus of Chaco Canyon. Some historians have suggested the name Tségai might apply to the canyon as well as the mesa.

✤ **Role in Hillerman Fiction:**

A Thief of Time: The employee housing at Chaco Canyon consists of eight bungalows backed up against the foot of this mesa (chap. 2).

Coyote Waits: Jim Chee sees Chacra Mesa from his Mesa Air Lines flight from Albuquerque to Farmington (chap. 15).

Sacred Clowns: This mesa is seen by Jim Chee some 40 miles away while he is visiting his singer mentor, Frank Sam Nakai, high in the Chuska Mountains (chap. 12).

CHACO WASH: (7000–5000 ft) McKinley County, NM. Shown on most maps as Chaco River. Navajos call this 135-mile-long, ephemeral streambed Tséyaa Chahałheeł Ńlíní, meaning "Flows Along in Darkness Under Rock." This tributary of the San Juan River heads in the barren flats 10 miles north of Star Lake Trading Post and flows 30 miles southwest, west, and northwest into Chaco Canyon, passing Pueblo Alto Trading Post and Pueblo Pintado en route. It drains the 20 miles of Chaco Canyon, and flows another 85 miles west, north, and west through the San Juan Basin, to merge with the San Juan River a mile south of U.S. Highway 550, a couple miles east of Shiprock.

Archaeologists have dated Navajo presence along the Chaco River since at least A.D. 1690, give or take 80 years. Trader Franc Newcomb suggested it was at the big bend of this river that a party of Mexican ranchers and soldiers under Captain Hinojos was ambushed and soundly defeated by Navajos led by Narbona in 1835. (However, historian Dave Brugge points out that nineteenth-century documentation places this battle at Narbona Pass.)

Coyote and Tunicha washes are substantive tributaries of this normally dry river; early Spanish documents presented a tangled misapplication of names to all three of these streams.

✤ Role in Hillerman Fiction:

People of Darkness: This place marks the end of the road that Jim Chee and Mary Landon were driving to see Rudolph Charley; from here they must take a Jeep trail to the isolated hogan where Charley is conducting a Peyote Way (chap. 28).

A Thief of Time: Chaco Park Supervisor Luna drives Joe Leaphorn and Bureau of Land Management law enforcement officer L. D. Thatcher on the road paralleling the wash to question the friends of the missing Eleanor Friedman-Bernal at Site BC 129 (chap. 2).

CHAOL CANYON: (4600–4300 ft) Coconino County, AZ. Also Choal Canyon. The Navajo name for this feature is Chá'oł, meaning "Piñon." This 1000-foot-deep canyon is tributary to Navajo Canyon approximately 18 miles upstream (east) of the latter's confluence with Lake Powell. When the lake is at its peak holding capacity, it actually encroaches so deeply into Navajo Canyon that Chaol Canyon can be said to empty directly into Lake Powell.

✤ Role in Hillerman Fiction:

The First Eagle: Joe Leaphorn finds Richard Krouse, wearing an "elephant suit," hunting mice along this creek, where it runs into Chaol Canyon, atop the Rainbow Plateau (chap. 20).

CHECKERBOARD RESERVATION: McKinley, San Juan, and Cibola counties, NM. Also known as the Checkerboard Area. There seems to be no Navajo name identifying this feature, which is apparent only on maps. The English name refers to a vast expanse of land (east of and contiguous to the New Mexico portion of the Navajo Reservation) in which alternating sections (square miles) of land were granted to the Santa Fe Railroad prior to the expansion of the reservation into this region. The grants extend 40 miles north and 40 miles south of the railroad tracks, from very near the Arizona–New Mexico line to the Rio Puerco of the East. Most of the non-Navajo sections now belong to the U.S. Bureau of Land Management.

The Checkerboard Area includes much territory occupied by the Navajos prior to the origin of the reservation established June 1, 1868. The Navajo Nation has since acquired some sections, half-sections, and quarter sections, by grant and purchase, and individual Navajos have acquired quarter-section tracts by federal allotment and by purchase. Other tracts have been sold to non-Indian interests.

Residents of this region live under a variety of legal jurisdictional issues. Federal and Navajo Nation courts (and law enforcement agencies) have traditionally had authority only over bonafide reservation land (established by act of Congress or presidential executive order). Conversely, state and county law enforcement maintained authority only in non-reservation tracts. With legal jurisdiction changing with land status every other square mile, making arrests and conducting investigations proved next to impossible.

This problem was finally addressed during the early 1980s, when the Navajo Nation passed legislation expanding their police authority over the Navajo-owned (but non-reservation) tracts, and the State Of New Mexico and the Navajo Nation entered into a "Joint Powers Agreement" giving each entity's law-enforcement agencies authority to act within the other's jurisdiction—provided the Navajo policemen received training at the New Mexico State Police Academy in Santa Fe.

✤ Role in Hillerman Fiction:

The Blessing Way: Anthropologist Bergen McKee recalls Greerson's stories of witches turning into owls and crows here (chap. 14).

People of Darkness: The Native American Church flourished in this region after World War II (chap. 2).

Skinwalkers: Joe Leaphorn falls into the "Checkerboard type" of Navajos, distinctive through blood/gene mix with the pueblo Indians (chap. 5).

A Thief of Time: Joe Leaphorn and Jim Chee finally find Slick Nakai's revival on the edge of the Checkerboard Area (chap. 4). Leaphorn had rarely worked in this part of Navajo country (chap. 4).

Sacred Clowns: Continental Collectors, with the apparent help of Tribal Councilman Jimmy Chester and the Bureau of Land Management, want to install a national garbage dump in the Checkerboard Area (chap. 1). Navajo Tribal Councilman Jimmy Chester, who apparently supports the installation of the national garbage dump in the Checkerboard Area, is a big cattle operator there (chap. 6).

The Fallen Man: Navajo Tribal Police Captain Largo is stirred up by recent cattle rustling, because he runs cattle in the Checkerboard (chap. 3). Mrs. Breedlove's Lazy B Ranch has public land leases in the Checkerboard Area, and is losing cattle to rustlers (chap. 3).

The First Eagle: Unlike the Tuba City area, where he's worked only a short time, Jim Chee knows every track in the Checkerboard Area (as well as the Navajo Mountain region) (chap. 2). Red pins in the Checkerboard Area on Joe Leaphorn's notorious map mark narcotics cases (chap. 6).

CHETRO KETL: (6200 ft) Also Rain Pueblo, Chettro Kettl, Cheto Kette, Ketro Kete, Shining Pueblo. Navajos call this Anasazi ruin in Chaco Canyon Tsé Bidádi'ní'ání, meaning "Scaled Rock." The meaning and origin of the name Chettro Kettle are problematic.

Located one-quarter mile east of Pueblo Bonito on the north side of Chaco Canyon, this site dates from A.D. 1010–30 until sometime after A.D. 1105, partially predating Pueblo Bonito. The site has at least 337 rectilinear rooms and 21 kivas, and some roomblocks were three or more stories high. Test excavations on the site's southeast corner took place in 1920–21, and the University of New Mexico Archaeology Field School excavated the ruin from 1929 to 1934. A room with murals preserved on the walls was discovered in 1936. Repair and stabilization projects were undertaken in 1948, 1950, and 1964.

Chaco Canyon is renowned for the unique masonry styles in its ruins, and masonry Types II, III, and IV dominate at Chettro Ketl between A.D. 1010 and 1059; Type III dominates between 1060 and 1109. Approximately 17,000 beads were recovered from a single feature in the ruin nicknamed "The Sanctuary" (due to numerous sealed niches). Another interesting feature of this site is the south wall of the north-central roomblock. Called "The Colonnade," this wall originally consisted of 13 or more masonry pillars joined by a low wall. At some later date, the spaces between the pillars were filled in with masonry, resulting in a solid wall.

The "modified D-shape" of the pueblo resulted in an enclosed plaza or courtyard, typical for this period, and is similar to that of its larger neighbor, Pueblo Bonito.

Navajos consider Chettro Ketl as a home of some Diné deities.

❖ Role in Hillerman Fiction:

A Thief of Time: Missing anthropologist Eleanor Friedman-Bernal had evidence connecting St. Johns Polychrome pottery from Chettro Ketl with pottery from Wijiji and Kin Nahasbas (chap. 10).

CHICO ARROYO: (6900–4900 ft) McKinley and Sandoval Counties, NM. This 35-mile-long, meandering arroyo heads in the flats near New Mexico Highway 509, in Indio Draw, about 10 miles south of White Horse. It flows primarily eastward, then southeast, to merge with the Rio Puerco of the East, about 15 miles southeast of Torreon.

❖ Role in Hillerman Fiction:

Sacred Clowns: Jim Chee and BIA Police Sergeant Harold Blizzard cross the south fork of this arroyo in search of Delmar Kanitewa (chap. 10).

CHILCHINBITO CANYON: (7500–6000 ft) Navajo County, AZ. The Navajo name for this location is uncertain, but features associated with it are named below. This canyon on the northeast face of Black Mesa lies just west of the community of Chilchinbito, called by the Navajos Tsiiłchin Bii'Tó, meaning "Spring in the Sumacs" (Rhus trilebata), though sometimes translated as "Scented Reed Water." The canyon forms the headwaters of Blackhorse Wash, which the Navajos call Łizhiin Bikooh, or "Black Creek." This is a tributary to Tyende Creek some eight miles northeast of the village of Chilchinbito. Another Blackhorse Creek in the Chaco Valley of New Mexico is said by geological surveyor Gregory to be named for a Navajo chief, but the origin of the name of Blackhorse Creek in Arizona remains problematic.

❖ Role in Hillerman Fiction:

Skinwalkers: Wilson Sam's dog is found here by Sam's nephew the day after Sam is killed (chap. 2).

CHINLE: (5058 ft) (Population: 5,590) Apache County, AZ. Also Chinlee, Chin Lee, Tsinlee. To traditional Navajos, this is Ch'ínílį́, "Water Outlet," referring to the mouth of Canyon de Chelly.

This thriving community at the junction of U.S. Highway 191 and Navajo Route 7 began as a government settlement along the south bank of the de Chelly fork of Chinle Wash, a mile west of the mouth of Canyon de Chelly. The community is the gateway to Canyon de Chelly National Monument, the western boundary of which now abuts Chinle's eastern margins. One of the largest and fastest growing towns on the reservation, Chinle is now a major trading center and tourism destination, with motels (most notably the Thunderbird Lodge, formerly a guest ranch) and multiple trading posts and galleries. A major school complex (Chinle Unified School District, Arizona Public Schools) has been constructed in Chinle, along with many recent, multi-family housing units. These latter have swelled the population of the community in a short time, causing serious socioeconomic problems.

Historically, the town has included such traders as Lorenzo Hubbell, C. N. Cotton, C. Garcia, L. McSparron, and Wallace Gorman. The Franciscan Fathers and the Presbyterians both hosted missions in Chinle. In 1910 the fifth boarding school on the reservation was located here. In the 1930s and 1940s, the U.S. Indian Irrigation Service located a maintenance camp here.

The vicinity has been known to Whites for nearly two centuries. Spanish and New Mexican expeditions of war and trade came here until the beginning of the American occupation. The first visit to the locality by American military forces occurred in the fall of 1849, under the command of Lieutenant Colonel John Washington, accompanied by the territorial governor, James S. Calhoun, Captain Henry Lafayette Dodge, Lieutenant James H. Simpson, artist Edward Kern, and other members of Washington's command.

On the small knoll some 100 yards north of the Thunderbird Lodge, they held a council with Navajo chiefs Mariano Chavez, Zarcillos Largos, and Chapiton. The council led to the signing of the Treaty of 1849, and the troops moved on, passing over the Defiance Plateau along approximately the same path as the present Navajo Route 7.

During the winter of 1864, at the location of the historic council, Colonel Christopher Carson, Captain Francis McCabe, and Captain Albert Pfeiffer accepted the surrender of about 50 de Chelly Navajos under Hastiin Chooyíní ("Mr. Humpback") and the Navajo female chief, K'íníbaa' ("She Made a Discovery While on the Warpath").

The first trading post was established at Chinle in 1882 by a Mexican the Navajos called Naakaii Yázhí ("Little Mexican") at a site later occupied by Dick Dunnaway. Naakaii Yázhí operated from a tent, and was ejected the following year by Navajo Agent Dennis M. Riordan. Samuel E. Day and Anson C. Damon established a small trading camp here in 1885, and Michael Donovan took over that post. In 1887, C. N. Cotton succeeded Donovan and in 1888–89, the Lingle Brothers ran a store at Chinle. Many others have followed these early traders.

The Franciscan Fathers established their first Navajo mission here in 1904, under the guidance of Father Leopold Osterman. In 1906, Navajo Agent Ruben Perry, while attempting to force Navajo children into school at Fort Defiance, was overpowered and held captive by Doo Yáłti'í, "Silent One," and his followers for two days. Soldiers later captured the rebels, who were sent for a year to Alcatraz Prison in San Francisco Bay before being transferred to Fort Huachuca, in extreme southern Arizona.

Figure 9. These apartment buildings along the west bank of Chinle Wash are examples of the high-density housing that has been growing in Chinle since the mid-1980s. The influx of people has brought to Chinle a host of problems normally associated with larger cities, like crime and gang activity.

In the Emergence story of the Navajo creation legend, a ceremony was held near Chinle to celebrate the "nubility" of 'Asdzą́ą́nádleehí, Changing Woman.

✤ Role in Hillerman Fiction:

The Blessing Way: Anthropologist Bergen McKee called Joe Leaphorn from the Gulf station here (chap. 8).

People of Darkness: Lieutenant Joe Leaphorn is stationed here (chap. 6).

The Ghostway: After failing to reach Frank Sam Nakai's winter place via Greasewood Flats, Jim Chee circles back and drives through Round Rock, Many Farms, and Chinle, to the south side of Black Mesa, past Cottonwood and Blue Gap, before attempting to mount Carson Mesa again from the south (chap. 24).

Skinwalkers: Navajo Police Officer Gorman at Shiprock had been loaned out to Chinle, and he investigated the murder of Wilson Sam (chap. 5).

Sacred Clowns: In their first meeting with Joe Leaphorn, Asher Davis and Roger Applebee rented a car in Farmington for Applebee to drive to Canyon de Chelly. Applebee then rode to Flagstaff with some other "big environmentalists" and flew to San Francisco from there, mailing Davis the keys to the rental car. Davis had called Chinle Police Substation and Leaphorn arranged for someone to return the car from Chinle to Farmington (chap. 19).

The Fallen Man: Joe Leaphorn had been stationed at Chinle when Harold Breedlove disappeared from the Thunderbird Lodge at Canyon de Chelly (chap. 2). Guide Amos Nez is hospitalized in the Indian Health Service facility here after being shot at Canyon de Chelly (chap. 3). The Chinle Substation of the Navajo Tribal Police is in charge of investigating the Amos Nez shooting; officers here tell Leaphorn that Nez is not cooperating with them (chap. 6). Joe Leaphorn returns a call to Sergeant Addison Deke at Chinle about a message from Deke concerning a "poacher" seen on the Black Rock Canyon rim of Canyon del Muerto above Amos Nez's home—where no one has seen a deer "since God knows when" (chap. 11).

Hunting Badger: Deputy Sheriff Cowboy Dashee is stationed at Chinle (chap. 8).

CHINLE WASH: (5058–4200 ft) Apache County, AZ, San Juan County, Utah. Also Chinle Creek. At least in the vicinity of Canyon de Chelly, the Navajo name is the same as the name for the community: Ch'ínílį ("Water Outlet").

This stream is formed by the confluence of De Chelly and Del Muerto Washes at the mouth of the Canyon de Chelly system, just east of the community of Chinle. From here it turns north and travels some 85 miles through Many Farms and Rock Point to empty into the San Juan River in Utah, approximately midway between Bluff and Mexican Hat. Along the way, it is fed by the major tributaries of Nazlini Wash, Black Mountain Wash, Lukachukai Wash, Laguna Creek, and Walker Creek.

Troops under Major Henry L. Kendrick called the wash Rio de Chelly (or Rio de Cheille or Rio de Chella) in 1853, since it came forth from the mouth of the canyon complex.

❖ Role in Hillerman Fiction:

The Blessing Way: In his search for the "Big Navajo," Joe Leaphorn determines that the man's Land Rover had crossed Chinle wash several times (chap. 15).

Skinwalkers: Dugai Endocheeney's hogan is at the confluence of Chinle Wash with the San Juan River (chap. 2).

Hunting Badger: Ute raiders would disappear along here, maybe Chinle Wash or Gothic Creek (chap. 13).

CHIVATO MESA: (8530–8917 ft) McKinley, Cibola, and Sandoval Counties, NM. The Navajo name remains uncertain. This feature is the northeastern extension of the San Mateo Mountains. It runs approximately 25 miles from the point where it emanates from the base of Mount Taylor to its northeastern terminus 15 miles south of Torreon.

❖ Role in Hillerman Fiction:

Sacred Clowns: Jim Chee and BIA Police Sergeant Harold Blizzard drive past Chivato Mesa as they search the Torreon region for Delmar Kanitewa (chap. 10).

CHUSKA MOUNTAINS: (approx. 7500–9365 ft) McKinley and San Juan counties, NM (and Apache County, AZ). Also Chuska Range. The Navajo

Figure 10. The Chuska Mountains as seen from the south, about five miles south of Tohatchi, New Mexico, on U.S. Highway 666.

name Ch'óshgai, which means "White Spruce," refers specifically to the Chuskas, the major component of the 90-mile-long Chuska-Tunicha-Lukachukai Range. (Some historians mistakenly have suggested that "Chuska" is an Americanization of the Spanish "Tunicha"—the closest the Spanish could come to pronouncing Tó Ntsaa, Navajo meaning "Abundant Water.")

These mountains snake along the New Mexico–Arizona line from New Mexico Highway 264 north to the Carrizo Mountains. Navajos refer to the entire range as Níłtsá Dził, meaning "Rainy Mountain." The mountain's highest point is just north of Narbona Pass (formerly Washington Pass); Chuska Peak (above Tohatchi) is 600 ft lower at 8765 ft.

In the Navajo Blessing Chant stories, the Chuskas comprise the body of Yo'dí Dził ("Goods of Value Mountain"), a male anthropomorphic figure, of which Chuska Peak is the head. Beautiful Mountain is his feet and the Carrizos his lower extremities; Shiprock is a medicine pouch or bow that he carries.

These mountains were a confirmed Navajo stronghold by 1796, and they were traversed by Governor José Antonio Vizcarra in 1823. Several important battles were fought in and around the Chuskas between Navajos against the Spanish, Mexican, and American militaries.

✤ Role in Hillerman Fiction:

The Blessing Way: Anthropologist Bergen McKee suggests these mountains (along with the Lukachukais and Kah Bihgi Valley) to Ellen Leon as a possible place to look for her wayward electrical engineer, Jimmy W. Hall, Ph.D. (chap. 3).

People of Darkness: While attending the University of New Mexico, Jim Chee would spend semester breaks at his mother's place in the Chuskas (chap. 11).

The Dark Wind: Captain Largo tells Jim Chee to go visit family in these

Figure 11. Whiskey Lake, a man-made reservoir, sits atop the Chuskas near the eastern escarpment, above Tohatchi, New Mexico. This lake is a favorite fishing and camping spot for Navajos across the reservation, as well as for non-Navajos from Gallup and Farmington, New Mexico.

mountains to minimize suspicion that he had anything to do with the missing cargo from Pauling's crashed airplane (chap. 12).

The Ghostway: The people around Shiprock and the Chuska Mountains call 81-year-old Joseph Joe "Hosteen," a term of general respect that means "old man" (chap. 1). Jim Chee, FBI Agent Sharkey, and San Juan Sheriff's Deputy Bales drive into these rugged mountains at night (without the use of their headlights) in search of Ashie Begay's hogan, where they expect to find Albert Gorman (chap. 2). Captain Largo surmises that Albert Gorman, after leaving the shooting at the Shiprock Economy Wash-O-Mat, must have laid up in the region bounded by the Shiprock pinnacle and the Chuska, Carrizo, and Lukachukai Mountains (chap. 2). A body assumed to be Albert Gorman is found buried near the hogan of Ashie Begay (chap. 2). Chee drives back into the Chuskas to re-scour Ashie Begay's camp and encounters Ashie's grand-daughter, Margaret Billy Sosi, and the horse stolen from Two Grey Hills Trading Post (chap. 8). Upon his return from his eventful trip to Los Angeles, Chee returns for the third time to Ashie Begay's hogan in the Chuskas to see if he can verify Bentwoman's assertion that Begay must be dead. In the chinde hogan, Chee finds Ashie Begay's Four Mountains Bundle, containing herbs and minerals from the four sacred mountains: the San Francisco Peaks in Arizona (sacred mountain of the west), Mount Hesperus in the La Plata Mountains of Colorado (sacred mountain of the north), Blanca Peak in the Sangre de Cristo Mountains of Colorado (sacred mountain of the east), and Mount Taylor in New Mexico (sacred mountain of the south) (chap. 22). Leaving the Chuskas in the snowstorm, Chee had to drive three hours to get to the graded road leading toward the Toadlena Boarding School (chap. 23).

Skinwalkers: A thunderstorm, which had built over the Chuskas and promised rain to parched Shiprock, had finally moved north into Utah with no moisture for Shiprock (chap. 1).

A Thief of Time: These mountains rise to Jim Chee's left as he drives up the Chuska Valley toward Tsaya, looking for evangelist Slick Nakai (chap. 13).

Talking God: Navajo Tribal Councilwoman Agnes Tsosie was known to just about everybody west of the Chuskas (chap. 2).

Coyote Waits: These mountains are described as a corner of the triangle in which the community of Red Rock is located (chap. 1). (The other two corners are the Carrizo Mountains and Shiprock Pinnacle.) Ashie Pinto's grandfather told him of two White men killed by Navajos south of the San Juan and east of the Chuska Mountains in the late 1800s (chap. 7).

Sacred Clowns: Jim Chee chose a smaller office in Window Rock because its window offered a view of the southern ragtag end of the Chuska range (chap. 8). Chee finds his mentor singer, Frank Sam Nakai, in higher summer pastures in the Chuskas (chap. 12). Chee and Nakai search for Hosteen Barbone, only to find he has gone from his home near Crystal to someplace in the Chuskas west of Two Grey Hills (chap. 24).

The Fallen Man: A power line from the vicinity of Shiprock travels in the direction of the Chuska Mountains (chap. 11).

The First Eagle: Jim Chee visits the dying Hosteen Frank Sam Nakai near the northern end of the Chuskas (chap. 21).

Hunting Badger: Jim Chee drives over the Chuskas traveling from Farmington to Lukachukai (chap. 8). Chee visits Frank Sam Nakai's home in the Chuska Mountains, but finds that neither Nakai nor his wife is home (chap. 10); discovers Nakai is in the hospital in Farmington. After visiting the hospital with Officer Bernadette Manuelito, Chee brings Nakai home (in an ambulance) to die (chap. 11).

CHUSKA VALLEY: (5500 ft) McKinley County, NM. The Navajo name is uncertain, though the English name is a derivative of the Navajo Ch'óshgai, the name of the nearby mountains. This designation refers to that portion of the San Juan Basin between the foot of the Chuska Mountains and the Chaco River.

Navajos occupied the Chuska Valley as early as A.D. 1750. It was in this valley that Spanish Governor Fernando Chacon met with Navajo headmen in May 1800.

❖ Role in Hillerman Fiction:

A Thief of Time: Jim Chee drives up this valley toward Tsaya, looking for Slick Nakai (chap. 13).

COCONINO RIM: (approx. 7500 ft) Coconino County, AZ. Also Coconino Point, Coconino Plateau, and Gray Mountain. The Navajo name Dził Łibáí ("Gray Mountain") refers to that vast highland plateau that comprises the South Rim of the Grand Canyon and gives rise to the San Francisco Peaks. Formerly Havasupai territory, this plateau was first entered by Navajos around the middle of the nineteenth century, according to Béésh Łigaii Atsidí ("Silversmith"), whose father and other Navajos from the Piñon region lived with the Havasupai on Gray Mountain over 100 years ago.

During the 1850s, Coconino Point was the scene of a fight between Navajos and a band of Mexican horse thieves and slave raiders. The Mexicans were all killed, except for two who escaped to Oraibi and, with the help of the Hopis, eventually returned to the Rio Grande.

Traditionally, many Little Colorado River Navajos would leave the treeless barrens of the river valley for the abundance of winter fuel growing on the plateau. A presidential Executive Order of 1918 and the additional purchases by the Indian Department gave the Navajos title to certain springs in the southern part of the highland over which there had been a great deal of trouble between Navajos and White stockmen.

❖ Role in Hillerman Fiction:

The Dark Wind: From where Jim Chee discovers the carryall hidden in the tributary of Wepo Wash, he can see thunderheads over the plateau (chap. 15).

COLORADO RIVER: (12,000–0 ft) Grand, Eagle, Garfield, and Mesa counties, CO; Grand, San Juan, Garfield, and Kane counties, UT; and Coconino and Mohave counties, AZ. Navajos call this, the largest river in the southwestern United States, Tó Nts'ósíkooh, meaning "Slim Water Canyon." An older name meant "Life Without End."

This river forms all or portions of the Arizona-Nevada and Arizona-California state lines. Originally, the name Colorado applied only to that portion below the confluence of the Green and Grand rivers in eastern Utah. The Colorado legislature changed the name of the Grand to the Colorado, in order to gain a claim on the massive amount of water this 1,440-mile-long river dumped into the Gulf of California. Along its length, the Colorado takes in such tributaries as the Gunnison, Green, San Juan, Little Colorado, Paria, Escalante, Virgin, Williams, and Gila rivers. It has been dammed at Glen Canyon (to form Lake Powell), Black Canyon (forming Lake Mead), and Davis (for

Lake Havasu). During the 1960s, the Department of the Interior even planned dams in Marble Canyon and the Grand Canyon, but these were thwarted by environmentalists.

This river is in serious danger today. During the 1960s, with the completion of Glen Canyon Dam and the intensive irrigation projects in southern California and Arizona, the water's salinity at the Mexican border rose from 200 parts per million to 1,500 parts per million, rendering the water unusable. With the OPEC oil embargo of the 1970s, however, when Americans began eyeing perceived Mexican oil reserves, the United States constructed the Yuma River Desalinization Plant, which now purifies water at a cost of $300.00 per acre-foot. (Irrigators along the river pay only $3.50 per acre-foot of water used.)

To the Navajos, the Colorado is female, mounted by the male San Juan River at what is now Lake Powell. The location of this union of waters, now submerged beneath the lake, is a highly ceremonial location to the Navajos.

✤ Role in Hillerman Fiction:

The Dark Wind: Largewhiskers Begay, accused of trespassing on Mary Joe Natonabah's grazing rights, lives at the Colorado River Gorge (chap. 18).

Coyote Waits: Cliffs of the Colorado River canyon are visible from murder victim Ashie Pinto's home on Blue Moon Bench (chap. 5).

Hunting Badger: Chee's mentor, Frank Sam Nakai, remembered the building of Glen Canyon Dam to form Lake Powell, impounding waters of both the San Juan and Colorado Rivers (chap. 11).

COMB CREEK: (7000–4400 ft) San Juan County, UT. Perhaps better known today as Comb Wash. According to the U.S. Indian Claims Commission, Navajos refer to this stream as Nagashi Bicho (*sic*), which the commission interpreted as "Mountain Sheep's Trail." However, Navajo linguist and ethnographer Robert Young says the Navajo translation of this English phrase would actually be Tsétah Dibé Bitiin, and he doubts "Nagashi" is a Navajo word. The section nearest Mexican Hat, though, is called Bicho'adahditiin ("Mountain Sheep's Testicle Trail Down").

This stream heads on the southeast tip of Milk Ranch Ridge, near the northern tip of Comb Ridge. It parallels the west face of Comb Ridge some 30 miles south, where it joins the San Juan River about 10 miles southwest of the town of Bluff.

✤ Role in Hillerman Fiction:

A Thief of Time: Joe Leaphorn searches the mouth of this creek while floating down the San Juan River looking for missing anthropologist Eleanor Friedman-Bernal (chap. 18).

COMB RIDGE: (5945 ft) Navajo and Apache Counties, AZ, and San Juan County, UT. In Navajo, this feature is Tsé Yík'áán ("Rock Extends in the Form of a Narrow Edge"). This substantial sandstone uplift runs northeast to southwest for 55 miles between Chaistla Butte and Cane Valley. It forms the southern boundary of the Little Capitan Valley (south of Monument Valley), about four miles north of U.S. Highway 160.

This formation is important in Navajo mythology. It is considered one of the arms of a female anthropomorphic figure known as Pollen Mountain. (Navajo Mountain is her head, Black Mesa her body, Balakai Mesa her feet, and Tuba Butte and Agathla Peak her breasts). It is also the edge of a massive furrow dug by the youngest brother in the Changing Bear Maiden legend of the Upward Reachingway chant of the Evilway Ceremony. It is the sharp edge of one of four arrowheads used to form the earth during the creative period, and it is considered the spine of the world, encircling the earth underground from its prominence in Arizona and Utah.

✤ Role in Hillerman Fiction:

Hunting Badger: Comb Ridge creates a zigzag of light and shadow as Jim Chee and Cowboy Dashee drive across the sagebrush flats of Nokaito Bench (chap. 8).

COPPERMINE, COPPERMINE MESA, and **COPPERMINE TRADING POST:** (6100 ft) Coconino County, AZ. Also called Keams District. The Navajo name is Tsinaabáás Habitiin, meaning "Ascending Wagon Road." Located on the Red Mesa portion of the Kaibito Plateau 25 miles north of the Gap, this tiny chapter seat and trading community is 10 miles due east of Bitter Springs and the junction of U.S. Highway 89 with Alternate 89 along the Echo Cliffs. Coppermine Trading Post opened in the early 1930s.

Thomas Varker Keam (of Keams Canyon) and associates prospected and located copper here in the 1880s. In 1915, the Pittsburgh Copper and Mining Company worked the mines and in 1917 the Navajo Copper Company reopened the 1882 diggings. The Arizona Copper and Chemical Company followed. In the 1940s, there was considerable activity mining and manufacturing copper sulphate, employing 15 to 20 Navajos. The surrounding region is good stock country, and a small band of antelope still roamed the plateau in the forties.

Two sets of three-toed, bipedal dinosaur tracks have been discovered in the Navajo and Wingate sandstones of the Kaibito Plateau, one a half mile north of Coppermine, the other two miles north.

✤ Role in Hillerman Fiction:

Coyote Waits: Mary Keeyani tells Joe Leaphorn that Ashie Pinto once found a horse for a man from Coppermine (chap. 3).

The First Eagle: Five days before his death, Anderson Nez had visited his mother's hogan four miles southwest of the trading post before joining Al Woody near Goldtooth (chap. 15).

CORN MOUNTAIN: (7100 ft) McKinley County, NM. Shown on most maps as Dowa Yalani Mountain; also Zuni Sacred Mountain, Thunder Mountain, Taaiyolone, Towayalani, and variations thereof. Navajos call this mesa Tséé'dóhdoon, "Rumbling Inside the Rock," and Tsé Hooghan, "Rock House." Located two miles southeast of the village of Zuni.

Figure 12. The people of Zuni took refuge atop Corn Mountain more than once during their encounters with the early Spanish exploration and conquest expeditions.

❖ Role in Hillerman Fiction:
    Dance Hall of the Dead: The Bowlegs's family home lay behind this mesa (chap. 3). Archaeologist Ted Isaacs is excavating a Folsom site near the eastern foot of this mountain sacred to the Zunis (chap. 4).

CORTEZ: (6198 ft) (Population: 7,284) Montezuma County, CO. Navajos refer to this southwestern Colorado agricultural community as Tséyaatóhí, meaning "Water Under the Rock." Located in the well-watered McElmo Creek Valley, Cortez was named for Spanish explorer Hernan Cortez by the first Anglo founders in 1887. The town was incorporated on November 2, 1902. The town is located on McElmo Creek, at the highway junction of U.S. Highways 164 and 666. The entry to Mesa Verde National Park is a short 11 miles east of the community.

In addition to serving the local farmers and ranchers, Cortez is a commercial center for residents of Colorado's Ute Mountain Ute and Southern Ute reservations, as well as for Navajos of southeastern Utah.

❖ Role in Hillerman Fiction:

Coyote Waits: According to the newspaper article Dr. Tagert discovered, the two escaping train robbers were observed passing through Cortez in the late 1800s (chap. 9).

The Fallen Man: Driving between Cortez and Mancos, Jim Chee and Officer Bernadette Manuelito run into the full brunt of a winter blizzard (chap. 25).

Hunting Badger: Joe Leaphorn calls a friend, Marci Trujillo, in Cortez, who confirms a rumor that $400,000 was taken in the Ute Casino robbery (chap. 24).

COTTONWOOD: (6600 ft) Apache County, AZ. Navajos call this vicinity Tsé Łání, "Many Rocks," or Tsigai Deez'áhí, "White Rock Point." This small trading settlement is located on Navajo Route 4, in the sloping foothill country with scant vegetation on the east side of Balakai Mesa, some 19 miles southwest of Chinle.

Here within a few scant miles lie two trading posts and the Tselani Chapter House. Cottonwood Trading Post is on the highway, as is the BIA Cottonwood Day School; Salina Springs Trading post, established about 1910, is four miles to the south. The Presbyterian Church established the Child's Community Center here, along with the Tselani Health Center, which closed in 1962.

Balakai Mesa, which dominates the whole horizon west of Salina, is the summer range for the Salina Navajos and is ceremonially important as the lower extremities of the female figure called Pollen Mountain of the Blessing Side Ceremony.

❖ Role in Hillerman Fiction:

The Dark Wind: Jim Chee stops here for directions to Fanny Musket's place (chap. 17); Joseph Musket and the son of Jake West (from Burnt Water Trading Post) had been schoolmates at the boarding school here (chap. 17).

The Ghostway: After failing to reach Frank Sam Nakai's winter place via Greasewood Flats, Jim Chee circles back and drives through Round Rock, Many Farms, and Chinle, to the south side of Black Mesa, past Cottonwood and Blue Gap, before attempting to mount Carson Mesa again from the south (chap. 24).

COUNSELORS: (7000 ft) Sandoval County, NM. Navajos refer to this trading post as Bilagáana Nééz, "Tall White Man," for trader Jim Counselor, who opened the post during the winter of 1922–23. It is situated on U.S. Highway 550 (formerly New Mexico Highway 44), about 30 miles west of Cuba. By the mid-twentieth century, a sheep ranch and guest ranch were added to the trading settlement in this wooded region west of the continental divide.

Prior to the Navajo acquisition of automobiles, this locale was the trading center for the Navajos living southwest of the Jicarilla Apache Reservation. It lies in the Dinétah (the traditional Navajo homeland), and has served as base for archaeological and historical investigations of the old Navajo country by the School of American Research, Columbia University, and the United States Indian Service (predecessor of the Bureau of Indian Affairs). The region abounds in old Navajo sites, and many stone watchtowers are located at vantage points on mesa rims. Counselor Chapter House is located here.

❖ Role in Hillerman Fiction:

A Thief of Time: Here Jim Chee finds out about Old Lady Daisy Manygoats's family (chap. 13), who were of Slick Nakai's congregation (chap. 13).

COW SPRINGS (TRADING POST): (5800 ft) Coconino County, AZ. The Navajos call this place Béégashii Bito' ("Cow Spring"). This trading post on U.S. Highway 160, some nine miles northeast of Tonalea, was established as a summer and fall post by George McAdams in 1882. It was run as a William and Babbitt post by 1895. Cow Springs Wash was encountered by men of Vizcarra's campaign of 1823, who called it "Arroyo de los Pilares," apparently in reference to the nearby Elephant's Feet pillars.

❖ Role in Hillerman Fiction:

Listening Woman: Joe Leaphorn listens to tapes of Listening Woman as he drives Navajo Route 1 from Tuba City, Arizona, to the turn-off to Cow Springs on his way to Low Mountain Trading Post (chap. 5).

Figure 13. Today the historic Cow Springs Trading Post is a hollow shell, covered with gang-oriented graffiti.

COYOTE CANYON and **COYOTE WASH:** (6100 ft) McKinley County, NM. Navajos call this locale Mą'ii Tééh Yítłizhí, meaning "Where the Coyote Fell into Deep Water." On Navajo Route 9, 10 miles east of U.S. Highway 666, this canyon, deeply eroded by the headwaters of Coyote Wash, heads five miles south of the highway.

It flows north, joining Tohatchi Wash, which, with the Red Willow and Standing Rock washes, merges with Chaco Wash at its Great Bend 30 miles north of Coyote Canyon Trading Post. A segment of Chacoan prehistoric road leads northward from this vicinity.

Navajos say the name Coyote Canyon came from the story of a coyote that, while trying to drink from a sinkhole in the rock, fell in and could not get out.

The first trading post at Coyote Canyon was established by George Washington Sampson (known to the Navajos as Hastiin Bái, "Gray Man") in the 1890s. It was sold to Dan Dubois in 1902.

Sampson also held posts at Sanders, Arizona (1883), Rock Spring (north of Gallup, 1887), Tohatchi, New Mexico (prior to 1892), and at Lukachukai and Chilchinbito, Arizona.

Charles Baker held Coyote Canyon Trading Post in 1909. James Brimhall expanded the post in 1919. The locale later became home to Coyote Canyon Chapter House.

✤ Role in Hillerman Fiction:

Dance Hall of the Dead: Shorty Bowlegs (George's father) married a woman from here (chap. 13).

People of Darkness: Jim Chee determines that Rudolph Becenti (survivor of the oil rig explosion) lived at Coyote Canyon (chap. 22).

A Thief of Time: At Coyote Canyon, Darcy Ozzie (of Old Lady Daisy Manygoats's outfit) tells Jim Chee that Slick Nakai had headed to a place between White Rock and Tsaya, and then was bound for Lower Greasewood (chap. 13).

Coyote Waits: Mrs. Greyeyes, a juror on the Ashie Pinto jury, is thought by the prosecuting attorney to be from Nakaibito, but she is actually from near Coyote Canyon (chap. 18).

Sacred Clowns: Leaphorn and Streib drive past Nazhoni Trading Post on their way to Crownpoint to meet with Lieutenant Ed Toddy concerning the murder of Thoreau teacher Eric Dorsey (chap. 4). The family of Eugene Ahkeah, suspected in the murder of Eric Dorsey, lives at Coyote Canyon, even though Ahkeah had a place in Thoreau (chap. 5). Jim Chee and BIA Police Sergeant Harold Blizzard pass through here returning from their Torreon region search for Delmar Kanitewa (chap. 11).

COYOTE PASS CHAPTER: A fictitious location.

✤ Role in Hillerman Fiction:

Sacred Clowns: The KNDN radio news transcripts from three days prior to Jim Chee's Crownpoint meeting with BIA Police Sergeant Harold Blizzard announced the death in Gallup of a former Chairwoman of Coyote Pass Chapter (chap. 8).

CROSS CANYON (TRADING POST): (7000–6800 ft) Apache County, AZ. A canyon at the head of Fish Wash, five miles south of the last Cross Canyon Trading Post on Arizona Highway 264. Navajos call this location 'Ah Ba Deel Hadisa ("Creek Connection") and Béésh Dich'ízhii ("Rough Flintstone"). The English name comes from a Navajo trail crossing a canyon at the head of Fish Wash, five miles to the south of the trading post. In the 1940s a collection of hogans here was called Burnt Piñon.

The trading post is on Arizona Highway 264, on the west slope of the Defiance Plateau, about 10 miles east of Ganado. The original post was built south of the present highway by C. C. Manning of Gallup at the turn of the century. Historian Richard Van Valkenburgh noted that some considerable Navajo-White violence occurred here between 1915 and 1922.

✤ Role in Hillerman Fiction:

Skinwalkers: Looking out his Window Rock office window, Joe Leap-horn knows it's raining at Cross Canyon while Chee is visiting the Dinnebito Wash country (chap. 19).

Coyote Waits: Joe Leaphorn daydreams of receiving his first math lesson on randomness while attending a sing-dance (song and dance) between Kin-leechee and Cross Canyon when he was a junior at Arizona State University (chap. 15).

Figure 14. Cross Canyon Trading Post was abandoned in the early-to-middle 1980s.

Figure 15. The Navajo Tribal Police Headquarters (and jail) in Chinle is a modern, brick building atop the hill on Navajo Route 9 near the western edge of town.

CROWNPOINT: (6943 ft) (Population: 2,108) McKinley County, NM. Navajos call this community T'ííst'óóz Ńdeeshgizh, meaning "Narrow-Leafed Cottonwood Gap"; also T'iists'ózí, "Slender Cottonwood." This largely government settlement is located at the junction of New Mexico Highway 371 and Navajo Route 9, 24 miles north of Thoreau. It is comprised of a chapter house, public schools, a BIA boarding school, and the Navajo Institute of Technology. An Indian Health Service medical center opened here in 1940, starting with a 65-bed hospital, and the Navajo Police maintain a substation here. Radio station KTGM operated from here in the 1940s, along with a U.S. Weather Bureau station, and the headquarters of the eastern division of the Civilian Conservation Corps–Indian Department. There was also a coal mine nearby.

Traders included two separate Crownpoint Trading Posts between 1905 and 1915, and E. B. Simm, trader. Traders Madison and McCoy also operated in the vicinity, between the late 1890s and 1920.

Crownpoint was founded in 1909 as the Pueblo Bonito Indian School (the sixth school on the reservation) by agent Samuel F. Stacher, whom Navajos called Nat'áanii Yázhí ("Little Boss"). Later it was known as the Eastern Navajo Agency until the Navajo Central Agency at Window Rock absorbed its jurisdiction in 1935. It reverted to Crownpoint subagency status in 1955, and a few years later became the Crownpoint Agency.

One of the most important Navajo figures of this region was Becenti (the son of Becenti Sani), who in 1868 met with the Navajo chiefs at Fort Wingate to determine where the Navajo boundaries were to lie. After many years of leadership and cooperation with the Indian Department, Becenti died in 1937 and was buried in the Gallup cemetery.

At the end of the Navajo Gun Shooter Red Antway Myth, the hero's youngest brother goes to Crownpoint and Hosta Butte.

✤ Role in Hillerman Fiction:

Crownpoint is one of the commonly mentioned places in the Hillerman series, appearing in eight of the 14 Chee/Leaphorn novels.

People of Darkness: Chee has transferred here from Tuba City; has been here less than a year (chap. 2). He attends a Crownpoint Rug Weavers Association Navajo rug auction, where he meets Anglo teacher Mary Landon (chap. 12), and sees Colton Wolf for the first time—talking to Tomas Charley (chap. 12). A sister of Windy Tsossie (a survivor of the oil rig explosion) lives between here and Thoreau (chap. 28).

The Dark Wind: Jim Chee had been transferred from this subagency of the Navajo Tribal Police just six weeks prior to the burglary at Burnt Water Trading Post (chap. 3).

The Ghostway: As he drives into the Chuska Mountains in search of Ashie Begay's hogan, Jim Chee remembers the relationship-ending discussion with Mary Landon in Crownpoint, about his application to the FBI (chap. 2). He also remembers when he first met Mary, at a Crownpoint Rug Auction (chap. 3). Mary Landon teaches fifth grade at Crownpoint Elementary School (chap. 6). Even while he is away in Los Angeles, Jim Chee thinks of Mary Landon in her Crownpoint classroom (chap. 6).

Skinwalkers: Jim Chee remembers happy times at Crownpoint, with schoolteacher Mary Landon (chap. 1).

A Thief of Time: Archaeologist Eleanor Friedman-Bernal once drove out of Chaco on the road toward Crownpoint to go target-shoot with her new pistol (chap. 1). Joe Leaphorn and Bureau of Land Management law enforcement officer L. D. Thatcher drive through here on their way from Window Rock to Chaco Canyon to investigate the disappearance of Friedman-Bernal (chap. 2). Once, a long time ago, Leaphorn called the dispatcher here for help when his car got stuck on the dirt road into Chaco Canyon (chap. 2). Children living at Chaco go to school in Crownpoint (chap. 10).

Talking God: Mary Landon (Officer Chee's erstwhile love interest) taught at the elementary school in Crownpoint when they first met (chap. 7).

Coyote Waits: Even officers from the Crownpoint office of the Navajo Tribal Police are dispatched to the scene of Officer Delbert Nez's murder, nearly 100 miles away (chap. 2).

Sacred Clowns: To aid in his search for Delmar Kanitewa, Jim Chee obtains a photo of Delmar taken from the Crownpoint High School yearbook (chap. 1). Joe Leaphorn and FBI Agent David W. Streib travel to Crownpoint to meet with Navajo Tribal Police Lieutenant Ed Toddy, in whose precinct Thoreau teacher Eric Dorsey was murdered (chap. 4). Most people Jim Chee knew when he was stationed in Crownpoint thought Navajo Tribal

Councilman Jimmy Chester was a jerk (chap. 6). Joe Leaphorn meets BIA Police Sergeant Harold Blizzard at the Crownpoint Navajo Tribal Police Substation to search again for Delmar Kanitewa (chap. 8). Kanitewa's best friend, Felix Bluehorse, lives with his mother in Crownpoint (chap. 9). On being interviewed by Jim Chee and BIA Police Sergeant Blizzard, Bluehorse tells them that Kanitewa is fleeing because Eric Dorsey's killer is chasing him. This connects Kanitewa to the second murder (his clown uncle being the first) (chap. 9). Chee had earlier earned Acting Sergeant stripes while stationed here, but he was busted for not following the rules (chap. 11). Joe Leaphorn calls the police substation here from his home in Window Rock, leaving a message for Lieutenant Ed Toddy to meet him at St. Bonaventure Mission in Thoreau (chap. 21). Leaphorn and Asher Davis had earlier crossed trails at a Crownpoint rug auction (chap. 21). On the way between Gallup and Aztec, Jim Chee and Janet Pete stop in Crownpoint to pick up Eugene Ahkeah (the lead suspect in the murder of Eric Dorsey) from the Crownpoint Navajo Tribal Police Substation (chap. 26).

CRYSTAL: (7800 ft) San Juan County, NM. Old name, Cottonwood Pass. Navajos call this place Tó Niłts'ílí, meaning "Clear Water" or "Sparkling Water," for Crystal Creek, on which the tiny community is situated. This trading post and village is located on Navajo Route 32 in the Chuska Mountains, at the west entrance to Narbona Pass (formerly Washington Pass). It is one of the half-dozen best-known trading posts on the reservation, having given its name to a fine weaving style, the "Crystal Rug."

Romulo Martinez was trading in Narbona Pass as early as 1873. Ben Hyatt was trading in 1882–84, and Stephen Aldrich and Elias Clark were present in 1884. Clark joined Charles Hubbell (brother of Lorenzo) the next year, followed by Walter Fales in 1885, Michael Donovan in 1886, and Perry Williams in 1887.

Government records show that the first trader at Crystal was Michael Donovan of Onondaga County, New York, who in 1884 established the post with Clarence Tooley and John H. Bowman (Navajo Agent 1884–85) as clerks. These early traders were followed by Joe Reitz (who had earlier traded with Joe Wilkin and Elmer E. Whitehouse) in 1894. They were bought out by John B. Moore during the winter of 1896–97. Moore, according to his own 1912 commercial brochure on Navajo weaving—with color plates—was one of the earliest traders to send Navajo wool away to be scoured, to grade the rugs, and to develop a mail-order business in Navajo rugs.

That same brochure listed Moore's Special Grade rugs (ER-20) as priced (according to size) from 90 cents to $1.00 per square foot. His second Tourist Grade (-TXX) rugs sold for $1.00 to $2.00 per pound, regardless of size. It also

Figure 16. The ruins of historic Crystal Trading Post sit near the front of the much newer Mormon church.

publicized one of Moore's top weavers, a young woman named Łį́į́łbáhí Be'esdzáán ("Gray Horse's Woman"). Many of the rugs shown in the catalogue are strikingly similar to those of the Two Grey Hills type of today, rather than the typical banded, vegetal-dyed rugs for which the region is now most renowned.

Moore sold the post to his manager, Jesse A. Molohon, in 1911. The post became part of the C. C. Manning company 1919–22, and Charlie Newcomb owned the post around 1936. Jim Collyer acquired the post and sold it to Don Jenson (in 1944), who held the post until 1981, when he moved to the Inscription House post after selling Crystal to Charlie and Evelyn Andrews. According to Navajo weaver H. P. James, Jenson was responsible for developing the current Crystal rug.

Crystal Creek was once known as Rio Negro (Black River), possibly because of the fact that it fed Laguna Negra (Black Lake). It may also be the stream that was named Simpson Creek by geological surveyor Herbert Gregory, in honor of cartographer Captain James Simpson, of the first Anglo-American expedition to cross the Chuska and Lukachukai Mountains (in 1849–50).

❖ **Role in Hillerman Fiction:**

Skinwalkers: Joe Leaphorn takes the "shortcut" through Crystal and Sheep Springs on his trip from Window Rock to Shiprock (chap. 11).

Coyote Waits: Joe Leaphorn and Professor Louisa Bourebonette stop and look around at Narbona Pass in the Chuska Mountains on their way from Window Rock to Shiprock (chap. 12).

Sacred Clowns: Old man Victor Todachenee, a hit-and-run victim, is from Crystal (chap. 3). Frank Sam Nakai promises to talk to old-timers living around Crystal to see if clan relationships will let Jim Chee be romantically involved with Janet Pete, whose family is from the Hunger People Clan (chap. 10). Jim Chee and Nakai drive past Crystal on a trip to see a hataali named Barbone in their quest to see if Chee can be romantically involved with someone from Janet Pete's father's Hunger People Clan (chap. 18).

DEFIANCE PLATEAU: (8304 ft at Fluted Rock, its highest point) Apache County, AZ. The Navajo name is uncertain, but it is generically referred to as Dził, "Mountain." A massive upland plateau west of the Chuska Mountains and east of the Painted Desert and Chinle Valley. It extends from the Rio Puerco of the West (near Houck) in the south 75 miles north to the vicinity of Lukachukai. From St. Michaels, in the east, it reaches west to Ganado. In all, it covers some 1,875 square miles. The English name is for Fort Defiance, situated at its eastern foot in the vicinity of today's community of the same name.

This upland is heavily forested in ponderosa pine, and has seen many episodes of logging prior to the moratorium placed on such extractive activities in the late 1980s. The village of Sawmill, once the site of the Navajos' own sawmill, sits high on the eastern slope of the plateau near Fluted Rock.

The western face is heavily eroded, with outcrops of red and pink sandstone common among the many resulting canyons—which include the Canyon de Chelly system.

❖ Role in Hillerman Fiction:

Talking God: Lieutenant Leaphorn drives over this upland on his journey from his office in Window Rock to Lower Greasewood to visit Agnes Tsosie (chap. 3).

DE NA ZIN WILDERNESS: (6100–6000 ft) San Juan County, NM. The Navajo name is uncertain. This small designated wilderness lies on Coal Creek, a tributary of De Na Zin (Dééł Náázíní) Wash, less than five miles northeast of the Bisti Wilderness. Some references erroneously equate Coal Creek with De Na Zin Wash itself.

❖ Role in Hillerman Fiction:

Sacred Clowns: Jim Chee can see the discoloration of this region from Frank Sam Nakai's place high in the Chuska Mountains (chap. 12).

DESERT CREEK: (4600–4500 ft) San Juan County, UT. The Navajo name is uncertain. This normally dry channel is a southern tributary of the San Juan River, rising on the eastern slopes of Casa del Eco Mesa. It flows approximately 10 miles to the northeast, meeting the San Juan two miles west of the mouth of Montezuma Creek (a more substantial, northern tributary of the San Juan).

✤ **Role in Hillerman Fiction:**

Hunting Badger: Joe Leaphorn crosses the Aneth Oil Field approaching Casa del Eco Mesa, as per Oliver Potts's map, on his way to Desert Creek in search of Everett Jorie (chap. 9).

DINÉTAH: (5500–9000+ ft) San Juan and Rio Arriba counties, NM. The Navajo name is Dinétah, roughly interpreted as "the old Navajoland." This is the area occupied by the Navajos during their earliest years in the Southwest—as early as A.D. 1550 or even prior to A.D. 1500.

There are some isolated and largely unsubstantiated tree-ring dates (from samples lacking the outside rings of growth, which indicate cutting date) elsewhere in Navajoland that suggest a possible earlier presence—including those found in the vicinity of Quemado, dating to the late 1300s. But the Dinétah is generally accepted by Navajo traditionalists and non-Navajo archaeologists and historians alike as the Navajo's earliest southwestern habitation.

The definition of the Dinétah most often quoted in the literature has it stretching approximately from the continental divide on the east to the juncture of the San Juan River with Canyon Largo on the west, and from the southern edge of Canyon Largo on the south to just above the Colorado state line in the north. Historian Dave Brugge, however, has noted that there are many definitions of the Dinétah, and suggests that it was in reality far more expansive.

On the other hand, historian Robert A. Roessel, Jr., has suggested a much broader area, based largely on Navajo land claims. While he defines it simply as including Blanco, Largo Carrizo, and Gobernador Canyons and their surrounding drainages in northeastern New Mexico, he goes on to suggest that it includes such important Navajo places as the La Plata Mountains (Dibé Ntsaa), Blanca Peak (Sisnaajiní), Hosta Butte ('Ak'iih Dah Nást'ání), Mount Taylor (Tsoodził, "Towered House") or Kinya'a Ruin (Kin Yaa'á), Shiprock (Tsé Bit'a'í), and Wide Belt Mesa (Sis Naateel). Brugge is skeptical, believing the truth lies somewhere in between the two definitions.

In any case, the Dinétah seems to be where the Navajos first contacted the Pueblo Indians, and it is where Spanish explorers in the region first encountered the Navajos. It is also the birthplace and home of Changing Woman ('Asdzą́ą́ Nádleehé—see Gobernador Knob and Huerfano Mesa).

In the seventeenth and eighteenth centuries, the Navajos spread southward and westward into the Chama Valley and Big Bead Mesa regions.

Within the Dinétah, the early Navajo material culture seems to concentrate in Largo and Gobernador Canyons. Here, on Bureau of Land Management land, a large number of important early Navajo sites have been recorded and investigated. These ruins were built during the Gobernador phase of Navajo history. This period of great population movements and hostilities started with the Pueblo Revolt of 1680, in which the Spaniards were driven from the region. With the return of the Spanish in 1692, many Pueblo people fled their Rio Grande homes, some venturing westward into Navajo territory.

There is evidence that the Puebloans and the Navajos lived together here, possibly intermarrying. The threat of attack by the Navajos' northern neighbors, the Utes, kept the sites in defensive locations, such as on mesa ridges and hilltops. The region was ultimately abandoned in the early 1750s, possibly hastened by a drought.

These ruins are all minor in stature, and are called collectively "Pueblitos" (Spanish, meaning "little villages"). The Navajo names are unknown today, but the generic Navajo term "Kits'iilí" (Shattered House) seems to apply to all of them.

Similar structures were discovered in 1978–79 on the east escarpment of the Chuska Mountains, and Brugge notes their appearance on Mesa de los Lobos, as well as near Manuelito, Klagetoh, Ganado, and Nazlini.

✤ Role in Hillerman Fiction:

Hunting Badger: Frank Sam Nakai warns Jim Chee that sometimes you can never return to the Dinétah, meaning you can lose your way as a Navajo and not return (chap. 11).

DINNEBITO WASH: (7200–4400 ft) Navajo and Coconino Counties, AZ. The Navajo name for this channel is Diné Bito', meaning "Navajo's Spring," though the upper reaches of the drainage are referred to as Hooghan Bijáád Łání ("Many Legged Hogan"), referring to an unusual construction style common to hogans in the region, in which walls are formed of stockaded logs planted vertically in the ground.

This 96-mile-long tributary of the Little Colorado River is one of the five major drainages of Black Mesa (the other four are Moenkopi, Oraibi, Polacca, and Wepo Washes). Enlarged by its union with East Fork Dinnebito Wash, it heads on the northeast escarpment of the mesa and flows southwest through the Hopi Reservation northwest of Third Mesa. It flows into the Little Colorado River five miles northwest of Grand Falls.

A portion of this wash was scouted by (Governor) Colonel Jose Antonio Vizcarra in July 1823.

The small trading community of Dinnebito is located in the sparsely vegetated Valley of the Dinnebito Wash where Navajo Route 62 and Dinnebito Wash cross the Navajo-Hopi boundary.

✤ Role in Hillerman Fiction:

The Ghostway: Frank Sam Nakai, medicine man and Jim Chee's teacher, tells Chee that only a few medicine men are left who can cure the ghost sickness, including one old man near Navajo Mountain who still conducts the nine-day ceremony. He learned it from his grandfather over near Dinnebito Wash on Moenkopi Plateau (chap. 24).

Skinwalkers: Jim Chee drives out toward this wash looking for the hogan of Hildegard Goldtooth, where he's supposed to perform a Blessing Way (chap. 5).

The First Eagle: The road Leaphorn had to take to find Jim Chee crosses Dinnebito Wash (chap. 14).

DINNEHOTSO (TRADING POST): (5000 ft) (Population: 616) Navajo County, AZ. Also spelled Dennehotso, Dennehatso, and Dinnehatso. The Navajo name for this location is Denihootso,meaning "Upper Ending of the Meadow," or, more literally, "Yellow-green Streak that Extends Up and Ends." This small chapter community was described by Granger (in 1960) and Van Valkenburgh (in 1941) as a summer camp for 500 Navajo families. It is situated in a shallow sandy valley called Dennehotso Canyon (of Laguna Creek), covered in places with growths of chico or black greasewood. It is located on U.S. Highway 160, some 15 miles west of its junction with U.S. Highway 191. The community hosts a day school and trading post.

Dinnehotso Trading Post opened between 1911 and 1915, and was one of some 20 in New Mexico, Arizona, and Utah owned by the Foutz Brothers (Junius, Alma, Hugh, Jess, Leroy, and Luff). Van Valkenburgh lists the trader in 1941 as Charles Ashcroft.

On the north side of the valley is Comb Ridge and on the south a rolling country that slopes east into Chinle Wash, which Van Valkenburgh calls a "concentrated agricultural area," with little timber for winter firewood.

Settlers from the Kayenta region established farming operations in the lower valley of the Laguna Creek at Tsé 'Awe' ("Baby Rocks") some 15 miles west of Dinnehotso. The floods of 1912 destroyed the natural earth dams in the upper Laguna Creek (or Segi) and released tremendous heads of water, cutting the channel of the lower Laguna Creek down to bedrock and making it impossible for the farm colony at Baby Rocks to divert water from the deep streambed.

Old Crank, leader of the Baby Rocks colony, then led a movement to establish Dinnehotso where there was a shallower channel and a natural dam site.

❖ Role in Hillerman Fiction:

The Ghostway: Jim Chee drives 70 miles over snowpacked highways, passing through Teec Nos Pos, Red Mesa, Mexican Water, and Dinnehotso, on his way to Frank Sam Nakai's winter place (chap. 24).

Skinwalkers: The nephew who found Wilson Sam's body in the tributary of Tyende Creek drove to Dinnehotso Trading Post to call police (chap. 5).

A Thief of Time: Jimmy Etcitty lives between Tes Nez Iha and Dinnehotso (chap. 8).

DULCE: (6800 ft) (Population: 2,438) Rio Arriba County, NM. Navajos call this, the capital of the million-acre Jicarilla Apache Reservation, Beehai, meaning "Jicarilla Apache Home." Located five miles south of the Colorado state line on U.S. Highway 64, this community is situated on a south fork of the Navajo River in a high mountain region of running streams, lakes, and grassy meadows amid ponderosa pine forests. The Denver & Rio Grande Railroad maintained a station here, and the U.S. Indian Service (predecessor of the Bureau of Indian Affairs) ran a cooperative trading post. The name Dulce is Spanish, meaning "sweet," and derives from a spring in the area.

Dulce is well known to the eastern Navajos, particularly to those in the Counselor region, due to a long contact with the Jicarilla Apaches and the appreciable amount of government work they have received from this Indian agency.

Most of the Jicarilla Apaches live in the mountainous region near Dulce in the north; the southern part of the reservation is used primarily for grazing.

For forty years, the trading post at Dulce was the property of Emmett Wirt, pioneer trader and stockman of northern New Mexico.

❖ Role in Hillerman Fiction:

A Thief of Time: Slick Nakai's partner, Reverend Tafoya, had his skin cancer cured by a laying on of hands in a revival tent in Dulce (chap. 4).

DURANGO: (Population: 12,480) La Plata County, CO. Navajos call this city Kin Łani, meaning "Many Houses." This tourist favorite at the junction of U.S. Highways 160 and 550 sits on the Animas River some 21 miles north of the New Mexico state line, at an elevation of 6,505 feet. "Durango" comes from a Basque word meaning "watering place," and the name was bestowed in honor of Durango, Mexico, which was in turn named for a city in Spain (originally "Urango," from "Ur," meaning water, and "Ango," meaning town). The town hosts the Durango-Silverton Narrow Gauge Railroad, fall hunters, winter skiers, and spring and summer kayakers and rafters and general tourists.

Durango was founded in 1880 by the promoters of the Denver & Rio

Grande Railroad, William Bell and Alexander Hunt. Governor Hunt was credited in 1881 with naming the town for its Mexican namesake, where he had traveled on business. However, a mine by the same name had existed by September 1879, and may have lent its name to the town.

Gobernador-phase Navajo pottery has been identified in the region, and archaeologist Florence Ellis suggested that Navajos may have collected obsidian nodules from the banks of the Animas River in the vicinity of Durango. More recent archaeological research indicates that Dinétah-phase Navajos lived along the nearby La Plata River as early as A.D. 1500. Though a sizable percentage of the students at Fort Lewis College are Navajo, Navajos and Utes have only occasionally been hired for menial chores in Durango at low wages.

❖ Role in Hillerman Fiction:

The Dark Wind: Police expect that the jewelry burgled from Burnt Water Trading Post will turn up in Durango, Phoenix, Albuqerque, or Farmington (chap. 3).

A Thief of Time: Jim Chee listens to a radio news program from Durango as he drives toward Farmington through the Bisti Badlands (chap. 13).

Hunting Badger: Everett Jorie, member of the Minutemen militia, once appeared on a radio talk show in Durango (chap. 7).

DZILIDUSHUSHZNINI PEAKS: Navajo County, AZ. From the description, this appears to be Little Black Spot Mountain, also known as Little Black Speck Mountain (elevation 7001 ft). The Navajos call this Dził Dah Zhin, meaning "Black Speck Mountain," or Dziłłátahzhiní, meaning "Black Mountain Peak."

This steep-sided mesa sits atop south-central Black Mesa, five miles southwest of Piñon. There has been considerable confusion between Black Speck Mountain and Big Mountain, as at least one Navajo name appears to apply to both. However, the better name for the latter is Dził Ntsaá, meaning "Extensive Mountain."

❖ Role in Hillerman Fiction:

The Dark Wind: As a boy, Jim Chee would accompany Hosteen Dashee here to collect herbs and minerals (chap. 17).

DZIL NA O DITH HLE SCHOOL: (5800 feet) San Juan County, NM. This BIA school, also spelled Dzilith-Na-O-Dilth-Hle, is called Dził Ná'oodiłii by the Navajos. It is located in the community of Huerfano, at the southern foot of Huerfano Mesa, also called Herfano Mountain, and El Huerfano. The Navajo name (Dził Ná'ooditii) is from the mesa, and means "People Encircling Around Mountain," which refers to a legend in which people moved around the mountain. A sacred name is Nłiz Dził, meaning "Mountain of Precious Stones."

This large, isolated mesa is situated a mile northeast of U.S. Highway 550 (formerly New Mexico Highway 44), 25 miles south of Bloomfield. The school lies between the highway and the southern tip of the mesa, in the vicinity of the old Huerfano Trading Post. (Historian Van Valkenburgh suggested the remains of two trading posts lay south of the mesa.) This post opened sometime prior to 1916, though historian Frank McNitt suggests that Stokes Carson founded it around 1920. The Carsons donated the land on which the Huerfano chapter house was built.

For additional information on this community, see Huerfano Mesa, below.

✤ Role in Hillerman Fiction:

A Thief of Time: Jim Chee had hoped to find Slick Nakai's revival tent between here and Nageezi (chap. 3).

EL DIENTE PEAK: Dolores County, CO. The Navajo name remains uncertain. This 14,159-ft peak is one of the highest in the San Juan Mountains. It rises near the San Miguel County line some 35 miles northeast of the community of Dolores. It is the headwaters for the Dolores River, which flows southwest into Montezuma County near the village of Stoner, before turning northwest near the community of Dolores and flowing into the Colorado River some 30 miles northeast of Moab, Utah.

✤ Role in Hillerman Fiction:

The Fallen Man: Jim Chee learned with disapproval that, before his death, Hal Breedlove had climbed this peak in the San Juan Mountains (chap. 5).

EL MALPAIS (NATIONAL MONUMENT): (6550 ft) Cibola County, NM. Also El Malpais Lava Flow, San Mateo Lava Flow. To the Navajos, this is Yé'iitsoh Bidił Niníyęęzhí, "Where Big God's Blood Coagulated." El Malpais (Spanish meaning "The Badlands") refers to a vast area covered with lava flows from volcanos in the San Mateo and Zuni Mountains. The flows extend from the Grants/Milan area south approximately 35 miles. They are most dense between New Mexico Highway 53 (on the west) and New Mexico Highway 117 (on the east), an area four to six miles wide. The National Monument lies west of New Mexico Highway 117 between 10 and 31 miles south of Interstate 40, extending west to the Ice Caves.

The Navajo name derives from that portion of the Navajo creation myth in which the Twin War Gods on Mount Taylor killed the monster Yé'iitso, "Big God." The lava flows are the coagulated blood of Yé'iitso. The Rio San José,

Figure 17. This portion of El Malpais Lava Flow sits between Interstate 40 and the foothills of Mount Taylor, at the junction of Interstate 40 and New Mexico Highway 117.

flowing west to east, has cut through the flows, separating a small portion at the northern end, near Grants. Legend holds that if the lava flows separated by the Rio San Jose ever grow together, Big God will live again.

In 1882, anthropologist Adolph F. Bandelier described the flows as "…like a frozen and bulged up jet-black river. Terribly broken and burnt. It follows the railroad and furnishes excellent opportunities for surprises and ambushes. Last year the Navajo killed many people here." (This last statement is somewhat perplexing, as the Navajos had been settled on their reservation for 14 years by that time, and, aside from occasional appropriation of livestock, they were predominantly peaceful.)

✤ Role in Hillerman Fiction:

People of Darkness: This is where Jim Chee and Mary Landon discover Tomas Charley and Chee is shot by assassin Colton Wolf (chaps. 13–14).

Coyote Waits: In studying rock formation photos in the darkroom of murdered Huan Ji, Joe Leaphorn and Louisa Bourebonette conjecture the formations photographed could be in numerous locations—including El Malpais (chap. 17).

ESCAVADA WASH: (7000–6200 ft) San Juan and Sandoval counties, NM. Also Escarvada Wash, Choukai Wash. Navajos call this tributary of the Chaco River Gah 'Adádí, meaning "Where You Can Block the Rabbit's Trail," or "Rabbit Ambush." It is formed about two miles southwest of Lybrook (on U.S. Highway 550 [formerly New Mexico Highway 44]), by the convergence of Bitani Tsosi (Bit'ahniits'ósí) Wash and Deesh Bik' Anii'á Bitó (Béésh Bíyaa 'Anii'á Bitooh) Wash.

Traveling some 26 miles southwest and west, it joins the Chaco River at the northwestern corner of the National Historical Park, at Tó Bíla'í, "Water Fingers," near what historian Richard Van Valkenburgh referred to as "Roy Newton's camp" and Penasco Blanco Ruin. "Escarvada" may be a corruption of Spanish "excavada," derived from "excavar," which means to excavate. It has been suggested that this relates to the many prehistoric ruins excavated in the vicinity, but historian David Brugge believes it refers to the fact that water can be found by excavating in the bed of the wash.

✦ Role in Hillerman Fiction:

A Thief of Time: Archaelogical Site BC 129, visited by Joe Leaphorn and BLM law enforcement officer L. D. Thatcher, was located beside this wash (chap. 2).

Sacred Clowns: Jim Chee and Janet Pete drive past this wash on their trip from Gallup to Aztec (chap. 26).

ESCRITO and **ESCRITO SPRING:** (7000 ft) Rio Arriba County, NM. Navajos call this place Tódóó Hódik'ą́adi, meaning "Where an Area Extending from the Water Is Slanted," or, more simply, "Slanted Water," but also translated as "Spring from a High Place." This spring is located near Lybrook on U.S. Highway 550 (formerly New Mexico Highway 44). It has Navajo clan associations, and there are many old Navajo sites in this vicinity.

✦ Role in Hillerman Fiction:

A Thief of Time: Jim Chee drives from Nageezi to Escrito, looking for Slick Nakai (chap. 13).

FAJADA BUTTE: (6450 ft) Also Mesa Fahada, Mesa Fachada, Mesa Fajada. To the Navajos this feature is Tsé Diyiní, or Tsé Diyilí, both of which mean "Holy Rock."

This 450-ft-high sandstone landmark between South Mesa and Chacra Mesa in New Mexico sits a mile and a half east of Fajada Wash, and an equal distance south of Chaco Wash. In the Navajo Windway, the butte's creation occurs when the hero becomes involved with Woman Who Dries People Up and is stranded on a rock that grows through the night, with both of them upon it. It is also one of the important stopping places in the story of the Male Shooting Chant, and nearby Navajos collect medicinal plants here.

A feature called the "Sun Dagger" near its summit has recently become the focus of a study on prehistoric astronomy. Here, a pair of petroglyph spirals have been discovered on a cliff wall beneath three huge slabs of sandstone leaning against the cliff. A remarkable "dagger" of light is formed by the sun shining through gaps between the naturally positioned sandstone slabs. The entire dagger passes across the spirals at the equinox and summer and winter solstices, as well as at major and minor standstills of the moon.

Although this may be nothing more than a shrine with coincidental shadowing, two additional sites with possible astronomical markings have been recorded on the east and west sides of the butte.

❖ Role in Hillerman Fiction:

A Thief of Time: Joe Leaphorn and Bureau of Land Management law enforcement officer L. D. Thatcher drive past this butte on their way to visit Site BC 129, the archaeological ruin where the beautiful Maxie Davis is excavating (chap. 2).

FAJADA WASH: (6575–6150 ft) McKinley and San Juan counties, NM. The Navajo name is uncertain. This wash heads in a series of ephemeral gullies converging a few miles north of Whitehorse, southeast of Pueblo Pintado. It flows northwest approximately 20 miles, merging with the Chaco River just east of Fajada Butte within the main body of the Chaco Culture National Historical Park. It has also been called Becenti Wash.

❖ Role in Hillerman Fiction:

Sacred Clowns: Jim Chee and Janet Pete cross this wash on their trip from Gallup to Aztec (chap. 26).

FARMINGTON: (5308 ft) (Population: 39,028) San Juan County, NM. The Navajo name is Tóta', "Between the Waters," referring to the fact that the community lies between the San Juan and Animas Rivers. This agricultural, Indian trading, and oil refining center was founded in the 1880s, and during its early days was the scene of many difficulties with the Navajos over land tenure.

The northeast corner of the Navajo Reservation is two miles west of Farmington, and Navajos have lived on the south side of the San Juan River in this vicinity for many years, coming to Farmington to barter their products for the excellent fruits grown in the region. They now shop in the town quite regularly all year round.

The Navajo Methodist Mission School was operated here by the Woman's Home Missionary Society beginning in 1890. Originally a grade school, it was developed into a vocational high school for 100 Indian children by the 1940s.

In 1932, the Soil Conservation Service identified a possible Chacoan prehistoric road in the vicinity of the town. The town's population grew wildly during the 1950s, from 3,637 to 23,786, due largely to the oil industry.

❖ Role in Hillerman Fiction:

The Blessing Way: Old Woman Gray Rocks gossiped to anthropologist Bergen McKee at her brush hogan about a son of Hosteen Tom having gone to Farmington to join the Marines, but instead ending up working in the coal mines near Four Corners (chap. 7). Murder victim Luis Horseman had a history of arrests here, as well as in Gallup and Tuba City (chap. 10).

Listening Woman: The nearest Lottaburger (the burger wrappings from which Leaphorn finds in Gold Rims's car) is in Farmington (chap. 2). According to Short Mountain trader "Old Man" McGinnis, Hosteen Tso's son, Ford, used to drink and whore here (chap. 5).

The Dark Wind: It is surmised that the jewelry stolen in the burglary of Burnt Water Trading Post would turn up in Albuquerque, Durango, Phoenix, or Farmington (chap. 3).

The Ghostway: Lerner apparently found Albert Gorman so easily at the Shiprock Economy Wash-O-Mat because the highway from Farmington runs through Shiprock and right past the laundromat parking lot (chap 6). While in the motel in Flagstaff (on his trip home from Los Angeles), Jim Chee wonders how Lerner knew to fly directly to Farmington and drive directly to Shiprock in search of Albert Gorman (chap. 21).

Skinwalkers: FBI Agent Jay Kennedy is stationed in Farmington (chap. 2). Joe Leaphorn wants to check with mobile home dealers here to see if anyone has recently studied the type Jim Chee owns, possibly to determine the most effective placement of shots (chap. 5). The autopsies of murder victims Wilson Sam and Dugai Endocheeney were performed in Farmington (chap. 7).

A Thief of Time: Missing anthropologist Dr. Eleanor Friedman-Bernal had told everyone at Chaco Canyon she would be driving to Farmington (chap. 1). She is unable to find ammunition for her unusual pistol here (chap. 1). Janet Pete goes to Farmington to buy her beautiful blue Buick Riviera (chap. 3). Jim Chee is traveling to Farmington when he spots the backhoe bandit (chap. 3). Jim Chee determines that a single tire dealer in Farmington sells Dayton tires; the dealer tells Chee that they sold a pair with the identified tread pattern to Farmington U-Haul, who in turn identify the renter of the truck with the new Dayton tires as Joe B. Nails (chap. 5). Nails has a record in Farmington, from which Chee discovers that Nails works for Wellserve, Inc. (chap. 5), which is based in Farmington (chap. 5). Missing anthropologist Eleanor Friedman-Bernal's travel agent here calls the Chaco community to tell Eleanor about flight changes, so everyone knows her plans (chap. 10). Bolak travel agent discloses to Jim Chee that Randall Elliot had lied, changing his plans and not taking a trip to New York (chap. 17).

Talking God: Since Farmington is the closest airport to Shiprock, Officer Chee flies Mesa Airlines there from Washington, D.C. (chap. 22).

Coyote Waits: Officer Jim Chee is hospitalized here with burns suffered trying to rescue Officer Delbert Nez from Nez's burning patrol car (chap. 3). FBI agents consider Farmington duty a form of exile (chap. 3).

Sacred Clowns: Someone once offered a craftsman only $2 for a silver pollen container later sold by Asher Davis for $250 (chap. 1). Farmington is the home of KNDN, the radio station to which Chee notices that Delmar Kanitewa's radio is tuned (chap. 3). Janet Pete reminds Jim Chee he once tried to "nail" her client in jail here (chap. 11). An anonymous person confesses on KNDN in Farmington to the hit-and-run death of Victor Todachenee, saying he did not know he hit the man (chap. 13). Jim Chee inquires about the confessor at KNDN, and learns about the man's onion odor, broken-billed baseball cap, and a bumper sticker that says "ERNIE IS THE GREATEST" (chap. 15). Envelope containing money, mailed by the anonymous confessor to Todachenee's family, was postmarked from Farmington (chap. 16). In their first meeting with Joe Leaphorn, Asher Davis and Roger Applebee rented a car in Farmington; Applebee drove it to Canyon de Chelly, then mailed Davis the keys from San Francisco. Davis had called Chinle Police Substation and Leaphorn arranged for someone to return the car to Farmington. Applebee had ridden to Flagstaff with some other "big environmentalists" and flew to San Francisco from there (chap. 19). While driving through Farmington, Jim Chee stops at the QuikPrint shop and orders three bumper stickers (chap. 24).

The Fallen Man: Acting Lieutenant Jim Chee meets Janet Pete at the Carriage Inn Restaurant here for dinner; she informs him of her pending trip to Washington, D.C., where her past flame, John McDermott (the former law professor who hired her when he went into private practice), lives (chap. 6). Joe Leaphorn and Gallup attorney Bob Rosebrough depart the Farmington airport by helicopter for a photography trip to Shiprock Pinnacle (chap. 22).

The First Eagle: Shirley Ahkeah was born here (chap. 2). Joe Leaphorn listens to KNDN on the limousine radio as he is driven to Santa Fe to meet Millicent Vanders; someone on the radio complains of having lost a wallet in the Farmington bus station (chap. 3). Nellie Hale, who lived north of Kaibito, died in the hospital here 10 days after being admitted—the year's first plague fatality (chap. 14). Pawn shops in Gallup, Farmington, and Flagstaff are questioned about receiving parts from the missing Catherine Ann Pollard's Jeep (chap. 17).

Hunting Badger: Teddy Bai, the Ute Casino guard (and County Sheriff Deputy), wounded in the casino robbery, is hospitalized in Farmington (chap. 2). Jim Chee gets information on the casino in Farmington (chap. 5). Police dispatcher Alice Deal tells Chee that wounded casino guard Teddy Bai has been taking flying lessons here (chap. 5). Jim Chee contacts Eldon Timms's insurance agent in Farmington to see how much insurance the rancher had carried on the missing plane (chap. 5). Jim Chee recognizes a helicopter he sees near the scene of the abandoned getaway truck near Bluff as one he saw at the Farmington airport (chap. 8). Chee discovers that his Hataali mentor,

Frank Sam Nakai, is in the hospital in Farmington (chap. 10). Chee meets Joe Leaphorn at the Anasazi Inn to compare notes in the search for the Ute Casino robbers (chap. 13).

FLAGSTAFF: (6905 ft) (Population: 56,657) Coconino County, AZ. The Navajo name is Kin Łání Dook'o'oosłííd Biyaagi, meaning "Many Houses Below San Francisco Mountains." (Several towns are named Kin Łání, so Flagstaff is differentiated by describing its location in relation to the mountains.) This is Arizona's largest city north of the Phoenix metropolitan area. It is nestled in the southern shadow of the San Francisco Peaks, near the east-west center of the state on the Burlington Northern Santa Fe Railway and Interstate 40 (at its junction with Interstate 17).

Flagstaff for many years has been the wholesale trade center for the Hopi and western Navajo reservations, and is a stock and lumber shipping point. It serves as a tourist center and home of Northern Arizona University (formerly Arizona Teachers' College) and the world-class Museum of Northern Arizona. This venerable institution hosts three annual exhibitions for Zuni, Hopi, and Navajo artisans. (Previously, a junior art show and an Arizona art and artisan show were held in May and August.) Until the early 1980s, Flagstaff also hosted the annual Southwest Indian Powwow held over the Fourth of July. In the nearby San Francisco Peaks is Lowell Observatory.

The first settler in the Flagstaff region was Edward Whipple, operator of the Texas Star saloon near Flagstaff Spring in 1871. Edwin Beale, however, of "Uncle Sam's Camels," is known to have camped near Le Roux and Eldon Springs in September 1857.

One scenario for the origin of the town's name is that in 1876 a party of eastern settlers known as the "Boston Party" attempted to settle in the Little Colorado River valley near the Mormon town of St. Joseph (present Joseph City) east of Flagstaff. Suspicious of the Mormons and discouraged with the country, they moved west to Prescott, founded 12 years earlier. That Fourth of July, a party of them camped at Antelope Park, a short distance southwest of present Flagstaff. They celebrated their Fourth by hoisting a flag on a pole made by stripping the boughs from a large pine tree. When the Atlantic and Pacific Railroad reached Flagstaff in 1882, the pine was still standing. This natural flagpole gave the name to the city of Flagstaff.

The arrival of the railroad and the creation of a sawmill by E. E. Ayer marked the beginning of extensive settlement. On February 4, 1886, a fire practically wiped out the town, destroying more than 20 buildings. Within 10 months, 60 buildings replaced those burned, but on a new site. This was called New Town to distinguish it from the original town, appropriately called

Figure 18. Part of the rejuvenated business district in downtown Flagstaff. This section of town is renowned for its specialty shops and restaurants.

Old Town. Flagstaff was incorporated as a town on July 4, 1894, and as a city in 1929.

❖ **Role in Hillerman Fiction:**
Flagstaff appears in eight of Hillerman's Chee/Leaphorn novels, but by far the most action here takes place in *The First Eagle.*

Listening Woman: Father Tso, Hosteen Tso's grandson, passed through here after returning from Rome, on his way to Hosteen Tso's hogan on Nokaito Bench (chap. 17).

The Dark Wind: Jim Chee attended the Arizona High School Cross Country Meet in Flagstaff in a younger day; trader Jake West informs him that Flagstaff is the closest place to Burnt Water for attending movies (chap. 6). Hopi Messenger Albert Lomatewa visited family here, where his granddaughter's family acted like a bunch of White people (chap. 10). Joseph Musket's probation officer in Flag tells Chee that Musket had been serving three to five years in prison for possession of narcotics with intent to sell. The Medical Examiner's Office here is asked to compare dental records of Joseph Musket with x-rays of the "John Doe" (with skinned hands and feet) found on Black Mesa (chap. 26).

The Ghostway: On his way home from Los Angeles following his saving 17-year-old Margaret Billy Sosi from Vaggan (who beat Chee so severely he was hospitalized for three days), Chee stops at a motel in Flagstaff for the night. While here, he wonders how Lerner knew to fly directly to Farmington and then drive directly to Shiprock in search of Albert Gorman (chap. 21).

Skinwalkers: Jim Chee bought his trailer house in Flagstaff (chap. 5). The Cambodian doctor in charge at Badwater Clinic tells Leaphorn that Bahe

Yellowhorse (founder of the clinic) was in Flagstaff when Jim Chee arrived at the clinic as a patient (chap. 22).

Coyote Waits: Associate Professor of American Studies (Northern Arizona University) Louisa Bourbonette lives in Flagstaff (chap. 3).

Sacred Clowns: Joe Leaphorn and Professor Louisa Bourebonette have dinner in Dowager Empress Restaurant to plan a trip to China; Leaphorn ends up spending the night on Bourebonette's couch (chap. 7).

The Fallen Man: On his way to Flagstaff, retired Joe Leaphorn stops at Canyon de Chelly National Monument to visit with old Amos Nez about his experience guiding the Breedloves up Canyon del Muerto 11 years earlier and about who might have shot him (chap. 7). Interstate 40 is closed at Flagstaff by the snowstorm hitting Jim Chee and Officer Bernadette Manuelito between Cortez and Mancos in Colorado (chap. 26).

The First Eagle: Anderson Nez dies in the Northern Arizona Medical Center in Flagstaff (chap. 1). An Arizona Highway Patrol secretary in Winslow claimed one of their officers had to break up a fight in Flagstaff between Officer Benny Kinsman and a Northern Arizona University student over a woman (chap. 2); this is where Kinsman's grandmother had relocated from the Joint Use Area (chap. 2). The missing Catherine Ann Pollard lives in Flagstaff (chap. 3), where Victor Hammar reportedly stalked her (chap. 3). A lawyer from Christopher Peabody's Flagstaff firm (Peabody, Snell & Glick) is unable to find any clues concerning Pollard's disappearance (chap. 3). Jim Chee meets Janet Pete in a worn, grungy dining room here to ask about the Jano case (chap. 7). Joe Leaphorn visits Louisa Bourebonette here (chap. 10). Pawn shop proprietors in Flagstaff, Gallup, and Farmington are questioned about receiving parts from the missing Catherine Ann Pollard's Jeep (chap. 17). Tommy Tsi first claims a friend from Flagstaff gave him the Jeep radio he tried to sell at Cedar Ridge (chap. 17). At the Public Health Service hospital in Flagstaff, Shirley Ahkeah tells Leaphorn that she remembers Al Woody bringing Nez in, and that the now missing Catherine Pollard was trying to find out where Nez picked up the plague flea (chap. 18). Janet Pete is defending Robert Jano in Flagstaff against the charge of murdering Officer Benny Kinsman (chap. 19). Al Woody, gravely ill with the plague, tries to get Leaphorn and Chee to drive him to the medical center in Flagstaff (chap. 27).

Hunting Badger: Joe Leaphorn's friend, Professor Louisa Bourebonette, was unable to return here from Window Rock (where she was visiting Leaphorn) (chap. 6).

FOREST LAKE: (6600 ft) Navajo County, AZ. Navajos call this locale Dibé Bighanteelí ("Wide Sheep Corral"), Dibé Be'ek'id ("Sheep Lake"), and Tsiyi'í Be'ek'id ("Forest Lake"). This tiny chapter-house community sits on Black

Mesa, where Navajo Route 41 crosses the East Fork Dinnebito Wash, about 25 miles north of Piñon, AZ.

✤ Role in Hillerman Fiction:

Skinwalkers: Jim Chee drives through Forest Lake on his way to Hildegard Goldtooth's hogan to perform the Blessing Way (chap. 21).

FORT DEFIANCE: (6892 ft) (Population: 4,489) Apache County, AZ. The Navajo name of this community is Tséhootsooí, meaning "Meadow in Between the Rocks," though most Navajos simply call it "Fort." It sits in Black Creek Valley at the mouth of Cañon Bonito and six miles north of Window Rock.

Fort Defiance began as an isolated military post, but was converted to the Navajo Agency in 1868 after the Diné returned from the Bosque Redondo. Today it houses a chapter seat, schools, and Public Health Service hospital (formerly a U.S. Indian Service Tuberculosis Sanatorium). After its transformation from a miitary post, Good Shepherd (Episcopal), Presbyterian, and Franciscan missions settled around the establishment in an effort to convert the sizable numbers of Navajos visiting the Navajo Agency.

Traders serving the agency have included Lehman Spiegelberg (whose July 1868 license was the first issued for trading on the reservation—though others traded in the vicinity prior to the establishment of the reservation), Neal and Damon (1870s), Hyatt (1880s), Weidemeyer (1890s–1960s), Dunn Mercantile, W. M. Staggs, and A. C. Rudeau.

The fort was constructed in a steep-walled basin at the eastern foot of the Defiance Plateau (named for the fort). This basin was first named Cañon Bonito ("Beautiful Canyon," not to be confused with nearby Tsé Bonito) by the Spanish, and was a favored Navajo rendezvous in the pre-American era. Here medicine men collected herbs known as Łe'éze' ("horse medicine"), and the bubbling springs were shrines into which white shell and turquoise were thrown either as payment for blessings received or as pleas for further blessings.

The first known visit by Americans to the site of Fort Defiance was in the fall of 1849, when the expedition led by Colonel John Washington stopped to rest by the lush cienega on the return journey to the Rio Grande after concluding the Treaty of 1849 with the Navajo chieftains at Chinle.

Fort Defiance was established under its present name by order of Colonel Edwin V. Sumner in the fall of 1851. It was not a true fortress, but rather a collection of adobe or log buildings. Captain Electus Backus laid out the buildings around a rectangular parade ground with an "entrance" opening to the south. It was first garrisoned by the Third Infantry, called the "Buff Sticks,"

Figure 19. This view of the buildings of Fort Defiance Indian Health Service hospital, taken from near the top of the Defiance Plateau west of the community, shows the vulnerable location chosen for the fort. Navajos could fire upon the soldiers from the plateau as well as from the mesa across the meadow (where the water tanks now sit).

and quickly reinforced by one artillery company and four companies of cavalry. The soldiers nicknamed the post "Hell's Gate" or "Hell's Hollow," largely because of its distance from civilization and the poor location that gave the Navajos the high ground above the fort. Between 1856 and 1863, the Navajos subjected the Army to continual guerilla warfare.

In April 1860, Fort Defiance was attacked by a reported one thousand to two thousand Navajos. They were driven off by the garrison of 150 soldiers of the First U.S. Infantry under Captain O. L. Shepherd. A single private, Sylvester Johnson, was killed and three other soldiers wounded. At least 20 Navajos, including a chief from Canyon de Chelly, were killed. Private Johnson's grave is marked by a tombstone in the old Fort Defiance Post Cemetery.

> *Author's Note:* Gatherings of this many Navajo warriors were rare, and a surprise night attack on the unwalled post with attackers outnumbering defenders nearly ten to one seems likely to have had a different outcome. Inflating the number of attackers would have improved the defenders' valor on paper, and would also have supported pleas to increase the garrison's size.

On April 25, 1861, at the beginning of the Civil War, Fort Defiance was abandoned in favor of Fort Fauntleroy (later named Fort Lyon and, still later, Fort Wingate). But the continued depredations of the Navajos led General Carleton to send Kit Carson and a group of Army officers from Fort Union (near Mora, New Mexico) into the Navajo country in the summer of 1863 to establish a military post on Pueblo Colorado Wash on the western slope of the Defiance Plateau (near present-day Ganado). After a survey of possible post locations, the party recommended the reestablishment of old Fort Defiance. That fall Carson led companies of New Mexico Volunteers, a few regular Army officers, and Ute, Zuni, and New Mexico Irregulars, to reoccupy the fort, which was temporarily renamed Fort Canby. Throughout the winter, the troops pursued and captured Navajos, and the fort served as a concentration point for captive Navajos prior to marching them 300 miles to the Bosque Redondo at Fort Sumner in southeastern New Mexico Territory. Many of the prisoners died from exposure, from eating food to which they were not accustomed, and at the hands of White soldiers and camp followers.

By the spring of 1864 the so-called Navajo War ended, and the majority of Navajos were sent on the "Long Walk" to the Bosque Redondo. The fort was again deserted on October 20, 1864. Roaming bands of Navajos who had eluded Carson's troops and scouts burned the cane and timbered sections of the fort, leaving only the thick sod and rubble walls.

Upon the signing of the Treaty of 1868 at Fort Sumner, which allowed the Navajos to return to a portion of their own country, Fort Defiance was selected as the site of the Navajo Agency. The treaty required the government to build a warehouse, an agency headquarters, carpenter and blacksmith shops, a school, and a chapel. But no troops were to be housed within the reservation boundaries, so the closest military presence was to be at Fort Wingate near Gallup—some 30 miles to the southeast.

Most of Fort Defiance's old buildings were repaired and Major Theodore Dodd, called Na'azísí Yázhí, "Little Gopher," by the Navajos, became the civil agent. On his death shortly after his appointment, he was succeeded by Captain Frank T. Bennett, whom the Navajos called Chąątsohi, "Big Belly." (The name is actually interpreted as either "Big Beaver" or "Big Excrement.") In the fall of 1869, Bennett issued the sheep and goats stipulated in the Treaty of 1868: over thirteen thousand ewes and 300 rams (purchased from Vicente Romero, a large operator in the vicinity of Fort Union, New Mexico) as well as 900 female and 100 male goats, forming the foundation of today's Navajo flocks.

The erstwhile military post slowly developed into an Indian agency. Article 6 of the Treaty of 1868 called for the U.S. government to provide for the education of Navajo children with a schoolhouse and teacher for every 30 children. But it also dictated that the Navajos would send all children between the ages of 6 and 16 to those schools, and therein lay the dilemma. Schooling was not fully understood nor accepted—nor even desired—by the average Navajo, and this provision provoked many bitter confrontations between the Diné and their White overseers.

The government first introduced schools by contracting with various missionary societies and churches. The first school was a mission school, opened by the Foreign Board of the Presbyterian Church (John Roberts, missionary, and Charity Gaston, teacher) in 1869. No students attended, and the school failed in less than a year. The same year the school failed, Missionary Roberts was "removed" for having performed a "mixed marriage." This was followed by the second mission, established by John Menaul in 1871, which also failed.

The Fort Defiance School became the reservation's first boarding school in 1880. At first the Navajos sent only sickly children, until the Navajo police began to enforce attendance in 1887. Still, by 1892, fewer than 100 students were enrolled in all reservation schools. The Fort Defiance Boarding School had a capacity of 300 students in 1941, but eventually gave way to day school preferences and was eventually replaced with Window Rock High School and an Arizona public school.

Until 1899, Fort Defiance continued as the agency for all Navajos and Hopis, but in that year a separate Hopi agency was established at Keams Canyon, and over the next 10 years four other Navajo agencies were organized to deal with this large reservation. In 1936 these were again centralized by Indian Commissioner Collier. The new agency was established at Window Rock, less than five miles southeast of Fort Defiance.

Regular medical service for the Navajos did not begin until 1880. The Episcopal Church sent medical missionaries to Fort Defiance in the 1890s, along with a nurse named Miss Eliza Thackara. They were kept very busy, and started a tradition lasting through the present. A 140-bed hospital and tuberculosis sanatorium were built in 1938, and by 1941, Fort Defiance was the Navajo medical center, with its 294-bed base hospital serving all parts of Navajoland. Since then, hospitals have been established at other reservation and bordertown communities, the largest (larger even than the one in Fort Defiance) in Gallup.

❖ Role in Hillerman Fiction:

Talking God: At the Public Health Service Hospital here, Agnes Tsosie is told that she is dying of cancer; she goes home over her doctor's objections (chap. 2).

FORT SUMNER (OLD): (4025 ft) De Baca County, NM. Navajos refer to this hated location simply as Hwéeldi, a corruption of the Spanish "fuerte," or "fort." Older Navajos called it T'iis Názbąs ("Cottonwood Circle," roughly equivalent to the Spanish name Bosque Redondo, "Round Grove").

This deserted site is four miles south of U.S. Highway 60, three miles east of the present town of Fort Sumner in southeastern New Mexico. The fort itself was built in the Bosque Redondo on the Pecos River in 1863, just north of the confluence of the Pecos River with Alamogordo Creek—a locale visited by Captain Arellano of Coronado's 1541 Quivira expedition, Gaspar Castaño de Sosa in 1590, the Rodriguez-Chamuscado expedition in 1581, and by Antonio de Espejo in 1583. Its purpose was to house an Army contingent overseeing the Indian residents of the new reservation.

Some 8,500 Navajos were removed from their homeland and were force-marched on the infamous 300-mile "Long Walk" to the Bosque Redondo in 1863–64. Here they were settled on a reservation 40 miles square, which they were to share with the Mescalero Apaches, under the watchful eyes of the troops at Fort Sumner. (The Apaches stayed until 1865 and decamped in one night.)

The Long Walk was devastating to the Navajos, and tales of cruelty on the part of their White guards persist today. It has been said that the trail to the Bosque Redondo reservation could be identified by the bodies strewn along the way. While many were the victims of brutality, even more were the unfortunate casualties of stupid oversights. For instance, the Army issued wheat flour to the Navajos, but did not give any instructions for cooking a substance so alien to the Indians, and many died of dysentery after eating flour mixed with water.

The Navajos tried to farm the alkaline soil from the irrigation system laid out by Army officers, but each year brought greater failure and a mounting death rate. Desertions (escapes) were numerous, and graft by military and civil agents robbed the Navajos of government supplies. Conditions became so deplorable that in the spring of 1868, General W. T. ("The only good Indian is a dead Indian") Sherman and Colonel Francis Tappan, Indian Peace Commissioners, were sent to Fort Sumner and there drafted the Navajo Treaty of June 1, 1868. Within one month, the Navajos were on their way home.

While at the Bosque, Navajos lived a rigidly controlled life. Article 6 of the treaty sending them to the Bosque read: "Any adult Indian who shall be found absent from his or her village between the hours of 7 o'clock pm and 5 o'clock am in winter, and between 8 o'clock pm and 4 o'clock am in summer, shall be imprisoned."

On June 6, 1868, the Navajo return to their homeland was nearly cancelled when renegades fled the reservation and killed six Whites on Twelve Mile Creek (12 miles from the post). The Army pursued these fugitives with the help of the Navajo headmen from the reservation, and all were killed or captured near Apache Springs. The planned Navajo release of June 18 took place as scheduled.

The fort (with the exception of the cemetery) was officially turned over to the Department of the Interior on February 24, 1871, though the reservation had been transferred back on October 31, 1867.

An odd historical footnote to the Navajo internment involved the famous outlaw Billy the Kid. The home of Lucien B. Maxwell, in which the famed bandit was killed on July 18, 1881, had served as the Army officers' billet during the Navajo incarceration. And Deluvina Maxwell, the woman who first entered the dark room where the dead or dying Billy lay after being shot by Sheriff Pat Garrett, was a Navajo from Canyon de Chelly, sold as a slave to Lucien Maxwell by Apache captors.

Today the site is a large grassy field with few visible remnants of the original fort. But no old Navajo forgets Hwéeldi and the four years spent in far eastern New Mexico. Many of that generation even calculated their age from the date of return.

✤ **Role in Hillerman Fiction:**

Skinwalkers: Bahe Yellowhorse wanted the U.S. government to pay for the fact that the treaty the Navajos signed at Fort Sumner was full of broken promises (chap. 23).

FORT WINGATE: (7000 ft) McKinley County, NM. Also Bear Springs and Big Bear Spring. To the Navajos this important location is Shash Bitoo, meaning "Bear Spring." The Spanish name for the region, Ojo del Oso ("Bear Spring"), came from the Navajo name.

Situated three miles south of Interstate 40, 12 miles east of Gallup, this site of the old Army fort (now a boarding school, and a farming, mining, and ranching community) has a colorful and convoluted history. The Navajos had known of the fine spring in the vicinity for quite some time before the arrival of the Whites. In 1821–22, and again in 1836 (both long before the military post was established), Navajos were killed in this vicinity by Spanish soldiers.

Navajo historian Richard Van Valkenburgh recorded a story related by 'Ayóó Ánilnézii ("Very Tall Man") in the the 1930s, concerning the origin of the Navajo name (Shash Bitoo):

> Many years ago when the Navajos were raiding on the New Mexicans, the war parties used to stop at Bear Spring. There was always a bear near the springs, and Hastiin Nihoobáa-nii, a Navajo warrior of the Nihoobáanii Dine'é Clan, stopped there on his second raid, and again saw a bear. Hoping to gain success, he cast offerings into the spring—which was located south and west of the present school and was sacred to the Navajos. Nihoobáanii's raid was successful and on his return from the Rio Grande he named the spring Shashbitoo. This was long over one old man's life ago.

Hastiin Nihoobáa-nii remains an obscure figure, but David Brugge suggests that perhaps he took part in the war of 1774–75.

The name Fort Wingate has referred to a total of four southwestern posts.

Three were in New Mexico, though only two (referred to as "Old" and "New") were actually named Wingate; the third, a garrison at Cebolleta (some 30 miles northeast of Old Fort Wingate) between 1846 and 1851, has sometimes been confused in the literature with the "old" Fort Wingate. To confuse matters even more, the second (or New Fort Wingate) was actually built first, but assigned "Wingate" as its third name. It had previously been known as Fort Fauntleroy and Fort Lyon. Further complication arises in the fact that the fourth post, Fort Wise in southern Colorado, also previously bore the names Fort Fauntleroy and Fort Wingate.

Fort Fauntleroy was established on August 31, 1860, by seven officers and 240 enlisted men of Companies C, E, F, and K, 5th U.S. Infantry. It was situated at the foot of the northwestern end of the Zuni Mountains (just three miles south of present Interstate 40), "126 miles west and a little north of Albuquerque, and 40 miles southeast of Fort Defiance." It was named for department commander Colonel Thomas T. Fauntleroy, 1st U.S. Dragoons. However, Fauntleroy left the Army at the outbreak of the Civil War to join the Confederacy, so the post's name was changed to Fort Lyon on September 25, 1861. This name honored Union Brigadier General Nathanial Lyon, killed at the Battle of Wilson's Creek, Missouri, on August 10, 1861.

The Union Army, being mauled by the Confederates, found soldiers in short supply, so regular Army troops were withdrawn from Fort Lyon in August and September 1861. They were replaced with New Mexico militia until the fort was closed about two months later.

While the post was under militia command, the Fort Fauntleroy Massacre (the post's new name had not yet caught on) was one of the most infamous events to occur at either fort. In August 1861, many Navajos had gathered at the fort for rations and a council with their new agent, Ramon Luna. A festive atmosphere was enjoyed by all, and Luna and special agent John Ward agreed to meet with the Navajos again in 40 days. Some 500 Navajos remained in the vicinity of the post and a series of horse races started on September 10.

Three days later, a race went sour when a Navajo named Pistol Bullet raced his horse against one owned by the post surgeon. Pistol Bullet lost control of his mount and lost the race. The Navajos accused the Whites of cutting his bridle rein, and pandemonium ensued. A dozen Navajos were killed by small arms and cannon fire. There were no White casualties.

Colonel Manuel Chavez, the commandant and known hater of Navajos, was accused by Navajos and his own subordinates of precipitating the hostilities and overreacting, causing the unnecessary deaths. He was temporarily relieved of command, but never placed on trial. The post was closed in November 1861.

(Old) Fort Wingate was established on October 22, 1862, at Ojo del Gallo

(Spanish, meaning "Chicken Spring"), some 50 miles to the east of the defunct Fort Lyon (Fauntleroy), and three miles south of present-day Grants, New Mexico. It was named for Captain (Brevet Major) Benjamin Wingate, 5th U.S. Infantry, who had previously served at Fort Fauntleroy (Lyon) at Bear Springs. Wingate died on February 21, 1862, of wounds received from Confederate soldiers on June 1, 1861, in the Battle of Valverde on the southern Rio Grande.

Navajos called this post Béésh Dáádílkał, "Iron Door," and it was one of the few western forts surrounded by a stockade. Plans for the fort called for 4340 ft of eight-foot-high wooden stockade, which required over a million feet of lumber. The post also incorporated 9,317 ft of foot-thick, eight-foot-high adobe walls. Much of these materials was salvaged from the previously abandoned Fort Lyon (Fauntleroy) at Bear Spring.

(Old) Fort Wingate was first garrisoned by Companies D and G, First Dragoons, and it served as Kit Carson's headquarters in rounding up the Navajos in 1863–64. Navajo chieftain Manuelito surrendered at the post, effectively ending the Navajo War.

When the Navajos returned to their homeland in the summer of 1868, (Old) Fort Wingate was too far away from the new reservation for the conducting of adequate guard duty. So, on July 25, 1868, that post was abandoned and its name transferred to the remains of what had been Fort Lyon (Fauntleroy), which became commonly known as New Fort Wingate, or Fort Wingate II.

The location of the future "New" Fort Wingate was shown as Ojo del Oso on the Miera y Pacheco maps of 1779, and the name seems to have been of common usage by then. The Treaty of Bear Springs was signed there between Narbona, Zarcillas Largo, and other Navajo chiefs and Colonel Alexander Doniphan of the 3rd Missouri Volunteers of the United States Army in 1846, and it was a regular stopping place on the military road between Albuquerque and Fort Defiance in the years 1851–54. In 1863, after the closure of Fort Lyon, the location was an express station for use during the Navajo War. It served as one of the stops for the Navajos traveling to Fort Sumner, though no military post existed at the springs at the time.

By an executive order of 1870, the 10-mile-square military reservation of 1860 was expanded to 100 square miles, and in 1881 it was enlarged again, to 130 square miles, to include certain timber resources. In 1911, after the military post was decommissioned, the entire Fort Wingate reserve became a part of the Zuni National Forest but remained under the control of the War Department for military purposes. Troops continued to be stationed there until 1912.

One of the most interesting military figures connected with Fort Wingate was Dr. Washington Matthews, called Hataałii Nééz, "Tall Medicine Man," by the Navajos. As surgeon at Fort Wingate 1880–84 and 1894–95, he became

Figure 20. Most of the remaining buildings of the historic Fort Wingate military post are in an even worse state of repair than this two-story barracks across from the parade ground. All of the buildings lie on the Wingate Boarding School grounds, and are in a state of limbo as they are too historic to be destroyed, but there is no funding to restore them, or even to stabilize them.

an outstanding authority on Navajo culture. His many publications remain standard references in scientific literature on Navajo ethnology.

Victorio, the chief of the Warm Springs band of the Chiricahua Apaches, and members of his band were interned at Fort Wingate in 1880 and later returned to their country by Agent Thomas V. Keam. Some of them, however, led by an Apache sub-chief called Loco, stayed in the Navajo country and left descendants in the Chíshí Dine'é (Chiricahua Apache) Clan of the Navajo—a number of whom still live in the vicinity of Fort Wingate.

During the Poncho Villa uprisings in Mexico, Fort Wingate was used to intern refugees from northern Mexico. A number died here, and their graves can be seen in the cemetery a half-mile east of the school. The Southwestern Range and Sheep Breeding Laboratory (U.S. Department of the Interior and U.S. Department of Agriculture) was installed three miles south of the depot, and became a district headquarters for the National Forest Service.

In 1925 the Indian Department (later Bureau of Indian Affairs) took over the buildings and an area around Fort Wingate under a lease from the War Department. The barracks and officers' quarters were turned into dormitories and residences for Indian students and their instructors. The original name, Charles H. Burke Vocational School and Hospital, was changed in 1937 to Wingate Vocational High School. In 1941 it had an enrollment of 500 pupils, predominantly Navajo. The curriculum stressed academic training and vocational work (adapted to preparation for living in the Navajo country) along with Navajo arts and crafts.

The Zunis used to acquire soapstone in the vicinity of the fort for making fetishes.

Today few of the old Army buildings remain standing; all are structurally condemned. A more modern complex of government buildings comprises Wingate High School and Elementary School, BIA boarding schools.

Three miles to the west of the fort, a U.S. Army munitions storage depot was established as a Magazine Area right after World War I. Over 46,000,000 pounds of TNT were stored here until the stock was sold to England, the last of it just one month before the Japanese attack on Pearl Harbor.

The depot expanded considerably during World War II, and served as a storage depot until it closed in January 1993. A large number of Navajos were employed at the depot during its heyday. As late as 1997, highly unstable munitions were still being removed from the bunkers with occasional accidental explosions.

Fort Wingate Trading Post (also known as Wingate Trading Post) was located at (New) Fort Wingate. It began as a combination military sutler and Indian trader under Willi Spiegelberg, the first officially sanctioned trader to the Navajos, appointed on July 8, 1868 (even though he was off-reservation and thus did not need a license). His brother Lehman was the first to receive a license to trade on the reservation, on August 28 of that year, trading at Fort Defiance eight years prior to Congress's formal creation of the position of civilian post traders. (Willi and Lehman were two of the German Jewish Spiegelberg Brothers—the others being Jacob, Levi, and Emanual—whose importation and wholesale and retail empire stretched from New York City to Santa Fe.

Spiegelberg left Fort Wingate in March of 1869, leaving the trading post (which, like the "fort," was really no more than a collection of tents) to one John L. Waters. Henry Reed was licensed to trade there from 1872 to 1877, employing a young Lorenzo Hubbell, who would become a giant in the Navajo trading industry. Lambert Hopkins took over in 1877, but was bankrupt by 1882. A post was operated here by Richard White in the 1930s and 1940s, and the Merrill family ran it through the middle 1990s, though it shifted its emphasis to restaurant and convenience store. By 2000, it was strictly a convenience store.

✤ Role in Hillerman Fiction:

Talking God: The body of a murder victim, apparently thrown from a passing train, is discovered just across Interstate 40 from Fort Wingate (chap. 3).

FOUR CORNERS: (4800 ft) San Juan County, NM, Apache County, AZ, San Juan County, UT, and Montezuma County, CO. The Navajo name for this location is Tsé 'Íí'áhí, "Rock Spire," an obvious reference to the stone monument erected by the Navajo Nation in 1964 to mark the only point in the United States where four states (New Mexico, Colorado, Utah, and Arizona) and two Indian reservations (Navajo and Ute Mountain) come together. The monument is situated on U.S. Highway 160, six miles northeast of Teec Nos Pos, AZ. A trading post that was operated here by Wilken and Whitecraft in 1910 is now abandoned.

The benchmark was set in 1875, and a small cement boundary marker was installed in 1912, replaced by the Navajo Nation monument 52 years later.

This location is not without its controversy. A 1925 survey proved the original 1868 survey of the 37th Parallel was in error, placing the New Mexico–Colorado and Arizona-Utah boundaries some 100 yards too far south. When the courts ruled that the original boundaries would stand, a problem was created between the Navajos and Utes, because the U.S. treaty with the Navajos gave them land north to the 37th Parallel, while the treaty with the Utes gave them land south to the New Mexico–Colorado state line. Thus, a strip of land 100 yards wide and 25 miles long remains contested by both tribes, with no solution in sight.

❖ Role in Hillerman Fiction:

The Blessing Way: Old Woman Gray Rocks gossiped to anthropologist Bergen McKee at her brush hogan about a son of Hosteen Tom having gone to Farmington in order to join the Marine Corps, but ending up working as a coal miner in the Four Corners region (chap. 7).

Hunting Badger: The Four Corners is the territory of the Shiprock substation of the Navajo Tribal Police (chap. 2), and was the scene of a massive manhunt in 1998 (chap. 2).

FRUITLAND: (5100 ft) San Juan County, NM. Navajos call this locale Bááh Díílid ("Burned Bread"); also Niinah Nízaad or Nenahnezad ("Long Upgrade"). This Mormon farming community and Navajo trading center is located on the north bank of the San Juan River, 18 miles east of Shiprock, and 11 miles west of Farmington, on U.S. Highway 550 (which roughly follows the route of the old Denver & Rio Grande Western Railroad). Trading concerns in the vicinity have included Albert Farnsworth (Fruitland Trading Post), Southside Trading Post, Fruitland Trading Co., Joe Hatch, Hatch & Ashcroft, and Ray Foutz.

The name Bááh Díílid was derived from Navajo observation of a Mormon burning a batch of bread. Early maps show this location as Burnham, a name bestowed in 1877–78 to honor Mormon Bishop Luther C. Burnham. The name Fruitland was selected to advertise the agricultural enterprise.

The vicinity was first settled by the Mormon families of Benjamin T. Boice and Jeremiah Hatch, in 1878. The population swelled in 1903 with the arrival of many Mormons displaced when their enclave at Tuba City was annexed to the reservation in a western extension of the reservation boundaries. In 1892 the mesa south of Fruitland was recommended as an experimental irrigation project for the Navajos along the San Juan River.

It was a precursor of the Navajo Indian Irrigation Project (NIIP). Located on the south side of the San Juan River, the Fruitland Project began as a narrow strip running some 16 miles from the dam (two miles west of Farmington) westward along the south river bank to near the Hogback. It consists of small farm tracts asigned to Navajo farmers who have individual rights to them as long as they plant regularly.

The first irrigation ditch in the vicinity was the Costiano Ditch, dug before 1880. When the Executive Order of 1880 added this section to the Navajo Reservation, White squatters refused to move off the lands. Violence was averted only by troops sent from Fort Lewis, Colorado, to eject the squatters.

Cornfield's Ditch, as the Costiano Ditch was later known, was replaced in 1939 by the New Fruitland Canal (or Fruitland Ditch), which served some 1400 acres of agricultural land and was the largest irrigation project of its time on the reservation. Under the Indian Service policy of conservation and development of Navajo resources, the lands under this canal were allotted to Navajos without livestock. Unfortunately, inept government leadership led to chaos and failure of the project. It was later replaced by the NIIP (see Navajo Agricultural Industries).

❖ **Role in Hillerman Fiction:**

The Blessing Way: A man whose daughter died here of tuberculosis shot four people he suspected of witchcraft (chap. 8).

FRY CREEK: (5800–5000 ft) San Juan County, UT. The Navajo name is uncertain. This steep canyon-walled creek is in the White Canyon region of Utah, between the San Juan and Colorado Rivers. It heads near Table of the Sun (approximately four miles west of Natural Bridges National Monument), and flows northwest some eight miles before merging with White Canyon from the South.

❖ **Role in Hillerman Fiction:**

Coyote Waits: According to a newspaper article discovered by Dr. Tagert, in the late 1800s three men robbed a train when it stopped to take on water along this creek. One was shot and died in the Blanding hospital (chap. 13).

GALLUP: (6506 ft) (Population: 20,120) McKinley County, NM. Navajos refer to this town as Na'nízhoozhí, meaning "Spanned Across," or, more simply,

"Bridge." An old Navajo name is T'iis Tsoh Sikaad, meaning "Big Cottonwood Sits."

This town is located 21 miles east of the Arizona state line in the rock-rimmed valley of the Rio Puerco of the West, at the junction of Interstate 40 (formerly U.S. Highway 66) and U.S. Highway 666. It serves as a wholesale distribution point for art and crafts and is a major tourist center (particularly in mid-August at the time of the Inter-Tribal Indian Ceremonial). The Burlington Northern Santa Fe Railway passes through the town, and Gallup is one of only three New Mexico stops for Amtrak passenger service. The Santa Fe Railroad used to maintain a station, roundhouse, shops, etc. in Gallup, but these dwindled over the years until virtually all remaining railroad personnel (some 300 families) were transferred to Belen, New Mexico, and to Winslow, Arizona, in the late 1980s.

Gallup has been known for brick manufacturing, uranium mining (until the late 1970s), and coal mining (until the late 1980s). Regional offices for the Bureau of Indian Affairs and a major Indian Health Service hospital have been mainstays to the economy.

The Gallup region was the scene of numerous clashes between the Navajos and the U.S. Army prior to the Navajo relocation of 1863–64. Historian Van Valkenburgh related one of these, in the summer of 1863, as described by "an old Navajo":

> We found out that more soldiers were being sent to Fort Wingate near Bear Springs. Some Navajos had been there and had spied on them. A band collected at Many Arrows [China Springs, four miles north of Gallup]. They hid behind the rocks—all in a line and not far apart. A troop of soldiers came up the road, and the Navajos all shot at once. Cháali Sání shot the soldier captain right in the middle of the back of the neck and the bullet came out through his eye. Other soldiers which we called Naago 'Adiłdoní ["Those Who Shoot From the Side"], were shot down. Some got away on their horses. The Navajos chased them and got some horses. Cháali Sání, who was the leader of the Navajos did not get any. (Van Valkenburgh 1941, 62)

> *Author's Note:* Other names for American soldiers were Bijaa' Yee Njahí ("Those Who Sleep on their Ears"), Bigod Doodilí ("Scorched Their Kneecaps"), Sha Bidiiłchii ("Sunburnt"), Táa'ji' 'Adeez'ahí ("Something Extends Out at the Forehead," so called after the shape of the military caps of the Civil War era).

The Atlantic and Pacific Railroad reached the vicinity of Gallup in the fall of 1881. The discovery of coal and shallow water encouraged the railroad to start mining coal at Mineral Springs (Gallup Hogback). Early in 1882 a station was

Figure 21. The FBI Office in Gallup, where Chee and Leaphorn have met with Special Agent Kennedy, now occupies an unmarked storefront in the recently renovated downtown section of Coal Avenue.

established at the present site of Gallup and named after David Gallup, the Comptroller of the Frisco Railway (associated with the Atlantic and Pacific during the building of the transcontinental railroad).

During the early days, Gallup and the surrounding villages were rip-roaring settlements. According to historian Van Valkenburgh, Indian Agent Eastman wrote the Commissioner of Indian Affairs on February 14, 1882:

I have hitherto governed these people through persuasion, and now all but a few heed my advice, but there is a condition of affairs at the four stations, viz. Bacon Springs or Coolidge, Gallup, Defiance Station and Defiance (formerly Sheridan) in the vicinity of Fort Wingate as is referred to in the Acting Governor Cosper's report to the President on the 9th instant, on conditions in southern Arizona. Bunco men and desperados collected there, including three or four hundred employees at the coal mines who are employed at the stations mentioned above. Two days since four men were killed at Crane's Station—or Coolidge as it is called. (Van Valkenburgh 1941, 63)

The evolution of Gallup beyond the railroad station and mining camp stage (populated largely by desperate characters) began after 1890, when traders on the reservation began opening outlets in Gallup in order to offer the Indian goods to the increasing numbers of travelers through the area. Clinton M. Cotton, formerly a partner of Don Lorenzo Hubbell of Ganado, was one of the first wholesalers to establish a business in Gallup. In 1890, there were fewer than 10 Navajo traders. The number increased until by 1941 there were over 200 firms doing business in various parts of the Navajo area, and then it declined to fewer than two dozen by the middle 1990s.

In 1941, Gallup's wholesalers handled nearly a quarter of a million dollars of Indian arts and crafts products per year. Today the figure is in the tens of millions. It has been estimated that 60 percent of Gallup's business is derived from Navajo, Zuni, and federal sources, and the remainder comes mainly from tourist trade (which is fed by the commerce of Indian arts). The town's population of 20,000 is estimated to swell to over 50,000 on weekends when Navajos and Zunis come to town.

The town continues a rocky relationship with the Indian tribes, as it houses dozens of liquor outlets that contribute to a severe addiction epidemic among the local Native Americans. It also plays host to two hospitals (one an Indian Health Service facility) and several addiction/mental health providers.

Gallup has been made world-famous by the annual Inter-Tribal Indian Ceremonial, held in the community every year since 1922 (except 1975). The defunct United Indian Traders Association flourished in the town between 1931 and 1950, as an effort to police an industry often permeated with fraud (imported and machine-made products labeled "Indian made").

✤ Role in Hillerman Fiction:

Along with Farmington, Tuba City, Shiprock, and Albuquerque, Gallup is one of the most common sites for activity and passive background in the Chee and Leaphorn epics. It appears in 12 of the 14 novels.

The Blessing Way: Luis Horseman "cut a Mexican" in Gallup, after which Horseman fled into hiding in Kah Bihgi Valley (chap. 4). Luis Horseman had a history of arrests here, as well as in Farmington and Tuba City (chap. 10).

Dance Hall of the Dead: Frank Bob Madman had gone to Gallup to buy salt when his wife died at home; he abandoned the hogan (after knocking a hole in one wall). It later became Jason's Fleece Commune (chap. 5).

Listening Woman: According to Short Mountain trader "Old Man" McGinnis, Hosteen Tso's son Ford died here (chap. 5).

The Dark Wind: Ashie McDonald is in Gallup when Chee arrives at McDonald's camp near Nipple Butte (in the Hopi Buttes region) to talk to him about the beating of McDonald's cousin (chap. 18). Joseph Musket's first rap (according to prison records in Santa Fe) was a drunk and disorderly charge in Gallup (chap. 19).

The Ghostway: Joseph Joe knows the driver who leaves the shooting in the Shiprock Economy Wash-O-Matic will turn either west and toward Teec Nos Pos, or south toward Gallup (chap. 1). Chee had seen prostitutes in Gallup and in Albuquerque at state fair time, but not like the children plying the trade in Los Angeles (chap. 14). The blizzard that caught Chee in the Chuska Moutains looking for Ashie Begay had closed U.S. Highway 666 from

Mancos Creek, Colorado, to Gallup (chap. 23). Upon learning of the Ghost-way being conducted on Margaret Billy Sosi at Cañoncito, Jim Chee calls Leroy Begay and suggests he meet Chee and Margaret at Cañoncito. He instructs Begay to drive south to Gallup, then east through Grants and past Laguna, before looking for the turnoff to Cañoncito (chap. 25).

Skinwalkers: A Gallup soup line for drunks gave rise to a nickname for the shakes as "Shakey Soup" (chap. 3). Doctors at the Public Health Service (PHS) hospital were taking care of Leaphorn's wife, Emma (chap. 5). Leaphorn wants to check mobile home dealers to see if anyone recently studied models like Jim Chee's to help them plan the most effective placing of shots (chap. 5). Irma Onesalt had visited a pathologist at Gallup with a list of names of people for whom she wanted dates of birth (chap. 8). Joe Leaphorn instructs Officer Jimmy Tso, liaison with the Gallup Police, to check pawn shops and jewelry supply shops to find out how bone beads could be obtained (chap. 10). FBI Agent Dilly Strieb is based in Gallup (chap. 16).

A Thief of Time: Joe Leaphorn's wife, Emma, died not long ago in the Indian Health Service hospital here (chap. 2). Slick Nakai is told he could get $30 for an Anasazi pot in Gallup (chap. 4). Leaphorn flies into Gallup from Albuquerque on a commuter airline, following his trip to New York City (chap. 14).

Talking God: The body of a murder victim, apparently thrown from a train, is found on the tracks east of Gallup (chap. 3). Also, FBI Agent Jay Kennedy is stationed here (chap. 3).

Coyote Waits: FBI agents consider duty in places like Gallup and Farmington a form of exile (chap. 3). FBI Agent Jay Kennedy calls Gallup home (chap. 10).

Sacred Clowns: Jim Chee used to go to movies here as a youngster, and learned to view the Cheyenne Indians as the "Indian's Indian" (chap. 3). Jim Chee romances Janet Pete by asking her to dinner and a movie in Gallup (chap. 6). The KNDN radio news transcripts from three days prior to Jim Chee's Crownpoint meeting with BIA Police Sergeant Harold Blizzard listed the death in Gallup of a former chairwoman of the Coyote Pass Chapter (chap. 8). Delmar Kanitewa's dad was driving to Gallup with Delmar, but dropped Delmar in Thoreau to pick up his friend's class project (a silver bracelet) from Eric Dorsey the afternoon of Dorsey's murder (chap. 9). The FBI agent in Gallup is suddenly interested in talking to Delmar Kanitewa; he blames Jim Chee for Kanitewa's escape (chap. 10). Jim Chee and BIA Police Sergeant Harold Blizzard meet at the Gallup Police Station, then depart for Torreon, looking for Delmar Kanitewa (chap. 10). Chee, Blizzard, and Janet Pete see "Cheyenne Autumn" in Gallup (chap. 11). Joe Leaphorn wonders why articles stolen from Eric Dorsey's classroom showed up under Eugene Ahkeah's mobile home instead of a pawnshop in Gallup or Grants (chap. 14). Father Haines of the St. Bonaventure Mission has a meeting in Gallup so he lets Joe Leaphorn have free rein in Haines's office (chap. 22). From Gallup, Jim Chee and Janet Pete drive through the red sandstone cliffs, and Chee points out where various movies were filmed (chap. 26).

The Fallen Man: Chee remembers the night he walked into Janet Pete's apartment in Gallup, carrying flowers and a videotape of a traditional Navajo wedding—just before their break-up (chap. 8). Leaphorn's wife, Emma, had died in the Indian Health Service hospital here (chap. 10). Lucy Sam had bought her father's telescope at a pawnshop in Gallup (chap. 11). Janet Pete shares an apartment here with another DNA attorney (chap. 13). Jim Chee ends up in the PHS hospital here after being shot at Maryboy's place (chap. 20). Gallup attorney Bob Rosebrough, an avid rock climber, takes photos of the climber's log atop Shiprock for Joe Leaphorn (chap. 22).

The First Eagle: Pawn shops in Gallup, Farmington, and Flagstaff are questioned about receiving parts from the missing Catherine Ann Pollard's Jeep (chap. 17).

Hunting Badger: Ute Casino security chief Cap Stoner, killed in the casino robbery, was formerly a New Mexico State Policeman stationed at Gallup (chap. 14). Frank Sam Nakai had driven Chee to Gallup after he graduated from high school. They watched drunks on Railroad Avenue, whose spirits had left the Dinétah (chap. 11).

GANADO: (6400 ft) (Population: 1,257) Apache County, AZ. Navajo: Lók'aahnteel, "Wide Band of Reeds up at an Elevation." This substantial chapter, school, mission, and trading settlement straddles Arizona Highway 264 and Pueblo Colorado Wash, 29 miles west of Window Rock. It is the home of Hubbell Trading Post National Historic Site, 164-bed Sage Memorial Hospital (which began as part of the Presbyterian mission in 1901), and a branch of Diné College (formerly Navajo Community College), which began as the Presbyterian-supported College of Ganado.

Traders have included Stover-Hubbell, opened in the early 1870s; Hubbell Trading Post, also opened in the early 1870s and now a National Historic Site; Round Top Trading Post; and Ganado Trading Post, opened in the late 1920s.

The settlement is named after Ganado Mucho (Spanish meaning "Much Livestock"), the last peace chief of the Navajos and the twelfth signer of the Treaty of 1868. Called Tótsohnii Hastiin ("Mr. Big Water") by the Navajos, Ganado Mucho was the head chief of the western division of the Navajos until his death in 1892.

Figure 22. Hubbell Trading Post, a National Historic Site, and one of the few genuine trading posts still operating on the Navajo Reservation, is located on the
southern perimeter of Ganado, Arizona.

The Ganado vicinity was sometimes labeled Pueblo Colorado on early
maps, after the nearby stream, which in turn was named for a pueblo ruin the
Navajos called Kin Dah Lichí'í ("Red House in the Distance"), located some
10 miles northeast of Ganado near Kin Lichee.

Ganado was one of the earliest centers of commerce developed on the
reservation. In 1871, Charles Crary settled at Ganado Lake and started a small
trading post. A short time later William ("Old Man") Leonard opened a post
on the site of the present Hubbell Ranch and Trading Post, and in 1878 was
bought out by Juan Lorenzo Hubbell, known to the Navajos both as Nák'ee
Sinilí ("Eye Glasses") and Naakaii Sání ("Old Mexican"). In 1884 Hubbell
formed a partnership with Clinton N. Cotton, a former telegraph operator on
the Atlantic and Pacific Railroad. Hubbell, conversant with Indian life after 10
years of wandering among the Paiutes, Hopis, and Navajos, handled the
Ganado end of the business, while Cotton mostly managed the affairs from
Gallup—though he lived at the Hubbell post for some time and was sole
owner from 1884 to the early 1900s. Cotton later went into banking in Gallup
while Hubbell divided his interests between Ganado and St. Johns, Arizona,
until the time of his death in 1930.

In the mid-1880s Cotton and Hubbell brought several Mexican silversmiths to Ganado, including Naakaii Dáádiil ("Thick Lipped Mexican") from
Cubero, New Mexico. Introducing the more easily worked Mexican pesos or
silver dollars, they taught the craft to local Navajos who had already started
rudimentary work in silver. By 1890, the value of the silver craft products in
the hands of Navajos was estimated by their agent as some $300,000.

For many years the Hubbell home at Ganado was the social and business
center of the western Navajo reservation. Among many notable White visitors

was E. A. Burbank, prolific artist of Indian life, who did much of his best work while visiting with the Hubbells.

✤ Role in Hillerman Fiction:

The Blessing Way: Joseph Begay was on his way to the bus stop here to pick up his daughter when he encountered the body of Luis Horseman in the road (chap. 5).

The Ghostway: Jim Chee and Frank Sam Nakai search the archives at the Navajo Community College in Ganado and find a medicine man at Two Story, over by Window Rock, who can conduct the five-day Ghostway (chap. 24).

Skinwalkers: Looking out his Window Rock office window, Joe Leaphorn knows it's raining in Ganado while Chee is visiting the Dinnebito Wash country (chap. 19). Joe Leaphorn stops in here for gas on his way to the Badwater Clinic, trying to reach the wounded Chee before Yellowhorse returns (chap. 22).

A Thief of Time: Evangelist and part-time pottery dealer Slick Nakai first met the missing anthropologist Eleanor Friedman-Bernal at Ganado (chap. 8).

Talking God: Lieutenant Leaphorn drives through Ganado on his journey from his office in Window Rock to Lower Greasewood to visit Agnes Tsosie (chap. 3).

The Fallen Man: Joe Leaphorn stops in Ganado to buy groceries for wounded Amos Nez, who lives in Canyon del Muerto (chap. 6). U.S. Highway 191 is closed here by the snowstorm hitting Jim Chee and Officer Bernadette Manuelito between Cortez and Mancos in Colorado (chap. 23).

GAP (TRADING POST): (approx. 5900 ft) Coconino County, AZ. The Navajo name is Yaaniilk'id ("Sloping Down"), or Tisnaabąąs Habitiin ("Wagon Trail Up Out"). A natural gap was discovered in the sandstone Echo Cliffs northwest of Tuba City, 36 miles north of Cameron on U.S. Highway 89. Being the only passage past the cliffs (the crest of which is known as Hamblin Ridge, named after Jacob Hamblin, the Mormon missionary and explorer) onto the Kaibito Plateau for a dozen miles north, this was a natural location for a trading post. Such a post was first operated at the base of the Echo Cliffs by Joseph Lee (son of John Doyle Lee of Lee's Ferry) sometime between 1876 and 1880. (In 1941, Joe Lee was the oldest living Navajo trader, then operating Black Mountain Store.)

Hamblin Creek passes by Gap Trading Post, and a partially graveled road, Navajo Route 20, runs northeast through the Gap to Coppermine.

In addition to Navajos, a small contingent of Paiutes (numbering 28 in 1941) led by Nomutz ranged in the vicinity.

✤ Role in Hillerman Fiction:

Coyote Waits: Hosteen Pinto's niece, Mary Keeyani, was shopping at this trading post when Pinto left his home, apparently heading for the Shiprock area (chap. 3).

GARCES MESA: (5000 ft) Coconino County, AZ. The Navajo name is uncertain. This flat highland south of Padilla Mesa—one of the Hopi Mesas—sits between Dinnebito and Oraibi Washes. Geological surveyor Gregory named it for Francisco Garces, the noted missionary who came to the Southwest in 1768 and was killed by Indians in 1781.

✤ Role in Hillerman Fiction:

The Dark Wind: Jim Chee drives past Newberry Mesa, Garces Mesa, Blue Point, and Padilla Mesa here on his way to the Hopi cultural center to see if Ben Gaines and Gail Pauling are still in residence (chap. 18).

The First Eagle: The road Leaphorn had to take to find Jim Chee crosses Garces Mesa (chap. 14).

GLEN CANYON: (4000–3000 ft) Coconino County, AZ. The Navajo name is uncertain, but probably Tséyi', the generic term for "Canyon." Currently the name Glen Canyon applies to that stretch of 1000-ft-deep Colorado River canyon lying between Lake Powell and Lee's Ferry. The true length of this canyon extends an additional curvilinear 100 miles upstream from Glen Canyon Dam, but this portion is now beneath the waters of Lake Powell, the first water for which was retained behind the dam in 1964.

The canyon was named in 1869 by explorer John Wesley Powell, who is the namesake of the lake and the National Recreation Area created by an act of Congress in 1972. Cass Hite, called Beesh Łigaii ("Mr. Silver") by the Navajos, mined in the canyon in the 1880s and 1890s.

Glen Canyon Dam, which the Navajos call simply Dá'deestł'in ("Dam"), sits across the Colorado River at the narrows of Glen Canyon. Authorized by Congress in 1956 as part of the Colorado River Storage Project, construction was initiated by the Bureau of Reclamation in 1959 and completed in 1964. The first water was held on March 13, 1963, after diversion tunnels were closed. The first power generated by Glen Canyon Generating Unit No. 1 began around midnight, September 4, 1964. Now 30,000 cubic feet of water pass through penstocks.

✤ Role in Hillerman Fiction:

Listening Woman: Leaphorn's perceived straight line connecting Gold Rims's abandoned car and the watering hole could be extended to the wilderness area around Glen Canyon (chap. 4).

Hunting Badger: Frank Sam Nakai remembered the building of the dam in Glen Canyon to form Lake Powell, damming up the San Juan and Colorado Rivers (chap. 11).

GOBERNADOR CANYON and **CREEK:** (6400–5700 ft) Rio Arriba and San Juan counties, NM. The Navajo name is uncertain. This 22-mile-long canyon is a tributary to the San Juan River, five miles west of Navajo Dam and Reservoir. The path of Gobernador Creek mostly parallels the route of U.S. Highway 64 east to Navajo City, and New Mexico Highway 539 for three miles before diverging into a deeper channel.

The canyon was traversed by Roque Madrid's expedition following their battle with Navajos in La Jara Canyon on August 11, 1705.

✤ Role in Hillerman Fiction:

A Thief of Time: This feature is scouted by Jim Chee in his search for Joe B. Nails, whom he believes to be the Backhoe Bandit (chap. 5).

GOBERNADOR KNOB: (7100 ft) Rio Arriba County, NM. The Navajo name is Ch'óol'į'í, meaning "Fir Mountain," though linguist Robert Young notes that this is a folk etymology and that the true meaning is unclear. The ceremonial name is Ntł'iz Dziil, which means "Hard Goods Mountain." This rounded, cone-shaped pinnacle rises above the broken mesas sloping west from the continental divide toward Canyon Largo, about seven miles south of the community of Gobernador (trading post and post office).

Gobernador Knob is one of the significant sacred mountains of the Navajos interior to their homeland, and can be seen as a small cone from great distances to the west. In the vicinity of the knob, archaeological investigations since the 1920s have identified a number of old Navajo remains, and the region is a part of the Dinétah or Old Navajo Country. Around 1925, Dr. Alfred V. Kidder of the Phillips-Andover Academy investigated what he believed to have been refuge sites of Puebloans fleeing Spanish vengeance during the troubled years following the Pueblo Revolt of 1680.

The Navajos have many traditions relating to Gobernador Knob, including one related by historian Richard Van Valkenburgh (1941, 66):

> Jiní. Times were bad. Everywhere there were Enemy Monsters who killed and ate people. One day a rain cloud came to rest on Gobernador Knob. Gradually it enveloped the mountain until on the fourth day it completely covered it.
>
> 'Átsé Hastiin ("First Man"), seeing this from Huerfano Mountain told 'Átsé 'Asdzáán ("First Woman") that something unusual was happening on Gobernador Knob. He went there to look things over and sang a Blessing Song as he went.

When he reached Gobernador Knob, he heard a baby cry. He found this baby lying with its head toward the west and its feet toward the east. Its cradle was made from two short rainbows. Across the baby's chest and feet lay the red beams of the rising sun. Arched over its face was another short rainbow. Four blankets covered the baby. One was black, another was blue, another was yellow and the fourth was a white cloud. Along both sides there was a row of loops made of lightning and through these sunbeams laced back and forth.

Not knowing what to do with the fastenings, First Man took the babe back to Huerfano Mountain to First Woman. He told her that he had found the baby in the darkness and rain on Gobernador Knob.

They heard the call of Haashch'é'élti'í ("Talking God"), as he came. They heard the call of Haashch'é'ohaagan ("Growling God"), as he came. Talking God clapped his hands over his mouth and then struck them together saying something important had happened. The baby was what the Holy People had been wishing for. Talking God placed the child on the ground and with one pull of the strings, the lacings came free.

"This is my daughter," said the First Woman. First Man said the same. The days passed—they were the same as years—and when two years had passed, the girl sat up. She was then dressed in white shell. She walked for two days, and in three days, she danced. On the tenth day, she was named. She was called Yoołgai 'Adszáán ("White Shell Woman"). Thus the benevolent goddess was brought to the Navajos by the Holy People from Gobernador Knob. (White Shell Woman is also known as Changing Woman.)

The Diné Habitiin ("Navaho Trail Up"), mentioned in the Navajo Beadway Story of the Navajo clans, is located west of Gobernador Knob. West of this trail and on the mesa above the trail is Ta'neeszah, the place where the Ta'neeszahnii (Tangle People Clan) of the Navajos are reputed to have lived at one time. It is claimed by Blanco Canyon Navajos that remnants of the old hogans and a "braided" wood fence were still in evidence in the 1940s. Indeed, there are many ruins in the area, some possibly early Navajo.

In 1705, Roque Madrid's expedition marched a short distance through this canyon south of Magdena Butte and Santos Peak between their second and third battles with Navajos. (The others took place at Los Peñoles and Largo Canyon.)

✤ Role in Hillerman Fiction:

A Thief of Time: Slick Nakai told his congregation that he sometimes went to pray at Gobernador Knob as a child (chap. 4).

THE GOOSENECKS: (5000 ft) San Juan County, UT. Also, "The Twist." The Navajo name is uncertain, but is reputed to translate as "The One who Crawls with her Body," referring to Big Snake, who created the deep, twisting canyons. This 30-mile stretch of extreme twists, turns, and switchbacks in deeply eroded canyons in the course of the San Juan River lies between Mexican Hat and Johns Canyon.

It takes six river miles to travel one mile in this region. This rugged, barren vicinity was visited by an Army contingent under Major Henry Lane Kendrick in August 1853. It is a favorite rafting location for today's tourism industry.

✤ Role in Hillerman Fiction:

Skinwalkers: Chee is instructed by Captain Largo to try to find out who is stealing from tourist cars at the parking places along the Goosenecks (chap. 6).

GOTHIC CREEK and **GOTHIC CREEK CANYON:** (5000–4400 ft) San Juan County, UT. The Navajo name is uncertain. This 20-mile-long, normally dry wash flows north from the northern foot of Boundary Butte. Skirting the west margin of Casa del Eco Mesa, it merges with the San Juan River from the south, opposite the community of Bluff. The name, reflecting the nature of the sandstone formations in the vicinity, was applied by U.S. Army Major Electus Backus in November 1858.

✤ Role in Hillerman Fiction:

A Thief of Time: Along this creek, Jim Chee finds Slick Nakai's car, out of gas, and surmises that Nakai is trying urgently to reach his friend's home (chap. 13).

Hunting Badger: The canyon appears as a crooked streak of darkness to Jim Chee and Cowboy Dashee as they drive to the scene of the abandoned getaway truck (chap. 8). Chee speculates that the casino robbers, after abandoning the pickup truck, moved down Gothic Creek Canyon to the San Juan River (chap. 8). Frank Sam Nakai tells Chee about an old Ute raider named Ironhand, who used to disappear with his men in Gothic Creek Canyon and reappear on the rim above (chap. 11). Chee and Officer Jackson Nez search the vicinity of Gothic Creek Canyon coal mines for signs of the Ute Casino robbers (chap. 15). Chee, assuming Ironhand would know his father's legendary escape trick for eluding Navajos in this region, wonders if there are still mine shafts in the canyon (chap. 15). Chee discovers three or four old coal digs in the canyon (chap. 19). Chee hitches a helicopter ride to look for the coal diggings in an EPA helicopter searching for waste dumps east of the Nokaito Bench (chap. 20).

GRAND CANYON: (8300 ft North Rim–2800 ft floor) Coconino County, AZ. The Navajos call this feature Bidáá' Ha'azt'i' ("Railroad Ends," or more literally translated as "Something [the Railroad] Extends in a Line to Its Brink"); Bikooh Ntsaa Ahkee ("Deep Canyon"); and Tsékoo Hatso ("Big Canyon").

This vast chasm located west of the Navajo Reservation is the most extensive canyon system cut by the Colorado River, and is one of the nation's largest (and most popular) national parks.

Here the waters of the Colorado River have cut a winding channel a mile deep through limestone, sandstone, shale, and igneous, Precambrian rock. Grand Canyon Village (formerly "El Tovar"), with complete tourist accommodations and its own school for Park employees, is located on the South Rim of the canyon, roughly opposite the smaller North Rim Village.

Many legends center about the canyon, which was first discovered by Whites when a detachment of Spaniards under Don Pedro de Tovar of the Coronado Expedition of 1540 dispatched Don Lopez de Cardenas to investigate the Hopi tales of a great gorge.

Little has been identified as relating to the Grand Canyon in Navajo folklore, perhaps reflecting the Navajos' relatively late arrival in this particular region. It is important, however, to both Zuni and Hopi mythology, serving as a winter dwelling place for kachinas of both tribes.

Yet, even before the 1863–64 exile to Fort Sumner, the canyon's South Rim, as far west as present-day Grand Canyon Village, was a favored camping place in the fall and when the piñon crop was good. This was Havasupai territory, but the tribes were usually friendly. Béésh Łigaii 'Atsidii ("Silver Smith") who was born near Cameron, Arizona, and died in 1939, told of a Navajo Dziłk'ijí Bi'áádjí (Female Mountain Top Ceremony) that was held near Desert View in 1862.

The Navajos also are known to have crossed the Colorado River at the Crossing of the Fathers upstream from the mouth of Navajo Canyon, traveling southwestward to hunt deer and wild horses along the north rim of the Grand Canyon, on Kaibab Plateau, in a region known to them as Nát'oh Dził ("Tobacco Mountain").

In the winter of 1863–64, numerous Navajos, fleeing Kit Carson's New Mexico Volunteers and raiding Utes, took refuge in the Grand Canyon. One group is known to have gone down the Tanner Trail from the canyon rim near present Desert View Tower (formerly Hopi Tower), some 30 miles east of Grand Canyon Village. When the refugees got halfway down the sheer walls of the canyon they stopped to rest and camp on a wide shelf. Here they were attacked by a band of Navajo renegades. After considerable fighting, the renegades were ambushed and killed.

The refugees then moved deeper into the canyon and stayed there until Round Moccasin, a Navajo emissary of Carson's, followed their trail and offered them food and protection. Most of the Navajos accepted the offer, and they left the canyon to go to Fort Sumner. A few decided not to surrender and stayed in the canyon, eventually ascending what is now Bright Angel Trail. They had to hoist their sheep up over the steep places with yucca-fiber ropes.

✤ Role in Hillerman Fiction:

The Fallen Man: Elisa Breedlove's brother-in-law, Demott, tells Leaphorn that Hal Breedlove had planned to take a Dartmouth chum and his girlfriend to visit Navajo National Monument, the Grand Canyon, and Canyon de Chelly, but Hal wanted to climb Shiprock before he turned 30, and his birthday was the day the two visitors were supposed to arrive (chap. 27).

GRANTS: (6470 ft.) (Population: 9,294) Cibola County, NM. Navajos call this town 'Anaa'task'ai'i, which historian Van Valkenburgh interpreted as "With Her Legs Spread," but which linguist Robert Young suggests is a garbled version of Naatooh Sik'ai'í, referring to an Isleta Indian prostitute. The town is nestled between Horace Mesa (foothills of the San Mateo Mountains) on the east and Black Mesa on the northwest. It is situated on the Rio San Jose, north of Interstate 40, 60 miles east of Gallup and 75 miles west of Albuquerque.

The community was formerly a station for the Santa Fe Railroad. Limited logging takes place in the nearby Zuni Mountains, a mere vestige of the former industry. Cattle and sheep raising and dry land farming are of growing importance. Mining activities include pumice, flurospar, and coal, and, until the 1980s, especially uranium.

The earliest event described in the Grants vicinity is known as the Comanche Massacre, and occurred before Europeans entered the region. A group of Navajos planting corn at the mouth of present Bluewater Canyon had posted sentinels about a mile from the corn field. These sentinels were attacked by a band of Comanches who stole all of their horses. The alarm was sounded and the main camp set out in immediate pursuit. The only water hole available to the Comanches (whom the Navajos call Naałání, meaning "Many Enemies") was a spring that came out of the Malpais near present Grants. The Navajos took a shortcut to the spring and watched from behind rocks while the Comanches killed and ate one of the stolen horses. They then attacked, killing all the Comanches.

The first White settler at Grants was Don Jesus Blea, who lived there prior to the Civil War. His home, still standing in the 1940s, was then the oldest building in Grants. The town was first called Grants Camp after the Grants Brothers, railroad contractors during the building of the Atlantic and Pacific Railroad. The community was called Alamitos (Spanish, meaning "Little Cottonwoods") in 1872, one year before the family of Don Ramon Baca moved into the village. Uranium was found in the vicinity of Grants in the 1950s, and the town boomed with mining activities during the 1970s.

Another community, Milan, grew adjacent to and west of Grants, and the two have grown together into a continuous line of homes and businesses.

Milan mining town incorporated in 1957, and was named for an early Hispanic settler, Salvador Milan.

✦ Role in Hillerman Fiction:

People of Darkness: In days preceding the formation of Cibola County, this is the location of the Valencia County Sheriff's Department, office of the objectionable Lawrence Gordo Sena (chap. 3).

The Ghostway: Upon learning of the Ghostway being conducted on Margaret Billy Sosi at Cañoncito, Jim Chee calls Leroy Begay and suggests he meet Chee and Margaret at Cañoncito. He instructs Begay to drive south to Gallup, then east through Grants and past Laguna, before looking for the turnoff to Cañoncito (chap. 25).

Sacred Clowns: BIA Law Enforcement Sergeant Harold Blizzard picks up Delmar Kanitewa near the bus station in Grants (chap. 8). Blizzard is phoning the Feds in Albuquerque that he has caught Delmar Kanitewa, when Kanitewa takes off (chap. 8). Joe Leaphorn wonders why articles stolen from Eric Dorsey's classroom showed up under Eugene Ahkeah's mobile home instead of a pawnshop in Gallup or Grants (chap. 14).

GRAY MOUNTAIN: (5040 ft) Coconino County, AZ. Navajo: Dził Łibáí, "Gray Mountain," though this designation also refers to Coconino Rim and Coconino Plateau. This tiny community on U.S. Highway 89 lies eight miles south of Cameron. It consists of several motels, Gray Mountain Trading Post (opened during the late 1930s), gas stations, and a giant Arizona Department of Transportation maintenance yard.

✦ Role in Hillerman Fiction:

The Ghostway: Upon leaving Flagstaff, Jim Chee drives to Shiprock via Gray Mountain and Tuba City (chap. 22). From Gray Mountain, he calls Captain Largo to discuss what he has found out, and to tell him he thinks the Grayson living in the aluminum trailer by the San Juan River is really Leroy Gorman, brother of the dead Albert Gorman (chap. 22).

GREASEWOOD FLATS: (5250 ft) Apache County, AZ. Also Greasewood Flat. This broad, barren pancake of a landscape is situated between U.S. Highway 160 (near Dinnehotso) and Tyende Creek. It is an area of sand dunes and slick rock.

✦ Role in Hillerman Fiction:

The Ghostway: Jim Chee tries to approach Frank Sam Nakai's winter place by driving across Greasewood Flats, Tyende Creek Canyon, and Carson Mesa in the deep snow, before turning back to Dinnehotso to try another approach (chap. 24).

Skinwalkers: The tributary of Tyende Creek in which Wilson Sam's body was discovered is south of Greasewood Flats (chap. 5).

GREASY WATER TRADING POST: Fictional location.

✤ Role in Hillerman Fiction:

Sacred Clowns: An antique saddle and other artifacts are stolen from this fictional location—a case that ends up on Jim Chee's desk (chap. 8).

HANO: (6200 ft) Apache County, AZ. Also called Tewa. The Navajos call this Hopi village Naashashí, meaning "Bear People," or, more literally, "Enemy Bears." The name apparently derives from the bear sandpaintings of the Tewas at Hano. The same name is applied to Santa Clara Pueblo in New Mexico. To the Hopis, this village is "Hanu," referring to the "ha" commonly heard in the Tewa language, and which has come to mean "Tewa" in Hopi.

This is the northeasternmost village on First Mesa. The village had a population of 285 in 1939.

According to Southwestern historian Albert Schroeder, around the year 1700 a portion of the population of the village of Tsewaii (also known as San Cristobal), in the Galisteo Basin southwest of Santa Fe, New Mexico, were invited by Hopi emissaries to leave their home and settle in the Hopi country. They were promised attractive lands in return for help in fighting the Utes and Navajos.

They first settled near Coyote Spring, but after a battle in which they defeated a Ute war party that had attacked Walpi, they were invited to settle atop First Mesa.

Although they lived in close proximity with, and even intermarried with, the Hopis, they have never been fully absorbed into that tribe, and still retain the Tewa language of the Rio Grande villages. Originally renowned warriors, they became the policemen for the Hopi Reservation.

The Navajo Rounded Man Red Antway Myth mentions this community in the hero's search for his family.

✤ Role in Hillerman Fiction:

The Dark Wind: Jim Chee and Deputy Sheriff Cowboy Dashee pass Sichomovi and Hano on their way to Piutki, where they learn who is vandalizing Windmill No. 6, and that there was a witness to Pauling's plane crash (chap. 21).

HARD GOODS CANYON: Fictional location(?) in the vicinity of Old Woman Gray Rocks's brush hogan.

❖ Role in Hillerman Fiction:

The Blessing Way: Old Woman Gray Rocks tells anthropologist Bergen McKee that her grandson has seen a van (possibly belonging to the missing Dr. Hall) in this canyon while he was trapping rabbits (chap. 7).

HEART BUTTE: (6970 ft) McKinley County, NM. This is most likely the sandstone formation shown on some maps as Heart Rock. The Navajo name is uncertain. It rises some 200 ft on the flat plains north of Mesa de los Lobos, seven miles east of Crownpoint. It is presumably the location of Heart Rock Trading Post, opened between 1946 and 1950, and closed by 1955.

❖ Role in Hillerman Fiction:

People of Darkness: Chee determines that Windy Tsossie (a survivor of the oil rig explosion) lived here (chap. 22).

HESPERUS PEAK: (13,232 ft) La Plata County, CO. (Also known as Mount Hesperus.) The Navajos call this highly sacred mountain Dibé Ntsaa, meaning "Big Sheep." Located approximately 11 miles north of Mancos (and U.S. Highway 160), this is the highest point in the La Plata Range of the San Juan Mountains. The English name commemorates the schooner in Longfellow's poem "The Wreck of the Hesperus."

This is the Navajo sacred mountain of the north, and in the Navajo creation myth, First Man impregnated it with jet, covered it with darkness (its symbolic color is black), and fastened it to the sky with a rainbow. It is one of the seven sacred mountains. Blanca Peak, Mount Hesperus, Mount Taylor, and the San Francisco Peaks mark the four cardinal directions and were once considered boundaries of Navajoland; Gobernador Knob, Hosta Butte, and Huerfano Peak are smaller features internal to Navajoland. Navajos consider Hesperus Peak and Mount Taylor (sacred mountains of the north and south) to be female, while the San Francisco Peaks and Blanca Peak (sacred mountains of the west and east) are thought of as male.

❖ Role in Hillerman Fiction:

The Ghostway: After returning from Los Angeles, Chee returns for the third time to Ashie Begay's hogan in the Chuskas to see if he can verify Bentwoman's assertion that Begay must be dead. In the chinde hogan, Chee finds Ashie Begay's Four Mountains Bundle, containing herbs and minerals from the four sacred mountains: the San Francisco Peaks in Arizona (sacred mountain of the west), Hesperus Peak in the La Plata Mountains of Colorado (sacred mountain of the north), Blanca Peak in the Sangre de Cristo Mountains of Colorado (sacred mountain of the east), and Mount Taylor in New Mexico (sacred mountain of the south) (chap. 22).

The Fallen Man: Elisa Breedlove tells Jim Chee that her late husband Hal had wanted his ashes scattered over the San Juan Mountains in the La Plata Range, specifically on Mount Hesperus; Chee gets angry when he learns Hal had climbed this sacred mountain before his death (chap. 5).

HOGBACK: (6200 ft) San Juan County, NM. The Navajos call this feature Tsé Kíniitíní ("Leaning Rock"); Tsétaak'áán ("Rock Extending into Water"); and Tsétaak'á ("Rock Ledge Slants into Water"). This 18-mile-long, vaguely S-shaped monocline is of Mesa Verde sandstone, and is similar in appearance to the Gallup Hogback. It begins 14 miles southwest of Shiprock, near Bennett Peak, and travels north through Waterflow, in the vicinity of the Chimney Rock Oil Lease.

In 1894 the Navajos constructed an early irrigation system—known as the Hogback Ditch or the Fruitland Ditch—at the point where the San Juan River bisects the Hogback. It irrigated some 75 acres. In 1941 a subsequent system irrigated 3500 acres of agricultural land on the north bank of the San Juan River, and that system later gave rise to the Navajo Indian Irrigation Project (NIIP, managed by the Navajo Agricultural Products Industries, or NAPI). This colossal undertaking was initiated in the late 1960s, and will eventually irrigate 110,000 acres.

In 1941, the Midwest Oil Company maintained a long-term lease in the region where the Hogback intersects the Chaco River, and the BIA operated a coal mine in the monocline some 20 miles southeast of Shiprock.

Hogback Trading Post is located on U.S. Highway 64, on the north bank of the San Juan River, where the highway cuts through a pass in the hogback (just 100 yards outside the eastern boundary of the Navajo Reservation). This post was established by Hank Hull at least by September 1871. Hull sold out to his nephew, Harry Baldwin, in 1900. Joe Tanner purchased the post from Baldwin in 1916, but sold it a year later to Wilfred Wheeler and Albert Hugh Lee. Wheeler became sole owner in 1918, and the post has since remained in the Wheeler family—a very long tenure by trader standards.

✤ **Role in Hillerman Fiction:**

A Thief of Time: Jim Chee finds that Slick Nakai's True Gospel had been here until recently (chap. 3). Nakai was approached here by Randall Elliot for pottery from Bluff that Nakai was to have for the missing Eleanor Friedman-Bernal (chap. 4).

The Fallen Man: Jim Chee receives reports of drug use and gang activity around Hogback. Roderick Diamonte, who owns a disreputable bar here, files a citizen's complaint against officer Bernadette "Bernie" Manuelito for harassment (chap. 8). Chee uses the phone at the Hogback Trading Post to call the

Farmington number Joe Leaphorn had left for him, but Leaphorn was already on his way back to Window Rock (chap. 13). Navajo police officers take turns dropping in on the disreputable bar here to make the owners and patrons nervous (chap. 16).

HOPI BUTTES: (5400–6740 ft) Navajo County, AZ. Also Moqui Buttes, Moki Buttes, Blue Peaks, and Rabbit Ear Mountain. The Navajos call these mesas Dibé Dah Sitíní, meaning "Mountain Sheep Lying Down Up at an Elevation." To the Hopis, each of the buttes has its own name.

This rough, broken, and strikingly barren country lies between the Hopi Mesas and Interstate 40. The area is dotted with many small and moderate-sized volcanic plugs that form buttes and mesas between 800 and 1000 ft high (Egloffstein Butte, Nipple Butte, Montezuma's Chair, Castle Butte, Chimney Butte, Star Butte, Badger Butte, Round Top, Elephant Butte, Janice Peak, Five Buttes, Flying Butte, Stephen Butte, Teshim Butte, Deshgish Butte, French Butte, Haystack Butte, Smith Butte, Mitten Peak, Hennesey Buttes, etc.). The region is the scene of early summer eagle harvesting by Hopis.

This picturesque region, visible for miles from the south and west, was shown on McComb's map of 1860 as Blue Peaks, and until about 1915 was known as Johnson's Extension. Parts of the region were acquired for the Navajos by successive Executive Orders and acts of Congress, the latest action being in 1934.

Historian Van Valkenburgh describes Moqui Butte (which the Navajos call Tsézhin Ch'inít'i', meaning "A Line of Lava Extends Horizontally Outward") as important to the western clans' eastern migration stories.

✤ Role in Hillerman Fiction:

The Dark Wind: Jim Chee travels to the Hopi Buttes region to see Ashie McDonald about someone having beaten his cousin (chap. 18), but Ashie McDonald is away at Gallup.

Talking God: These formations are visible from Agnes Tsosie's home. Also, Agnes Tsosie's place is east of Nipple Butte, one of the Hopi Buttes (chap. 2).

Coyote Waits: In studying rock formation photos in the darkroom of murdered Huan Ji, Joe Leaphorn and Louisa Bourebonette conjecture the formations photographed could be from several locations, including the Hopi Buttes region (chap. 17).

HOPI MESAS (HOPI RESERVATION): (4650–7220 ft) Navajo and Coconino Counties, AZ. Also Moqui or Moki, a word believed to be derived from the Zuni or Hopi spelling of an archaic word, "mókwi." This term was commonly used after 1598, but was changed to Hopi, a more modern term used by the Hopi themselves, because the English pronunciation of the older term was offensive to the Hopi (it was too similar to their word móki, meaning "dies, or is dead"). The Navajos call this region 'Ayahkinii, meaning "Underground People."

Calling themselves Sinome, the Hopis are a pueblo tribe living in 13 villages located on the 2,472,320-acre Hopi Reservation in north-central Arizona. The population in 1939 was 3248; in 1990 it had reached 11,173. The villages are mostly located on three peninsular mesas that are the southwestern "fingers" of Black Mesa. Their agency is located at Keams Canyon. The language falls into the Shoshonean family of the Uto-Aztecan stock.

The Hopi Reservation is entirely surrounded by the larger Navajo Reservation, and incorporates a portion of southern Black Mesa in the north and the barren Painted Desert region to the south. The southern—and lowest—portion of this parcel of desert land is some of the most desolate country in the United States, yet the Hopi Indians have lived for centuries in numerous small villages situated among their three mesas. Although the region is dotted with sporadic small streams, it has no permanent rivers. The predominant ephemeral channels are Moenkopi, Dinnebito, Wepo, Oraibi, and Jadito Washes.

The traditional Hopi homes were pueblos of the classical style, and these are still in evidence atop the three mesas. Between the mesas, however, many individual family units have sprung up, both as isolated farmsteads and aggregated into villages like Polacca.

The Hopis are the oldest continuous inhabitants of northern Arizona; some of their ancestors may have lived in the region as early as A.D. 700. The ample and permanent springs fed from seepages carried along non-filterable strata from Black Mesa have had a great deal to do with their stability. Tradition relates that some of their early ancestors were immigrants from the Tsegi and Canyon de Chelly Anasazi ruins. Later groups came from Chavez Pass, Homolovi, and other southern pueblos, joined still later by Tewas and Keres from the Rio Grande region in New Mexico.

The first Europeans to visit the Hopis were Don Pedro de Tovar and Father Juan Padilla in 1542 on a side exploration from the Coronado Expedition. At that time all the pueblos, with the exception of Oraibi, were described as located on the foothills below the mesas and on the lower terraces, placing them closer to the springs and water channels. (This, however, brings the longevity of Walpi into question.) The Spaniards called the general Hopi region "Province of Tusayan."

The Franciscans established the first mission among the Hopis in 1629 and introduced peaches and other domesticated plants, as well as domesticated animals. Most of the missions were destroyed and their priests killed in the Pueblo Revolt of 1680. Seeking refuge from the possible reprisals during the reconquest of New Mexico, and from increasing Ute and Navajo raids, the Hopis moved from the foothills and terraces to the more defensible positions on the mesa rims, leaving only Oraibi occupying its original site. Soon after the Spanish Reconquest, groups of Tewa from the Rio Grande moved in and established themselves among the Hopis.

Until 1906, there were seven main villages and the farming village of Moenkopi (an offshoot of Oraibi) located some 40 miles to the west near Tuba City. The Hopis had had difficulty with the U.S. government since 1880, for refusing to send children to school or allow the introduction of modern sanitation and medical practices necessitated by epidemics of smallpox. In 1904 the Hopi Indian Agent was attacked at Shungopovi over the forced schooling issue, and a number of Hopis were sent to Alcatraz Penitentary for a year.

Oraibi had split into two factions in the 1890s, the "Unfriendlies," or Conservatives, and the "Friendlies," or Non-conservatives, the labels indicative of their attitude toward the U.S. government. Conservatives left to establish the present village of Hotevilla. With them went certain ceremonials, including the Snake Dance. A lowering of the water table and loss of agricultural lands through floods led to a further decline of Old Oraibi, until there are now fewer than 100 inhabitants. Many former residents moved off the mesa and settled at Kykotsmovi (known until about 1982 as New Oraibi).

The economic basis of Hopi life rests upon an extremely specialized form of agriculture. No permanent streams flow through the Hopi country, and rainfall annually averages less than 12 inches and comes almost solely in the summer months. There is little snow in winter.

The majority of the farm lands lie along washes, where temporary dams of brush, earth, or stone divert the flood waters over the fields. These are usually bordered or "diked" following the natural contour of the land in an effort to conserve all the moisture. On the mesa tops as well as on the plains below them, the Hopi farmers construct brush barriers of any shrub or tree available in order to accumulate the wind-blown sand for mulch.

Hopi agricultural products include corn of the flint type, a quick-growing and hardy species commonly known as "Indian corn," over 20 varieties of beans, melons, and squash, as well as fruit trees (particularly peach tees, which are planted on sand and talus slopes near springs and sub-irrigated places). In the past, some native cotton was raised, but little if any is now grown. Some families also own cattle and/or sheep.

Hopi women manufacture decorated and undecorated pottery. All of the decorated pottery was made on First Mesa until the 1970s. The men weave blankets and engage in silversmithing, painting, and woodcarving. Basketry is made on Second and Third Mesas.

✦ Role in Hillerman Fiction:

Skinwalkers: Looking out his Window Rock office window, Joe Leaphorn knows it's raining in Hopi country while Chee is visiting the Dinnebito Wash country (chap. 19).

Sacred Clowns: From his office window, Joe Leaphorn can see rain building over Hopi country (chap. 2).

The First Eagle: The land about Yells Back Butte, next to the Hopi Reservation, is unfamiliar to Jim Chee, who has worked out of the Tuba City substation of the Navajo Tribal Police only a short time (chap. 2). Yells Back Butte, the site of Navajo Tribal Policeman Benny Kinsman's murder, is on the edge of the Hopi Reservation (chap. 3).

HORSE FELL CANYON: A fictitious location, near Many Ruins Canyon, which would place it in the vicinity of Red Rock Valley on the Arizona–New Mexico state line west of Shiprock Pinnacle.

✦ Role in Hillerman Fiction:

The Blessing Way: Luis Horseman knows that the moving dust plume in the distance means that a truck or Jeep is on the dirt track leading to Horse Fell and Many Ruins Canyons, and ultimately to Tall Poles Butte, the site of the Army radar station (chap. 1).

HOTEVILLA: (6000 ft) (Population: 869) Navajo County, AZ. Also Hotavilla. The Navajos call this community Tł'ochintó, "Wild Onion Spring." To the Hopis, it is Hitaveli ("Skinned Back"). This Hopi village lies on the west flank of Third Mesa, and is off Arizona Highway 264. The 1939 population was 507.

The name Hitaveli was taken from a spring that was located in a low cave, so that one entering to get water often skinned his back. This spring was visited by Colonel (Governor) Jose Antonio Vizcarra in 1823.

This village was born as a result of strife in the "mother" village, Oraibi, in 1905–6. The population was sharply divided into two factions, the Conservatives (or Hostiles), and the Progressives (or Friendlies). After a confrontation, the Conservatives, under the leadership of Youkeoma, left Oraibi in 1906 and established the village of Hotevilla. (Youkeoma and a couple dozen others were arrested and imprisoned at Fort Wingate shortly after the fracas at Oraibi.) A further split at Hotevilla in 1907 led to the founding of the village of Bacabi one mile to the east.

For two decades the people of Hotevilla refused to send children to school, and on one occasion the U.S. Cavalry was called out to round up the children hidden in the houses. The people also refused to allow their sheep to be dipped, and for this Youkeoma was banished to California. Today, Hotevilla is one of the most conservative of the Hopi pueblos, producing high-quality baskets and textiles. It hosts the Snake Dance every even-numbered year.

Navajos from the Dinnebito region carry on considerable trade in Hotevilla.

✤ Role in Hillerman Fiction:

The Dark Wind: Jim Chee passes through the villages of Oraibi, Hotevilla, and Bacavi on his way to see if Ben Gaines and Gail Pauling are still residing at the motel in the Hopi Cultural Center on Second Mesa (chap. 18).

Sacred Clowns: Deputy Sheriff Cowboy Dashee believes the clowns from Shongopovi, Hotevilla, and Walpi villages are "better" than those from Tano (chap. 1).

HUERFANO MESA: (7470 ft) San Juan County, NM. Also Huerfano Mountain, El Huerfano. The Navajo name is Dził Ná'oodiłii, "People Encircling Around Mountain," referring to a legend in which people moved around the mountain. A sacred name is Nłiz Dził, "Mountain of Precious Stones." This large, isolated mesa is situated 25 miles south of Bloomfield, a mile northeast of U.S. Highway 550 (formerly New Mexico Highway 44). The old Huerfano Trading Post lies between the highway and the southern tip of the mesa, in the vicinity of Dził Ná'oodiłii BIA school.

The mesa is steep-walled and angular, with one arm extending east, the other south. It is topped with four cupolalike sandstone crags. It dominates the country south of the San Juan River for 40 miles, and can be seen from the Chuska Mountains, 50 miles to the west. By 1941, it had been ascended by relatively few White men, and traditional Navajos disapprove of efforts to climb it, preferring that only their medicine men visit the top. However, since Van Valkenburgh's writing, the mesa has been crowned by a veritable fence of radio and microwave towers—an affront to Navajos, and placed there without their consent.

Huerfano is one of the four sacred mountains interior to the traditional Navajo homeland (see also Hosta Butte, Gobernador Peak, and Navajo Mountain), and is said to be suspended from the sky with sunbeams. It is reputed to be the home of Yódí Ashkii (Goods of Value Boy), and Yódí At'ééd (Goods of Value Girl), as well as one of the homes of Átsé Hastiin (First Man) and Átsé 'Asdzáán (First Woman). Navajo mythology tells that in the beginning it was decorated with pollen, rugs, hides, cloth, and male rain. It was also the scene of First Girl's puberty rites and is mentioned in the Blessingway and Coyoteway myths.

In 1967, the Bureau of Land Management (earlier responsible for the microwave towers) proposed to make a recreation area of the east wing, complete with picnic tables. Navajo singers protested, and the Navajo Tribe sent historian Dave Brugge to investigate. His report enabled Edward O. Plummer of the tribe to negotiate a land exchange with BLM, returning the east wing to the tribe. While the Navajos did not get all that they had hoped, the east wing is now a sort of "sacred wilderness" accessible only to Navajo singers and those accompanied by singers.

The mesa and surrounding area was the scene of a bitter protest by Navajos in 1992 to prevent a Farmington firm from establishing an asbestos dump on private land about seven miles north of the mesa beneath the "line-of-sight" between Huerfano and Gobernador Knob. (The line-of-sight is said to have led First Man to the infant Changing Woman in Navajo mythology.) The company eventually withdrew its proposal.

✤ Role in Hillerman Fiction:

A Thief of Time: Slick Nakai expounds to his congregation about the defamation of Huerfano Mesa by radio towers all over the top, where he and his uncle carried Aghaal when he was a child (chap. 4).

Coyote Waits: Joe Leaphorn's uncle, Hoskie Jim, had used the story of how Coyote had scattered the stars from the blanket of First Man and First Woman near Huerfano Mesa to illustrate a discussion of randomness (chap. 15).

INSCRIPTION HOUSE TRADING POST: (6850 ft) Coconino County, AZ. The Navajo name is Ts'ah Bii' Kin, "House in the Sage." This old trading location (and former tourist lodge) was opened in the early 1920s. It is situated on the Shonto Plateau, east of the head of Navajo Canyon, on Navajo Route 16, five and a half miles north of Arizona Highway 98. In 1954, S. J. Richardson sold this post to Stokes Carson, who operated it until his death in 1974. Carson's daughters inherited the lease, and granddaughter Wy and her husband Al Townsend operated it until the lease expired in 1990. Al Grieve took over management briefly in 1991 with intent to purchase, but this deal fell through. The location is also a chapter seat.

The name comes from the nearby Inscription House Ruin, a famed Anasazi structure, with an almost illegible cliff-wall inscription interpreted by some to read "Carlos Arnais 1661," or "S-haperio Ano Dom 1661." More recent investigations show it probably dates to the late nineteenth century, probably 1881.

Navajo Mission church is located across the road from the Trading Post.

✤ Role in Hillerman Fiction:

The First Eagle: Returning to Krouse's office, Joe Leaphorn finds a note saying that Krouse has gone to Inscription House, then to Navajo Mission (chap. 25).

IYANBITO: (7000 ft) McKinley County, NM. The Navajo name is 'Ayáníi Bitó', meaning "Buffalo Spring." This Navajo community is located at the foot of the red sandstone cliffs three miles north of Interstate 40, and seven miles east of Church Rock. It formerly housed a BIA day school in the 1940s, and now includes a chapter house. Navajo ethnohistorian Klara Kelley has identified a Buffalo Springs Trading Post that may have been located here for about a decade beginning in the late 1940s.

The name 'Ayáníi Bitó' is of recent origin, having been given after imported buffalos for an early Gallup Inter-Tribal Indian Ceremonial were watered nearby. Previously the name was Tł'ízí Łigai ("White Goat") after the English Goat Ranch operated here in the 1880s by an English "remittance man." An older name was Naakaii Haayáhí ("Mexican's Ascent"), after a trail up the sandstone cliff ascended by a Mexican through the cove that opens at the site of the old day school.

✤ Role in Hillerman Fiction:
Sacred Clowns: Jim Chee recognizes this locale as the background for the movie "Cheyenne Autumn" (chap. 11).

IYANBITO MESA: (8200 ft) McKinley and Cibola Counties, NM. The Navajo name remains uncertain. This is the name Mr. Hillerman has applied to the imposing mesa that parallels Interstate 40 from Gallup eastward nearly all the way to Milan. This feature is surprisingly nameless on virtually all maps. The north face of the mesa is sheer, red sandstone, towering 800 ft high in places. The mesa's peninsulas jut south like the prows of huge, red warships. The mesa is comprised of layer set upon layer of deep red sandstone topped with dark evergreen trees.

Other names applied by writers include Wingate Cliffs, Red Rock Mesa, and Mesa de Los Lobos ("Wolf Mesa"—although this name refers primarily to the highest layer on the northern periphery above Crownpoint).

✤ Role in Hillerman Fiction:
Talking God: A murder victim, apparently thrown from a passing train, is found in this vicinity (chap. 3).

JADITO WASH: (7485–4900 ft) Navajo County, AZ. Also Jeddito Wash, Jedito Wash. Navajos call this Jádító, meaning "Antelope Spring." A 65-mile-long wash draining Balakai Mesa, flowing southwest across the Hopi Reservation. Jadito Wash merges with Polacca Wash to form Corn Creek Wash, which then flows another eight miles into the Little Colorado River.

Pedro de Tovar, of Coronado's expedition of 1541, was the first White man to visit this region.

✤ Role in Hillerman Fiction:

Coyote Waits: Officer Delbert Nez lived between here and Birdsprings Trading Post before he was killed (chap. 10).

JEMEZ (PUEBLO): (5575 ft) (Population: 1,783) Sandoval County, NM. The Navajos call this place Mą'ii Deeshgiizh ("Coyote Pass"), named for a gap eight miles north of the current village. This Towa pueblo is located on the east bank of Rio San Jose at the southern end of the Jemez Mountains. It is situated on New Mexico Highway 4, 45 miles north of the junction of that road with U.S. Highway 550 (formerly New Mexico Highway 44). The name Jemez is from the Towa "Hay Mish," meaning "the people." (Towa is a branch of the Kiowa-Tanoan language family, and Jemez is related by language stock solely to the now-abandoned Pecos Pueblo, situated about 30 miles to the east).

The present site of the pueblo was established after many movements of the Jemez people in the region. Many of these relocations were precipitated by the Navajos, whom the Jemez called Wangsave, meaning "Jemez-Apaches." Navajo raids and difficulties with the Spanish nearly depopulated Jemez in the latter part of the sixteenth century. At the time of the Pueblo Revolt of 1680, there were three villages (Asti'olakwa, Guisewa, and Patoqua). After the Reconquest of 1692, the old village was rebuilt on Jemez Creek, and is the present village of Jemez.

In 1541, Pedro de Castañeda, chronicler for Francisco Vásquez de Coronado, wrote of seven Jemez pueblos in the vicinity of Jemez Hot Springs (Aguas Calientes). Mission San José de Guise was founded in 1622. In 1639, Fray Diego de San Lucas was killed during a Navajo attack on the pueblo. Between 1644 and 1647, Governor of New Spain Luis Arguello hanged 29 Jemez leaders after the pueblo allied itself with the Navajos and killed Diego Martinez Naranjo, a Spaniard. In 1662, Fray Miguel Sacristán hanged himself at the pueblo, and during the Pueblo Revolt of 1680, Fray Juan de Jesus Matador was killed by the pueblo's occupants.

Following the Reconquest of 1692, the Jemez were less than totally supportive of the Spanish and their allies—the Keresan pueblos of Zia and Santa Ana. Over the next two years, the people of Jemez raided these two nearby villages, eventually killing four Zia men. This led to a punitive expedition of 120 Spanish soldiers and auxiliaries from Zia, San Felipe, and Santa Ana, led by de Vargas. A battle on the mesa above the pueblo led to the deaths of 84 Jemez people and the capture of 361. Legend states that during the battle, a likeness of San Diego appeared on a cliff from which many people were leaping to their deaths; all leapers landed on their feet with no harm after the appearance. Today a likeness of the saint can still be seen on the red sandstone cliff above Jemez Hot Springs.

On June 4, 1696, another friar, Francisco de Jesus, was killed at Jemez, which led to another battle (this one in San Diego Canyon) in which 28 to 40 Indians were killed (including eight Acomas who had allied themselves with the Jemez). Thereafter, only a portion of the Jemez people returned to the pueblo; many sought their ancestral homeland in northwestern New Mexico (Canyon Largo or "Stone Canyon" to the Jemez), or went to live among the Navajos and Hopis to the west. (Some went as far as the White Mountain Apache country to the southwest in Arizona.)

Most eventually returned to Jemez, although some stayed with the Navajos. They even formed a new clan, Mą'ii Deeshgiizhinii, within that tribe. Washington Matthews stated that the village from which these people originated was called Klogi; but historian David Brugge points out that Tłogi is the Navajo name for Zia Pueblo.

Many Jemez refugees settled at Hopi First Mesa. Between 1730 and 1734 a drought drove them eastward to Canyon de Chelly, where they met with other Mą'ii Deeshgiizhii who had previously joined the Navajos.

Navajos attacked Jemez Pueblo on June 8, 1708; in March 1714; in 1796; from 1826 through 1829; in 1833; and in 1835. Spruce Baird, the first Indian agent to the Navajos, established his agency at Jemez in 1852. The pueblo was the staging area for many incursions into Navajo country throughout the Spanish, Mexican, and American periods. In January of 1824, and again in 1839 and December 1851, peace talks between the Navajos and New Mexicans were held at Jemez. In 1838, people abandoning Pecos Pueblo to the southeast moved into Jemez.

In 1863–64, the Jemez sheltered Navajos fleeing the U.S. Army (under Kit Carson), refusing to surrender them until the pueblo was surrounded by the Army. Anthropologist Adolph F. Bandelier stated around 1890 that "Jemez is more than half Navajo, and one of their leading men, whom unsophisticated worshipers are not wont to admire as typical and genuine pueblo, the Nazlo, was Navajo by birth, education, and inclination. We ought to consider, for instance, the Indians of Zuni have married with, and plentifully absorbed Navajo, Tegua (Tewa) and Jemez blood."

Traditionally many Navajos would travel to Jemez on feast days to trade, and regularly Jemez traders traveled through the Navajo country trading vegetables and fruits for sheep, blankets, and silver. Today a close friendship exists between the Navajos of Torreon and the Jemez, their eastern neighbors and relatives.

✤ Role in Hillerman Fiction:

The Ghostway: In Los Angeles, the ancient and blind Bentwoman tells Chee that the missing Ashie Begay is part Jemez, because his grandmother was from Jemez (chap. 17).

Sacred Clowns: In Eric Dorsey's room in Thoreau, Joe Leaphorn finds a flyer from an earlier environmental protest that had taken place at Jemez to stop the mining of perlite (used to wash "pre-washed" bluejeans). But Father Haines's secretary tells him that Dorsey was far more concerned with people than with the environment, so Leaphorn wonders how the flyer came to be in Dorsey's room (chap. 19).

JEMEZ MOUNTAINS: (6550–11,254 ft) Sandoval, Rio Arriba, and Santa Fe counties, NM. The Navajos call this range Dził Łizhinii or Dziłizhiin ("Black Appearing Mountains"), and 'Aniłt'ánii Dził ("Corn Beetle Mountain"). This heavily wooded mountain range straddles the boundary between the Rocky Mountain Province and the Basin and Range Province. The range stretches some 45 miles between the junction of the Rio Grande and Jemez Creek on the south and Los Alamos on the north. On the east it is bounded by the Rio Grande Valley, and on the west lies the upper Rio Puerco of the East. These mountains are of volcanic origin, which distinguishes them from both the Rocky Mountains and the basin-and-range mountains. Valle Grande, a broad valley west of Los Alamos, is the result of a tremendous volcanic explosion.

The San Pedro Mountains, the Nacimiento Mountains, and Cejita Blanca Range are all physically a part of the Jemez Range, dominated by 11,254-ft Redondo Peak west of Los Alamos.

The Jemez Mountains are well known to the Navajos. Pelado Peak, called Dził Dijool ("Round Mountain" or "Globular Mountain", though Van Valkenburgh translated this as "Big Buttocks Place"), was a favored hunting ground of the old-time Navajos. It is one of several promontories hypothesized as being the Navajo sacred mountain of the east. (Also suggested are Pelado Peak, Wheeler Peak, and Blanca Peak, which is considered by most authorities as the correct mountain.) Pedernal Peak in the Jemez is known as Noolyínii (technically meaning "Obsidian," but generally any flaking material).

Pajarito Peak is called Tł'iish Jik'áhí ("Grinding Snakes"), and is an important place in the Navajo Wind Chant stories. Cejita Blanca Ridge is known as Bistah ("Among the Adobes"). According to the Rounded Man Red Antway Myth, the first home of the Ant People was in the Jemez Mountains. In the Navajo creation myth, Déélgééd ("Horned Monster") was killed by the Twin War Gods in the Jemez Mountains.

Throughout the entire Jemez Range there were old Navajo hunting and raiding trails as well as camp sites: Yé'ii Bikék'eh ("Yei's Footprints") at Piedra Lumbre, and Táála Hooghan ("Flat-topped Hogan") are well-known old Navajo camps and fields. Under the name Dził Łizhin, they are mentioned in the Navajo Ghostway tradition of the Male Branch of Shootingway.

❖ Role in Hillerman Fiction:

Coyote Waits: From the overlook at Washington Pass, Joe Leaphorn can see the Zuni Mountains to the south, the Jemez Mountains to the east, and the San Juan Mountains (in Colorado) to the north (chap. 12).

JICARILLA APACHE RESERVATION: Sandoval and Rio Arriba counties, NM. Navajos call this region Beeha, meaning "Always Winter People." This tribe of Apacheans is now situated on a reservation located in north-central New Mexico near the Colorado state line. The agency is at Dulce, New Mexico. The language spoken is Jicarilla Apache of Athapaskan stock, and is similar to Navajo.

The former habitat of the Jicarilla was in central and eastern New Mexico and southern Colorado in an area bounded by the Canadian, the Arkansas, and the Chama Rivers, and the region of Mora, New Mexico. There were two main divisions, or bands, of the tribe. The eastern was known as the Cooxgaen, or Plains People, called the "Llanero" in contemporary literature. They ranged east of the Rio Grande, having their favorite retreat in the Sangre de Cristo Range north of Taos. The other division lived west of the Rio Grande and called themselves Shaindeh, or Sand People. In Spanish and early American documents they were known as the Ollero (pronounced Oyero).

The Jicarillas were the only Apaches to join in the Pueblo Revolt of 1680, aiding the Taos Indians in ridding northern New Mexico of Spanish settlers and missionaries. During the 1700s, the Jicarillas greatly feared their neighbors to the east, the Comanches, who had obtained guns from the French to the north, while the Spanish forbade supplying the Apaches with firearms.

The Jicarilla under Chief Chatto were subdued in military campaigns conducted by Lieutenant Colonel Philip St. George Cook and Lieutenant Davidson in 1854. They were placed in the nucleus of their present reservation in 1873, the agency at Dulce established in 1900.

Until the 1930s, the Jicarilla were dying at an alarming rate from tuberculosis and other conditions of abject poverty. A program of physical and economic rehabilitation was inaugurated by the Indian Department (later BIA) with the support of Emmett Wirt, pioneer trader. Since the 1940s, the Jicarilla have been increasing in population. They are a relatively wealthy tribe, deriving revenues from oil and gas and from taxes they impose on mining. They recently outbid the State of New Mexico to purchase an extensive and valuable Chama Ranch property. In 1937, the Jicarilla Apache Cooperative Store was established to manage all sheep and wool sales.

The Jicarilla are essentially stockmen, having little interest in agriculture. Arts and crafts are not considerable, but there is some work in basketry, bead-ing, and tanning, and there has been a recent revival of Jicarilla micaceous pottery.

✤ Role in Hillerman Fiction:

A Thief of Time: Joe Leaphorn suspected that some of Nakai's congregation were not Navajo but Jicarilla Apaches (chap. 4).

Coyote Waits: The San Juan County Sheriff supposedly hired a half-Apache deputy, T. J. Birdie, to get votes from the Jicarilla Apache Reservation—even though Birdie was Mescalero Apache (chap. 16).

The Fallen Man: The Granger-Smith law firm had dealings in water rights on the Jicarilla reservation when Janet Pete worked for their Albuquerque office (chap. 6).

Hunting Badger: A BIA cop sent from the Jicarilla Reservation spotted the truck stolen from the gas station assault in the Aneth Oil Field—within walking distance of Gothic Creek Canyon (chap. 17).

JOINT USE RESERVATION (JOINT USE AREA): (5000–7000 ft) Apache and Navajo Counties, AZ. The Navajo name remains uncertain. According to Presidential Executive Order of December 16, 1882, this "buffer zone" surrounding the Hopi Indian Reservation was intended "for the use of the Moqui (Hopi) and such other Indians (Navajo) as the Secretary of the Interior may see fit to settle thereon." Many attempts were made over the years to divide the land equitably between the two tribes, but technicalities and each tribe's desire to retain its perceived share of a wealth of resources in the region stymied all such attempts until 1974, when the U.S. government forced both tribes into a settlement. Actual compliance with this agreement led to the forced relocation of 26 Hopi families and over 3,600 Navajo families. Delays in the relocation of some families continue to the publication date of this volume.

✤ Role in Hillerman Fiction:

The Dark Wind: Virtually all the action of this novel takes place within the Joint Use Area.

Talking God: Officer Chee recognizes a type of White person as being "Lone Rangers," who have declared themselves spokesmen for (and guardians of) Navajo families faced with eviction from the Joint Use Area in the infamous Relocation (chap. 6).

KAH BIHGHI: (6500 ft) Apache County, AZ. The common English spelling is Kah Bihgi or Kah Bizhi; Hillerman spelled it Kam Bimghi, which is how the name seems to be spelled on the popular Southern California Automobile Association maps. The Navajo name for this region is K'aabizhii (Biznauga

Figure 23. This unique feature in the Kah Bihgi valley obviously resembles a thumb, complete with thumbnail. However, it is some five miles northwest of the conical feature labeled "The Thumb" on the renowned AAA Indian Country map and USGS maps. (Could the maps be in error?)

species of cactus), or K'aabizhiistł'ah ("A Corner Where a Small Stubby Cactus with Interlocking Thorns Grows").

In this valley a tiny trading and day-school community is centered around Cove Trading Post, 10 miles west of Red Valley, on the northeast slope of the Lukachukai Mountains. Broken by many blind and hidden canyons and coves among the forests of the Lukachukai Mountains, this remote region was an excellent, defendable hiding place and served as a Navajo rendezvous.

Historian Van Valkenburgh told of a Navajo tradition involving a sheer rock in Mexican Canyon prior to the removal of the Navajos to Fort Sumner in 1864:

> A long time ago in the time of our grandfathers, the Navajos had a citadel on top of Tsénikání ("Round Rock"). In times of trouble they moved up there to live in security until the enemies left. Once the Mexicans came, but they could not climb the sides of the rock so they camped below and tried to starve the Navajos out. After a few days the Navajos knew they had to do something and held a meeting.
>
> Among them was a man who was supposed to be a witch and they asked him to try his power on the Mexican captain. That night he made evil medicine. In the morning, when the Navajos were all together again, the witch said, "I killed the Mexican captain." They looked down and the captain lay dead and the Mexicans were moving out. (Van Valkenburgh 1941, 45)

In 1859, Captain John Walker led the first American military party to cross the Lukachukai Mountains, marching around the eastern flanks of the Carrizos, crossing Cove Mesa, and passing over the Lukachukais near the head of

Tsaile Creek or Spruce Creek. That same year, Major J. S. Simpson also crossed Cove Mesa, and Lieutenant W. O. Brown visited the vicinity in 1892. Brown noted a small mud spring four and a half miles northeast of Shiprock Pinnacle near Mitten Rock—a name he apparently applied. Brown described the Cove region as an area with "good agricultural possibilities," needing only good irrigation. He remarked that the locality was the finest he had observed and that not a wagon or plow had been used in the entire valley. At this time the cove was under the control of a local Navajo headman named Black Horse. (See Round Rock for more information on this leader.)

The red sandstone country between the Carrizo and Lukachukai Mountains is rich in Anasazi ruins and old Navajo sites. During the 1930s, Earl Morris of the Carnegie Institute investigated this region, considered at the time one of the most untouched archaeological areas left in the Navajo country.

The Navajos call Cove Mesa (lying to the north of the community of Cove) Chooh Dínéeshzheé, meaning "Fringed with Roses." This mesa sits between the Lukachukai and Carrizo Mountains, north of Mexican Cry Mesa.

✤ **Role in Hillerman Fiction:**
The Blessing Way: Luis Horseman keeps a lookout over this valley from his hideout (chap. 1). Anthropologist Bergen McKee suggests that Ellen Leon look for her Ph.D. electrical engineer (Jimmy W. Hall) in these mountains, as well as in the Lukachukais and Kah Bihgi Valley (chap. 3).

KAIBITO: (6070 ft) (Population: 641) Coconino County, AZ. Navajos call this small community K'ai' Bii' Tó, meaning "Spring in the Willows." This trading, chapter, and school community lies in the upper canyon of the Kaibito, the southern branch of Navajo Canyon on the Kaibito Plateau (about half a mile south of Arizona Highway 98). The region was a stronghold for Navajo refugees of the war and Bosque Redondo years of the 1860s, under headman Dághaa' Sikaad.

✤ **Role in Hillerman Fiction:**
The First Eagle: When Joe Leaphorn visits the Tuba City lab of Richard Krouse, he finds a note saying that Krouse went mouse hunting at Kaibito (chap. 20). Mrs. Gracia Nakaidineh at the Kaibito Chapter House remembers Leaphorn from when he used to patrol the Kaibito area out of Tuba City (chap. 20).

KAIBITO CREEK: (7900–3800 ft) Coconino County, AZ. (See Kaibito for the Navajo name.) This stream heads in a deep canyon of White Mesa, some eight miles east of Kaibito. It flows west and north, some 30 miles, past Kaibito and

into Navajo Creek (Navajo Canyon), a tributary of the San Juan River Arm of
Lake Powell.

✤ **Role in Hillerman Fiction:**

The First Eagle: Joe Leaphorn finds Richard Krouse, wearing an "elephant suit," hunting mice along this creek, where it runs into Chaol Canyon,
atop the Rainbow Plateau (chap. 20).

KAM BIMGHI VALLEY: See Kah Bihghi.

KAYENTA: (5800 ft) (Population: 4,372) Navajo County, AZ. Navajos call this
community Tó Dínéeeshzhee', translating as "Fringed Water" or "Fingers of
Water." Historians have suggested that the name Kayenta is an English rendering of "Téé'ndééh" ("Animals fall into Deep Water"—a place one mile downstream from the old Indian Service irrigation dam), or that it means "Three
Springs Come out of the Side of a Hill." U.S. Army Captain John Walker and
his Mounted Rifles named the place "Laguna" in 1860, due to the pools and
lush vegetation then found along the creek.

This chapter community lies south of Monument Valley at the junction of
U.S. Highways 160 and 163. An early day school was established here, along
with a USIS tuberculosis sanatorium, which evolved into an Indian Health
Service hospital. Trading posts in the vicinity have included Wetherill and
Colville Trading Company (opened prior to 1910); Babbitt Trading Company
(opened prior to 1915); and Joe Kerley. The Wetherills even had a ranch in the
vicinity, and the U.S. Indian Service (precursor of the BIA) helped establish
Navajo agricultural work in the area.

The first White visitor in 1823, Colonel Francisco Salazar, traveled north
from the Hopi Mesas, and east to Chinle Valley to rejoin the main body of
Vizcarra's Navajo expedition. During the Kit Carson campaign of 1863–64,
Hashké Neiniihí led his people into deep canyons of the region, where they
waited out the return of the bulk of the Navajos from the Bosque Redondo internment. Hashké Neiniihí (namesake of Hoskininni Mesa) died in 1909.

According to Van Valkenburgh, traders John and Louisa Wetherill settled
here about 1910, having moved from their post at Oljeto, Utah, which they
had founded in 1906. The Wetherills advertised their post office as the most
distant of all from a railroad in the United States. The community served as a
base for numerous archaeological and exploratory expeditions into the great
wild country that spreads northward like a fan.

✤ **Role in Hillerman Fiction:**

Listening Woman: This is where Leaphorn, as a boy, first experienced a
female pair of blue eyes staring at him as though he was an interesting object;
and where he saw his first bearded man (chap. 6).

The Ghostway: Jim Chee's mother owned a summer hogan near Kayenta when he was a child (chap. 3). Chee remembers seeing Shiprock pinnacle from his mother's place near Kayenta (chap. 7). [*Author's note:* Actually, because of the Carrizo Mountains, Shiprock cannot be seen from Kayenta.] The blizzard that caught Chee in the Chuska Moutains looking for Ashie Begay had closed Navajo Route 1 from Shiprock to Kayenta (chap. 23).

A Thief of Time: Leaphorn had been stationed at Kayenta when Harrison Houk's crazy son Brigham went berserk years ago, killing the boy's own mother, sister, and brother before disappearing under the waters of the San Juan River (chap. 2).

Coyote Waits: According to Mary Keeyani, people would come from as far as Kayenta to have Pinto perform crystal gazing on them (chap. 3).

Sacred Clowns: KNDN radio news transcripts from three days prior to Jim Chee's Crownpoint meeting with BIA Police Sergeant Harold Blizzard discussed a plan to improve the runway here (chap. 8).

The First Eagle: Shirley Ahkeah was born here (chap. 1). Joe Leaphorn listens to KNDN on the limousine radio as he is driven to Santa Fe to meet Millicent Vanders; a speaker invites all friends to a yeibichai north of Kayenta (chap. 3).

KEAMS CANYON: (6400 ft) (Population: 393) Navajo County, AZ. To the Navajos, this is Lók'a'deeshjin, meaning "Reeds Extend in a Black Line," though some interpret it as "Black Reeds in the Distance." Hopis simply call it Pongsikvi ("Government community"). This village is located in a deep canyon of buff Mesa Verde sandstone that runs west to join Polacca Wash near the village of Polacca. The Hopi Indian Agency is located here, with a hospital, boarding school, missions of the Franciscan Fathers and Rainbow Baptists, and a post office.

Originally a Hopi farming area, this site was called Peach Orchard Spring at the opening of the American era, when Billy Dodd—brother of Navajo Agent Major Theodore Dodd—opened a trading post in the canyon in the 1860s. The settlement received its present name from Thomas Varker Keam, an Englishman who fought under Kit Carson, and later acted as agent and inspector for the Navajos. Keam moved to present Keams Canyon in 1880 and established a trading post and ranch, and was instrumental in opening the first Hopi school in 1881. When the decision was made to separate the Navajo and Hopi agencies in 1899, Keams Ranch was selected as the site for the Hopi Agency. In 1902 the agency was moved down the canyon to its present site.

On the canyon walls near the ruins of Keam's old ranch is an inscription made during the Navajo Wars bearing the name "C. Carson-63." Carson passed through the Hopi country in 1863 while on a sortie against fleeing Navajo "ricos" as far west as the Little Colorado River.

The name applies equally to the community and the canyon itself—a deep, steep-sided channel heading on Balakai Mesa at ephemeral Bighams Lake some four miles south of Low Mountain. It flows southwest through the community of Keams Canyon (10 miles downstream), then turns west to flow into Polacca Wash 15 miles farther downstream. This canyon is mentioned in the hero's search for his family in the Navajo Rounded Man Red Antway Myth.

The existing trading post was constructed by Thomas and William Keam on August 31, 1875, in the canyon that eventually took on their name. The original site was upstream from the present location. When the government purchased the original land and buildings for a school in 1887, Keam rebuilt at the present site.

Exactly when Keam sold the post to Lorenzo Hubbell, Jr., is problematic, but Hubbell sold it to Joseph Schmedding in 1914. Schmedding sold the post to E. P. Halderman in 1924, following a nasty fight to keep it after tarnished Secretary of the Interior Albert B. Fall tried unsuccessfully to strip him of his license. Another trader whose tenure is not well documented was Freeman H. Hathorn, sometime after 1908.

✤ Role in Hillerman Fiction:

The Dark Wind: The Office of Hopi Partitioned Land to the Joint Use Administration Office is located in Keams Canyon (chap. 3).

The Ghostway: The blizzard that caught Chee in the Chuska Moutains looking for Ashie Begay had closed Navajo Route 3 from Two Story to Keams Canyon (chap. 23).

The Fallen Man: Officer Bernadette Manuelito's family lived here before moving to Red Rock (chap. 11).

KENBITO WASH: See Kimbeto Wash.

KIMBETO WASH: (7000–6200 ft) San Juan County, NM. Also Kenbito, Kinbito, or Kinnebito Wash. Navajos call this feature Giní Bit'ohí, meaning "Sparrowhawk's Nest," after circular Anasazi ruins found in the vicinity north of Kimbeto Wash. This 16-mile-long tributary of Escavada Wash heads in the barren, broken flats east of U.S. Highway 550 (formerly New Mexico Highway 44) about two miles south of Nageezi and the junction of New Mexico Highway 56 and U.S. Highway 550. It joins Escavada Wash three miles upstream from that wash's confluence with the Chaco River.

Kimbeto Trading Post sits on the sandy north bank of Kimbeto Wash and New Mexico Highway 56, approximately four miles southeast of Nageezi. The original post was half a mile north of the present location. In the 1930s, the U.S. Indian Service constructed a sheep dip here, and nearby Anasazi pueblo ruins drew archaeologists and tourists alike. Paleontological expeditions of the American Museum of Natural History made their headquarters at Kimbeto while excavating for fossils in the eroded badlands of the vicinity in the 1930s.

The circular ruin north of Kimbeto Wash figures in the story of Nááhwiiłbįįhí (the Gambler from the Bead Chant), which tells how the Navajos obtained their sheep.

The trading post was in operation by 1901 and was closed by 1975. Between 1914 and 1920 it was operated by a White man named Shorty Woody. The post was robbed twice, by Whites, between 1914 and 1938.

❖ Role in Hillerman Fiction:

Sacred Clowns: Jim Chee and Janet Pete drive past this location on their trip from Gallup to Aztec (chap. 26).

KIN HAHASBAS: See Kin Nasbas.

KINLEECHEE: (6600 ft) Apache County, AZ. Also spelled Kinlichee and Kin Lichee. The Navajo name is Kin Dah'lichi'i, which means "Red House in the Distance," and refers to an Anasazi ruin in the vicinity (now a Navajo Nation park). A BIA boarding school located two miles north of Arizona Highway 264 on Navajo Route 39, closed in 1979–80. The school was situated along the deeply eroded Sage House Wash. In the 1940s, the U.S. Indian Service had 130 acres under irrigation here. A trading post opened here between 1881 and 1885, but closed within 15 years.

The Anasazi ruin has also been called Pueblo Colorado (Spanish for "Red Town"). During the Navajo War of 1863–64, U.S. Army Camp Florilla, an outpost and remount camp, was located here by a large spring. Robert Young, linguist and historian of the Navajos, believes the Navajo name for the ruin is Táala Hodijool, "Flat-Topped Round Area," erroneously interpreted by at least one other historian as "Round Place Where a Sing was Held." However, David Brugge, another authority on Navajo history, places Táala Hodijool (consisting of an Anasazi structure and several Navajo hogans dating to the 1760s) northwest of Ganado and not in the vicinity of Kinlichee.

❖ Role in Hillerman Fiction:

Skinwalkers: The principal from the Kinlichee Boarding School complains to Leaphorn that bootleggers are going into the dorms at night (chap. 2).

Coyote Waits: Joe Leaphorn remembers receiving his first math lesson on randomness while attending a sing-dance (song and dance) between

Kinleechee and Cross Canyon while he was a junior at Arizona State University (chap. 15).

KIN NASBAS: (6200 ft) In Navajo this ruin in Chaco Canyon is Kin Názbąs, meaning "Circular House." Called by Hillerman Kin Nahasbas. An isolated great sanctuary a quarter-mile northeast of Una Vida Ruin, Kin Nazbas was excavated by the School of American Research in 1935.

✤ Role in Hillerman Fiction:

A Thief of Time: Missing anthropologist Eleanor Friedman-Bernal had evidence connecting St. Johns Polychrome pottery from Chettro Ketl with pottery from Wijiji and Kin Nahasbas (chap. 10).

KIRTLAND: (5150 ft) (Population: 3,552) San Juan County, NM. To the Navajos, this is Dághaa' Łichíí', meaning "Red Mustache." This small farming community 10 miles west of Farmington on the north bank of the San Juan River is situated approximately one mile east of Fruitland.

An Army column led by Lieutenant Robert Ransom visited this fertile, tree-lined vicinity next to the San Juan on November 17, 1853—long before there was a settlement here.

✤ Role in Hillerman Fiction:

Sacred Clowns: Someone used the KNDN open mike in Kirtland to broadcast the tape of Navajo Tribal Councilman Jimmy Chester's apparent discussion of bribes in the national garbage dump case (chap. 16).

KISIGI SPRING: This is the site of a Hopi spruce shrine, and the location is therefore being withheld.

✤ Role in Hillerman Fiction:

The Dark Wind: The body of "John Doe" is found near this shrine by Hopi Messenger Albert Lomatewa (chap. 3). The tributary of Wepo Wash in which Jim Chee finds the concealed carryall leads upstream to this spring (chap. 16).

KLAGETOH (TRADING POST): (6200 ft) Apache County, AZ. Navajos call this place Łeeyi'tó, which means "Water in the Ground." The trading post was located in a small basin on U.S. Highway 191, 13 miles south of Ganado and 10 miles north of Wide Ruins. It was opened in the early 1920s, possibly by artist Nils Hagner and his Navajo wife, Teeklee, who were known to have run it later that decade; Wheeler ran it during the 1960s and 1970s. The post has closed, but there are now a chapter house and several homes in the area, along with a day school.

At Sagebrush Spring south of here, Navajo headman Zarcillos Largos was killed by New Mexican militia and Pueblo auxiliaries in October 1860. A twelfth-century Anasazi ruin is also present.

✤ Role in Hillerman Fiction:

The Blessing Way: Luis Horseman, who met his end in Red Rock Valley, and whose body was found near Ganado, lived here at Klagetoh (chap. 8).

Skinwalkers: Looking out his Window Rock office window, Joe Leaphorn knows it's raining at Klagetoh here while Chee is visiting the Dinnebito Wash country (chap. 19). Joe Leaphorn considers calling for officers here to try to reach Jim Chee; they could do so before Leaphorn expects to reach him, since Many Farms is closer to Dinnebito Wash than is Window Rock (chap. 21).

LADRON BUTTE: Fictional location?

✤ Role in Hillerman Fiction:

Coyote Waits: According to Pete's grandfather, this location was a source of old Ute raids on Navajos (chap. 7).

LAGUNA PUEBLO: (5800 ft) (Population: 3,731) Cibola County, NM. Navajos call this village Tó Łání, "Much Water," referring to the lake (originally a beaver pond) at which the pueblo was originally constructed. (This was just north of present-day Interstate 40, about 40 miles west of Albuquerque and the Rio Grande.) The Keresan name is Kawiaka, "Laguna Pueblo." The Spanish name, "San José de la Laguna" (conferred upon the pueblo by New Spain Governor Cubero on July 4, 1699), refers to the pond as well. It disappeared when the beaver dam washed away in 1855.

The main village is situated on the Rio San José (earlier called the Rio Cubero), a tributary of the Rio Puerco of the East, which lies 25 miles to the east. The Keresan language ties the village to nearby Acoma, as well as the Rio Grande pueblos of Zia, Santa Ana, San Felipe, Santo Domingo, and Cochiti. The Laguna people now reside in six villages in addition to Old Laguna: Seama, Mesita, Encinal, Paguate, Paraje, and New Laguna.

Historians believe the pueblo was established by refugees from the Spanish Reconquest of 1692 who fled Cochiti, Jemez, Santo Domingo, and Cieneguilla in 1697, along with some people from Acoma Pueblo. There may be some Plains Indian heritage at the pueblo as well. Laguna was visited by Governor Don Pedro Rodriguez on July 4, 1699, at which time the occupants declared their allegiance.

In the early 1870s Laguna was sharply divided over religious quarrels. The native hierarchy crumbled into two factions, the pro-White "Progressives" and the anti-White "Conservatives." The latter moved out of the original pueblo (which they called "Punyana") to the village of Mesita, though some ended up living at Isleta Pueblo, having aborted a planned migration to Sandia Pueblo. (The lands given the Laguna at Isleta were called Oraibi, possibly after the name of a nearby hill.) Old Laguna became rapidly depopulated and the former farming communities of Casa Blanca (Seama), Encinal, Santa Ana, Paraje, Paguate, and Tsisma became permanent villages. The old village has been gradually changing from its original pueblo cluster to a scattered village of modern, individual adobe-stucco houses. Atop the hill above the old village sits the old church of San José de Laguna, which opens its doors during the feast days of San José held annually in September.

The pueblo was raided by Navajos in 1796 and 1851. A scalp dance over four Navajo scalps was observed at Laguna by Army Lieutenant Colonel Congreve Jackson in October 1848.

The Navajo name Tó Łání refers to the people of Laguna as well as the physical location, unless they are grouped with the people of Acoma Pueblo, when they are called Haa'kohnii.

Although the Navajos were largely peaceful following their return from the Bosque Redondo in 1868, George H. Pradt, a surveyor of the Navajo Reservation in 1869, helped organize Laguna volunteers against raiding Navajos and Apaches in 1882.

✤ Role in Hillerman Fiction:
The Ghostway: When Jim Chee discovers that the medicine man at Two Story (who can conduct the five-day Ghostway) is in Cañoncito performing the ceremony on a girl named Sosi, he is at once elated at finding Margaret Billy Sosi once again, but dismayed at the distance he will have to travel—to the region near Acoma and Laguna Pueblos (chap. 24). Upon learning of the Ghostway being conducted on Margaret Billy Sosi at Cañoncito, Jim Chee calls Leroy Begay and suggests he meet Chee and Margaret at Cañoncito. He instructs Begay to drive south to Gallup, then east through Grants and past Laguna, before looking for the turnoff to Cañoncito (chap. 25).

LA JARA WASH (and **CANYON**): (7800–6200 ft) Sandoval County, NM. Navajos call the village of La Jara K'ai' Ch'íneeltł'ó, meaning "Willows Extending Out Tangled," and the same name could apply to this wash. This 40-mile-long canyon is north of Gobernador Canyon. It flows east to west, heading some 10 miles south of Dulce and merging with the San Juan River about seven miles northeast of Navajo Dam. On August 11, 1705, Roque Madrid's expedition's first combat with Navajos took place near the junction of La Jara and La Fragua canyons, during which many Navajo *"milpas"* (fields of maize) were burned.

✤ Role in Hillerman Fiction:

A Thief of Time: This feature is scouted by Jim Chee in his search for Joe B. Nails, whom he believes to be the Backhoe Bandit (chap. 5).

LAKE POWELL: (3711 ft at high water) San Juan and Kane counties, UT, Coconino County, AZ. According to Navajo linguist Alan Wilson, Navajos call this lake Tólá Dah Siyíní, meaning "Large Body of Water at an Elevation." This enormous, man-made lake fills the former Glen Canyon and many side canyons above and below the confluence of the Colorado and San Juan rivers. To the Navajos, the confluence of the (male) San Juan and the (female) Colorado is To Ahidiidlíní, "Waters Come Together," a very sacred location.

The lake is named for John Wesley Powell, the one-armed scientist and Civil War veteran who led the first Colorado River float expedition with eight men in four wooden boats in 1869. Three million people anually visit the national recreation area (authorized in 1972). The surface of the lake is never to be allowed to drop below 1083 ft above sea level. The lake has nearly two thousand miles of shoreline, equal to the Pacific Coast between San Diego and Seattle. It peaked at 3707 ft above sea level on July 14, 1983.

Full, the lake contains 27,000,000 acre-feet of water, and it took 17 years to rise 560 feet. It covers the equivalent of 252 square miles, reaching 186 miles up the Colorado River and 75 miles up the San Juan River in 1980.

The lake was controversial among naturalists when the dam was constructed, because of the deep and beautiful canyons it inundated, and because of long-range plans to dam the Grand Canyon itself. Little discussion, however, concerned the Navajo sacred sites to be inundated.

✤ Role in Hillerman Fiction:

Listening Woman: Leaphorn's perceived straight line connecting Gold Rims's abandoned car and the watering hole could be extended to this vast body of water (chap. 4). The cave to which the hostages are taken is on the San Juan River Arm of the lake (chap. 18).

Hunting Badger: Frank Sam Nakai remembers the construction of the dam in Glen Canyon to form Lake Powell, damming up the San Juan and Colorado Rivers (chap. 11).

Figure 24. Navajo Mountain looms high above the blue waters of man-made Lake Powell. The lake fills the ancient Glen Canyon and its network of side canyons.

LAKE VALLEY: (5900 ft) San Juan County, NM. Also Juan's Lake. To the Navajos this region is known as Be'ek'id Łigaií, "Small White Lake." The name refers to what most maps show as Juan's Lake, but applies to the region immediately east of Lake Valley Chapter House community in Yellow Point Valley (about 20 miles north of Crownpoint). A government day school was constructed here on the banks of a shallow, ephemeral lake surrounded by low mesas and sparsely covered grasslands.

This chapter community is in the "Checkerboard Area," a vast region in which the government granted every odd-numbered section (or square mile) of land to the railroad. Even-numbered sections vary in ownership and have changed hands often, rendering patterns of ownership difficult to determine. Most of the land around Juan's Lake is now in trust status, some being allotted land, and some withdrawn from public domain for the BIA school. There are even a few state school sections.

Historian Van Valkenburgh mentioned a Delawoshih (Navajo) family having operated large herds in this region for many years.

✤ Role in Hillerman Fiction:

Sacred Clowns: Jim Chee and Janet Pete drive past this location on their trip from Gallup to Aztec (chap. 26).

LA PLATA MOUNTAINS: (12,000–13,000 ft) La Plata and Montezuma Counties, CO. Also Sierra de la Plata (Spanish for "Silver Mountains"), a name apparently applied by the Dominguez and Escalante expedition of 1776. The Navajos call this mountain range Dibé Ntsaa ("Big Mountain Sheep"), and Dził Bíni' Hólóonii ("Mountain that Has a Mind"). Its ceremonial name is Baashzhinii Dziil ("Jet Mountain," jet referring to the black stone). The range runs roughly north-south for 50 miles, from Silverton to Mesa Verde. It includes such noted heights as Snowstorm Peak (12,511 ft), Lewis Mountain (12,720 ft), Parrot Peak (11,857 ft), Madden Peak (11,972 ft), Gibbs Peak (12,286 ft), Spiller Peak (13,123 ft), Mount Moss (13,192 ft), Banded Mountain (13,062 ft), Mount Hesperus (the highest at 13,232 ft), and Sharkstooth (12,462 ft), all with heavily timbered zones and many lakes and streams.

Many gold and silver mines are found in the range; the earliest mentions of "metallic veins and rocks" came during the Dominguez-Escalante Expedition.

Mount Hesperus in this range is the Navajos' northern sacred mountain, said to be fastened to the heavens with a rainbow and decorated with jet, dark mist, and wild animals. It is the home of mythological Tádídíín 'Ashkii (Pollen Boy) and 'Aniłt'ánii 'At'ééd (Corn Beetle Girl). It is also the traditional northern Blessingway boundary mountain, and is mentioned in the Navajo Mountain Chant and the Coyoteway Ceremony.

In the northern end of the La Platas, seven miles west of Silverton, a small island sits in the center of Island Lake, surrounded on the four cardinal directions by four high peaks. This is thought to be Hájíínáí, the Navajo "Place of Emergence," where the Diné emerged from the underworld, and where the spirits of the dead pass to the nether world.

❖ Role in Hillerman Fiction:

A Thief of Time: Jim Chee sees a storm building beyond these mountains as he searches for Kin Kletsoh to find missing anthropologist Randall Elliot (chap. 17).

The Fallen Man: Elisa Breedlove tells Jim Chee that her late husband Hal had wanted his ashes scattered over the San Juan Mountains in the La Plata Range—specifically on Mount Hesperus (chap. 5).

LEUPP: (4714 ft) Coconino County, AZ. The Navajo name is Tsiizizí, meaning "Scalps," though it is also referred to as Tó Naneesdizi, which translates as "Tangled Water" (or, more accurately, "Place of the Water Rivulets"). This vicinity is important in the Navajo Coyoteway Ceremony.

This small village began as a government settlement, and sits on the north bank of a treeless bottom of the Little Colorado River at the junction of Arizona Highway 99 and Navajo Route 15. Old Leupp was located two miles to the southeast; the current settlement grew around the old Sunrise Trading Post, and includes a chapter seat. It was named for Indian Bureau Commissioner Francis E. Leupp, who served from 1905 to 1908. The U.S. Indian Service operated a hospital here.

The Navajo name is said by some Navajos to be derived from the story of a fight between the Navajos and the Walapai Indians, called Dilzhí'í ("Small Jay Bird"), near Sunrise Trading Post. In this fight the Navajos took three Walapai scalps. A less exciting explanation is that the name refers to a wig worn by a bald-headed former agent named Maxwell.

The Leupp Jurisdictional Agency was founded in 1908, and located on a bar or islet in the river bottom. The shifting of the river channel made it necessary to erect high dikes, but it was practically inundated in the spring floods of 1937. In 1909, the reservation's fourth boarding school opened at Leupp.

Traders have included Leupp Trading Company (formerly Lower Sunrise Springs, opened in the first decade of this century) and Upper Sunrise Trading Post (opened a mile to the north in the early 1890s). The first Navajo Business Council (one of the earliest steps toward self-government) was established in Leupp in 1904. It consisted of two Navajo Court judges and three "elected" headmen. The community hosted a prisoner-of-war camp during World War II.

✤ Role in Hillerman Fiction:

Coyote Waits: According to Mary Keeyani, people would come from as far as Leupp to have Pinto perform crystal gazing on them (chap. 3). Angie, a secretary in the Shiprock Navajo Police Substation, is from Leupp (chap. 15).

LITTLE BLACK SPOT MOUNTAIN: (7001 ft) Navajo County, AZ. Also Little Black Speck Mountain. The Navajos call this feature Dził Dah Zhin, "Black Speck Mountain." This steep-sided mesa sits upon south-central Black Mesa, five miles southwest of Piñon. Some chroniclers have applied the Navajo name to Big Mountain, 15 miles to the northeast, but that feature is more properly known as Dził Ntsaá ("Extension Mountain").

✤ Role in Hillerman Fiction:

The Dark Wind: Pauling could see Low Mountain and Little Black Spot Mountain ahead of him as he piloted his plane across Balakai Mesa (chap. 2).

LITTLE PAJARITO ARROYO: (8200–5500 ft) San Juan County, NM. The Navajo name is uncertain. The location of this feature is uncertain. Since Hillerman mentions it in the same sentence as Salt Creek Wash and the San Juan River, it stands to reason that it is in the same vicinity. However, the only feature with a remotely similar name is Pajarito Creek, which is a tributary of Dead Man's Wash, which is tributary to Chaco Wash less than half a mile from the confluence of that stream with the San Juan River. Pajarito Creek heads on the southwest flank of Beautiful Mountain (at an elevation of 8200 ft), and its confluence with Dead Man's Wash is some 15 miles southwest of Shiprock (at 5500 ft). Further confusion is seen in the fact that the Southern California Automobile Association's Indian Country Map (which Hillerman used extensively in his reservation travels and his writing) errs in naming Dead Man's Creek as Pajarito Creek.

✤ Role in Hillerman Fiction:

The Ghostway: Aside from the banks of the San Juan River, the only places in the Shiprock vicinity where a silver trailer house (like that in the photo Albert Gorman showed Joseph Joe) could be sitting in a cottonwood grove would be Salt Creek Wash and Little Pajarito Arroyo (chap. 10).

LITTLE SHIPROCK WASH: (7600-5000 ft) San Juan County, NM. The Navajo name is uncertain. This perennial stream heads high on the west face of Beautiful Mountain, then flows northwest and north, through the sandy lowlands around White Rock and Mitten Rock. It merges with Shiprock Wash near Rattlesnake, some 25 miles from its headwaters. There are occasional clusters of cottonwoods and other local vegetation in the streambed, but the channel is usually dry—except after rain storms.

✥ Role in Hillerman Fiction:

The Fallen Man: The Sam family built a home between this wash and Red Wash (chap. 11).

LITTLE WATER: (5600 ft) San Juan County, NM. The Navajo name is most likely Tó Áłts'íísí ("Little Water"). This trading location is on U.S. Highway 666 at Sanostee Wash, 24 miles south of the village of Shiprock.

(The name also applies to Little Water Chapter, located on Navajo Route 48, approximately five miles southeast of Crownpoint, about halfway between Crownpoint and Borrego Pass.)

Figure 25. Little Water Trading Post on U.S. Highway 666 is now a convenience store and gas station.

✥ Role in Hillerman Fiction:

The Ghostway: Captain Largo determines that Albert Gorman did not go toward Teec Nos Pos or west of Little Water (chap. 2).

Skinwalkers: Jim Chee drives through Little Water on his way to meet Joe Leaphorn at Sanostee (chap. 13).

LITTLE WATER WASH: (8400–5500 ft) San Juan County, NM. Most likely Sanostee Wash. Also known as Sanastee Wash. Tsé 'Ałnáozt'i'í ("Overlapping Rocks") is a name applied by non-Navajos to a nearby location. Also known as Tó Yaagaii ("Water Rises in a White Column"), referring to a now inactive artesian well that used to geyser.

The headwaters of this intermittent stream are in the Chuska Mountains, a few miles southeast of Roof Butte. It flows east 21 miles, passing south of Beautiful Mountain, just north of Sanostee, and through Little Water, before joining Tocito Wash.

Slim Woman's family hid from Ute raiders in a canyon of this arroyo during the period of the American Civil War. The Utes burned the Navajos' hogans and killed their sheep.

✤ Role in Hillerman Fiction:

Skinwalkers: Jim Chee drives through here on his way to meet Joe Leaphorn at Sanostee, whereupon they will go to Roosevelt Bistie's place (chap. 13).

Coyote Waits: According to Ashie Pinto's grandfather's story, Delbito Willie saw two White men riding between Rol Hai Rock and Little Water Wash, apparently traveling toward Beautiful Mountain (chap. 11). In studying rock formation photos in the darkroom of murdered Huan Ji, Joe Leaphorn and Louisa Bourebonette conjecture the formations photographed could be many locations, including Little Water (chap. 17).

LIZARD HEAD PEAK: (13,113 ft) San Miguel and Dolores Counties, CO. This peak in the La Plata Mountains is about 10 miles southwest of Telluride, Colorado, in the vicinity of Wilson Peak, Mount Wilson, and El Diente Peak. It has a tenuous tie to the Yellow Jacket Ruin, possibly the largest known Anasazi Pueblo III–era ruin, and one of eight major ruins in the Montezuma Basin (near Yellow Jacket, Colorado). This ruin has the highest concentration of kivas in the known Anasazi realm—minimally 120, including at least one Great Kiva, a Chaco phenomenon. It has been suggested that the site was solstice-predicting, as the sun rises over distant Lizard Head Peak as viewed from the southern part of the ruin 16 days prior to the summer solstice.

✤ Role in Hillerman Fiction:

The Fallen Man: Before his death, Hal Breedlove had climbed this peak in the San Juan Mountains (chap. 5).

LONE TULE WASH: (7800-6600 ft) Apache County, AZ. The Navajo name remains uncertain. This sometimes dry creekbed on the west flank of the Defiance Plateau heads at Segatoa Spring, near Fluted Rock. It flows southwest some 18 miles before it merges with the waters of Sage House Wash, Kinlichee Creek, and Fish Wash in Ganado Lake. Emanating from the south end of this man-made reservoir is Pueblo Colorado Wash.

✤ Role in Hillerman Fiction:

Skinwalkers: Looking out his Window Rock office window, Joe Leaphorn knows it's raining in this vicinity while Chee is visiting the Dinnebito Wash country (chap. 19).

LOS GIGANTES BUTTES: (6460–6490 ft) Apache County, AZ. Navajos call these features Tsé Ch'ídeelzhah, meaning "Rocks Jut Out." These sandstone buttes are located five miles west of Mexican Cry Mesa, and two miles south of Hasbidito Creek.

✤ Role in Hillerman Fiction:

The Blessing Way: Old Woman Gray Rocks tells Bergen McKee that George Charley was warned by men in trucks to move his sheep away from Los Gigantes, because there would be explosions near here (chap. 7).

LOWER GREASEWOOD: (5900 ft) (Population: 196) Apache County, AZ. To the Navajos, this small community near Greasewood Spring is Díwózhii Bíí'Tó, meaning "Spring in the Greasewood." A trading post (opened prior to 1915) and a school comprise the bulk of this village in the wide, barren valley of the Pueblo Colorado Wash, some 20 miles south of Ganado. (Lower Greasewood is not to be confused with Greasewood Trading Post near Lukachukai.) A possible Chacoan prehistoric road has been identified in the vicinity.

In some of the literature, this community seems interchangeable with Sunrise Springs (Sháá' Tóhí, meaning "Sunnyside Spring") actually located about eight miles northeast of Lower Greasewood. Sunrise Springs was occupied as early as 1907 and also sits on Pueblo Colorado Wash.

The vicinity of Lower Greasewood (and nearby White Cone and Indian Wells) is the home of various Ant People in the Navajo Rounded Man Red Antway Myth.

✤ Role in Hillerman Fiction:

A Thief of Time: At Coyote Canyon, Darcy Ozzie (of Old Lady Daisy Manygoats's outfit) tells Jim Chee that Slick Nakai had headed to a place between White Rock and Tsaya, and then was bound for Lower Greasewood (chap. 13).

Talking God: This is the home of Agnes Tsosie. It is also the scene of a Yeibeichai ceremony where Jim Chee spots the elusive Henry Highhawk (chaps. 2, 4).

LOW MOUNTAIN: (6760 ft) Navajo County, AZ. Navajos call this feature T'áásahdii Dah 'Azkání or Jeeh Deez'áhí ("Pitch Point"). This broad, low mound between the root of First Mesa and Balakai Mesa is flanked by Polacca Wash and Tsé Chizi (Tséch'ízhí) Wash. Schmedding Trading Post opened here in the early 1950s. Today Low Mountain Trading Post operates here.

The name refers as well to the small community that grew up around the trading post (today including a chapter house), on the south flank of the geological feature. A few miles to the east of the community is Smoke Signal Trading Post, opened in the late 1960s.

✤ Role in Hillerman Fiction:

The Dark Wind: Pauling could see Low Mountain and Little Black Spot Mountain ahead of him as he piloted his plane across Balakai Mesa (chap. 2). Pauling could see the light bulb over the lonely gas pump as he piloted his plane over Low Mountain Trading Post (chap. 2).

LUKACHUKAI: (6433 ft) (Population: 113) Apache County, AZ. Navajos refer to this location as Lók'a'jígai ("Reeds Extend White") or Lók'a'ch'égai ("White Streak of Reeds Extends Horizontally Out"). This chapter and day school community is located near the base of Lukachukai Pass, in a broad cove at the western foot of the Lukachukai Mountains, about four miles northeast of the junction of U.S. Highway 191 and Navajo Route 64. This prosperous agricultural area is drained by Tótsoh ("Big Water"), Tł'ézhiitóhí ("Horsefly Creek"), Na'asho'iito'í ("Big Lizard Creek"), and Díwózhii Bii' Tó ("Greasewood Creek").

An annual fair used to be held here every September. A new housing development has expanded the community to the junction of Highway 191 and Navajo Route 13.

The first trading post, called Chéh'ilyaa ("Under the Oaks") by the Navajos, was established here in 1892 by George N. Barker. George Washington Sampson—known to the Navajos as Hastiin Báí ("Gray Man")—operated the post at the turn of the century. Rico Menapace is mentioned in some records and may have managed it between Sampson and the next confirmed owner, W. R. Cassidy, who is known to have sold the post to Earl Kennedy in October 1928. Following Earl's death in 1921, his son Kenneth took over the post. It was closed in 1979, and only the foundations of the old buildings remain, seen just north of Navajo Route 13, a mile east of U.S. Highway 191. Trading is now conducted at Totsoh Trading Post, operated by Bradley and Victoria Blair just east of the original post.

In 1916, St. Isabel Mission, established by Franciscan Father Berard Haile, operated a school that was taken over by the government in 1933.

✤ Role in Hillerman Fiction:

Skinwalkers: Irma Onesalt was killed between here and Upper Greasewood (chap. 2). Roosevelt Bistie's daughter tells Chee that her father visited a hand trembler between Roof Butte and and Lukachukai to find out what was making him sick (chap. 16).

The Fallen Man: Jim Chee receives a report of a drunken brawl at a girl dance at the Lukachukai Chapter House (chap. 8). When Officer Bernadette

Manuelito finds the loose fence posts near Shiprock, she was actually supposed to be searching the Burnham area for the Roanhorse couple, who had witnessed a shooting at a dance near Lukachukai (chap. 9).

Hunting Badger: Jim Chee meets Deputy Sheriff Cowboy Dashee at the Lukachukai Chapter House (chap. 8).

LUKACHUKAI MOUNTAINS: (9460 ft) Apache County, AZ. Navajos call this range Shį́į́k'eh ("Summer Place"). It is a narrow strip of rugged mountains forming a northern extension of the Chuska Mountains, lying between the Chuskas and the Carrizo Mountains. The Lukachukais are mentioned in the Navajo Coyoteway.

The first uranium mining on the reservation was at the Vanadium Corporation of America mine in the Lukachukais, during World War II. There were other mines later at Monument Valley, Tuba City, Mexican Hat, and Shiprock, as well as near Grants and Gallup.

Figure 26. The Lukachukai Mountains have the unique appearance of a mountain range sitting atop a red sandstone mesa. The village of Lukachukai sits at the western foot of the mountains; its long-legged water tanks are barely visible in the center of this picture.

❖ Role in Hillerman Fiction:

The Blessing Way: This mountain range looms above Luis Horseman's hideout in Kah Bihgi Valley (chap. 1). Anthropologist Bergen McKee suggests these mountains (along with the Chuska Mountains and Kah Bihgi Valley) to Ellen Leon as a possible place to look for her Ph.D. electrical engineer, Jimmy W. Hall (chap. 3).

The Ghostway: Captain Largo surmises that Albert Gorman, after leaving the shooting at the Shiprock Economy Wash-O-Mat, must have laid up in the region bounded by the Shiprock pinnacle and the Chuska, Carrizo, and Lukachukai Mountains (chap. 2).

Skinwalkers: Roosevelt Bitsie, who was wanted for the killing of Dugai Endocheeney, lived here (chap. 1).

MANCOS: (7032 ft) Montezuma County, CO. The Navajo name for this community remains uncertain. However, Tó Nts'ósíkooh ("Slim Water Canyon") is the Navajo name for Mancos Creek, and Tó Hasłeeh ("Where the Water Comes Up") refers to that portion of Mancos Creek that traverses Mesa Verde. Mancos is Spanish for "One-handed" or "Crippled," and comes from the name of the creek. Some say the name was bestowed by the Dominguez-Escalante Expedition of 1776.

The town of Mancos straddles U.S. Highway 160, approximately 17 miles east of Cortez. The community served as the shipping point for the La Plata district mining activities.

❖ Role in Hillerman Fiction:

The Fallen Man: Hal Breedlove's widow lives near Mancos, on the Lazy B Ranch, which she and her brother inherited upon Hal's death (chap. 3). Jim Chee and New Mexico Brand Inspector Dick Finch drive to Mancos to see if the widow Mrs. Breedlove can identify any of the Fallen Man's equipment as belonging to her late husband, missing some 11 years (chap. 5). Joe Leaphorn interviews banker Cecilia Rivera about the Breedlove finances, both now and at the time of Hal Breedlove's disappearance (chap. 12). Driving through a winter blizzard, Jim Chee and Officer Bernadette Manuelito visit Elisa Breedlove and get the final details on the disappearance of her husband 11 years ago (chap. 25).

MANCOS CREEK: (10,800–4800 ft) Montezuma County, CO (and San Juan County, NM). Navajos call this feature Tó Nts'ósíkooh, or "Slim Water Canyon." The Spanish name "Mancos" means "One-handed" or "Crippled," applied, according to legend, by the Dominguez Escalante expedition of 1776, during which a member of the party fell from his horse while fording the river, injuring his hand. Historian Dave Brugge, however, notes that although there is apparently no entry in the Escalante Journal to substantiate this story, Escalante was aware of this name, though he preferred Rio de San Lázaro.

Three branches of this creek (East, Middle, and West, all draining the La Plata Mountains in the vicinity of Sharks Tooth Mountain) merge before the Mancos passes through the Mesa Verde country. It travels another 67 miles before crossing into New Mexico, where it enters the San Juan River approximately five miles farther downstream (approximately 15 miles downstream from Shiprock, New Mexico).

In the Mesa Verde region, Mancos Creek forms the long and deep Mancos Creek Canyon. There are many important Anasazi ruins in the canyon and its branches, the most prominent being those of Mesa Verde National Park.

Mancos Creek plays an important role in Navajo mythology and ceremonialism. The point where the creek and the San Juan River meet is especially powerful to the Navajos, and may be where Navajo warriors prayed for victory in combat. The Ant People of the Navajo Antway moved to Mancos Creek after the Restoration Rite. It is also mentioned in the Navajo Coyoteway myth, and figures heavily in the stories of Monster Slayer and Born for Water, and the teachings of Female Mountainway.

✤ **Role in Hillerman Fiction:**

The Ghostway: The blizzard that caught Chee in the Chuska Mountains looking for Ashie Begay had closed U.S. Highway 666 from Mancos Creek, Colorado, to Gallup (chap. 23).

MANKI CANYON: This fictional canyon is in the vicinity of Cow Springs.

✤ **Role in Hillerman Fiction:**

Listening Woman: Joe Leaphorn drives through this canyon to reach the Short Mountain Trading Post (chap. 5).

MANUELITO PLATEAU: (8100 ft) McKinley County, NM. The Navajo name is uncertain. This 10-mile-long mesa is actually part of the western foothills of the Chuska Mountains, near the southern terminus of that range. The southern end is approximately five miles east of Fort Defiance, Arizona.

✤ **Role in Hillerman Fiction:**

Hunting Badger: Hillerman has Joe Leaphorn and Professor Louisa Bourebonette head south from here toward the Painted Cliffs (chap. 24). However, this is most likely a typographical error; from his description of features to the east and west, they would have been traveling north.

MANY FARMS: (5304 ft) (Population: 1,294) Apache County, AZ. The recent Navajo name is Dá'ák'eh Haláni, meaning "Many Fields," but an older name was Tó Naneesdizí ("Water Stringing Out in Rivulets"). This small farming, trading, and chapter community sits in the alluvial flats of the Chinle Valley, at the juncture of U.S. Highway 191 and Navajo Route 59, 14 miles north of Chinle. In 1940, there were about 650 acres under irrigation here. The region is the site of Many Farms Lake, a small ephemeral sink on the east margin of the village, fed by Sheep Dip Wash. Navajo farms were seen in the vicinity by the first Spanish expeditions, who called the area La Labor, "The Tillage."

The vicinity was visited by Captain John G. Walker's 1858 expedition, at which time Walker noted "a succession of fields growing corn, some of them containing from forty to sixty acres."

The first trading post opened here about 1920, roughly the same time as the Many Farms project. By 1937 the subjugation of 500 acres was undertaken. The headworks of this project, a loose rock-weir diversion dam and concrete headworks feeding into the irrigation ditch, were located three miles north of Frazier's Trading Post.

In 1941, Many Farms was the site of the Navajo Tribal Slaughter House and Cannery, which supplied fresh and canned meat from livestock purchased from Navajos for school and hospital use on the reservation.

❖ **Role in Hillerman Fiction:**

The Blessing Way: Joe Leaphorn drove past Many Farms, Agua Sal Creek, Round Rock, and Seklagaidesi while trying to figure out what the Big Navajo was doing on Ceniza Mesa (chap. 15).

Listening Woman: According to Short Mountain trader "Old Man" McGinnis, a singer from Many Farms conducted a ceremony at (fictional) Yazzie Springs (chap. 5).

The Dark Wind: Hosteen Nakai lived at Many Farms when he would take the young Jim Chee to collect herbs and minerals at Blue Gap and Dzilushzhinih Peaks (chap. 17).

The Ghostway: After failing to reach Frank Sam Nakai's winter place via Greasewood Flats, Jim Chee circles back and drives through Round Rock, Many Farms, and Chinle, to the south side of Black Mesa, past Cottonwood and Blue Gap, before attempting to mount Carson Mesa again from the south (chap. 24).

Skinwalkers: Officer George Benaly (*sic*), of Shiprock, used to work out of Many Farms with Joe Leaphorn, many years ago (chap. 5). Joe Leaphorn, leaving Window Rock, considers calling for officers at Many Farms to try to reach Jim Chee, since they are closer to Dinnebito Wash and could reach Chee before Leaphorn could (chap. 21).

A Thief of Time: L. D. Thatcher and Joe Leaphorn stop for breakfast in Many Farms on their way to Bluff to visit old man Houk because of a note left on missing anthropologist Eleanor Friedman-Bernal's calendar (chap. 8).

Talking God: Nancy Yebenny, clerk-typist at Navajo Timber Industries and a crystal gazer, travels from Many Farms to Lower Greasewood for Agnes Tsosie's ceremony (chap. 2).

MANY RUINS CANYON: This fictional canyon is tributary to Kah Bihgi Canyon.

✤ Role in Hillerman Fiction:

The Blessing Way: Luis Horseman knows that the moving dust plume in the distance means that a truck or Jeep is on the dirt track leading to Horse Fell Canyon and Many Ruins Canyon, and ultimately to Tall Poles Butte, the site of the Army radar station (chap. 1).

A Thief of Time: The canyon with this name in *A Thief of Time* appears to be a different feature than that with the same name in *The Blessing Way*. In *A Thief of Time,* the canyon is tributary to the San Juan River, and is also called "Watersprinkler Canyon" and "Canyon Where Watersprinkler Plays His Flute." It turns out to be the source of the mysterious pottery so important to the missing Dr. Eleanor Friedman-Bernal (chaps. 14, 19).

MESA DE LOS LOBOS: (7000–8000 ft generally; highest point 8748 ft) McKinley County, NM. Also Lobo Mesa. A specific Navajo name remains elusive, but it is called by the Navajos from the north by the general descriptive term "Dził," or "Mountain."

On maps, this feature seems to refer only to the higher, northern extremity of the long mesa formation that separates Wingate Valley from the San Juan Basin to the north. However, many apply the name to the entire mesa formation, including the imposing, south-facing red cliffs along the Wingate Valley. The name of the mesa goes back to the McComb map of 1860.

The brown and buff sandstone of the upper, northern portion sits atop the much more spectacular red sandstone layer. The latter is called Wingate sandstone, originally named for these red cliffs forming the northern boundary of the Wingate Valley. Ironically, after the name was applied, testing determined that the closest outcropping of the true Wingate layer is some 60 miles to the north, along the northeastern edge of the Chuska Mountains.

On October 1, 1858, troops under Captains Andrew J. Lindsay and George McLane battled Cayetano's band of Navajos in a canyon of this mesa. Two privates (Paulman and Neugent) were killed, along with seven Navajos. Sergeant John Thompson and several Navajos were wounded.

✤ Role in Hillerman Fiction:

Skinwalkers: Referring to the entire red sandstone formation, Hillerman notes that the mesa east of Gallup is visible from the wounded Joe Leaphorn's hospital-room window (chap. 15).

MESA GIGANTE, NM: (6657 ft) Cibola County, NM. The Navajo name is uncertain. Another name in English is Bell Rock Mesa. This starfish-shaped mesa rises some 900 ft from the valley floor about 15 miles west of the Rio Puerco of the East, about five miles north of Interstate 40. The mesa is bifurcated by the western boundary of the Cañoncito Band Navajo Reservation. The summit is unusually level (even for a mesa), and the talus slopes below the sheer cliffs of the mesa are littered with slablike boulders of friable, reddish brown sandstone.

✤ Role in Hillerman Fiction:

The Ghostway: Jim Chee arrives at Cañoncito and discovers the Ghostway ceremony for Margaret Billy Sosi is out at Jimmy Yellow's place on Mesa Gigante, on the eastern fringe of Mount Taylor. From Jimmy Yellow's place, the view is extraordinary, taking in the valley of the Rio Puerco, the Sandia Mountains and the lights of Albuquerque to the east, and the Sangre de Cristos to the north. Being on the wrong side of Mount Taylor (Turquoise Mountain), some strictly traditional medicine men would have refused to perform the ceremony here (chap. 25).

MESA VERDE: (approx. 8393–6000 ft) Montezuma County, CO., San Juan County, NM. Navajos call this feature Gad Deelzhah, meaning "Cedars in an Undulating Line." Also sometimes erroneously referred to as Nóódá'í Vi' Dziil, by those confusing the uplands with the nearby Ute Mountains; it may also have been called Tó Nts'ósí ("Slim Stream [Canyon]"). The Spanish name, Mesa Verde, means "Green Tableland," descriptive of the juniper and piñon trees capping the mesa.

This abruptly rising, extensive plateau in southwest Colorado is a massive deposit of whitish Cliff House Sandstone, laid down 75 million years ago. Bounded on the north and west by Montezuma Valley, on the east by the La Plata River, and on the south by the Mancos River, the highland is cut by an extensive series of deep canyons running north and south. A portion of the mesa has been set aside as a national park eight miles wide and 15 miles long, but the majority of the landform lies within the Southern Ute Indian Reservation.

The origin of the Spanish name of the mesa itself is problematic. It has been speculated that it was named by the Dominguez-Escalante expedition of 1776, but their map refers only to the Sierra Datil (Sleeping Ute Mountain to the east) and the Mancos River—both tantalizingly close. In any case, the name was in common use by 1859, when Dr. J. S. Newberry listed it in his report on the exploration of the San Juan region. Captain J. F. McComb's map of 1860 gives the name Mesa Verde.

Humans have been exploiting the mesa for at least three thousand years. Prehistoric Desert Culture inhabitants were growing corn on the mesa by 1000 B.C. The Anasazi, generally considered to be ancestral to today's Pueblo Indians of Arizona and New Mexico, were living in caves on the mesa and building rudimentary habitation structures by the Basketmaker I period (so called because of the excellent baskets and dearth of pottery found with their remains).

Later they started building settlements of small pithouses, which, by about A.D. 800, were giving way to rectangular surface "jacal" structures constructed of interwoven branches covered with mud.

By the Pueblo II period, dwellings were linked in long rows, with open "plazas" in front of the buildings and one or more subterranean chambers that became ceremonial kivas.

During the twelfth century, a large portion of the population of Mesa Verde moved into the most desirable caves and built cliff houses, like Cliff Palace. Those remaining on the mesa tops built larger communal houses with as many as 200 rooms in three or four stories, such as Far View House.

Then these sedentary occupants abruptly left the mesa around A.D. 1300, coincidentally at the beginning of a great drought that struck most of the Colorado Plateau, though there is no proven correlation. Their descendants are believed to be living in the modern Rio Grande, Zuni, and Hopi pueblos.

After the Anasazi came the Ute Indians, but probably not for 100 years. Historians believe the Navajos arrived later still, though archaeological investigations continue to push back their earliest demonstrable arrival dates.

By the middle 1700s, two centuries after the first Spanish incursions into the American Southwest, rumors of mineral wealth in the San Juan Mountains prompted Governor Juan de Rivera to launch three expeditions to the region from Santa Fe between 1761 and 1765. These probes, reaching the confluence of the Uncompahgre and Gunnison Rivers, established trade with the Utes, and fur trappers later explored the region.

The territory was ceded to the United States as a result of the Mexican-American War of 1849, and Captain John William Gunnison's first official American expedition entered the region in 1853, searching for a railroad route from Leavenworth, Kansas. The expedition was set upon by hostile Paiutes in the valley of the Sevier River in Utah, and Gunnison and all but four of his men were killed. For the next three decades railroaders, miners, ranchers, and soldiers overwhelmed the indigenous Indians of southwestern Colorado.

Ferdinand Hayden and William H. Jackson explored the Mesa Verde region for the Department of the Interior in 1874–75, recording the flora, fauna, geologic formations, and the first written descriptions of Indian ruins. A year later, Professor William H. Holmes, later chief of the Bureau of American Ethnology, passed through the Mancos and reported remarkable stone watch-towers.

In 1880–81, the Wetherill family, formerly of Leavenworth, Kansas, homesteaded the Alamo Ranch in the Mancos Valley to the east of Mesa Verde, and, owing to a good relationship with the Ute Indians, began running cattle on the mesa. In 1888, Richard Wetherill and Charley Mason discovered a great 200-room cliff dwelling, which they named the Cliff Palace. In the years that followed, the Wetherill brothers discovered hundreds of Anasazi ruins.

Scientific explorations began with the 1891 excavations of Kodak House, Long House, and Step House by the young Swedish archaeologist, Baron Gustof Nordenskiöld of the Stockholm Museum, guided and assisted by the Wetherills. Uncontrolled excavations ravaged the mesa for nearly two decades, leading Dr. Edgar L. Hewitt of Santa Fe's School of American Research to lead a drive for the protection of all Indian ruins. The result was the Federal Antiquities Act of 1906—the same year that the 52,000-acre Mesa Verde National Park was established on July 29. Mrs. Virginia McClurg of Colorado Springs worked tirelessly for many years toward the establishment of the park.

Navajos hunted on the mesa, and medicine men traveled up Mancos Canyon on their way north to the La Plata Mountains for ceremonial purposes. The cliff dwellings must have been known to the Navajos, for they are crystallized in Navajo mythology and play important parts in the Ha'neełnée-hee (Upward Reachingway), and the Dziłk'ijí Ba'áádjí (Mountaintop Way, Female Branch) ceremonies. It is also mentioned in the Navajo Flintway rites and in traditions of Two-Faced Monster.

Mesa Verde also figures in the Zuni migration narrative and is important to their Sword Swallower Society, as are Chaco Canyon and Canyon de Chelly. Interestingly, very few (if any) of the ruins today retain readily remembered Navajo names.

✦ Role in Hillerman Fiction:
The Fallen Man: Jim Chee and New Mexico Brand Inspector Dick Finch drive past Mesa Verde on their way to visit the widow Mrs. Breedlove. The mesa throws shadows on nearby Bridge Timber Mountain (chap. 3).

MEXICAN HAT: (4150 ft) (Population: 259) San Juan County, UT. The Navajo name is Ch'ah Łizhin ("Black Hat") or Naakaii Ch'ah ("Mexican Hat"). This community sits on the San Juan River at the east end of the Goosenecks, where the suspension bridge on Utah Highway 47 first crossed the river in 1909 (near the mouth of Gypsum Creek, some 30 miles southwest of Bluff). The community is named for a rock formation, a few miles north of the San Juan River, that resembles a Mexican sombrero resting upside down atop a spire of sandstone. The country here is rough and broken by many tributaries of the San Juan River.

The community was first known as Goodridge, after E. L. Goodridge, a prospector in the region in 1882. Goodridge was the first to boat down the San

Juan River in search of gold. Instead, he found oil in 1882, and founded the settlement and named it for himself.

Between 1906 and 1910, a man named Nevill opened a trading post on the north side of the river, a mile and a half southeast of the rock formation for which the town was named. Five miles downstream are the famed Goosenecks of the San Juan River, great scalloping curves cut through the badlands and terraces of crumbly shales. Flat-bottomed boats that used to float down the San Juan River from Mexican Hat have largely been replaced by rubber rafts. Some Navajos live south of the river along Gypsum Wash and others reside on Douglas Mesa.

The region is known among the Navajos for the presence of Big Snake, a powerful supernatural being, and a nearby butte is called Dził Náhineests'ee' ("Mountain that is Coiled Up"). This rounded formation has the appearance of a series of coils very much like the pattern of a coiled bullsnake. Navajos believe the region is dangerous to those who do not show proper respect to these beliefs.

In 1892–93, a gold rush brought nearly two thousand prospectors to Mexican Hat, and the town was the site of uranium milling between World War II and the 1980s.

✤ Role in Hillerman Fiction:

Skinwalkers: Roosevelt Bistie's daughter says sick Bistie went looking for someone around Mexican Hat of Montezuma Creek (chap. 3).

A Thief of Time: Pottery that interested missing anthropologist Eleanor Friedman-Bernal was supposedly taken from a private ranch between Bluff and Mexican Hat (chap. 4). Anthropologist Maxie Davis remembers that the missing Friedman-Bernal seemed happy upon returning from a trip to Mexican Hat and Montezuna Creek (chap. 6). Mexican Hat is the only place downstream from Bluff for many miles where one can leave the San Juan River (chap. 16).

MEXICAN WATER (TRADING POST): (4800 ft) Apache County, AZ. To the Navajos, this is Naakaii Tó ("Mexican Water"), though an older name is Naakaii Tó Hadayiiznilí ("Mexicans Dug Shallow Wells"). This small community with a trading post and a chapter house is north of U.S. Highway 160, west of U.S. Highway 191, on Walker Creek a mile south of the Utah state line.

It is situated at a steep rocky crossing of Chinle Wash some 21 miles east of Dinnehotso. Boundary Butte, the feature that served as the northwestern corner of the Treaty Reservation of 1868, is located some 10 miles southeast of Mexican Water.

In this rough country the soil covering is generally quite thin and "baldy," with small wind-blown hillocks scattered over tracts of bare rock. Before the paving of U.S. Highways 160 and 190, roads were marked in places only with piles of rocks.

The trading post was built by Hamblin Noel in 1907, two years after he had opened Teec Nos Pos Trading Post, and about seven years after he and brother Henry took over Two Grey Hills Trading Post from another brother, Frank Noel. At least one source suggests the name Mexican Water came from the trading post, which was so named because this portion of Walker Creek used to be called Mexican Water.

Until July 1939, the crossing of Chinle Wash, some three miles west of Mexican Water Trading Post, was made over a treacherous 30-degree grade dropping down to the bedrock of the channel, skirting the flash floods. Mexican Water Bridge, a 250-foot steel bridge, was completed on July 1, 1939. This bridge, in turn, was replaced about 20 years later. Numerous Anasazi ruins are found in the region.

✤ Role in Hillerman Fiction:

Listening Woman: Short Mountain trader "Old Man" McGinnis advises Joe Leaphorn that he may not find old Margaret Cigaret at home because she had gone to Mexican Water (chap. 5).

The Dark Wind: A girl here pawned a necklace Jake West accused Joseph Musket of stealing in the Burnt Water Trading Post burglary (chap. 18).

The Ghostway: Chee is assigned the case of a man beaten with a hammer by his brother-in-law at a sheep camp near Mexican Water (chap. 6). Jim Chee drives 70 miles over snowpacked highways, passing through Teec Nos Pos, Red Mesa, Mexican Water, and Dinnehotso, on his way to Frank Sam Nakai's winter place (chap. 24).

Skinwalkers: Officer Gorman meets Joe Leaphorn at Mexican Water to go over the scene of Wilson Sam's death (chap. 10).

A Thief of Time: L. D. Thatcher and Joe Leaphorn cross the state line into Utah just north of Mexican Water on their way to see old man Houk because of a note left on missing anthropologist Eleanor Friedman-Bernal's calendar (chap. 8). North of here, Jim Chee runs into Slick Nakai's abandoned trailer (chap. 13).

Sacred Clowns: The KNDN radio tape given to Jim Chee, containing the confession of the hit-and-run driver who killed Victor Todachenee, starts with a plea to relatives of a recently deceased Navajo woman to gather in Mexican Water for the funeral and distribution of her belongings (chap. 16).

Hunting Badger: Joe Leaphorn and Louisa Bourebonette stop for lunch at the Mexican Water Trading Post on their way to Red Mesa (chap. 6). The widow Eleanor Ashby tells Jim Chee and Deputy Sheriff Cowboy Dashee that

Eldon Timms has another place near Mexican Water, and that she heard his plane the day it was reported stolen (chap. 8). Chee and Dashee drive to Mexican Water looking for Elden Timms's airplane (chap. 8). An "old fella" tells Joe Leaphorn that a slide, cut down the cliff on the south side of the San Juan in the canyon across from Bluff, was operated in the 1880s to move coal to the canyon bottom for ferrying across the river to Bluff (chap. 19).

MISHONGNOVI: (5750 ft) Navajo County, AZ. Also known as Second Mesa. Navajos call this location Tsétsohk'id, meaning "Big Boulder Hill." (This is the same name as Shipaulovi, and a variant is applied to Toreva. It appears to refer to Second Mesa itself rather than to individual communities.) Hopis call it Moshangnovi ("Place of the Black Man."). A less accepted name means "the other of two sandstone columns remains standing," referring to the fact that one of two sandstone pillars several hundred yards from the village had collapsed.

This Hopi village sits on the eastern rim of Second Mesa, at the junction of Arizona Highways 264 and 87. The town had a population of only 227 in 1939.

An older village of the same name was established in the thirteenth century, then abandoned sometime prior to 1680. Its ruins are on the first terrace below and south of the present village. The Hopi name might refer to a chief, Mosahng, or Mishong, a member of the Crow Clan who led his people to the Hopi towns from the San Francisco Mountains sometime before the thirteenth century. The people of old Shungopovi refused to allow them to settle in their village because they had performed no service. Finally, they were given permission to build a town near Corn Rock on condition that they protect the rock, which was a shrine for the people of Walpi. (Another, though not as plausible, story of the founding is that the village was originally founded by female survivors of the massacre at Awatovi in 1700.)

The Franciscan mission of San Buenaventura, established at the old village in 1629, was destroyed during the Pueblo Rebellion of 1680, and the villagers fled to the top of the mesa where they established the present town.

The Snake Dance is held here at the same time as at Walpi in odd years; Shungopovi, Hotevilla, and Shipaulovi hold theirs in even years.

✦ Role in Hillerman Fiction:

The Dark Wind: Jim Chee and Deputy Sheriff Cowboy Dashee visit a woman at Mishongnovi about witchcraft killing the "John Doe" found on Black Mesa. They are sent to Shipaulovi (chap. 10).

Sacred Clowns: At Mishongnovi, County Sheriff Deputy Cowboy Dashee's relatives previously sold Asher Davis an owl kachina made in Taiwan (chap. 1).

The First Eagle: This village is the home of Robert Jano, arrested in the murder of Navajo Tribal Policeman Benny Kinsman (chap. 2).

MOENKOPI: (4750 ft) (Population: 924) Coconino County, AZ. Also Moencopi. Navajos refer to this community as 'Oozéí Hayázhí, meaning "Little Oraibi," a reference to another Hopi village. Hopis call the place Moncapi ("Place of Running Water"). This scattered Hopi farming village was founded in the 1870s on the north bank of Moenkopi Wash by "Tuvi" (also Tlvi, Tivi, Toobi, etc., a chief from the Hopi village of Oraibi, and the chief for whom nearby Tuba City is named). Originally about a half mile south of Arizona Highway 264 at its juncture with U.S. Highway 160, the village has grown to the intersection itself. In 1941, the population was 416.

The community is situated on the sloping north terrace of the Moenkopi Wash, which the Navajos call Naak'a' K'éédílyéhé ("Where Cotton is Cultivated"), and early Spanish documents refer to this region as Los Algodones, "The Cotton Fields."

Juan de Oñate visited this site, formerly occupied by a fifteenth-century Anasazi pueblo, in 1604 and called it Rancheria de Gandules. It was part of the old Havasupai habitat and is shown on the Dominguez-Escalante map of 1776 as a point of the Cosoninas trail to the Colorado River from Cosoninas Wash (which became known as Moenkopi Wash in 1870). (The name Cosoninas was derived from the Hopi name for the Havasupai, Kohninih, of obscure origin.) Father Garcés visited the Havasupai village here in 1776.

Tuvi was friendly with the Mormons, and made a trip to Salt Lake City with other Hopis while certain Mormons stayed with the Hopis as hostages. It was through his friendship that the first Mormon colony in Navajo country was established at Moenkopi.

In 1870, John W. Young, a son of Brigham Young, built a woolen mill at Moenkopi, with 192 spindles to be operated by Indian labor. The mill, still standing in 1941, was not successful and was soon abandoned. On the outskirts of the present Hopi village is the old Mormon cemetery with many headstones bearing names familiar in the Navajo country today. Lot Smith, the founder of Sunset, Arizona, was killed in 1894 by Chách'osh, a Navajo, in a fracas over pasture and water at Spring Canyon, three miles north of Moenkopi.

The village became a refuge for polygamists in 1880, as did the Bluff, Utah, region. Mormons shipped 1400 pounds of wool from Moenkopi to Provo in 1883, the same year Navajos and Hopis there raised 5000 bushels of grain.

The Mormon settlement at Moenkopi was within 1,575,369 acres added to the reservation by presidential Executive Order on January 18, 1900, and the Mormons were evicted in 1903. (See Tuba City.)

✤ **Role in Hillerman Fiction:**

The Blessing Way: Old Woman Gray Rocks gossiped to anthropologist Bergen McKee at her brush hogan about a nephew of an uncle by marriage having left his wife and taken up with a woman from Moenkopi (chap. 7).

The Dark Wind: Jim Chee drives past this village of stone walls on his way to Burnt Water Trading Post (chap. 13). Chee meets Deputy Sheriff Cowboy Dashee at Moenkopi to discuss the carryall Chee discovered in the tributary of Wepo Wash, near the site of Pauling's plane crash (chap. 16).

The First Eagle: Joe Leaphorn and Louisa Bourebonette drive through here on their way from Flagstaff to Tuba City (via Cameron) (chap. 14).

MOENKOPI PLATEAU: (5000–5400 ft) Coconino County, AZ. The Navajo name is uncertain. This vast, flat terrain lies to the west and southwest of the Hopi Mesas, and to the south of the communities of Moenkopi and Tuba City. It is a fairly barren, sandy, and desolate country, though both Hopis and Navajos graze livestock in the region. Howell Mesa marks the northeast margin, while the western boundary is marked by Ward Terrace. The southern perimeter is difficult to discern, but the approximate dimensions of the plateau are 30 miles north-south by 20 miles east-west.

✤ **Role in Hillerman Fiction:**

The Ghostway: Frank Sam Nakai, medicine man and Jim Chee's teacher, tells Chee that only a few medicine men are left who can cure the ghost sickness, including one old man near Navajo Mountain who still conducts the nine-day ceremony. He learned it from his grandfather over near Dinnebito Wash on Moenkopi Plateau (chap. 24).

The First Eagle: Crossing this plateau, Jim Chee drives through the track of a rain shower on his way to assist Officer Benny Kinsman (chap. 2). The road Leaphorn had to take to find Jim Chee crosses the Moenkopi Plateau (chap. 14).

MOENKOPI WASH: (7400–4200 ft) Navajo and Coconino Counties, AZ. Navajos call this channel Naak'a' K'éé'dílyéhé, meaning "Where Cotton is Cultivated." Ninety miles in length, Moenkopi Wash is one of the major tributaries of the Little Colorado River. The stream heads on northeastern Black Mesa, near Lolomai Point, and it is one of the five major drainages of the mesa (see also Dinnebito, Oraibi, Wepo, and Polacca Washes), though all are ephemeral.

The wash exits Black Mesa through Blue Canyon, called Bikooh Dootł'ish ("Blue Canyon)" by Victor Mindeleff in 1891. This canyon takes the channel west to the village of Moenkopi, after which the wash turns south for 25 miles before it joins the Little Colorado River a couple of miles west of Cameron.

Moenkopi Wash was traversed by Colonel (Governor) Jose Antonio Vizcarra's expedition of 1823. Early Spanish explorers called this wash Arroyo de los Algodones ("Stream of the Cotton Fields"), and Los Pilares, an apparent reference to the twin pillars known today as the Elephant Feet. The Dominguez-Escalante Expedition of 1776 called it Cosmisas Wash (etymology uncertain).

✣ Role in Hillerman Fiction:

The Dark Wind: Jim Chee spends the night in this wash beside his pickup truck after evading an ambush set at his trailer house in Tuba City (chap. 26).

MONTEZUMA CREEK: (8600–4300 ft) San Juan County, UT. Navajos call this creek Díwiózhii Bikooh, meaning "Greasewood Canyon." This 55-mile-long stream rises on the northeast flank of 11,360-ft Abajo Peak, some seven miles east of Blanding. The stream flows east, past Monticello, then turns south, flowing through Montezuma Canyon and entering the San Juan River approximately 11 miles downstream of Aneth and the mouth of McElmo Creek.

Like the Bears Ears, this was a major trading region for Utes and Navajos. Utes traded buckskins, buckskin clothing, elk hides, buffalo robes, saddlebags, horses, beaded bags, beaver skins, buffalo tails (for rattles), and pitch (for ceremonial whistles and baskets). Navajos traded woven blankets, silver, and agricultural produce.

The name also refers to a trading center on the north bank of the San Juan River and Utah Highway 163, a couple of miles west of the junction of that highway with Navajo Route 35 and Utah Highway 262. Here there are schools and a natural gas plant. Sunrise Trading Post, established between 1916 and 1920, is now closed. The bridge spanning the San Juan River here was dedicated on December 7, 1958.

This community, first known as Fort Montezuma, was established by Peter Shirts, who for some reason believed Aztec leader Montezuma was captured and killed near here.

✣ Role in Hillerman Fiction:

Skinwalkers: Roosevelt Bistie's daughter says a sick Bistie went looking for someone around Mexican Hat or Montezuma Creek (chap. 3). Refinery workers are angry because someone has been stealing drip gasoline out of the collector pipeline (chap. 6).

A Thief of Time: Anthropologist Maxie Davis remembers that the missing Eleanor Friedman-Bernal seemed happy upon returning from a trip to Mexican Hat and Montezuna Creek (chap. 6). The Houk kid who went

Figure 27. The small town of Montezuma Creek sits on the north bank of the San Juan River, amid some of the most rugged and barren land in Navajo territory. The town seems to be composed of as many petroleum storage tanks as houses.

berserk and killed most of his family had gone to high school in Montezuma Creek (chap. 6). From Jimmy Etcitty's description, Joe Leaphorn figures that the pots in which missing anthropologist Eleanor Friedman-Bernal is so interested were excavated somewhere west of here (chap. 14).

Coyote Waits: Ashie Pinto's grandfather had told him that the Utes used to cross the San Juan River near Montezuma Creek here to raid on the Navajos (chap. 7). A Mormon rancher spotted the two surviving train robbers in this vicinity (chap. 11).

Hunting Badger: Bandits from the Ute Casino robbery reportedly stole a private plane from rancher Timms, south of Montezuma Creek (chap. 2). This is the closest community to Ray Gershwin's ranch (chap. 3). George (Badger) Ironhand runs cattle north of Montezuma Creek (chap. 9). Captain Largo places Jim Chee in Montezuma Creek to search for Ute Casino robbers; the gathering place for officers in the search is the Montezuma Creek Chapter House (chap. 12).

MONUMENT VALLEY: (4800–5700 ft), San Juan County, UT, and Navajo County, AZ. Navajos call this region Tsé Bii' Ndzisgaii, meaning "Stretches of Treeless Areas" or "Clearings Among the Rocks." Straddling the Arizona-Utah state line about 20 miles north of Kayenta, Arizona, this expanse of desert highland measures some 20 miles by 30 miles. About 100 square miles (30,000 acres) is now a Navajo Tribal Park, containing some of the most astonishing—and, thanks to movie westerns, some of the most familiar—natural geological formations in the world. These include Mitchell and Spearhead mesas, Merrick, Mitchell, and The Mittens buttes, and Mystery Valley—sheer, isolated mesas and sandstone pillars of various sizes and shapes. The majority of the park is in Arizona, but the entrance is in Utah.

The valley floor is actually higher in elevation than the southwestern perimeter, near Monument Pass, and the northern boundary, the San Juan River at Mexican Hat. Many of the monuments loom 1000 ft above the valley floor.

Gouldings, the famed trading post/guest ranch, is located a mile northwest of the main road at Monument Pass. It was established in October 1925, when Harry Goulding and his wife, "Mike," arrived in the valley and claimed a stake. Colorful and determined Harry was personally responsible for bringing the motion-picture industry to the valley.

This awesome landscape was formed by geologic and environmental activity that began 25 million years ago, during the Cenozoic era, when the entire region was under a vast inland sea. When the sea receded, beds of sand compacted into stone some hundreds of feet thick. While the receding waters (and rain since then) may have affected some of the general topography, the great monuments for which the valley is noted today were formed primarily by wind-driven grains of sand in a relentless sculpting of the landscape.

Monument Valley lies in the old Paiute Strip, and was the original northwest corner of the Treaty Reservation of 1868. The western and northern part of the region was annexed to the Navajo Reservation by an executive order of 1884. A portion later was restored to public domain, but again became the property of the Navajos by Act of Congress in 1934. Today, its population is almost totally Navajo, with some Paiutes married to Navajos.

In December–January, 1879–80, two White prospectors, Ernest Mitchell and James Merrick, were killed in the northern portion of the valley. Navajos, Utes, and Paiutes all blamed one another, though it seems Paiutes were the most likely culprits. Separated, each prospector died at the foot of a different sandstone monument that would later bear his name—Mitchell Butte and Merrick Butte.

In another story with many parallels, two prospectors named Sam Walcott and James McNally were killed in 1884, south of the valley near Agathla Peak (El Capitan), by Navajos led by Hashké Neiniihí Biye' (often spelled Hoskinini Begay) Dinéts'ós'ósí. A military expedition accompanied by the Navajo agent, John Bowman, and his interpreter, Henry Chee Dodge, went to Monument Valley. The killers, with the exception of Hashké Neiniihí Biye', were apprehended. Unfortunately, Hashké Neiniihí, father of Hashké Neiniihí Biye', and the headman of the region, was imprisoned for some time for his son's misdeed.

In Navajo mythology, this region is a giant hogan, with Gouldings sitting in its fireplace and Sentinel and Gray Whiskers Mesas being doorposts.

Many Anasazi ruins are found in Monument Valley, most of them small. In the 1930s, the Rainbow Bridge–Monument Valley expeditions conducted considerable research in the valley. Monument Valley Tribal Park contains 30,000 acres and was established by the Navajo Tribal Council on July 11, 1958.

✦ Role in Hillerman Fiction:

The Blessing Way: In order to cover his kidnapping of anthropologist Bergen McKee and Ellen Leon, and the murder of Jeremy Canfield, the Big Navajo forces McKee to leave a note that says he and Canfield were moving their operation to Monument Valley (chap. 14).

A Thief of Time: From Jimmy Etcitty's description, Joe Leaphorn figures that the pots in which missing anthropologist Eleanor Friedman-Bernal is so interested were excavated somewhere north of Monument Valley (chap. 14).

Coyote Waits: In studying rock formation photos in the darkroom of murdered Huan Ji, Joe Leaphorn and Louisa Bourebonette conjecture the formations photographed could be in several locations, including Monument Valley (chap. 17).

MORGAN LAKE: (5300 ft) San Juan County, NM. This man-made body of water is the cooling pond for the Four Corners Power Plant. It is located three miles south of the San Juan River, directly south of the community of Waterflow. It measures approximately a mile and a half long (east-west) by one mile.

✦ Role in Hillerman Fiction:

The Fallen Man: The mirror surface of this pool reflects the sun as Joe Leaphorn and Gallup attorney Bob Rosebrough fly by helicopter from Farmington to Shiprock Pinnacle (chap. 22).

MOUNT HESPERUS: See Hesperus Peak.

MOUNT TAYLOR: (11,301 ft) Cibola County, NM. Also San Mateo Mountain, San Mateo Peak, Cebolleta Mountains. In Navajo this feature is Tsoodził ("Mountain Tongue" or "Tongue Mountain"). In sacred terminology, it is Dootł'izhii Dziil ("Turquoise Mountain" or "Blue Bead Mountain").

The name Mount Taylor generally refers to the highest peak in the San Mateo Mountains, 10 miles north of Interstate 40, about 15 miles northeast of Grants. Formerly called Seboyeta (Spanish for "Little Onion") Mountain. The English name commemorates Zachary Taylor, the twelfth President of the United States and Army general of Mexican War fame. When Colonel Alexander W. Doniphan's column traversed this mountain in November 1847, it was referred to as the Sierra Madre.

Figure 28. The west slope of Mount Taylor, as viewed from Interstate 40, about 15 miles west of Grants, New Mexico.

The mountain is visible from points in the Navajo country as far west as Chuska Peak, some 70 miles away. Projecting to the south and northeast from Mount Taylor are large lava flows forming mesas that sheer off from their forested tops in irregular and ragged escarpments.

Navajos refer to Mount Taylor as their sacred mountain of the south, indicating the southern boundary of their old country. It is said in the creation myth that First Man placed turquoise in this mountain, covered it with blue sky, and fastened it to the sky with a great stone knife. Its symbolic color is blue or turquoise, and it is referred to in mythology as the Turquoise Mountain. It is decorated with dark mist, female rain, and all species of animals and birds. It is the home of Dootł'izhii 'Ashkii ("Turquoise Boy") and Naadá'áłtsoii 'At'ééd ("Yellow Corn Girl"). It is also said to be the home of one of the Haasch'é'ooghaan, beings that defy etymology.

Mount Taylor is important in the Blessing Side ceremonies and the 'Anaa'jí (Enemyway Ceremony). Navajo mythology considers the mountain female, along with Hesperus Peak, the sacred mountain of the north. (Blanca Peak and the San Francisco Peaks, sacred mountains of the east and west, are considered male.) Three lesser landforms considered sacred mountains internal to Navajoland are Gobernador Knob, Hosta Butte, and Huerfano Peak.

Mount Taylor, legends say, was once the home of Yé'iitsoh ("Giant Yé'ii"), chief of the Enemy Gods, but it does not have the sacred significance of the other sacred mountains of the cardinal directions. The Twin War Gods killed Yé'iitsoh here, his blood running down and coagulating as the Malpais Lava Flows around Grants. The mountain also figures in the Navajo Mountain Chant. It was the territorial center of the Diné 'Ana'í (Enemy Navajos), Navajos who generally allied with the Whites against the main body of the tribe.

This mountain is also sacred to the Zunis, especially the Medicine and Big Fire Societies.

❖ Role in Hillerman Fiction:

The Blessing Way: This mountain was visible to Joseph Begay as he stood in the doorway of his hogan 70 miles to the west (chap. 5).

People of Darkness: The Frank Lloyd Wright home of Alice and Benjamin T. Vines is situated in the foothills of this mountain; Dillon Charley, a Navajo, is buried near the home (chap. 2). Years earlier, a drilling crew (of which Dillon Charley was a member) was killed in an explosion northeast of Mount Taylor (chap. 5).

The Ghostway: After returning from Los Angeles, Chee returns for the third time to Ashie Begay's hogan in the Chuskas to see if he can verify Bentwoman's assertion that Begay must be dead. In the chinde hogan, Chee finds Ashie Begay's Four Mountains Bundle, containing herbs and minerals from the four sacred mountains: the San Francisco Peaks in Arizona (sacred mountain of the west), Hesperus Peak in the La Plata Mountains of Colorado (sacred mountain of the north), Blanca Peak in the Sangre de Cristo Mountains of Colorado (sacred mountain of the east), and Mount Taylor in New Mexico (sacred mountain of the south) (chap. 22). From Jimmy Yellow's place on Mesa Gigante (on the eastern fringe of Mount Taylor), the view is extraordinary, taking in the valley of the Rio Puerco, the Sandia Mountains and the lights of Albuquerque to the east, and the Sangre de Cristos to the north. Being on the wrong side of Mount Taylor (Turquoise Mountain), some strictly traditional medicine men would have refused to perform the ceremony here (chap. 25).

Skinwalkers: The wounded Joe Leaphorn sees clouds building over this sacred mountain from his hospital room (chap. 15).

A Thief of Time: Joe Leaphorn wonders how the Chacoans could have hauled roof beams all the way from Mount Taylor (chap. 2).

Coyote Waits: Hosteen Pinto recounts to Jim Chee part of the creation myth dealing with Mount Taylor (chap. 14). In studying rock formation photos in the darkroom of murdered Huan Ji, Joe Leaphorn and Louisa Bourebonette conjecture the formations photographed could be in several locations, including Mount Taylor (chap. 17).

Sacred Clowns: Mount Taylor is seen in the distance as Jim Chee and BIA Police Sergeant Harold Blizzard search the Chico Arroyo area for Delmar Kanitewa (chap. 19).

The Fallen Man: The snow-covered crest of Mount Taylor is visible to climbers Bill Buchanan and John Whiteside at the top of Shiprock before they discover the skeleton in the recess below the crest (chap. 1). From partway up Shiprock Pinnacle, Elisa Breedlove could see Ute Mountain, Casa del Eco Mesa, the Carrizo Mountains, and Mount Taylor (chap. 5).

Hunting Badger: Joe Leaphorn and Professor Louisa Bourebonette can see Mount Taylor and Sleeping Ute Mountain from the top of Narbona (Washington) Pass (chap. 24).

NA AH TEE (TRADING POST): (6150 ft) Navajo County, AZ. Also Na-ah-tee, Naahtee, Naahtee Canyon. The Navajo name, Náá'á Diih, is interpreted as "Without Eyes," but actually means "toadstool," with a literal meaning of "Eyes Become None." This small community is located in the Hopi Buttes region, four miles west of Arizona Highway 77, 10 miles south of White Cone.

The trading post here is one of several owned at one time by Lorenzo Hubbell, though he apparently spelled it "Na-ah-tah." The post was opened about 1900, and closed during the mid-1920s.

✤ Role in Hillerman Fiction:

Talking God: Joe Leaphorn has to pass Na Ah Tee Trading Post on a dirt road on his way to visit Agnes Tsosie (chap. 3).

NAGEEZI (TRADING POST): (6950 ft) San Juan County, NM. This place is called Naayízí in Navajo, translating as "Squash" (the vegetable). The trading post and chapter house sit on U.S. Highway 550 (formerly New Mexico Highway 44), 26 miles south of Bloomfield. A post office has operated here since 1941. The trading post was opened by Jim Brimhall around 1920.

✤ Role in Hillerman Fiction:

A Thief of Time: Jim Chee finds Slick Nakai preaching just north of Nageezi (chap. 4). This region is scouted by Jim Chee in his search for Joe B. Nails, whom he believes to be the Backhoe Bandit (chap. 5). Joe Leaphorn and Jim Chee drive through Nageezi on their way to Chaco from the scene of the pothunter murder (chap. 10).

NAHODSHOSH CHAPTER: A fictitious location.

✤ Role in Hillerman Fiction:

Sacred Clowns: Leaphorn and Streib drive past Nazhoni Trading Post, Coyote Wash, Standing Rock, and Nahodshosh Chapter on their way to Crownpoint to meet with Lieutenant Ed Toddy concerning the murder of Thoreau teacher Eric Dorsey (chap. 4).

NAKAIBITO (also MEXICAN SPRINGS): (6500 ft) (Population: 242) McKinley County, NM. The Navajos call this place Naakaii Bító', meaning "Mexican's Water." An old name is Naakaii Chííhí Bitó' ("Long Nosed Mexican's Water"). This trading, chapter, and government community is located at the base of the foothills of the east slope of the Chuska Mountains, five miles west of U.S. Highway 666.

The trading post was operated by Edward Vanderwagen around the turn of the century. In the spring of 1939, a group of Navajos at Mexican Springs took over the Mexican Springs Trading Post, turning it into a cooperative venture with an outside (White) manager.

✤ Role in Hillerman Fiction:

Coyote Waits: Mrs. Greyeyes, a juror at the Ashie Pinto trial, is thought by the prosecuting attorney to be from Nakaibito, but she is actually from near Coyote Canyon (chap. 18).

Sacred Clowns: Jim Chee receives a report of fence cuttings and cattle thefts in the Nakaibito area (chap. 8).

NARBONA PASS: (8800 ft) San Juan County, NM. Also Washington Pass and, erroneously, Cottonwood Pass. The Navajo names attributed have included Sǫ' Silá ("Twin Stars") and Béésh Łichí'í Bigiizh ("Red Metal Pass" or "Copper Pass"), but neither of these seems accurate. Sǫ' Silá actually refers to the Sonsola Buttes to the west (in Arizona), and Béésh can also mean "flint" or "chert" (according to cultural historian Dave Brugge). Thus, Béésh Łichí'í Bigiizh may actually be "Red Pass Flint," referring to Washington Pass chert, which was used as far back as Anasazi times for chipped stone tools. In any case, due to the recent name-change, the feature is labeled Washington Pass on all but the most recent of maps.

This passage separates the Chuska Mountains on the south from the Tunicha Mountains on the north, and stretches between the communities of Sheep Springs and Crystal. It is traversed by New Mexico Highway 134 and Navajo Route 32.

Mexican Colonel (Governor) Jose Antonio Vizcarra crossed the Chuska Mountains through this pass on his wide-ranging expedition of 1823. Blas de Hinojos led an expedition into a Navajo ambush in this pass in 1835. Hinojos and several others were killed by Navajos.

The name Washington Pass was bestowed in 1859 by Captain J. F. McComb, commemorating Lieutenant Colonel John M. Washington, the military governor of New Mexico in 1848–49. Washington passed through the vicinity as he led an expedition to the Navajos in 1849. His route led him down the eastern face of the Tunicha Mountains near Two Grey Hills and westward over the pass.

According to older Navajos, Navajo warriors skirted the flanks of Washington's soldiers, stopping at a spring near the summit. The soldiers missed the camp, but walled up the spring before moving on westward. The stones were still visible in 1941, and the Navajos today consider the spring a minor shrine, depositing fragments of white shell, turquoise, abalone shell, and jet into it as offerings for rain.

Figure 29. The heart of Narbona Pass, facing east.

Washington's troops subsequently summoned Narbona and other Navajo leaders to a council near the pass, but when a soldier tried to claim an Indian horse as one stolen days earlier, shooting erupted and Narbona was killed.

Captain Henry Lafayette Dodge established the second Navajo agency at the eastern mouth of the pass, having moved there from Chupadero. Ruins of the agency are still visible in the pass. Also on the east slope, near the summit, there is a sheer lava crag, called "Sun Resting." Nearby is a tsé ninájihí, a pile of rocks and twigs upon which traveling Navajos add further rocks and twigs as offerings to the success of their journeys. Owl Spring, developed during the 1930s, lies beside the roadbed, also on the eastern slope.

The region of Narbona Pass is known to produce numerous bear, and is a prime deer-hunting area, although historian Van Valkenburgh notes that by 1941 deer were a rarity. Wild turkey also declined almost overnight in the last decade of the 1800s. Chee Dodge told that they migrated to the San Francisco Mountains following a particularly harsh winter (possibly the winter of 1892). They have made a modest comeback. The pass is blanketed with aspen, spruce, and dense thickets of Gambel oak and ponderosa pine. One of the few stands of birch in these mountains is found along Cottonwood Creek, which flows from the west side.

In 1993, the U.S. Geological Survey was successfully petitioned by members of the Navajo Nation to change the name of Washington Pass to Narbona Pass, honoring Navajo Headman Narbona (Hastiin Naat'áanii, "Mr. Chief"), rather then the White man responsible for his death.

It is fitting that the name of Colonel Washington be erased from this Navajo landmark deep within their own country. It is also fitting that it be re-placed with the name of one of the earliest Navajo leaders to combat the encroachment of the Whites into Navajoland, Narbona. Yet, naming a place after a person is a break with Navajo tradition, since such an act may bring unwanted attention of his spirit, and saying his name aloud is believed likely to attract that spirit—something traditional Navajos dread. It also seems ironic that the name chosen should be the name Spaniards applied to this chieftain, rather than his Navajo name. However, former Navajo Tribal Museum Director Martin Link, who played a role in getting the name changed, says that the selection of the chief's Hispanic name was a compromise between the various chapters that had to approve the petition to USGS.

❖ Role in Hillerman Fiction:

Coyote Waits: Joe Leaphorn and his female companion, Professor Bourebonette, traverse Narbona Pass in the Chuska Mountains, passing through Red Lake, Arizona, and Crystal, New Mexico, on their way from Window Rock to Shiprock (chap. 12).

Hunting Badger: Joe Leaphorn and Professor Louisa Bourebonette cross the pass in a "thinking" expedition (chap. 24).

> *Author's Note:* In this passage, Hillerman gives erroneous historical information concerning the original English name applied to the pass; see above paragraphs for correct history.

NASCHITTI (TRADING POST): (5950 ft) (Population: 323) McKinley County, NM. Also Drolet's, Naschiti. To the Navajos, this is Nahashch'idí, meaning "Badger." This chapter community is located on present-day U.S. Highway 666, 16 miles south of Newcomb and 42 miles north of Gallup. The name is a derivative of Nahashch'idí Bito' ("Badger Springs"), which surface on the south fork of Salt Springs Wash, near the present store. In the 1940s, this community was known for its silversmiths, including one woman.

Figure 30. Naschitti Trading Post in fall, 2000. It has long since become a convenience store.

Navajos call the trading post Bíchį́į́h Digiz ("Crooked Nose"), referring to trader Thomas C. Bryan's flat, twisted nose. The post was established by Bryan and his partner Charlie Verden in 1880–81, as one of the first posts on the eastern slopes of the Chuska Mountains. Gallup trader C. C. Manning purchased the post in 1902, employing as manager Charlie Newcomb, who became a noted trader in his own right (see Newcomb below).

✤ **Role in Hillerman Fiction:**

Talking God: Eight middle-aged men from Naschitti perform the Night Chant of the Yeibeichai at Lower Greasewood for Agnes Tsosie (chap. 4).

Sacred Clowns: Jim Chee drives past Naschitti on his way to see Frank Sam Nakai, his mentor singer (chap. 12).

NASHODISHGISH MESA: Hillerman uses this name (as well as Iyanbito Mesa and Mesa de los Lobos) to describe the massive red sandstone cliffs that line the north perimeter of Wingate Valley, the corridor through which Interstate 40 and the Burlington Northern Santa Fe Railroad pass east of Gallup, New Mexico. (See Mesa de los Lobos.)

The variety of names is typical in Navajo territory, where, with the dearth of maps and written materials, places tended to take on different names for different isolated groups of Navajos.

Hillerman's name is actually a typographical error, and should be Nahodishgish, which in turn is an English corruption of the Navajo name for Dalton Pass: Náhodeeshgiizh (meaning "Pass Coming Down"). This mountain community and pass on the north face of Mesa de los Lobos is also known as Łį́į́' Haa'nah, or "Where the Horse Crawls Up."

✤ **Role in Hillerman Fiction:**

Talking God: Joe Leaphorn drives along the base of the pink cliffs marking the southern edge of this mesa. From the entrance to the old Fort Wingate Army Ordnance Depot, east to the Shell Oil Refinery, he looks for evidence relating to the appearance of the body known as Pointed Shoes near the Santa Fe Railroad tracks (chap. 6).

> *Author's note:* Since Hillerman's writing of this book in 1989, the refinery has been taken over by Giant Petroleum, and the railroad tracks now belong to the Burlington Northern Santa Fe Railroad.

NATANI TSO: (6400 ft) San Juan County, NM. The Navajo spelling is Naat'áanii Tsoh, meaning "Big Boss." This large flat-topped mesa sits at the north end of the Red Rock Valley, eight miles northeast of Red Rock Trading Post.

✤ **Role in Hillerman Fiction:**

The Blessing Way: Luis Horseman watched the dust from a vehicle follow the track toward the west end of Natani Tso (chap. 1).

NAVAJO AGRICULTURAL INDUSTRIES: (6200 ft) San Juan County, NM. Based on the Navajo Indian Irrigation Project (NIIP), managed by the Navajo Agricultural Products Industry (NAPI). Navajos refer to this as Dá'ak'eh Ntsaa, meaning "The Big Farm."

The seeds of this enormous, federally sponsored project atop Gallegos Mesa were sown in 1894, when the Navajos constructed an early irrigation system, known as the Hogback Ditch, at the point where the San Juan River bisects the Hogback. It irrigated some 75 acres. In 1941 a subsequent system irrigated 3500 acres of agricultural land on the north bank of the San Juan River, constituting the largest functioning irrigation project in Navajo country. That system later gave birth to the Bureau of Indian Affairs Navajo Indian Irrigation Project (NIIP).

Authorized on June 13, 1962, the massive irrigation project lies between U.S. Highway 550 (formerly New Mexico Highway 44) and the Chaco River, and extends some 40 miles south of the San Juan River.

The project calls for 216,843 acres, of which 110,630 will be irrigated. Only 40,343 of the acres are within the Navajo Reservation; the remaining 176,000 acres have been—or will be—purchased by the Navajo Nation. The irrigated acreage is divided into eleven 10,000-acre plots, not all of which are contiguous. Irrigation on Block I was started in 1975, and by the end of 1998, some 50,000 acres were being watered. The irrigation will eventually require 508,000 acre-feet of water per year, and the project will potentially employ 4400 Navajos.

✤ **Role in Hillerman Fiction:**

Sacred Clowns: Clement Hoskie, Jim Chee's suspect in the hit-and-run death of Victor Todachenee, lives 10 miles south of the southernmost boundary of the agriculture project plot. Chee and Janet Pete park near Hoskie's house and meet Hoskie's retarded son, Ernie (chap. 26).

NAVAJO LAKE: (7200 ft) San Juan County, NM. Also Navajo Reservoir. The Navajo name is uncertain. This 35-mile-long, 110,000-acre lake was created some 18 miles east of Aztec by the closing of Navajo Dam on the San Juan River in 1962. A New Mexico State Park and recreation area surround the lake.

The lake covers Tó Aheedłí or Tóalnaazli Tó Bil Dahsk'id, which has been tentatively translated as "Place Where the Waters Crossed," referring to the juncture of the San Juan and the Los Pinos Rivers. The site was a highly sacred location to the Navajos, especially to medicine men, as are the junctures of the San Juan and Colorado rivers and the San Juan with Mancos Creek.

Here ripples in the sand were "read" by medicine men. Such readings reportedly predicted both the Bosque Redondo internment of the Navajos during the 1860s and the Navajo livestock reduction of the 1930s.

At least one scholar suggests that the location of Navajo emergence from the fourth world into the present one was near present Navajo Dam. However, this is arguable.

❖ Role in Hillerman Fiction:

A Thief of Time: Joe Leaphorn tells the Luna family that a possible reason for the county sheriff not responding to the report of missing anthropologist Eleanor Friedman-Bernal is the extent of his duties—including such trivial things as vandalism at Navajo Lake (chap. 10).

NAVAJO MISSION: (6850 ft) Coconino County, AZ. The Navajo name is uncertain. This church and mission is located across the road from the old Inscription House Trading Post. It is situated on the Shonto Plateau, east of the head of Navajo Canyon, on Navajo Route 16, five and a half miles north of Arizona Highway 98.

❖ Role in Hillerman Fiction:

The First Eagle: Returning to Krouse's office, Joe Leaphorn finds a note saying that Krouse has gone to Inscription House, then to Navajo Mission (chap. 25).

NAVAJO MOUNTAIN: (10,388 ft) San Juan County, UT, Navajo County, AZ. Also Sierra Panoche (Spanish meaning "Corn Mountain"). Navajos call this peak Naatsis'áán, which, according to historian Richard Van Valkenburgh, refers to the head of the sacred female and pollen range of Navajo mythology. A traditional, nonreligious Navajo name is thought to have translated as "Enemy Hiding Place," indicating it was in Paiute territory.

This high, rounded mountain straddles the Utah-Arizona state line, with most of it—including the highest peak—lying in Utah. It is situated east of Aztec Creek and south of the confluence of the San Juan and Colorado River arms of Lake Powell, some 90 miles north of Tuba City, Arizona. It is the dominating landmark in western Navajo country.

John Wesley Powell first named it Mount Seneca Howland, for one of three men killed by parties unknown after the three left Powell's 1869 expedition partway through the first exploration of the Grand Canyon; the term Navajo Mountain reportedly was coined by Almon Thompson.

Today, the name also refers to a chapter community sitting on the east slope of the mountain.

> *Author's Note:* For decades, the deaths of Seneca and his companions were blamed on the Shivwitz Indians, but an 1883 letter from William Leany (a resident of Harrisburg) to John Steele (of Toquerville) suggests that Mormons led by Eli N. Pace (a son-in-law of John D. Lee) killed the men in the Toquerville church ward.

The mountain was visited by Antonio de Espejo's troops in 1583, and Espejo applied the label Sierra Panoche, the name shown on McComb's map of 1860. In 1856, Major J. S. Simpson at Fort Defiance received information from friendly Paiutes that the Mormons had invited Navajos, Utes, and Mohaves to a council at Navajo Mountain. At this meeting, it was reported, arms were distributed to the Indians, and the United States government and its military were represented as natural enemies of the Indians.

This region was a stronghold for Navajos as early as the first Spanish incursions into Navajoland. Headmen Hashké Neiniihii and Spane Shank led refugees in the area during the Navajo Wars and the Bosque Redondo period. A wagon road to the foot of the mountain was not completed until 1925.

This mountain is regarded as sacred by the Navajos. They tell in their Blessing Side stories that Navajo Mountain represents the head of the female and pollen figure of Navajoland, called Tádídíín Dził ("Pollen Mountain") or Ni'go 'Asdzáán ("Earth Woman"). This anthropomorphic formation includes Black Mesa as her body and Balakai Mesa as her feet. Comb Ridge is one arm, and a monocline near Marsh Pass is the other. Tuba Butte and Agathla Peak are her breasts.

Navajo Mountain is also a home of the Bear People of the Rounded Man Antway Myth, and figures prominently in the Navajo Coyoteway myth. T'áá'neiyá ("Place of Raising") and Béésh Bee Hooghaní ("Flint Hogan"), both Navajo sacred places, sit atop the mountain.

Traditional Navajos are reluctant to climb above the lower elevations of the mountain and fear underground rumblings that are reported on the west slopes. Until the 1940s, very few Navajos would go north of the mountain into the broken country between there and the Colorado River.

The only stand of limber pine (Pinus flexilis) in the Navajo country is found on Navajo Mountain. Rainbow Lodge and Trading Post on the southeast slope conducted business from the early 1920s until the mid-1950s, and was formerly owned by the late Arizona Senator Barry Goldwater. This was only 50 straight-line miles from Gouldings, but 100 miles by road.

Rumors of silver being discovered on Navajo Mountain circulated in the 1860s, but the riches never materialized.

Located in a side canyon of Piute Canyon, on the southeast slope of Navajo Mountain (four miles east of the highest peak), the post was opened between 1931 and 1935. This was also the site of a USIS day school that today is a public day school.

✢ Role in Hillerman Fiction:

The Blessing Way: Anthropologist Bergen McKee recalls Greerson's story of a witch turning into a bear on Navajo Mountain (chap. 14).

Listening Woman: An extension of Leaphorn's mental straight line connecting Gold Rims's abandoned car to the water hole passes between Navajo Mountain and (fictional) Short Mountain (chap. 4).

The Dark Wind: Huge thunderheads building over the San Francisco Peaks are visible all the way to Navajo Mountain (chap. 21).

The Ghostway: Frank Sam Nakai, medicine man and Jim Chee's teacher, tells Chee that only a few medicine men are left who can cure the ghost sickness, including one old man near Navajo Mountain who still conducts the nine-day ceremony (chap. 24).

A Thief of Time: Paiute Clansman Amos Whiskers tells Jim Chee that the pots in which missing anthropologist Eleanor Friedman-Bernal is interested come from over near Navajo Mountain (chap. 13).

Talking God: "Lone Rangers" (Whites) had flocked here and declared themselves spokesmen for (and guardians of) Navajo families being evicted from the Joint Use Area in the infamous Relocation (chap. 6).

The First Eagle: Unlike the Tuba City area, where he's worked only a short time, Jim Chee knows every track in the Checkerboard Area and the Navajo Mountain region (chap. 2).

NAVAJO NATIONAL MONUMENT: (7286–5800 ft) Coconino and Navajo counties, AZ. The Navajo name is Bitát'ahkin ("House on a Rock Ledge"), referring to Betatakin Ruin in the monument.

During the winter of 1895, Richard Wetherill and Charlie Mason spent four months in the Monument Valley, Marsh Pass, and the Tsegi Canyon Region of the Shonto Plateau, discovering Keet Siel (Kits'iil) Ruin in the canyon. Wetherill became the first superintendent of Navajo National Monument in 1909.

The monument is a series of isolated islands of territory around three major ruin complexes. Construction of all three ruins is attributed to the Kayenta branch of the Anasazi, with occupation of the region beginning during the Basketmaker II period, about the time of Christ. Although the Kayenta Anasazi graduated from pithouses to aboveground dwellings as early as A.D. 600, construction of the multi-storied, many-roomed structures at these three ruins did not begin until about A.D. 1250—after the abandonment of the larger villages at Chaco Canyon to the east. The Navajo National Monument villages seem to have peaked about A.D. 1290, and were largely abandoned within the next decade.

Tsegi Canyon and its numerous side canyons and rincons house hundreds of prehistoric Anasazi ruins, but the best known are Betatakin, Keet Siel, and Inscription House. Other important ruins are Rubbish Ruin, Turkey Cave, Bat Woman, Twin Caves, and Swallow's Nest.

Dinosaur tracks are also known in the sandstone of the monument. Snake House, a minor, 19-room pueblo, is located near the larger Inscription House.

Betatakin Ruin, also called Kin Łání ("Many Houses") at one time, is located near the head of Betatakin Canyon (a two-mile-long southern branch of Tsegi Canyon), and is the most accessible ruin of the Navajo National Monument group. The overhanging red sandstone cliff rises 500 ft above the 135-room ruin situated at the base of the north wall of the canyon. Discovered in 1909 (14 years after the discovery of Keet Siel) by John and Richard Wetherill, Betatakin is the second largest cliff dwelling in the Tsegi region, and dates to A.D. 1260–77. This ruin is open to the public via scheduled three-hour tours of no more than 20 persons.

Inscription House, which the Navajos call Ts'ah Biis Kin ("House in the Sagebrush"), is a 74-room ruin with granaries and a kiva. It is located on the north side of the mouth of a branch of Nitsin Canyon, on the east bank of Navajo Creek, some four miles northwest of historic Inscription House Trading Post. The ruin was recorded by Byron Cummings in 1909, just a few days before Betatakin Ruin was discovered. The English name results from a non-decipherable inscription noted on the cliff wall, generally attributed to Spanish explorers. This ruin is closed to the public indefinitely, pending desperately needed stabilization.

Keet Siel Ruin (also spelled Kiet Siel and Keet Seel) is called Kits'iil ("Shattered House") by the Navajos. This name has also been erroneously interpreted as "Broken Pottery," which is Kiits'illi, and the ruin is also called Kin Yits'ill ("Empty House"). Yet another interpretation refers to a large spruce log lying across a retaining wall.

The ruin was first called Long House by Whites. In 1895, Keet Siel was the first of the Navajo National Monument ruins to be discovered, as Richard Wetherill searched for his wayward mule, "Neephi." Situated in Keet Siel Canyon, it is the largest cliff dwelling in Arizona, with 160 rooms and five or six kivas. Keet Siel was constructed between A.D. 1274 and 1286. Visitation to the site is limited to 20 persons per day and 1,500 annually, and visitors must register with the Park headquarters. Some overnight camping is allowed during the summer.

❖ Role in Hillerman Fiction:

The Fallen Man: Elisa Breedlove's brother-in-law, Demott, tells Leaphorn that Hal Breedlove had planned to take a Dartmouth chum and his girlfriend to visit Navajo National Monument, the Grand Canyon, and Canyon de Chelly, but Hal wanted to climb Shiprock before he turned 30, and his birthday was the day they were supposed to arrive—and the day he disappeared (chap. 27).

NAZHONI TRADING POST: (6100 ft) McKinley County, NM. The Navajo name is uncertain, although the name shown on maps sounds suspiciously like a corruption of the Navajo "Nizhoni" ("Beautiful"). This trading post was located on the south side of Navajo Route 9, midway between its juncture with U.S. Highway 666 and Coyote Canyon. It no longer exists.

❖ Role in Hillerman Fiction:

Sacred Clowns: Leaphorn and Streib drive past Nazhoni Trading Post, Coyote Wash, Standing Rock, and Nahodshosh Chapter on their way to Crownpoint to meet with Lieutenant Ed Toddy concerning the murder of Thoreau teacher Eric Dorsey (chap. 4).

The First Eagle: Nellie Hale, who died of the plague in the Farmington hospital, had visited her mother at Nazhoni Trading Post before contracting the plague; a prairie dog burrow was dusted for fleas, which proved to be plague carriers (chap. 23).

NAZLINI WASH: (7600–6000 ft) Apache County, AZ. The Navajo name is possibly the same as the community of Nazlini, which Navajos call Názlíní, meaning "Makes a Turn Flowing" (as a bend in a river).

❖ Role in Hillerman Fiction:

The Blessing Way: Between Chinle and Ganado, Leaphorn drives past the "lifeless depression" known as Beautiful Valley, which falls away from the highway into Nazlini and Biz-E-Ahi (Bis'ii Ah) Washes (chap. 4).

NEWBERRY MESA: (5039 ft) Coconino County, AZ. The Navajo name is uncertain. This 15-mile-long, 400-ft-high mesa sits in the approximate center of the Painted Desert, about 30 miles east of Sunset Crater National Monument. It was visited by U.S. Army Captain John S. Newberry (for whom it is named) in August 1859.

❖ Role in Hillerman Fiction:

The Dark Wind: Jim Chee drives past Newberry Mesa, Garces Mesa, Blue Point, and Padilla Mesa here on his way to the Hopi cultural center to see if Ben Gaines and Gail Pauling are still in residence (chap. 18).

Figure 31. Newcomb Trading Post today sells far more groceries and gasoline than the Navajo rugs for which it was once famous.

NEWCOMB: (5850 ft) (Population: 388) San Juan County, NM. Also called Newcomb's. Navajos refer to it as Bis Deez'áhí (meaning "Clay Point") or Bis Dootł'izh Deez'áhí ("Blue Clay Point"); trader Arthur Newcomb preferred "Trader at Blue Point."

This trading-post and school community is located on U.S. Highway 666, 60 miles north of Gallup, on the south bank of Captain Tom Wash. The mesa behind the trading post, called Blue Mesa, led to the post itself often being referred to as Blue Mesa Trading Post.

Newcomb is distinguished for its Two Grey Hills Navajo rugs, developed by trader Arthur J. Newcomb, who may have picked up the designs from J. B. Moore while trading at Crystal. (Early photographs of the rugs of J. B. Moore, who traded at Crystal from the 1890s until 1912, show a great similarity to the present Two Grey Hills type.) These finely woven rugs in natural grays, whites, browns, and blacks have characteristic geometrical designs and run to elaborate borders.

A renowned medicine man, Hastiin Klah (Tł'ah), lived in the Newcomb vicinity before his death in 1937. He was a weaver of rare, but well known, sandpainting blankets and the subject of the 1964 book by Franc Newcomb, *Hasteen Klah: Navajo Medicine Man and Sandpainter* (University of Oklahoma Press). A feature known as the Anthill, located near Nava, is important to the Navajo Mothway myth.

John Oliver built a post just south of Captain Tom Wash in 1904, which White men called "Crozier," after Captain Tom Crozier (U.S. Army), who had led troops on a reconnaissance through the area in 1846. Historian Frank McNitt suggested that Oliver sold the post to Charles Nelson in 1911, at which time the post came to be known as "Nelson's Trading Post" (or simply "Nelsons"), until Arthur J. Newcomb purchased the post in 1913–14, changing the name to "Nava," though it was sometimes called "Drolet's" (or Drolet's Trading Post), after J. M. Drolet (a subsequent owner) or "Newcomb's" after Charlie Newcomb.

However, McNitt's scenario may be in error. The 1929 "Automobile Club of Southern California Automobile Road Map of the Indian Country" (which evolved into the currently popular and annually revised "AAA Guide to Indian Country") identifies and pinpoints four separate locations for Crozier, Nava, Newcomb, and Drolet's. The map places both Crozier and Nava on the south side of the road from Newcomb to Toadlena, and Drolet's is shown on U.S. Highway 666, about 16 miles south of Newcomb.

In any case, the post was also known as Blue Mesa Trading Post; it burned to the ground in 1936 and was rebuilt.

✤ Role in Hillerman Fiction:

The Ghostway: Jim Chee calls the trading posts at Newcomb, Sheep Springs, and Two Grey Hills in search of the 17-year-old runaway, Margaret Billy Sosi (granddaughter of the missing Ashie Begay). He finally finds a Continental Trailways bus driver who remembers picking Margaret up just north of the Newcomb Trading Post, looking for a ticket to Los Angeles, but only able to afford a ticket to Kingman, Arizona (chap. 11).

Coyote Waits: A woman customer at the Red Rock Trading Post mentions that a sing-dance (song and dance) is taking place at the Newcomb School (chap. 1).

Sacred Clowns: Jim Chee drives past Newcomb on his way to see Frank Sam Nakai, his mentor singer (chap. 10).

NIPPLE BUTTE: See Hopi Buttes.

NOKAITO BENCH: (5000 ft) San Juan County, UT. Also Nakaito Bench. Navajos refer to this feature as Naakaiitó ("Mexican Spring"). It consists of a slightly elevated plain running north-south between Chinle Wash (on the west) and Gothic Creek. It extends from the juncture of Walker Creek and Chinle Wash in the south to the San Juan River in the north.

✤ Role in Hillerman Fiction:

Listening Woman: Hosteen Tso's hogan is located on Nokaito Bench (chap. 1), as is the secret cave with sand paintings (chap. 16). Leaphorn draws a mental line from Gold Rims's abandoned car to the water hole to Tso's hogan (chap. 6).

Skinwalkers: Dugai Endocheeney's hogan is on Nokaito Bench, near the confluence of Chinle Wash and the San Juan River (chap. 2).

A Thief of Time: L. D. Thatcher and Joe Leaphorn cross Nokaito Bench on their way to visit old man Houk because of a note left on missing anthropologist Eleanor Friedman-Bernal's calendar (chap. 8).

Hunting Badger: Comb Ridge creates a zigzag of light and shadow as Jim Chee and Cowboy Dashee drive across the sagebrush flats of Nokaito Bench (chap. 8). Navajos would chase Ute raiders along Nokaito Bench (chap. 13).

NOKAITO MESA: Fictional? Possibly Nokai Mesa?

✤ Role in Hillerman Fiction:

A Thief of Time: From Jimmy Etcitty's description, Joe Leaphorn figures that the pots in which missing anthropologist Eleanor Friedman-Bernal is so interested were excavated somewhere east of Nokaito Mesa (chap. 14).

NUTRIA LAKE: (6800 ft) McKinley County, NM. Also known as Nutria, Upper Nutria and Lower Nutria, Las Nutrias, and Nutrioso. Navajos call this region Tsé Dijįhí, meaning "Rock Starts to Extend Along Black." The same name applies to the lake as well as the community. Zunis call it Ts'iakwin, meaning "Seed Place" or "Planting Place." The Spanish name Nutria means "Otter."

These two small Zuni farming villages sit on Rio Nutria (north branch of the Zuni River) in the Zuni Mountains, 23 miles northeast of Zuni. Formerly occupied only during planting and harvesting, these communities are now permanent villages, with many Navajos living immediately to the north. During the latter part of the nineteenth century the Navajos were prone to impose on the people at Nutria. Historian Richard Van Valkenburgh stated that Pinto, the Navajo headman of the region, actually waged warfare on the Zunis, though David Brugge suggests that this was more a matter of intertribal boundary disputes.

Village of the Great Kivas is a well-known Anasazi ruin in the Nutria Valley, some seven miles southwest of Lower Nutria, on the north bank of Nutria Creek. This large ruin, occupied between A.D. 1000 and 1030, was excavated in the summer of 1930 by Dr. Frank H. H. Roberts, an archaeologist with the Bureau of American Ethnology.

The land around Nutria was given to Zuni Pueblo by the Spanish crown but was contested by the Navajos until their removal to the Bosque Redondo from 1864 to 1868. A trading post operated here in the 1930s.

A series of four man-made reservoirs along Rio Nutria, three to five miles downstream from the village of Lower Nutria, are called collectively Nutria Lakes, offering fishing for Navajos and non-Navajos.

✤ Role in Hillerman Fiction:

Dance Hall of the Dead: A third postulated location for the Zuni sacred site of Kothluwalawa (see also Zuni Wash and Ojo Caliente) (chap. 13).

OJO CALIENTE: (6400 ft) Cibola County, NM. Navajos call this place Tó Sido, "Hot Water," the same as the Spanish name. The Zunis call it I'iapwainakwin, "Place Whence Flow Hot Waters."

This small Zuni farming village is located about 13 miles southeast of Zuni, in the vicinity of Hawikku and at least 30 other prehistoric ruins. It is on the southernmost boundary of the Zuni Reservation, just inside the Cibola County line.

In February 1844, Spaniards attacked the Navajo rancheria here, killing 19 Navajos and capturing 19. They also took 1600 sheep and 200 other livestock. Two Navajos were killed here by Zunis in 1865, when most Navajos had been removed to the Bosque Redondo.

❖ Role in Hillerman Fiction:

Dance Hall of the Dead: This is a second postulated location for the Zuni sacred site of Kothluwalawa (see also Zuni Wash and Nutria Lake) (chap. 13).

OJO ENCINO: (6700 ft) McKinley County, NM. The Navajo name is Chéch'iizh Bii' Tó, meaning "Spring in the Rough Rocks," from a number of fallen sandstone pinnacles around the fine springs seeping out of a barren sandstone cove above one of the upper branches of the Torreon Wash (some nine miles northeast of Star Lake). Also Chéch'il Dah Lichí'í ("Red Oak Up at an Elevation").

These springs, first developed for a sheep dipping vat, were on the allotment of an old Navajo woman named "Old Lady Salvador Toledo." Robert (Bob) Smith, of Star Lake, formerly had a trading post here from about 1916 until the late 1920s.

❖ Role in Hillerman Fiction:

People of Darkness: Jim Chee determines that Roscoe Sam (a survivor of the oil rig explosion) lived either at Ojo Encino or at Standing Rock; and that Joseph Sam (another survivor) lived either here or at Pueblo Pintado (chap. 22).

A Thief of Time: Canyons near Ojo Encino are scouted by Chee in his search for Joe B. Nails, whom he believes to be the Backhoe Bandit (chap. 5).

ORAIBI: (6050 ft) Navajo County, AZ. Also Old Oraibi. The Navajo name for this place is 'Oozéí Biyashi (from Odzai, "Many Eagle Nests"), or simply 'Oazéí ("Eagle Traps"). To the Hopis it is Oraivi ("Place of a Rock Called Orai"). This village sits on the southeast tip of Third Mesa, on Arizona Highway 264, a mile or so west of Oraibi Wash.

The population in 1941 (in combination with New Oraibi, now called Kykotsmovi) was only 75 persons. The village contains the ruins of an old

Mennonite mission built by H. R. Voth in 1901 and destroyed by lightning in 1942. A trading post operated by Hopi Howard Sekestewa was situated five miles to the northwest.

Though its age has not been extensively studied, Oraibi shares with Acoma Pueblo (in New Mexico) a claim to be the oldest continuously occupied community in the United States. Tree-ring data indicate that certain beams used in Oraibi buildings were growing between A.D. 1260 and 1344. According to Hopi tradition, these beams were hauled from the San Francisco Mountains almost 100 miles to the west. The Franciscan Mission of San Fernando, established here in 1629, was destroyed during the Pueblo Revolt of 1680.

The village was visited in 1823 by troops of Vizcarra's expedition. In 1837, Oraibi was almost destroyed by the Navajos. Navajo medicine men used to visit a Hopi priest named Na'ashja' for certain medicines until his death in 1957. Navajos regarded Oraibi as a favorite place to obtain ló K'aatsoh ba'ádí, a large cane used in the manufacture of certain types of Navajo k'eet'áán, or prayer sticks.

Unrest was common at Oraibi during the last decade of the nineteenth century, between Hostiles (Conservatives) and Progressives, which resulted in 19 Hostiles, led by Chief Lomahongyoma, being arrested and incarcerated at Alcatraz on January 3, 1895. (They were released August 7 of the same year, having exhibited good behavior.) Internal dissension continued to simmer.

In 1906 Chief Tewaquaptewa ousted all villagers who were Christian or intended to become Christian. They founded the village of New Oraibi, now called Kykotsmovi. Then, on September 8, 1906, the Hostiles themselves were forced to leave Oraibi, establishing the village of Hotevilla. (A subsequent rift at Hotevilla sent the most conservative element to establish the village of Bacavi in 1908.)

Oraibi's population, which numbered in the thousands in the seventeenth century, declined to fewer than a hundred by the middle of the twentieth century. Smallpox epidemics were recorded in 1760, 1840, and 1898. Between 1890 and 1904 the Hopi country was visited by alternating drought and torrential rains; clan lands were swept away, and Oraibi Wash was cut to bedrock, seriously lowering the water table.

Arrows for the Navajo Male Branch of Shootingway were made from reeds obtained at either Oraibi or Taos, New Mexico.

❖ Role in Hillerman Fiction:

The Dark Wind: Jim Chee passes through the villages of Oraibi, Hotevilla, and Bacavi on his way to see if Ben Gaines and Gail Pauling are still residing at the motel in the Hopi Cultural Center on Second Mesa (chap. 18).

Sawkatewa tells Jim Chee and Deputy Sheriff Cowboy Dashee about the Fog Clan coming to Oraibi at the end of its migration cycle (chap. 21).

ORAIBI WASH: (7600–4950 ft) Navajo and Coconino Counties, AZ. The Navajos call this 'Asdzání 'Ayáásh Bitooh ("Lady Behind's Spring"), or 'Asdzání Bitł'aa' Bikooh ("Woman's Derriere Canyon"). This 85-mile-long, intermittent stream heads on Black Mesa, near the northeast rim of the mesa, and flows south through the Hopi Reservation, passing a mile east of the village of Oraibi. It joins Polacca Wash a mile east of Red Lake.

✣ Role in Hillerman Fiction:
   The Dark Wind: Pauling flies his plane across Oraibi Wash on his way to landing in Wepo Wash (chap. 2).

OWL SPRING: (8400 ft) San Juan County, NM. The Navajo name is uncertain. This permanent water source is located at the east mouth of Narbona Pass (formerly Washington Pass).

✣ Role in Hillerman Fiction:
   The Ghostway: A young boy getting off the bus from Toadlena school tells the police he saw a green sedan on the road from Two Grey Hills (Hillerman spells it Gray) toward Owl Spring (chap. 2).

PADILLA MESA: (6000–6300 ft) Coconino County, AZ. To the Navajos, this place is Gad Dah Yisk'id ("Juniper Hill"), or Tsin Dah Yiskid ("Woody Hill"). This feature is actually a lower, 10-mile-long, southwesterly extension of Hopi Third Mesa. The English name was applied by geological surveyor Gregory in honor of Fray Juan Padilla of Coronado's 1540 expedition. Padilla was killed on the Great Plains by Kiowa or Kansas Indians.

   This region has been identified as being a pre–Bosque Redondo (pre-1864) Navajo grazing area.

✣ Role in Hillerman Fiction:
   The Dark Wind: Jim Chee drives past Newberry Mesa, Garces Mesa, Blue Point, and Padilla Mesa on his way to the Hopi cultural center to see if Ben Gaines and Gail Pauling are still in residence (chap. 18).

PAGE: (4310 ft) (Population: 6,598) Coconino County, AZ. Navajos call this town Da'deestł'in Hótsaa ("Big Dam") or Na'ní'á Hótsaa ("Big Span"). The largest community along a 720-mile stretch of the Colorado River, this town on the south shore of Lake Powell was born of the need for a place to house the construction crews building Glen Canyon Dam.

   On March 22, 1957, a 24.3-acre tract of land on Manson Mesa was traded to the Bureau of Reclamation from the Navajo Tribe in return for a similar parcel on McCracken Mesa (near Aneth, Utah). The community was first labeled "Page Government Camp," honoring John C. Page, a commissioner of the Bureau of Reclamation from 1937 to 1943, who died in 1955.

The camp was designed with a park, a school complex, a warehouse district, churches, and 300 permanent homes and 1000 mobile homes. After several major fluctuations in population following the completion of the dam project, the townspeople incorporated in 1975.

This community is also the home of Navajo Generating Station, constructed between April 22, 1970, and June 1976. The plant employs 700, and produces 2.5 million kilowatts with coal provided via a slurry pipeline and electric trains from the Peabody mines on Black Mesa. It uses 36,000 acre-feet of water per year, which comes out of Arizona's meager 50,000-acre-foot allotment of Colorado River water. The Navajos actually had first rights to this water, but they relinquished them in favor of employment preference at the plant and the privilege of purchasing power from the plant.

✤ Role in Hillerman Fiction:

The First Eagle: Gas suppliers from Page charge old man McGinnis a surcharge for hauling gas to his remote Short Mountain trading post (chap. 6). The deceased Anderson Nez had been spending most of his time in the region between Page and Tuba City when he contracted the plague (chap. 9). Five days before his death, Anderson Nez drove to Page with his mother before going to work with Al Woody; he showed no signs of illness (chap. 15).

PAINTED DESERT: (4400–6000 ft) Coconino, Navajo, and Apache Counties, AZ. The Navajos call this region Halchíítah, meaning "Among the Red Areas," a general descriptive term for this type of country. This huge crescent of badlands extends from the northern end of Marble Canyon southeast to Winslow and Holbrook, then northeast to the western periphery of the Defiance Plateau near Houck. This swath extends some 300 miles along the north bank of the Little Colorado River, and in places is over 25 miles wide. The name is derived from the variety of hues presented by the various exposed strata of sandstone, clay, volcanic soils, and rock—usually occurring in parallel layers.

One of the most accessible parts lies in the northern portion of Petrified Forest National Park, some 28 miles northeast of Holbrook, Arizona. Here the Fred Harvey Company once operated the Painted Desert Inn, which housed the well-known Adolph Schuster Indian basketry collection. The inn is now a Park Service facility.

Spanish explorers first came upon this vast region of grotesquely eroded desert in 1540. Its brilliant colors, ever-changing with the intensity of sunlight, led them to name it El Desierto Pintado—the Painted Desert. The name was officially applied by Lieutenant Ives in 1861.

✤ Role in Hillerman Fiction:

The Dark Wind: That portion of Wepo Wash where Pauling's plane crashed is in the Painted Desert (chap. 14).

Skinwalkers: A vast rain drenched the landscape from here north, all the way to Sleeping Ute Mountain (chap. 22).

Talking God: Just about everyone living north of the Painted Desert (and west of the Chuska Mountains) knew about Navajo Tribal Council-woman Agnes Tsosie (chap. 2).

PICURIS PUEBLO: (7500 ft) (Population: 1,882) Taos County, NM. The Navajo name is uncertain. Situated on the Rio Pueblo on the west slope of the Sangre de Cristo Mountains, about 18 miles south of Taos Pueblo, its sister northern Tiwa Pueblo. They are closely related linguistically to the Southern Tiwa pueblos of Sandia and Isleta. Excavations during the 1960s at Pot Creek Ruin near Picuris suggest that Picuris was occupied by at least A.D. 1250.

The first recorded European contact with Picuris was by the Gaspar Castaño de Sosa expedition of 1591. By 1620 Spanish missionaries had arrived and forced the occupants of Picuris to build the Mission of San Lorenzo. This church was ruled by Fray Martin de Arvide, a harsh believer in taxation to the point of starvation.

Picuris warriors were known to join other pueblos and the Spaniards in raids on the Navajos during the seventeenth century. Spanish Governor Don Bernardo Lopez de Mendizabal traded cattle for two Navajo captives from Picuris in the 1660s.

In 1680, Luis Tupato, governor of Picuris, was instrumental in the planning and leading of the Pueblo Revolt. About 20 Spaniards were killed and the mission destroyed at Picuris. Following the 1692 "peaceful" reconquest by Don Diego de Vargas, Picuris revolted twice more—in 1694 and 1696. Following the final revolt the Picuris Indians abandoned the pueblo and lived on the plains with Apachean groups for 10 years, returning—at about one-tenth their previous strength—in 1706. At least one Navajo was baptized here in October 1837, and again in October 1857. The first serious impact of American culture on the pueblo was when the United States opened a day school in 1899.

✤ Role in Hillerman Fiction:

Sacred Clowns: Santa Fe gallery owner Desmond Clark tells Joe Leaphorn that Pojoaque, Tesuque, and Picuris Pueblos may have lost their Lincoln Canes during troubled times (chap. 22).

PIÑON: (6315 ft) (Population: 468) Navajo County, AZ. Navajos call this community Be'ek'id 'Ahoodzání, meaning "Lake that has a Hole in It." This is a chapter village located in the rolling, partly wooded mesa country on southeast Black Mesa, at the junction of Navajo Routes 4 and 41, some 41 miles west of Chinle. The Spanish name is for the nut-bearing evergreen.

Captain John Walker and two companies of Mounted Rifles were the first Americans known to have traversed this wild region, traveling northwest from near Salina to Marsh Pass in 1859. Walker described the region as a largely uninhabited series of broken hills, mesas, and canyons.

Walker warned that in case of war with the United States, the Navajos could easily conceal themselves in this "…labyrinth of hills, valleys and arroyos. Discovering their hiding places would be as difficult as it was to find the Seminoles in the Everglades of Florida." To this day, the region remains isolated, and is populated by extremely conservative Navajos.

In October 1939, Ramon Hubbell and Evon Vogt found old Spanish inscriptions in this vicinity, near a spring the Navajos called Naakaiitó ("Mexican Water"). The Navajos thought that the inscriptions had been left there by a party of Spanish or Mexicans who had killed some Navajos near Ganado and then proceeded northwest. A part of the cliff had fallen off, covering the inscriptions, and the explorers lacked the tools for the removal of the rocks.

Piñon Trading Post opened during the first decade of this century, possibly founded by Lorenzo Hubbell, Jr. His cousin George Hubbell (and George's wife, Madge) ran it during the 1930s. It was operated at one time by the Foutz brothers, and later by Bruce McGee. Bill Malone managed it for McGee in the late 1970s, before moving to Hubbell Trading Post.

A new 25,000-square-foot shopping center was completed in Piñon on Sunday, December 12, 1993, replacing 13.1 acres of juniper scrub land in the heart of the Navajo Nation with a grocery store, a video rental outlet, and a pizzeria.

✤ Role in Hillerman Fiction:

Skinwalkers: Figuring Jim Chee has to drive through here to get from Badwater to Dinnebito Wash, Joe Leaphorn tries to have him intercepted by Officer Leonard Skeet, the policeman assigned to work out of the Piñon Chapter House (chap. 19). Later, Leaphorn himself drives through here in pursuit of Chee (chap. 21).

PIUTKI: Hillerman borrows the name of an ancient Hopi settlement for this village, which is the scene of some key action in *The Dark Wind*.

✤ Role in Hillerman Fiction:

The Dark Wind: In this First Mesa village, Chee finds the elusive vandal of Windmill No. 6, as well as a witness to the crash of Pauling's airplane (chap. 21).

POJOAQUE PUEBLO: (5905 ft) (Population: 2,556) Santa Fe County, NM. The Navajo name remains uncertain. The Spanish name Pojoaque is probably borrowed from the Tewa "posuwaege," meaning "drink-water place," although another possibility is that it is a corruption of "povi age," Santa Clara meaning "place where the flowers grow along the stream."

This small Tewa village located 16 miles north of Santa Fe, on the Pojoaque River, is related linguistically to Nambe, San Ildefonso, Santa Clara, San Juan, and Tesuque Pueblos. It is the least "pueblo-like" village, conducting no ceremonies, and having no cacique (the last died in 1900). It has always been one of the smallest Tewa villages.

As with all the Rio Grande Pueblos, Pojoaque's ancestors were in the area by A.D. 900. The community likely was initiated in the 1300s, with an influx of Tewas into the region. The pueblo probably saw first European contact in the mid-sixteenth century, and its inhabitants took an active role in the Pueblo Revolt of 1680. For this they suffered greatly during de Vargas's "peaceful" Reconquest in 1692, and subsequently lost great chunks of its fertile land through the years.

By 1712, only 79 people lived at Pojoaque. After the village was very hard hit by the 1918 influenza epidemic, it was described as being abandoned. Those occupying the pueblo since it was resettled in 1934 are a mixture of Tewas, Tiwas, and Hispanic.

During the 1990s, the pueblo constructed a casino and became almost militant in defense of its rights to operate such a facility. More than once, the governor of the pueblo threatened to close the highway between Santa Fe and Los Alamos if the state of New Mexico tried to force closure of the casino.

This was the first pueblo to elect a female governor.

✤ Role in Hillerman Fiction:

Sacred Clowns: Santa Fe gallery owner Desmond Clark tells Joe Leaphorn that Pojoaque, Tesuque, and Picuris Pueblos may have lost their Lincoln Canes during troubled times (chap. 22).

POLACCA WASH: (7200–4900 ft) Navajo County, AZ. The Navajo name remains uncertain. One of five major drainages of Black Mesa (the others are Dinnebito, Oraibi, Wepo, and Moenkopi Washes), Polacca Wash heads 10 miles north of Lohali Point on the easternmost point of the mesa. The 85-mile-long wash flows southwest between Whippoorwill Spring Mesa and Balakai Mesa and northwest of Low Mountain. It skirts southeast of Polacca and continues another 45 miles before joining Jadito Wash to form Corn Creek Wash. A tributary of the Little Colorado River.

The earliest Spanish maps of this region, dating to the early 1700s, refer to this as Arroyo de Moqui ("Moqui Wash"). (The Spanish referred to the Hopi as Moqui.)

✤ Role in Hillerman Fiction:

The Dark Wind: This normally dry channel, filled to a raging torrent by a heavy thunderstorm, becomes backdrop to the confrontation between Burnt Water trader Jake West and DEA agent Johnson (chap. 30).

POPPING ROCK: (6000 ft) San Juan County, NM. The Navajo name is uncertain. This 200-foot-high sandstone outcrop stands at the southern end of a small peninsula of Mesa Verde, above Salt Creek Canyon. It is about 15 miles northwest of the community of Shiprock, less than two miles south of the Colorado state line. Approximately two miles to the east is Thieving Rock.

✤ Role in Hillerman Fiction:

The Fallen Man: Jim Chee has been spying on possible rustlers here when he's confronted by a Ute Mountain Tribal cop over jurisdiction (chap. 2).

PUEBLO PINTADO: (6480 ft) McKinley County, NM. In Navajo, the Anasazi ruin is called Kinteel ("Wide House"), or Kinteel Ch'ínílíní ("Wide House Outflow"), a name also applied to the Aztec West great house at Aztec National Monument. The same names have come to refer to the community, about a mile and half south of the ruin.

This trading and BIA school point on Navajo Route 9, just north of the "big bend" of New Mexico Highway 197, is some 60 miles northeast of Thoreau. A trading post was erected here between 1910 and 1915.

Pueblo Pintado Ruin is also known as Pueblo Colorado, Pueblo Montezuma, Pueblo Grande (and, erroneously, Pueblo Alto). This Chacoan greathouse community—with a Mesa Verdean reoccupation—overlooks the Chaco River, and dates to A.D. 1060. It contains 161 rectilinear rooms (including many that are two- and three-story) in an "L" shape. Two single-story wings connect the larger roomblocks to an enclosed plaza in near "D" shape. A great kiva lies near the southwest corner. A prehistoric road extends from the southwest corner to Chaco Canyon. There are about a dozen other Anasazi ruins of smaller size within a mile of the main structure.

This ruin is named in the Navajo Excessway, Waterway, and Shootingway, and is the starting point of Beadway. It is important to the tales of the Navajo Tsé Ńjíkiní, "Honey Combed Rock People" Clan. Navajo traditions on clan development include Pueblo Pintado:

> Jiní. Fourteen years after the Hashk'ąą Hadzohó Dine'é, "Yucca Fruit Strung Out in a Line People," came to join the nuclear Navajo clans, the tribe moved to Pueblo Pintado. It was deserted then. They spread out and camped there at night. Their many camp fires attracted the attention of some wanderers on Chacra Mesa.
>
> On the next morning, the strangers came down to see who the numerous people were who had made the camp fires. When asked from whence they came, the wanderers said that they came from Nihoobá, south of Zuni. [Note that Young and Morgan, in their 1987 volume *The Navajo Language* (University of New Mexico Press), locate Nihoobá between Torreon and Mount Taylor.] They had been driven from their country by enemies. The Navajos called them Nihoobáanii ["Gray Line Ending People"]). They made their camp with the Nihoobáanii Dine'é and the Dził Ná'oodiłnii Dine'é [people of the place called "Mountain that People Go Around"—see Huerfano Mountain]. These people then became members of the Navajo tribe. (Van Valkenburgh 1941, 117)

❖ Role in Hillerman Fiction:

People of Darkness: Jim Chee determines that Roscoe Sam (a survivor of the oil rig explosion) lived either here or at Ojo Encino. This ruin is named in the Navajo Excessway, Waterway, and Shootingway, and is the starting point of Beadway (chap. 22).

RAINBOW PLATEAU: (4800–5726 ft) Coconino County, AZ, San Juan County, UT. The Navajo name is uncertain. This extensive highland rises on the south bank of the San Juan River and extends approximately 25 miles to the south. It is bounded on the west by Navajo Canyon, and on the east by Piute Creek, a distance of about 30 miles.

The plateau gives rise to Navajo Mountain, Cummings Mesa, and Nasja Mesa, and houses Rainbow Bridge (probably the source of the plateau's name), Forbidding Canyon, Oak Canyon, Cha Canyon, and countless other cuts and ravines.

❖ Role in Hillerman Fiction:

Listening Woman: Leaphorn (with assistance from Corporal Emerson Bisti) had to search for Gold Rims in this broken, canyon-laced country along the Utah-Arizona state line (chap. 41). Rainbow Plateau is also the location of the (fictional) Short Mountain Trading Post (chap. 4).

The First Eagle: Joe Leaphorn finds Richard Krouse, wearing an "elephant suit," hunting mice along this creek, where it runs into Chaol Canyon, atop the Rainbow Plateau (chap. 20).

RAMAH: (6950 ft) (Population: approx. 1,000, of whom 194 are Navajo) Cibola County, NM. Formerly Seveyo, a corruption of Cebolla, Spanish for "Onions." The Navajo name is Tłohchiní, "Wild Onions" (Allium palmeri). This Mormon farming community straddles New Mexico Highway 53 in a wide, green valley on a south fork of upper Zuni River, eight miles east of El Morro National Monument. It is surrounded by scenic mesa country breaking from the southeastern slopes of the Zuni Mountains.

The town is the trading center for the Ramah Navajos (Tłohchin Dine'e or "Wild Onion People"). Schools are operated by Gallup-McKinley County Schools. Several trading posts have operated in the vicinity, including Red and White; Ramah; Bond Brothers, opened between 1916 and 1920, and Lambson, opened between 1931 and 1935, both closing before 1950; and Ashcroft Trading Post.

The first Mormon missionaries in the region were sent by Brigham Young to Zuni in 1876, forming a colony at the foot of the Zuni Mountains some five miles west of the present village. In 1877, the colony was nearly wiped out by smallpox, and it was largely abandoned by 1880. Bishop Joseph Tietjen and one Pitkin, Mormon missionaries, left the town of Sunset with their families and settled at Seboyeta, some three miles north of the present townsite, and named it Navajo. It was changed to Ramah (pronounced *Ray*-mah, the name of a hill where, according to the Book of Mormon, sacred records are stored) because another village was already named Navajo. The community's first post office came later, in 1886.

Other families from the decaying Sunset soon joined them and a dam was built across Seboyeta Canyon, one mile east of Ramah. The impounded waters of Ramah Lake provided permanent water storage. In 1915, the population was augmented by the arrival of five families from the Mexican Mormon colonies of Chuchupa, Colonia, and Naco in the state of Chihuahua, brought north by unsettled political conditions in Mexico. During the 1920s a number of Texan ranchers moved into the area.

The Ramah Navajo Reservation is an isolated section of the Navajo Reservation lying mostly south of New Mexico Highway 53, in the vicinity of Ramah and El Morro National Monument. The reservation is roughly 25 miles north-south by 15 miles east-west. Its chapter house, BIA school, and compound sit on Navajo Route 125, about six miles south of El Morro.

❖ Role in Hillerman Fiction:

Dance Hall of the Dead: At Ramah Leaphorn receives instructions by radio to go to Zuni because of the disappearance of 14-year-old George Bowlegs, a Navajo (chap. 2). Shorty Bowlegs's family is from Ramah (chaps. 9, 13).

RATTLESNAKE: (5200 ft) San Juan County, NM. Navajos call this place Siláo 'Atiin, meaning "Soldier Road" or "Soldier Trail." This oil-pumping station is located in the rolling plains north of Shiprock (Pinnacle). A trading post existed here from the early 1940s until the early 1960s.

Here, beside Shiprock Wash, is a 4,800-acre oil field opened in 1923 by the Continental Oil Company (Conoco), which was producing some 500 barrels of high-gravity crude oil daily by 1941. The contract with the Navajo Nation called for the Navajos to receive $3,000,000 plus a 12.5 percent royalty on oil produced.

In 1926, the Navajo Tribal Council signed an agreement that extended the lease indefinitely, making it possible for the oil company or its successors to operate as long as oil and gas are available. A pipeline connected the field with a small refinery at Farmington. The wells also supply a limited amount of natural gas for use in government establishments on the reservation.

❖ Role in Hillerman Fiction:

The Fallen Man: Jim Chee has to go rescue Officer Bernadette Manuelito, who has gotten her police cruiser stuck in snow south of here as she was investigating rustling (chap. 9). This area is linked to the outside world by Navajo Communications Company lines (chap. 11).

RECAPTURE CREEK: (9000–4000 ft) San Juan County, UT. The Navajo name is Dził Dił'oo'í Bikooh ("Fuzzy Mountain Creek"). This 35-mile-long stream rises on the southern slope of the Abajo Mountains, and flows south, skirting to the east of White Mesa. It drains Bluff Bench and enters the San Juan River five miles east of Bluff.

This creek was named around 1877 by a man named Peter Shirts, who, for some reason, believed that the Aztec emperor Montezuma had escaped his Spanish captors in Mexico and was recaptured here.

❖ Role in Hillerman Fiction:

Hunting Badger: Joe Leaphorn visits Oliver Potts at his ranch on Recapture Creek, five miles northwest of Bluff, Utah, one mile down a dirt road (chap. 7). Everett Jorie's computer file suggests looking for Ironhand and Baker near Recapture Creek, below the Bluff Bench and south of White Mesa Ute Reservation (chap. 9). Officer Bernadette Manuelito mans a roadblock between Recapture Creek and the Montezuma Creek bridge; Chee arrives to assist—uninvited, thinking she is not prepared for real circumstances (chap. 16).

RED LAKE: (7000 ft) Apache County, AZ. Navajos call this body Be'ek'id Halchíí ("Red Lake"), for its reddish color, created by silt. This small, semi-artificial lake sits at the north end of Black Creek Valley (north of Fort Defiance) between the Chuska Mountains and the Defiance Plateau.

Fed by ephemeral streams—mostly originating on the western slopes of the Chuska Mountains and flowing through Todilto (Tó Dildǫ', "Popping Water") Park in New Mexico—the lake is held in check by a dam constructed by the Indian Service (later to become the BIA) to replace an earlier one built by to the south by Navajos. It watered 128 acres of farm land below it in Black Creek Valley.

Black Creek flows south from this lake through Black Lake and on to the Rio Puerco of the West.

Red Lake is important in the Navajo Sǫ'tsohjí ("Big Star") Ceremony. The volcanic plugs near Red Lake are reputed to have once been giant ant hills, and the long white ridge running along the east side of the lake from the base of Fuzzy Mountain and cut by Todilto Wash was once the home of a big snake.

This Red Lake is not to be confused with Tolani Lake(s), also called Red Lake, approximately 15 miles northwest of Leupp.

❖ Role in Hillerman Fiction:

Coyote Waits: Joe Leaphorn and Professor Louisa Bourebonette traverse Narbona Pass in the Chuska Mountains, passing through Red Lake, Arizona, and Crystal, New Mexico, on their way from Window Rock to Shiprock (chap. 12).

RED LAKE TRADING POST: (5500 ft) Coconino County, AZ. Also Tonalea. The Navajo name is Tó Nehélįįh ("Water Flows and Collects"). This small trading center sits on U.S. Highway 160, about 21 miles northwest of Moenkopi, below the north rim of Black Mesa.

George Washington McAdams founded this post at the location later to become known as Tonalea around 1878. In 1881, it was run by Joseph M. Lee (son of John D. Lee of Lee's Ferry) as a canvas-topped shack that occupied two different locations. In 1885, George McManus moved the store back to its original location, and sold out to "Ditt" Dittenhoffer, who was killed in a lover's quarrel at the post in 1890. Babbitt Brothers moved the post to its present location and built the two-story structure.

According to Navajo rug expert H. L. James, subsequent managers were

Figure 32. Rustic Red Lake Trading Post remains in business as of this publication, despite the large, modern convenience store and gas station a mile to the west at Tonalea.

Sam Preston (1891–97), H. K. Warren (1897–1905), Earl Boyer (1905–18), Johnny O'Farrell (1918–35), Floyd Boyle (1935–53), Coit Patterson (1953–55), Harold Lockhart (1955–73), and Jerry Norris (1973–87).

Red Lake Trading Post became famous for storm-pattern Navajo rugs, and its businesses eventually gave rise to a chapter community.

❖ Role in Hillerman Fiction:

The First Eagle: Al Woody admits to Leaphorn that he'd seen the missing Catherine Ann Pollard in the area earlier, up at Red Lake (chap. 13). (Since she was filling the gas tank on a Health Service Jeep, it must have been Red Lake Trading Post in Arizona, as opposed to the body of water named Red Lake in New Mexico.)

RED MESA and **RED MESA CHAPTER:** (5500 ft) Apache County, AZ. Navajos call this area Tsé Łichii Dah' Azkání, meaning "Red Rock Mesa." Located 15 miles west of Teec Nos Pos, at the juncture of U.S. Highway 160 and Navajo Route 35. An Arizona Public School district is located here to serve students of the region. The Red Mesa Chapter house is actually about five miles to the north, in San Juan County, Utah.

In Navajo mythology, Monster Slayer killed Déégééd here, staining the sand red with the monster's blood.

❖ Role in Hillerman Fiction:

The Ghostway: Jim Chee drives 70 miles over snowpacked highways, passing through Teec Nos Pos, Red Mesa, Mexican Water, and Dinnehotso, on his way to Frank Sam Nakai's winter place (chap. 24).

Coyote Waits: According to Ashie Pinto's tape, his grandfather told him that Utes from the Ladron Peak region used to travel down Tsitah Wash to raid on Navajos in the Red Mesa vicinity (chap. 7).

Hunting Badger: Professor Louisa Bourebonette needs to talk to anthropological informants at the Red Mesa Chapter House and Towoac (chap. 6). Eldon Timms's "missing" L-17 airplane is found in a hay shed near Red Mesa (chap. 10).

RED ROCK and **RED ROCK TRADING POST:** (5800 ft) Apache County, AZ. Also called Red Valley. Navajos call this vicinity Tsé Łichíí Dah 'Azkání, which means "Red Rock Mesa" (the same as Red Mesa, above). This small trading community lies on the Arizona side of the Arizona–New Mexico state line, but the only paved road offering access is in New Mexico (Navajo Route 13, which intersects U.S. Highway 666 roughly six miles south of Shiprock village).

The scenery is both stark and beautiful. Red sandstone buttes and ridges intermix with black lava plugs (including the massive Shiprock Pinnacle 12 miles to the east) in a sandy region (that appears to have been badly overgrazed), all nestled at the foot of the forested Lukachukai and Carrizo Mountains.

The first trading post at Red Rock was built in 1900 by James Walker and Walter Whitecroft. Olin C. Walker managed the post between 1906 and 1908. In 1918, the post was purchased by Willis Martin, who hired as manager Roswell Nelson, son of Charlie Nelson of Newcomb Trading Post.

The walls were 18 inches thick, constructed by the unusual method of pouring a mixture of adobe and stone into forms made of wood placed directly on the wall.

✤ Role in Hillerman Fiction:

Skinwalkers: Roosevelt Bistie's daughter does her laundry in Red Rock on the second Monday in July (chap. 3).

A Thief of Time: After wrecking Janet Pete's car, Jim Chee spends most of the morning at Red Rock, trying to figure out how to tell her what he'd done (chap. 5).

Coyote Waits: Officer Nez, pursuing his "rock-painter," is murdered near Red Rock—while Officer Jim Chee flirts with the clerk at the Trading Post (chap. 1). The community is located in a triangle created by Shiprock, the Carrizo Mountains, and the Chuska Mountains (chap. 1).

The Fallen Man: Jim Chee receives a report of rustling from a grazing lease west of Red Rock (chap. 8). Officer Bernadette Manuelito is from the Red Rock area, conveniently close to Shiprock, where she works (chap. 9). This area is linked to the outside world by Navajo Communications Company lines (chap. 11).

RED WASH: (8000–4800 ft) San Juan County, NM, Apache County, AZ. The Navajo name is uncertain. Contrary to what is shown in the venerable AAA Indian Country Map, 30-mile-long Red Wash heads on the west face of Beautiful Mountain (not in the Carrizo Mountains). It flows northwest past The Thumb and through Red Rock village before turning to a more north-north-easterly route. It merges with the San Juan River about halfway between Shiprock community and Teec Nos Pos.

✤ Role in Hillerman Fiction:

The Fallen Man: The Sam family built a home between Red Wash and Little Shiprock Wash (chap. 11).

RIO PUERCO (OF THE EAST): (approx. 8000–4600 ft) Sandoval, Bernalillo, Valencia, and Socorro counties, NM. To the Navajos, this is Na-sisitge, possibly a rendering of Na'azísí Tó, meaning "Gopher Water." This river heads some five miles northeast of Cuba, and flows into the Rio Grande at Bernardo, approximately midway between Belen and Socorro. It is the second longest tributary of the Rio Grande, and, early in the American period, this was the only tributary that did not run dry before merging with the larger river.

Navajos ranged freely throughout the watershed of the Rio Puerco of the East prior to the Bosque Redondo period. After they returned from the Bosque, some settled in this region rather than within the boundaries of the reservation.

✤ Role in Hillerman Fiction:

The Ghostway: From Jimmy Yellow's place on Mesa Gigante, the view is extraordinary, taking in the valley of the Rio Puerco, the Sandia Mountains and the lights of Albuquerque to the east, and the Sangre de Cristos to the north (chap. 25).

ROL HAI ROCK: (5600 ft) San Juan County, NM. Also spelled Rol Hay Rock. The Navajo name is uncertain, though Rol Hai may be a corruption of a Navajo word or term. This gigantic boulder of sandstone lies just north of the northern tip of Table Mesa, and was likely part of the same structure. It measures over 200 feet in height.

✤ Role in Hillerman Fiction:

Coyote Waits: According to Ashie Pinto's grandfather's story, Delbito Willie saw two White men riding between Rol Hai Rock and Little Water Wash, apparently traveling toward Beautiful Mountain (chap. 11).

The Fallen Man: The road to Maryboy's hogan leads Jim Chee toward Rol Hai Rock and Table Mesa (chap. 19).

Figure 33. The black basalt of Rol Hai Rock contrasts sharply with the red and buff sandstone of the larger Table Mesa, just a few hundred yards to the south.

The First Eagle: Newly graduated officer Joe Leaphorn had driven from Shiprock to investigate skinwalkers near Rol Hai Rock and Table Mesa (chap. 6).

ROOF BUTTE: (9784 ft) Apache County, AZ. Navajos call this striking formation Dził Dah Neeztínii, "Mountain that Lay Down," although it is also translated as "Where the Mountain Went Out on Top." It is also called 'Adáá Dik'á, "Slanted (roof-shaped) Rim," which is apparently the source of the English name.

This remarkable, majestic butte—the highest point in the Lukachukai Mountains—is located 10 miles northeast of Lukachukai. The butte is sacred to the Navajos.

The name Roof Butte was first applied to another high elevation near Dził Dah Neezłínii, by Professor Sin, a school teacher and farmer at Lukachukai.

Figure 34. Roof butte stands higher than the surrounding mesas and buttes, surpassing even the Chuska Mountains in its reach for the sky.

That butte is actually called 'Adáá'dilkóóh ("Smooth on Edge"), and rises to 9340 ft. Yet another peak named Roof Butte rises in the White Mountains of west-central Arizona.

The Navajo medicine men tell of Dził Dah Neezłínii:

> Tsé Nináhálééh ("Picking Up Feathers"), a big bird that lived on top of Shiprock Pinnacle came to Dził Dah Neeztínii to get men. Never Women. He went there every day. He is not here any more, but lives in the Sun's house. He was the child of the Sun and Changing Woman. This is told in the Naayée'ee Hatáál. (Van Valkenburgh 1941, 127)

❖ Role in Hillerman Fiction:

Skinwalkers: Roosevelt Bistie's daughter tells Chee that her father saw a hand trembler between Roof Butte and and Lukachukai to find out what was making him sick (chap. 16).

ROUGH ROCK: (6500 ft) (Population: 523) Apache County, AZ. The Navajo name is Tséch'ízhí, which means "Rough Rock." This trading point and chapter house on Navajo Route 59 sits at the foot of the eastern scarp of Black Mesa, almost midway between Many Farms and Chilchinbito. The first trading post was opened here in the late 1920s.

After an abortive effort at Lukachukai, the Navajo Nation's first operative community school, called a "demonstration school," was opened at Rough Rock in 1966. It showed that the Navajo communities could govern their own schools, relieving the Bureau of Indian Affairs of that responsibility.

❖ Role in Hillerman Fiction:

People of Darkness: Rough Rock is the home of Jim Chee's clan, the Slow Talking Diné (chap. 2). Frank Sam Nakai sometimes taught Chee about ceremonialism here (chap. 11).

Figure 35. The old Rough Rock Trading Post sits at the foot of Black Mesa, amid the administration and maintenance buildings for the schools of the community.

Skinwalkers: Officer Leonard Skeet, working out of the Piñon Chapter House, is at Rough Rock when Joe Leaphorn urgently tries to contact him to intercept Jim Chee at Piñon (chap. 19).

A Thief of Time: When Slick Nakai's mother died at Rough Rock, his uncles came and took her body away and put it where the ravens and coyotes couldn't get at it (chap. 4).

Hunting Badger: Jim Chee grew up at Rough Rock, where people could obtain coal by digging shallow pits (chap. 19).

ROUND ROCK: (6020 ft) Apache County, AZ. The Navajos call this feature Tsé Nikání, or "Round Flat-Topped Rock." It is a rounded sandstone butte some 600 ft high, midway between Chinle Wash and Agua Sal Creek, a couple miles north of U.S. Highway 191.

According to historian Lynn R. Bailey, Round Rock is likely the "Piedra Rodilla" (Spanish possibly meaning "Knee Rock") explored by Captain John G. Walker's 1858 expedition.

Traditional Navajos will not climb the precipitous sides of this sacred rock for fear of punishment by lightning, snakes, whirlwinds, or bears. They tell the following tradition of the rock:

> It was during the time when the Navajos were at war with the Utes. The Navajos made two arrows with eyes. As they were going down the Chinle Valley, the Navajos saw the Utes coming from the north. As soon as the Utes got behind Round Rock, the Navajos shot one of the arrows and clipped off the top of the mesa. The sliding rock killed most of the Utes and the rest ran off because they were outnumbered. (Van Valkenburgh 1941, 127)

About six miles east of the butte, at the junction of U.S. Highway 191 and Navajo Route 12, is a trading post called Bis Dootł'izhí Deez'áhí ("Blue Clay Point") by the Navajos. This post, cited by historian Van Valkenburgh as the first in the region, was established by Stephen Aldrich of Manuelito, a former cavalryman and veteran of the Apache campaigns in 1885. It was managed by Chee Dodge, and was visited by Benjamin Alfred Wetherill and Baron Gustof Nordenskiöld of the Stockholm Museum in November 1891. C. N. Cotton purchased the post from Aldrich in 1911.

Combative Navajo Agent Henry F. Shipley took shelter in this post in October 1892 after an abortive meeting with Navajo headman Black Horse and his followers, who were resisting the taking of Indian children to the distant boarding schools. The badly beaten Shipley, already suffering a broken nose and bruises, was dragged into the trading post by Chee Dodge and others, saving his life. They were besieged in the post for 36 hours, during which time

Figure 36. Round Rock, the isolated, round, sandstone mesa for which the community was named.

Black Horse's followers continuously jeered them and threatened to kill them. A Navajo policeman accompanying Shipley slipped away and returned with a contingent of 11 soldiers, breaking up the siege. Shipley returned to Fort Defiance without any children from the Round Rock area.

Interestingly, Black Horse apparently was not resisting the forced education, but was protesting the crowded conditions of the boarding schools, the rampant illnesses among their students, and the poor food.

East of Round Rock and beyond the trading post, there is a Navajo shrine called Yé'ii Shijéé' ("Ye'iis Lying Down"), first discovered around 1840 by Washington Matthews's great informant, Hataałii Nééz. The Navajos tell that he went to sleep in a cave that is across the canyon from an Anasazi ruin. He heard singing in the cave where the shrine is, and in the morning went up and saw sculptured figures about 18 inches high. Navajos question whether they are of Navajo or Anasazi origin. Offerings of turquoise are made to them.

✤ Role in Hillerman Fiction:

The Blessing Way: After inquiring about Luis Horseman at Shoemaker's Trading Post, Joe Leaphorn travels through Round Rock on his way back to Window Rock (chap. 4). Joe Leaphorn drove past Round Rock, Agua Sal Creek, Many Farms, and Seklagaidesi while trying to figure out what the Big Navajo was doing on Ceniza Mesa (chap. 15).

The Ghostway: After failing to reach Frank Sam Nakai's winter place via Greasewood Flats, Jim Chee circles back and drives through Round Rock, Many Farms, and Chinle, to the south side of Black Mesa, past Cottonwood and Blue Gap, before attempting to mount Carson Mesa again from the south (chap. 24).

ROUND TOP TRADING POST: (approx. 6400 ft) Apache County, AZ. The Navajo name is uncertain. This is one of three trading posts historian Van

Valkenburgh identified as doing business in Ganado in 1941. (The others were Hubbell Trading Post and Ganado Trading Post.) In the early 1990s it was operated by Norman Gorman, Navajo.

✤ **Role in Hillerman Fiction:**
Skinwalkers: Shy Girl, from the Beno camp, watched Jim Chee as he stopped at Round Top Trading Post for a Pepsi (chap. 1).

SABITO WASH: (6500–5500 ft) Apache and Navajo Counties, AZ. The Navajo name is uncertain. This 20-mile-long tributary of Leroux Wash lies in the flats of the Painted Desert, a few miles north of the northern boundary of Petrified Forest National Park. Leroux Wash, a tributary of the Little Colorado River, was named Leroux Fork by Lieutenant Whipple in 1856, for Antoine Leroux, the guide for his expedition across Arizona. It may well be that this expedition also visited Sabito Wash.

✤ **Role in Hillerman Fiction:**
The Blessing Way: Luis Horseman calls this region home (chap. 4).

ST. JOHNS: (5733 ft) (Population: 3,443) Apache County, AZ. To the Navajos, this community is Tsézhin Deez'áhí ("Ridge that Runs Out to a Point") or Chézhin Deez'áhí ("Lava Point"). A Mormon farming and livestock community, St. Johns is situated on the Little Colorado River at the junction of U.S. Highways 666 and 180. It has been the Apache County seat since 1879.

Early Spanish explorers named this vicinity El Vadito del Rio Chiquito Colorado ("Little Crossing of the Little Colorado River"). The location was later called San Juan ("Saint John"), possibly after the Feast of San Juan (held June 24), or after a woman named Senora Maria San Juan Baca de Padilla.

In 1863, U.S. troops attacked Navajos in this vicinity. In 1866, W. R. Milligan, one of the first White settlers in Apache County, settled in a valley near the future St. Johns (though he later moved to Round Valley). Four years later, Frank Walker, a mail and express carrier between Fort Wingate, New Mexico, and Fort Apache, Arizona, built a shack at The Meadows, a crossing of the Little Colorado River some five miles north of the present site of St. Johns. In 1871 a few Spanish-Americans gathered in the vicinity, and in the spring of 1872 they established an agricultural settlement at the town's present location.

Solomon Barth and his brothers, Nathan and Morris, began farming activities in 1873. In 1879, a Mormon named Ammon M. Tenney bought out Barth's activities. In 1880, Wilford Woodruff, President of the Mormon Church, picked a spot about a mile north of St. Johns for a Mormon settlement, but later moved it to higher ground adjoining the Spanish-American settlement. By 1884, there were 586 Mormons living at St. Johns. The first newspaper was published by C. A. Franklin in July 1882.

In addition to being a major Mormon stronghold (Jacob Hamblin, famed Mormon missionary and Indian agent, is buried at Alpine, a village some 60 miles south of St. Johns), this rough, remote region was a favorite haunt for many notorious bad men, and was used as a base and hideout for operations in southern Arizona.

The location is mentioned prominently in the Navajo Mothway myth. The U.S. Indian Claims Commission studies suggest that Navajos have traditionally gathered nuts and berries in this region, and between 1870 and 1890, Navajos did considerable business in St. Johns. The region is also a traditional grazing area for Zunis.

✦ Role in Hillerman Fiction:

Skinwalkers: The Apache County Sheriff's office, based at St. Johns, could conceivably respond to a call at Sanostee, especially if the call was "officer down" (chap. 14).

ST. MICHAELS: (7000 ft) (Population: 1,119) Apache County, AZ. Navajos refer to this community as Ts'íhootso, meaning "Yellow Meadow" or "Area that Extends Out Yellow and Green." This Franciscan mission and school and chapter community on the eastern slope of the Defiance Plateau is situated on Arizona Highway 264 three miles west of Window Rock. Early Spanish documents called this locale Cienega Amarilla ("Yellow Meadow"). In 1850, in the first English mention of the place, Lieutenant James H. Simpson called it Cienega de Maria (almost certainly a corruption of Cienega Amarilla).

The mission is located above a well watered, wooded, and verdant meadow on the west slopes of Black Creek Valley. Traders in the region have included Stewart-Weid (opened in the early 1880s and closed about 1900); Wilkin-Wyatt (opened in the late 1880s); Sam Day (opened shortly after 1900); Osborne and Walker (opened in 1902); and Frazier, Kuhn, and McMahon Trading Posts.

In the 1850s the hillside near St. Michaels was the scene of a planned ambush by the Mexicans on the Navajos. It was frustrated by Chách'oshnééz ("Tall Syphilis") of the Diné 'Ana'í ("Enemy Navajos"—see Cañoncito, New Mexico), who accompanied the Mexicans from Cebolleta. While the Navajos and Mexicans were making arrangements to exchange slaves, the Mexicans planted a cannon in a hidden spot, planning to fire it into the Navajos when they were all assembled. Chách'oshnééz went to the Navajo camp and warned them. They invited him to join them. He accepted and was later one of the signers of the Treaty of 1868 under the name of Delgadito.

The Franciscan mission and school were established in 1898 by Father Juvenal Schnorbus with Father Anselm Weber as assistant. The site was donated by the Reverend Mother Katherine Drexel, head of the Sisters of the Blessed Heart of Philadelphia. The mission was for many years the headquarters of Father Weber's fight for protection of Navajo lands. These missionaries are often credited with being the first to reduce the Navajo language to writing, but linguist/historian Robert Young notes that the first extensive writing of Navajo was actually by Captain J. H. Eaton at Fort Defiance beginning in 1852. Eaton's extensive word lists were published in Henry Roe Schoolcraft's 1856 "History, Condition and Prospects of the Indian Tribes of the United States."

The Franciscans operate from here in general field work with the Navajos. The Sisters of the Blessed Heart manage the boarding school.

✤ **Role in Hillerman Fiction:**

The Fallen Man: To Jim Chee, Hosteen Sam's handwriting is reminiscent of the padres from St. Michaels School (chap. 18).

SALMON RUIN: (5400 ft) San Juan County, NM. The Navajo name for this large Anasazi ruin is Kin Dootłizhí, or "Blue House" (the same name applied to Wijiji in Chaco Canyon). A Chacoan great-house community, or "outlier," this ruin is located on a bench above the valley floor of the north bank of the San Juan River two miles west of Bloomfield. It dates to A.D. 1088–1263, and contains at least 183 rectilinear rooms and 18 round rooms in a shallow U-shape. A great kiva lies in the plaza. As at nearby Aztec Ruin, Type II Chacoan masonry occurs here long after its apparent demise at Chaco Canyon. A prehistoric road may run from the opposite bank of the San Juan River toward Kutz Canyon.

Archaeologists have determined that Salmon was built and occupied by Chacoans, who abandoned it about A.D. 1150. It was then reoccupied and partially rebuilt by Mesa Verdeans around A.D. 1210. Forty years later, some 50 children and one adult female died in a fire when a kiva roof on which they were standing collapsed. The ruin appears in the Navajo Enemyway, Blessingway, Waterway, and Beautyway.

The name Salmon came from a nineteenth-century homesteader, George Salmon, on whose land the ruin was discovered.

✤ **Role in Hillerman Fiction:**

A Thief of Time: Anthropologist Eleanor Friedman-Bernal had traced one of her potter's pots to Salmon Ruin (chap. 6).

SALT CREEK WASH: (6500–4900 ft) San Juan County, NM. Also Salt Creek. The Navajo name is Tó Dík'ǫ́ǫ́zh Bikooh ("Salt Water Canyon"). The upper reaches are labeled Salt Water Canyon on USGS maps.

This tributary of the San Juan River northeast of Shiprock and south of

Mancos Creek is important in the Navajo Emergence myths, which place Navajo ancestors in this vicinity.

❖ **Role in Hillerman Fiction:**

The Ghostway: Aside from the banks of the San Juan River, the only places where the silver trailer house could be sitting in a cottonwood grove would be Salt Creek Wash and Little Pajarito Arroyo (chap. 10).

The Fallen Man: Acting Lieutenant Jim Chee is approaching the wash on U.S. Highway 666 when he is passed by a Porsche doing at least 95 mph (chap. 2).

SANDIA MOUNTAINS: (10,678 ft at highest point) Bernalillo, Sandoval, and Santa Fe Counties, NM. In Navajo, this is Dził Nááyisí, or "Mountain that Revolves." This mountain range with a sheer western face runs generally north-south immediately east of Albuquerque, and extends from Tijeras Pass (and Interstate 40) 15 miles north to Placitas. (The mountains to the south of Tijeras Canyon are the Manzano Mountains.) "Sandia" means "watermelon" in Spanish, and reportedly refers to the color of the range at sunset. However, it is more likely that the mountains were named for San Diaz (Saint Diaz).

There is some evidence that prior to 1864, the deep canyons and high peaks of the Sandias were the base of operations for Navajo forays on the Rio Grande settlements. A contingent of Diné Ana'í (Enemy Navajos) may have lived in the Sandias under the half-breed Francisco Baca, around 1826, where they were plagued by Zuni raiders.

On their winter 1864–65 journey to the Bosque Redondo (Fort Sumner), Navajos skirted the southern edge of the mountains, passing through Tijeras Canyon. As closely as can be determined from the hazy memory of aged informants, the captive Navajos crossed the Rio Grande at Isleta and Albuquerque, and passed through Tijeras Canyon to Canyon Blanco and the Pecos River. Here they turned southward to Fort Sumner.

These are the southern sacred mountains of the Tewa Indians and are revered as sacred by the Keres and the Zunis. The Zunis call these mountains Chis Biya Yalanne and consider them the place of origin of their Big Fire Society. They are also a shrine for the Shua:que Society.

❖ **Role in Hillerman Fiction:**

The Ghostway: From Jimmy Yellow's place on Mesa Gigante, the view is extraordinary, taking in the valley of the Rio Puerco, the Sandia Mountains and the lights of Albuquerque to the east, and the Sangre de Cristos to the north (chap. 25).

SAND ISLAND: (4600 ft) San Juan County, UT. The Navajo name is uncertain. This tree-shaded, sandy beach on the north bank of the San Juan River is just a mile or so west of the community of Bluff. A recreation area with camping and picnicking now occupies the site.

❖ **Role in Hillerman Fiction:**

A Thief of Time: L. D. Thatcher and Joe Leaphorn cross the San Juan River on a bridge just below Sand Island on their trip to see old man Houk because of a note left on missing anthropologist Eleanor Friedman-Bernal's calendar (chap. 8).

Coyote Waits: Ashie Pinto's grandfather had told him of two White men killed in the late 1800s by Navajos between the Chuskas and the San Juan River (chap. 7).

SAN FRANCISCO PEAKS: (6000–12,633 ft) Coconino County, AZ. To the Navajos, these mountains are Dook'o'osłííd ("Never Thaws on Top"), or Dził Gháʼniłts'įjlii ("Faultless Mountain"). The sacred name is Diichiłí Dziil, meaning "Abalone Shell Mountain." The Hopis call them Nuvatekiaqui ("Place of Snow on the Very Top"), and the Havasupan name is Hvehasah-patch ("Big Rock Mountain").

This cluster of volcanic mountains north of Flagstaff contains the tallest peaks in Arizona: Humphreys Peak (12,633 ft), Agassiz Peak (12,340 ft), and Fremont Peak (11,940 ft). These mountains may have been more than 15,000 ft high before they collapsed into an empty magma chamber 500,000 years ago.

The name San Francisco was probably applied by Father Marcos de Niza in 1539. The mountains are shown as Sierra Sinagua by Fanforan and Quesada in 1598, and in 1776, Father Garcés called them the Sierra Napoc. They are the Corn Mountain and Jewel Mountain mentioned in Navajo Coyoteway.

The peaks comprise the Navajo sacred mountain of the west, believed by traditional Navajos to mark the tribe's rightful western boundary. According to Navajo creation mythology, First Man adorned them with diichiłí ("abalone shell"), yellow clouds, male rain, and all animals, and fastened them to the sky with sunbeams. They are also the home of Haashch'ééłti'í ("Talking God"), Naadą́'áłgaii 'Ashkii ("White Corn Boy"), and Naadą́'áłtsoii 'At'ééd ("Yellow Corn Girl"). Their symbolic color is yellow.

The Navajos consider these peaks and Blanca Peak, Colorado (sacred mountain of the east), to be male, while Mount Taylor, New Mexico, and Hesperus Peak, Colorado, are female. (Three additional New Mexico peaks—Gobernador Knob, Hosta Butte, and Huerfano Peak—are sacred mountains internal to the Navajo Reservation, as is Navajo Mountain on the Utah-Arizona line.)

The San Francisco Peaks are remarkable for their variety of vegetation. Climbing from base to peak, one passes through flora characteristic of arid zones and to the meager herbage of arctic regions. They are a favored place for the Navajo collection of herbs and medicine, and among traditional Navajos, only those bound to obtain medicine ascend the mountains.

To the Hopis, the peaks are the mythological home of the Kachina People and they are looked upon with awe and reverence. The northwestern slopes were formerly Havasupai habitat, and they also figure in the Zuni migration narrative.

✦ Role in Hillerman Fiction:

Listening Woman: These mountains are visible from Leaphorn's carryall as he receives the radio message about the Boy Scouts camping at Canyon de Chelly (chap. 12).

The Dark Wind: According to Hopi Albert Lomatewa, the Messenger, these peaks are the home of the Hopi kachinas (chap. 1). Jim Chee sees a huge rain cloud forming over these mountains as he visits Piutki on First Mesa (chap. 21).

The Ghostway: From the Gray Mountain store, Jim Chee can see the east face of the San Francisco Peaks (the Navajo sacred mountains of the west), which made him feel at ease for the first time since he left the reservation for Los Angeles (chap. 22). After returning from Los Angeles, Chee returns for the third time to Ashie Begay's hogan in the Chuskas to see if he can verify Bent-woman's assertion that Begay must be dead. In the chinde hogan, Chee finds Ashie Begay's Four Mountains Bundle, containing herbs and minerals from the four sacred mountains: the San Francisco Peaks in Arizona (sacred mountain of the west), Hesperus Peak in the La Plata Mountains of Colorado (sacred mountain of the north), Blanca Peak in the Sangre de Cristo Mountains of Colorado (sacred mountain of the east), and Mount Taylor in New Mexico (sacred mountain of the south) (chap. 22).

SANGRE DE CRISTO MOUNTAINS: (14,345 ft at Blanco Peak, the highest point in the range). Fremont, Saguache, Custer, Alamosa, Huerfano, and Costilla Counties in Colorado, and Taos, Colfax, Santa Fe, Mora, and San Miguel Counties in New Mexico. The Navajo name is uncertain. The Spanish name means Blood of Christ. The Sangre de Cristo is one of the longest mountain ranges in the world, stretching 204 miles from Poncha Pass (12 miles southwest of Salida, Colorado) in the north, to Glorieta Pass (10 miles southeast of Santa Fe, New Mexico) in the south. The range contains ten peaks over 14,000 feet high, and two dozen more over 13,000 feet. The highest is Blanca Peak, the Navajo Sacred Mountain of the east. The highest point in New Mexico is Wheeler Peak, northeast of Taos, at 13,161 feet.

The mountains are perhaps best known as the backdrop for such cities as Santa Fe and Taos, New Mexico's tourist Meccas.

✤ **Role in Hillerman Fiction:**

The Ghostway: From Jimmy Yellow's place on Mesa Gigante, the view is extraordinary, taking in the valley of the Rio Puerco, the Sandia Mountains and the lights of Albuquerque to the east, and the Sangre de Cristos to the north (chap. 25).

SAN JUAN BASIN: (4900–6800 ft) San Juan and McKinley Counties, NM. The Navajo name is uncertain. This vast lowland, drained by the San Juan River watershed, is exemplary of the wide-open spaces and sparse population and vegetation common to the Navajo Reservation. In broadest terms, it extends from the southern reaches of Mesa Verde, northwest of Farmington, some 90 miles south to the north rim of Mesa de los Lobos, near Crownpoint. From the Jemez Mountains on the east, it stretches all the way to the Chuska Mountains, a distance of 120 miles.

The San Juan Basin is characterized by flat, broken, sandy terrain, cut by numerous mostly-dry washes and accentuated with rough-edged mesas and hills. Grasses and low shrubs dominate, with areas of piñon and juniper.

The Bisti Badlands, Chaco Canyon, the Navajo Indian Irrigation Project, oil fields, and coal mines all lie within the San Juan Basin.

✤ **Role in Hillerman Fiction:**

The Ghostway: Jim Chee views the velvety panorama of the San Juan Basin unrolling below him from the precipice in the Chuska Mountains where the grave of Albert Gorman is located (chap. 4).

Coyote Waits: Janet Pete and Jim Chee drive through the Basin on their way to visit the scene of Delbert Nez's killing (chap. 6).

SAN JUAN MOUNTAINS: (10,000–14,246 ft) Montezuma, San Juan, La Plata, Archuleta, Rio Grande, San Miguel, and Hindsdale Counties, CO. The Navajos call this extensive range Dził Łigaii ("White Mountains"). (Most authorities limit the name applied by the Franciscan Fathers, Dibé Ntsaa, meaning "Big Sheep," to Mount Hesperus.) This is the predominant mountain range in south-central and southwestern Colorado and includes, among others, the La Plata Range.

The San Juans are likely the range shown on the Dominguez-Escalante map of 1776 as the Sierra de las Grullas ("Crane Mountains"). This name was used by Captain Roque Madrid, who explored the mountains in 1705, and he used the name as though it was already well known. The Dominguez-

Escalante map indicates it as the source of the Rio Nabajoe, Rio San Juan, Rio de la Piedra Parada ("Standing Rock River"), and the Rio los Pinos ("Pine River"). To the north the map shows the Sierra de la Plata (Silver Mountain), which would lie in the vicinity of present Mount Elous (14,060 ft), and Mount Nebo (13,191 ft.), some 50 miles north of Durango.

To the Navajos (and the Jicarilla Apaches), this is a place of great importance, containing, according to some authorities, the Navajo Place of Emergence (in the La Plata Range). At least one authority suggests Trout Lake is the location. Traditionally, Navajo hunting parties avoided the vicinity of this lake, and call it by a name translated as Spirit Lake. On the maps of the Hayden Survey, this pool is called San Miguel Lake. However, this lake has no small island in the center as described by the Navajos. A more likely candidate for the Hájíínáí, the Place of Emergence, is Island Lake in the northern end of the La Platas, about seven miles west of Silverton. A small island sits in the center of the lake, surrounded on the four cardinal directions by four high peaks, and it is thought by many scholars to be where traditional Diné believe they emerged from the underworld, and where the spirits of the dead pass to the nether world.

The San Juans are noted for their high scenic mountains, fine streams for fishing, and for deer and elk hunting. Heavy snow in the winter usually closes all mountain passes. Navajos hunted deer and elk all through this country, even though it was Ute territory. Hunting parties went into the region as late as 1895, but were eventually excluded from the region by the White population and the game laws.

✤ Role in Hillerman Fiction:

Coyote Waits: From the overlook at Washington Pass, Joe Leaphorn can see the Zuni Mountains to the south, the Jemez Mountains to the east, and the San Juan Mountains to the north (chap. 12).

The Fallen Man: Early snowpack atop the highest peaks is seen from the top of Shiprock (chap. 1). Elisa Breedlove tells Jim Chee that her late husband Hal had wanted his ashes scattered over the San Juan Mountains in the La Plata Range, specifically on Mount Hesperus (chap. 6).

SAN JUAN RIVER: (4800–3400 ft) Montezuma and Mineral Counties, CO., San Juan and Rio Arriba Counties, NM, and San Juan County, UT. The common name among the Navajos is simply Tooh, meaning "Water." Other names include Sá Bitooh ("Old Age River"), Tooh Biką'í ("Male Water," as opposed to the Colorado, which is female), Bits'iis Nineezí ("One with Long Body"), Bits'iis Nteelí ("One with Wide Body"), and Nóóda'í Bito' ("Utes' River").

Figure 37. The San Juan River, facing east off the U.S. Highway 191 bridge, just southwest of Bluff, Utah.

This is one of the Southwest's major rivers. It heads in the vicinity of Wolf Creek Pass in Mineral County, Colorado (well beyond the scope of this volume), and flows 80 miles into the northeast corner of man-made Navajo Lake. From here the river snakes into New Mexico and back into Colorado before passing into Utah, 125 miles downstream. It continues west another another 125 miles before its waters merge with the Colorado River in what is now Lake Powell.

This river is sacred to the Navajos. Its junctures with Los Pinos River (a place called Tó 'Aheedlí, "Water Flows in a Circle," now submerged under the waters of Navajo Lake), Mancos Creek, and the Colorado River are among the most sacred of all places in Navajoland. This is probably the most important river to the Navajos, and it figures heavily in Blessingway, Enemyway, and Evilway legends, and the Mountain Chant. The Navajos alternately describe the river as an older man with hair of white foam (who "mounts" the female Colorado River); as a snake wriggling through the desert (particularly at the Goosenecks in Utah); as a flash of lightning; and as a black club of protection keeping invaders from the Navajos.

Recent evidence from locations near the San Juan River documents Navajo presence in the Southwest since at least A.D. 1500.

The river's relationship to the Navajos is reflected in the fact that early Spanish maps refer to it as "Rio Navajoo," or "Navajo River."

✤ Role in Hillerman Fiction:

Listening Woman: Leaphorn is surprised to realize that the sounds of this river could be heard from murder victim Hosteen Tso's hogan on the Nokaito Bench (chap. 8).

The Ghostway: Hosteen Joseph Joe sees Shiprock pinnacle above the line of yellow trees lining the San Juan River (chap. 1). The last late Canada geese appear along the San Juan as the investigation of the Gorman case unfolds in Shiprock (chap. 5). On the bank of the San Juan River in Shiprock, Jim Chee finds a silver trailer house about a mile downstream from the San Juan Bridge, surrounded by cottonwood trees, matching the trailer Joseph Joe told him was in the photo of Leroy Gorman shown to him by Albert Gorman just before the shootout in the parking lot at the Shiprock Economy Wash-O-Mat (chap. 10).

Skinwalkers: Jim Chee's trailer house and the feral cat's den are next to the San Juan River just outside of Shiprock (chap. 1). Dugai Endocheeney's hogan is situated on the Nokaito Bench near the confluence of Chinle Wash with the San Juan River (chap. 2). Besides the only road into Badwater Clinic, the only other way to reach the isolated location is to float down the San Juan River (chap. 6). The Kayonnie boys, who smelled of beer the morning that Jim Chee arrived at the Badwater Trading Post, run sheep along the San Juan River north of Badwater (chap. 6).

A Thief of Time: Harrison Houk's crazy son reportedly drowned in this river after killing his own mother, sister, and brother (chap. 2). Jim Chee's trailer house is parked in a cottonwood grove next to the river outside Shiprock (chap. 7). Mr. Dumont's certification on the pot he purchased through Nelson's claimed it was found in a side canyon of the San Juan River, 10 miles downstream from Sand Island (chap. 12). Joe Leaphorn floats down the river in a Kayak, looking for Many Ruins Canyon and missing anthropologist Eleanor Friedman-Bernal (chap. 18).

Talking God: Officer Chee's aging aluminum house trailer is on the banks of the San Juan just outside Shiprock (chap. 7).

Coyote Waits: Jim Chee's scuffed and dented aluminum trailer is on the bank of the San Juan just outside Shiprock (chap. 6). Ashie Pinto's grandfather told him of two White men killed by Navajos south of the San Juan and east of the Chuska Mountains (chap. 7).

Sacred Clowns: The Navajo Nation's water rights from the San Juan River are used for the Navajo Agricultural Industries (chap. 17).

The Fallen Man: Jim Chee's trailer house is on the banks of the San Juan River just outside the community of Shiprock (chap. 2).

Hunting Badger: As when Jim Chee previously lived in Shiprock, his trailer house is located on the banks of the San Juan River just outside of town (chap. 2). Chee speculates that the Ute Casino robbers, after abandoning the pickup truck, moved down Gothic Creek Canyon to the San Juan River (chap. 8). Frank Sam Nakai remembered the building of the dam in Glen Canyon, damming up the San Juan and Colorado Rivers to form Lake Powell (chap. 11).

Figure 38. Graffiti now cover the walls of Sanostee Trading Post, exemplifying a gang problem that is growing in frequency and gravity.

SANOSTEE: (6000 ft) San Juan County, NM. Also Sanastee. The Navajo name is Tsé 'Ałnáozt'i'í ("Overlapping Rocks"). This name was applied by non-Navajos to a nearby location. Also Tó Yaagaii ("Water Rises in a White Column"), referring to a now inactive artesian well that used to geyser.

This trading community is located on Sanostee Wash, on the eastern slope of the Tunicha Mountains 20 miles south of Shiprock community, and eight miles west of U.S. Highway 666.

Lieutenant W. C. Brown of the U.S. Army resource survey of the Navajo country visited farms in the Sanostee region in 1892 and inspected the Indian irrigation system on Sanostee Wash. Today there are several areas irrigated out of this wash between Beautiful Mountain and the wash's juncture with the Peña Blanca Wash.

Some 12 miles southwest of Sanostee is an abandoned sawmill established in 1907 to cut lumber for the Shiprock and Toadlena schools. The Sanostee BIA boarding school has been closed, and is in the process of being torn down. The ruins give the impression of a bombed-out, evacuated community. A couple dozen new government-subsidized houses have been built east of the school, while at least as many government-owned houses, once occupied by teachers, now stand empty, boarded up and/or vandalized. A day-school sits in the middle of the ruined boarding school complex.

Sanostee Trading Post was built by Will Evans in 1899, for Joseph Wilken. In 1905, Frank Noel purchased it. Still later it became a Foutz Brothers enterprise.

While Noel owned it, the post played an important role in the Beautiful Mountain Uprising. In this colorful escapade of autumn 1913, the followers of Hostiin Bizhóshí (sometimes spelled Bi-Joshii), an old Navajo medicine man, resisted Superintendent Shelton's edict against plural marriages by freeing from the Fort Defiance jail three wives of his son, Hataałii Yázhí ("Little Singer").

Going into hiding on Beautiful Mountain, they defied all efforts to dislodge them for two months. No less than four troops of cavalry (261 men armed with 300 rounds of ammunition each) under General Hugh L. Scott were dispatched from Fort Robinson to Gallup by train, and then to Beautiful Mountain by horseback to confront the 12 or so men with Hostiin Bizhóshí. Negotiations between Bizhóshí, Scott, and Fr. Anselm Weber (from St. Michaels) took place at Noel's Sanostee post, leading to the surrender of Bizhóshí on Thanksgiving Day, November 27, 1913. As reported by Frank McNitt in *The Indian Traders* (University of Oklahoma Press, 1962), Bizhóshi was the last of the renegades to surrender, telling General Scott, "But I am not afraid of you!" This incident marked the last time U.S. Army troops were called out against American Indians.

Today the post houses a weaving museum filled with hundreds of exquisite historical and modern Two Grey Hills rugs and blankets, along with extensive genealogical information collected on the weaving families in the region.

✚ Role in Hillerman Fiction:

Skinwalkers: Joe Leaphorn picks Sanostee as a "halfway" point between Window Rock and Shiprock for his meeting with Jim Chee. From here, they drive northward to Roosevelt Bistie's place (chap. 13).

Coyote Waits: In studying rock formation photos in the darkroom of murdered Huan Ji, Joe Leaphorn and Louisa Bourebonette conjecture the formations photographed could be in several places, including Sanostee (chap. 17).

SANTA FE: (7000 ft) (Population: 67,879) Santa Fe County, NM. Navajos call the capital of New Mexico Yootó, meaning "Bead Water," referring to the Tewa name for the Santa Fe River. This city is located in the western foothills of the Sangre de Cristo Mountains, on Interstate 25, about 60 miles north of Albuquerque. The city's downtown sits atop at least two major puebloan ruins.

The community was founded in 1610 as the capital of the Province of New Mexico, by Don Pedro de Peralta, who named it La Ciudad de Santa Fe de San Francisco de Assisi ("The City of Holy Faith of St. Francis of Assisi"). The town was abandoned during the Pueblo Revolt of 1680, though many of the refugees returned in 1692–93 with Don Diego de Vargas.

The first Americans entered the area about 1820, as traders violating dictates from Mexico City. Until the 1940s and 1950s, when the population hovered around 15,000 people, the city was a center for the weaving of Spanish-

American textiles and wood-carving. It has gradually become better known as a retail center for Native American goods. It is a Mecca for tourists, artists, and writers.

Santa Fe is an arts community, and among its more notable facilities are the Museum of New Mexico, the Laboratory of Anthropology, School of American Research, Saint Francis Art Museum Historical Society, the Wheelwright Museum of Indian Culture (originally the Church of Navajo Religion), and the Institute of American Indian Art. The Palace of the Governors (housing the Museum of New Mexico's major exhibits) was under constant construction from 1601 to 1614, and the oldest house (still standing) in the United States was erected in Santa Fe, prior to 1636. Saint Francis Cathedral was built 1711–14 (though it remains unfinished, as it began to sink into the ground before the towers were completed). Guadalupe Church was built in the early 1800s.

Fort Marcy (erected on the city's northern perimeter in 1846) was the source of many of the U.S. Army expeditions into Navajo country prior to the opening of Fort Wingate and Fort Defiance.

In 1680 the governor, Capitan General Don Antonio Otermin, was driven out of Santa Fe (and the province) for 13 years by the Pueblos in rebellion. When Don Diego de Vargas reconquered New Mexico in 1692–93, he found some Tanos living in Santa Fe.

From the beginning of Spanish contacts, all Navajo official business with the Spanish government was conducted in Santa Fe—even while other Navajos continued to raid just beyond the city limits.

Santa Fe remained under the Spanish crown until the Mexican Revolution in 1821, when it became a part of Mexico. It was the western terminus of the famous Santa Fe Trail as well as the northern terminus of the Chihuahua Trail out of Old Mexico.

In 1837, it was the scene of a revolt of the outlanders, called Los Chimayosos, from Rio Arriba to the north. The city (and the state of New Mexico) became part of the United States when General Stephen W. Kearny marched in on August 18, 1846. (A U.S. post office was established three years later.) The Stars and Bars of the Confederacy flew over Santa Fe under General Sibley for a short time during the Civil War.

✤ Role in Hillerman Fiction:

Listening Woman: Several years earlier, the Buffalo Society pulled off a $500,000 armored truck robbery in Santa Fe. A helicopter leased at the Santa Fe airport lifted the robbers from the scene; it was later reported flying over parts of the Navajo Reservation (chap. 3).

The Dark Wind: Jim Chee visits the New Mexico state prison in Santa Fe and learns that DEA Agent Johnson visited Joseph Musket while the latter was an inmate (chap. 18).

The Ghostway: Captain Largo tells Jim Chee to begin a search for Margaret Billy Sosi, granddaughter of the elusive Hosteen Begay, who has run away from St. Catherine Indian School in Santa Fe (chap. 5) after receiving a letter from her grandfather, warning her about some danger, and telling her to stay away from Shiprock and Gorman (chap. 9).

Sacred Clowns: The office of Roger Applebee, "big gun" in the conservationist organization Nature First, lives in Santa Fe, and it is here that Applebee and Asher Davis went to high school (chap. 1). Ed Zeck runs a branch of his law firm in Santa Fe (chap. 6). Roger Applebee suggests putting the proposed national garbage dump in Santa Fe, rather than on the Navajo Reservation (chap. 6). In Santa Fe, "tree huggers" are called "fern fondlers" (chap. 6). Joe Leaphorn calls the Desmond Clark Gallery here to discuss the values of the Lincoln Canes (given to the pueblo governors by President Lincoln) (chap. 22). Joe Leaphorn calls the Santa Fe office of Nature First, establishing a nebulous connection between the group's leader and the murders of the Tano clown and Eric Dorsey (chap. 28).

The First Eagle: Joe Leaphorn rides in a limousine to the summer home of Mrs. Millicent Vanders in Santa Fe; she hires him to investigate the disappearance of her niece, Arizona Health Department Vector Contract Supervisor Catherine Ann Pollard; Pollard was last seen investigating the bubonic plague near Yells Back Butte in Arizona, the same day Navajo Tribal Policeman Benny Kinsman was killed (chap. 3).

SCATTERED WILLOW DRAW: (8000–7000 ft) Apache County, AZ. Also Scattered Willow Wash. The Navajo name is uncertain. This tributary of Kinlichee Wash heads on the west slope of the Defiance Plateau, roughly six miles south of Fluted Rock. It flows southeast only five miles before merging Black Soil and Kinlichee Washes. This vicinity is mentioned in the hero's search for his family in the Navajo Rounded Man Red Antway Myth.

❖ Role in Hillerman Fiction:

Skinwalkers: Looking out his Window Rock office window, Joe Leaphorn knows it's raining here while Chee is visiting the Dinnebito Wash country (chap. 19).

SECOND MESA: (6200–6450 ft) (Population: 929) Navajo County, AZ. It can be surmised that Navajos refer to this feature as Tsétsohk'id ("Big Boulder Hill"), since that is the name used to refer to all the villages on the mesa.

This is the middle of the three peninsular Hopi Mesas, projecting "fingerlike" from the southern edge of Black Mesa. Second Mesa is 20 miles long, and two to 10 miles wide, splitting into two smaller peninsulas. It is bounded on the west by Oraibi Wash, and on the east by Wepo Wash. It houses the Hopi villages of Shungopovi, Second Mesa, and Shipolovi.

✤ Role in Hillerman Fiction:

The Dark Wind: Here is located the Hopi Cultural Center where attorney Ben Gaines and Gail Pauling have a motel room while visiting the site of Gail's brother's fatal plane crash on Black Mesa (chap. 8).

The First Eagle: Robert Jano, arrested for the murder of Navajo Tribal Policeman Benny Kinsman, lives at Mishongnovi on Second Mesa (chap. 2).

SEGE BUTTE: Fictional location.

✤ Role in Hillerman Fiction:

Skinwalkers: The dirt track leading to Chilchinbito Canyon leads past Sege Butte (chap. 10).

SEKLAGAIDESI: See Seklagidsa Canyon.

SEKLAGIDSA CANYON: (7000–5600 ft) Apache County, AZ. The name is Navajo, and means "Prominent White Cliffs," as named by Emery. This is the north fork of Walker Creek. It rises on the west slope of the Carrizo Mountains, five miles southwest of Pastora Peak (the highest point). It flows southwest seven miles to join Alcove Canyon to form Walker Creek.

✤ Role in Hillerman Fiction:

The Blessing Way: Joe Leaphorn drove past here, along with Agua Sal Creek, Round Rock, and Many Farms, while trying to figure out what the Big Navajo was doing on Ceniza Mesa (chap. 15).

SHEEP SPRINGS: (5900 ft) San Juan County, NM. To the Navajos, this is Tooh Haltsooí ("Spring in the Meadow"), or Tó Haltsooí ("Water in the Meadow"), and Dibé Bitooh ("Sheep Spring"). This trading and chapter village is situated at the foot of the barren eastern foothills of the Chuska Mountains, at the junction of U.S. Highway 666 and New Mexico Highway 134. The latter, also designated Navajo Route 32, traverses Narbona Pass (formerly Washington Pass). Charles Newcomb established a trading post near the springs in 1912; it was called Taylor Trading Post in 1941, and is one of many posts once owned by Foutz and Sons. This chapter community now boasts a Navajo housing development of several dozen newer homes.

Some 10 miles to the southwest, on a bench of the Chuska Mountains, U.S. Army Captain Reid and a small command held council with Narbona and the

Figure 39. Like all of the "trading posts" on U.S. Highway 666 between Gallup and Shiprock, New Mexico, Sheep Springs Trading Post (at the juncture of U.S. Highway 666 and New Mexico Highway 134) has shifted its commerce to primarily that of a convenience store.

Navajo chiefs in 1847. Only the intervention of Narbona saved Reid and his men from the fury of Narbona's wife and other Navajos. Two years later Narbona was killed by Army troops near the pass that now bears his name.

The springs, located nearly a mile and a half west of the trading post, were visited by First Lieutenant W. C. Brown in 1892, who reported them as a well-known camping site. Several stone and adobe homes were standing at the time, and the local Navajos had built two small tanks for catching runoff. The remains of the buildings were still standing in 1941.

The Navajos of this region spend their winters on the lower benches of the Chuska Mountains and the flats that slope east to the Big Bend of the Chaco. They summer in the high pine- and aspen-covered Chuskas. Some 60 years ago, these seasonal shifts covered more territory, some outfits moving as far as 75 miles east to the continental-divide country. Descendants of Sheep Springs Navajos now live permanently in the eastern portion of their old range.

✤ Role in Hillerman Fiction:

The Ghostway: Captain Largo determines that, although Albert Gorman must have turned south from Shiprock after the shooting in the Shiprock Economy Wash-O-Mat parking lot, he did not travel as far south as Sheep Springs (chap. 2). Jim Chee calls the trading posts at Newcomb, Sheep Springs, and Two Grey Hills in search of the 17-year-old runaway, Margaret Billy Sosi (granddaughter of the missing Ashie Begay) (chap. 11).

Skinwalkers: Joe Leaphorn takes the "shortcut" through Crystal and Sheep Springs on his trip from Window Rock to Shiprock (chap. 2). Alice Yazzie's letter asking Jim Chee to perform a Blessing Way uses this trading post for a return address (chap. 11).

Sacred Clowns: Jim Chee drives past Sheep Springs on his way to see Frank Sam Nakai, his mentor singer (chap. 12).

SHIPAULOVI: (6050 ft) Navajo County, AZ. Also Shipolovi, Sipaulovi. Navajos call this community Tsétsohk'id ("Big Boulder Hill"). (This is the same name as Mishongnovi, and a variant is applied to Toreva. It appears to refer to Second Mesa itself rather than individual communities.) Hopis call it Shopaulovi, "Place of the Mosquitos." This is one of three Hopi villages atop Second Mesa (see also Mishongnovi and Shongopovi). Shipaulovi and Mishongnovi are located at the distal end of the easternmost peninsula of the mesa, with Shipaulovi the more northerly of the two. This village was founded about 1750, with beams from the old mission at Shungopovi, indicating that at least some of the population came from that village. The Hopi name of the village, "Place of the Mosquitos," was first applied to the village of Homolovi, from whence the population was forced by a plague of mosquitos. These people settled at Shipaulovi, and currently comprise the largest clan there.

In 1940 the population was 130 persons, and two traders, Secakuku and David Talawittima (both Hopi), were present.

✤ **Role in Hillerman Fiction:**

The Dark Wind: This is the home of Coconino County Deputy Sheriff Cowboy Dashee (chap. 9). When Jim Chee and Dashee visit Albert Lomatewa (the Messenger who first encountered the body of "John Doe" on a pilgrimage for spruce boughs on Black Mesa) at Shipaulovi, they learn that he concealed the knowledge of the body for days (chap. 10).

SHIPROCK (COMMUNITY): (4965 ft) (Population: 7,687) San Juan County, NM. To the Navajos, this community is Naat'áani Nééz ("Tall Boss"), or Tooh ("River," the same name applied to the San Juan River). The largest Navajo community in New Mexico, Shiprock is located on the San Juan River at the junction of U.S. Highways 666 and 64, about 13 miles northeast of the pinnacle for which it was named.

In 1872 this location was first scouted by Thomas Keam, as the Indian Service hoped to open a subagency here. (This did not materialize until September 11, 1903.) This locale was first called "Needles," and was little more than a verdant meadow when Agent Miller was killed by the Indians in the cottonwoods and willows in 1873. The community began as a cluster of ranches and farms on the north bank of the San Juan prior to 1884.

Shiprock was founded on September 11, 1903, as the San Juan (agricultural) School and Agency. The U.S. Indian Service opened a northern Navajo agency

Figure 40. The Shiprock Navajo Police Headquarters, housing the office of Jim Chee in several of the Hillerman novels, sits on the east side of U.S. Highway 666, about a mile north of the San Juan River.

here the same year. It was originally called San Juan Agency, but later became known as Shiprock Agency (after the nearby pinnacle). The school became the third boarding school on the reservation in 1907. Superintendent William T. Shelton, from whom the name Naat'áani Nééz originated, opened the school and administrative agency for the northern Navajos with a staff of three White and three Navajo employees.

In 1909, Agent W. T. Shelton began the Shiprock Fair during the first week of October. This annual event continues today.

Franciscan and Christian Reformed churches moved in early on, and traders have included the Shiprock Trading Company and Bruce M. Bernard (both opening just after 1900), Bond (opening in the late 1920s), Manning Brothers (opening in the late 1950s), and B and B Trading Co. A garage and a hotel were important facilities in the 1940s.

The settlement was laid out originally on land belonging to a Navajo named Tsenayabegay. According to one of Shelton's reports, Indians had been irrigating here for many years, and there were 275 Navajo farms under some 25 ditches drawing water between Shiprock and Farmington. Shelton immediately pushed an agricultural program, improved and extended the irrigation system, developed a fine dairy herd, initiated the Shiprock Fair, built a sawmill near Sanostee, and opened a coal mine in the Shiprock Hogback. Shelton was a stern disciplinarian and ruthless in his prosecution of moral lapses. He is to this day respected throughout the region for his staunch championship of the Navajos and for his efforts in adding the Utah-Colorado extension to the reservation.

The first buildings in Shiprock were constructed of logs and adobe. These were largely replaced with brick structures after a disastrous flood in 1912. A bridge was built to replace Jimmy the Boatman's ferry in 1909. A new concrete bridge was completed in 1938.

Shiprock was the site of a large uranium mill until the mid- 1970s, and it serves as a chapter seat.

The first trading post here was established by Robert Baker, who sold out to Bruce Bernard in 1909. Bernard held on to the post until 1952. Another post was built in 1911 by Walker and Hubbell; this was sold to Will Evans two years later. Evans sold the post to the Jacks Brothers in 1948, and Russell Foutz purchased it in 1954. Ed Foutz became the owner in 1972, and was still operating the post in 1990.

✦ **Role in Hillerman Fiction:**

The Blessing Way: Joe Leaphorn had been in charge of the Shiprock subagency of the Navajo Tribal Police when four suspected witches were shot by a man whose daughter had died of tuberculosis (chap. 8).

Dance Hall of the Dead: Leaphorn receives orders from the Navajo Police substation in Shiprock to go to Ramah, concerning the diappearance of George Bowlegs (a Navajo) and Ernest Cato (chap. 2).

Listening Woman: A Greyhound Bus driver reported seeing the helicopter used in the Santa Fe armored truck robbery fly over U.S. Highway 666 northwest of here (chap. 3).

People of Darkness: Jim Chee attended high school here (chap. 11).

The Ghostway: The book begins with a killing in the parking lot of the Shiprock Economy Wash-O-Mat. The people around Shiprock and the Chuska Mountains call 81-year-old Joseph Joe "Hosteen," a term of general respect that means "old man" (chap. 1). On the bank of the San Juan River in Shiprock, Jim Chee finds a silver trailer house surrounded by cottonwood trees, matching the trailer Joseph Joe told him was in the photo of Leroy Gorman shown to him by Albert Gorman just before the shootout in the parking lot at the Shiprock Economy Wash-O-Mat (chap. 10). Chee considered the housing in Gorman's Los Angeles neighborhood a little worse than the neighborhood Chee had lived in while attending the University of New Mexico in Albuquerque, but a little better than the average housing in Shiprock (chap. 12). While in Flagstaff, an exhausted Jim Chee realizes that Abert Gorman had not been followed to Shiprock where the shootout took place. He wonders how Lerner knew to fly to Farmington and drive directly to Shiprock to find Gorman (chap. 21). Upon his return from Los Angeles, Jim Chee stops at his trailer in Shiprock just long enough to strap on his pistol and get something to eat. Then he stops at the police substation and picks up a horse and trailer, before heading back to Albert Gorman's hogan in the Chuska Mountains (chap. 22). The blizzard that caught Chee in the Chuska

Moutains looking for Ashie Begay had closed Navajo Route 1 from Shiprock to Kayenta (chap. 23).

Skinwalkers: Shiprock's lights faintly light up a glow at night, as if attempting to civilize the town at night (chap. 1). Roosevelt Bistie spent the night here the night someone shot at Chee's trailer house (chap. 3). Roosevelt Bistie was locked up here after his arrest for killing Endocheeney (chap. 7). The attorney Janet Pete works for DNA Legal Services out of Shiprock (chap. 9).

A Thief of Time: Archaeologist Eleanor Friedman-Bernal had called ahead to Bo Arnold's place in Bluff from here to make sure the house was empty (chap. 1). Joe Leaphorn could not remember his drive to Shiprock the night his wife, Emma, died (chap. 2). A backhoe is stolen from the highway maintenance yard under the eyes of Officer Jim Chee (chap. 3).

Talking God: Throughout this book, Officer Jim Chee works out of the Shiprock office of the Navajo Tribal Police.

Coyote Waits: Captain Largo is in charge of the Shiprock subagency of the Navajo Tribal Police (chap. 3). Officer Jim Chee lives in a mobile home along the San Juan River on the outskirts of Shiprock (chap. 4). Shiprock High School Teacher Huan Ji is killed in his home at the school teacherage (chap. 12).

Sacred Clowns: The Chief of the Navajo Nation Police was in Shiprock when the report of Old Man Victor Todachenee's hit-and-run death came in; he investigated the accident himself (chap. 2). Jim Chee was stationed in Shiprock before his transfer to Window Rock (chap. 8).

The Fallen Man: Acting Lieutenant Jim Chee is stationed at the Shiprock substation of the Navajo Tribal Police; his trailer house is on the banks of the San Juan River just outside the community (chap. 2). At the Navajo Tribal Police substation here, Acting Lieutenant Jim Chee meets the colorful, obnoxious New Mexico Brand Inspector, Dick Finch (chap. 4). Officer Bernadette Manuelito tells Acting Lieutenant Jim Chee that she wants to transfer from Shiprock to—anywhere (chap. 9).

The First Eagle: A neurologist from Flagstaff is called to Shiprock to pronounce Benny Kinsman brain dead (chap. 4). Newly graduated officer Joe Leaphorn had driven from Shiprock to investigate skinwalkers near Rol Hai Rock and Table Mesa (chap. 6).

Hunting Badger: Jim Chee and Officer Bernadette Manuelito have both transferred from Tuba City back to Shiprock (chap. 2). Chee had worked here a long time before transferring to Tuba City (chap. 2). The Minutemen, a militia unit, had an organizing meeting at Shiprock a year ago (chap. 7). Law enforcement from New Mexico State Police, Navajo Tribal Police, FBI, and Apache and Navajo County Sheriffs' Offices gather at the Navajo Tribal Police substation at Shiprock to coordinate the search for the Ute Casino robbers (chap. 10).

SHIPROCK (PINNACLE): (7178 ft) San Juan County, NM. Also The Needle and Wilson Peak. Navajos call this Tsé Bit'a'í ("Winged Rock" or "Wings of Rock"). This 1800-ft-high volcanic plug is situated in the high plains country 13 miles southwest of Shiprock community, at a point eight miles west of U.S. Highway 666 (and six miles south of New Mexico Highway 504).

High volcanic trap-dikes run north and south of the main spire, which has been ascribed ceremonial significance through several Navajo legends. Based on the fact that the earliest treatments of Navajo ceremonialism do not mention the peak or its myths, any ceremonial significance may be of recent origin rather than based in antiquity. (Yet it seems highly unlikely that a feature so striking and unique would go without ceremonial significance among a people prone to apply such importance to unusual features.)

The pinnacle, visible for many miles in all directions, and which, from some angles, is said to resemble a full-rigged sailing schooner, was called The Needle by Captain J. F. McComb in 1860. The name Shiprock apparently came into use in the 1870s as indicated by the U.S. Geological Survey Maps. The pinnacle was first scaled in October of 1939, by climbers from the Sierra Club of California. Navajos resent such invasion of their sacred places, as illustrated in the following myth:

> A long time ago they tell that the Navajos were hard pressed by the enemy. One night their medicine men prayed for the deliverance of their tribe. Their prayers were heard by the Gods. The earth rose, lifting the Navajos, and it moved like a great wave into the east. It settled where Shiprock now stands. This is the way they escaped from their enemies. After this, the Navajos lived on the rock, only coming down to plant their fields and get water.
>
> They tell that for some time all went well. One day during a storm, and while the men were at work in the fields, the trail up the rock was split off by lightning and only a sheer cliff was left. The women and children and old men on top starved to death. Their bodies are still up there. Therefore, the Navajos do not wish any one to try to climb Shiprock for fear they might stir up the ch'į́įdii (ghosts), or rob their corpses. (Van Valkenburgh 1941, 144)

According to historian Richard Van Valkenburgh, Shiprock is associated with a number of Navajo ceremonies, including the Bead Chant; and the Naayee'ee Ceremony (for dispelling evil monsters) has a story of a large bird

Figure 41. Shiprock, in the distance, viewed from the southern trap dike, where it is bisected by Navajo Route 33 near Red Rock, New Mexico.

called Tsé Nináhálééh ("It Puts People Down on a Rock"—as eagles do when eating their prey). It also appears in stories from the Enemy Side ceremony, and is said to be either a medicine pouch or a bow carried by the mythological Goods of Value Mountain (in which the Chuska Mountains comprise the body and Chuska Peak the head; the Carrizo Mountains the legs; and Beautiful Mountain the feet.

The pinnacle is also the scene of Monster Slayer legends. After Monster Slayer destroyed Déélgééd at Red Mesa, he went to Shiprock and killed two adult Tsé Nináhálééh, and dispersed two young ones as an eagle and an owl. It is also mentioned in the Navajo Mountain Chant.

Medicine men used to climb to a point called Lightning Struck Tree on the highest reaches until the rock was profaned by the 1939 Sierra Club climb.

Shiprock's English name gave rise to a White man's myth in the first half of this century: that the Navajos once lived on the Pacific Coast and so named the rock when they came into the Southwest.

There are a number of Anasazi sites of undetermined age in the open country west of Shiprock, and the first oil on the reservation was discovered in the San Juan Basin near the pinnacle in 1921. Helium was pumped in the 1940s.

❖ Role in Hillerman Fiction:

The Ghostway: Hosteen Joseph Joe sees Shiprock pinnacle, blue-black and ragged against the glow of sundown from the parking lot of the Shiprock Economy Wash-O-Mat. Joseph Joe lives near the pinnacle at his daughter's place (chap. 1). Captain Largo surmises that Albert Gorman, after leaving the shooting at the Shiprock Economy Wash-O-Mat, must have laid up in the region bounded by the Shiprock pinnacle and the Chuska, Carrizo, and Lukachukai Mountains (chap. 2).

A Thief of Time: The peak is visible to Joe Leaphorn and Jim Chee from the site of the backhoe pothunter murders (chap. 9).

Coyote Waits: This volcanic plug is described as a corner of the triangle in which the community of Red Rock is located and in which there are no radio transmissions (chap. 1). (The other two corners are the Chuska Mountains and the Carrizo Mountains.) Officer Delbert Nez is killed between Shiprock and Beautiful Mountain, just south of Navajo Route 33 (chap. 10). In studying rock formation photos in the darkroom of murdered Huan Ji, Joe Leaphorn and Louisa Bourebonette conjecture the formations photographed could be near Shiprock (chap. 17).

The Fallen Man: Two climbers discover the skeleton of a man concealed in a niche (chap. 1). Black basalt makes for a hot climb, despite the elevation (a mile above sea level), yet the surface can be coated with ice in winter, and snowpacks where it's shaded (chap. 3). Local Navajos would sometimes try to prevent climbers from ascending the peak by recording and reporting to Tribal Police the license plate numbers of their cars (chap. 9). On a back road leading to Shiprock, Jim Chee and Officer Bernadette Manuelito find a spot in a fence line obviously prepared by rustlers (chap. 11). One of Hosteen Sam's log notations notes the presence of a "funny, green van" with three climbers at Shiprock, about the time Hal Breedlove disappeared (chap. 18).

SHONTO: (6500 ft) (Population: 710) Navajo County, AZ. Also Shato, Shanto. Navajos call this location Sháá'tóhí ("Spring on the Sunny Side," also interpreted as "Sunshine Water"). This same name is applied to Sunrise Spring. Located at the end of Arizona Highway 98, this isolated trading and chapter center sits on Shonto Wash some 20 miles upstream of the confluence of Shonto and Begashibito Wash. Shonto was once a lush meadow with many small lakes like the Segi Canyon, but in 1912 floods broke the natural earth dams and released the impounded waters.

Sháá'tóhí is located a mile and a half up-canyon from the Shonto Trading Post. For years, Navajos in the vicinity have used wells at the trading post. The Navajos were led into this canyon from Black Mountain by Tséyí' Sizíní and Hashké' some time before the majority were deported to Fort Sumner and the Bosque Redondo. Navajos state that the soldiers of Colonel Kit Carson were in the canyon in 1864.

In 1915 John Wetherill and Joe Lee started a trading post here and later sold out to Harry Rorick. Many Anasazi ruins, mostly open pueblos, are found along the floor of the canyon.

In Navajo traditions, one arm of Corn Pollen Woman mountain of the Blessingway lies in this vicinity. Other portions of her body are Navajo Mountain, Comb Ridge, Black Mesa, and Balakai Mesa.

❖ Role in Hillerman Fiction:

The First Eagle: On his third visit to Krouse's office, Joe Leaphorn finds a note saying Krouse has gone to Shonto, west of the landing strip (chap. 25).

SHORT MOUNTAIN TRADING POST: Fictional location west of Black Mesa, east of Tuba City, which shows up in several Hillerman novels. It is run down, sees little business, and is perpetually for sale. (This description fits almost any trading post on the Navajo Reservation.)

❖ Role in Hillerman Fiction:

Listening Woman: Joe Leaphorn visits the Trading Post to interview the trader, "Old Man" (John) McGinnis, concerning the murder of Hosteen Tso, and how to find Margaret Cigaret (chap. 5). Leaphorn encounters Theodora Adams at the trading post following the interview, and reluctantly takes her to the Tso hogan (chap. 6). McGinnis tells Leaphorn about the letter McGinnis wrote for Hosteen Tso to Tso's grandson about someone named Jimmy (chap. 9).

Skinwalkers: Joe Leaphorn visits the trading post here to see if trader McGinnis can tell him anything about Wilson Sam; he learns that Sam had just received a letter from Irma Onesalt (chap. 17).

Coyote Waits: Trader "Old Man" McGinnis tells Leaphorn he read Tagert's letter to a broke Ashie Pinto, and relates how Tagert used to give Pinto whiskey (chap. 5).

The First Eagle: Shirley Ahkeah's grandmother's hogan is located at Short Mountain, her grazing lease adjoining that of a Nez family (chap. 1). The cluster of black pins at Short Mountain on Joe Leaphorn's notorious map denoted reports of skinwalkers (chap. 6). Leaphorn talks to old John McGinnis, the trader at Short Mountain, about whether he'd heard anything about the missing Catherine Ann Pollard's Jeep (chap. 6).

SHUNGOPOVI: (6440 ft) (Population: 730) Navajo County, AZ. Also New Shungopovi, Shongopavi, Shongopovi, Shungopavi, Chimopovy. Navajos call this village Kin Názt'i' ("Houses Strung in a Circle"). Hopis call it Shung-o-hu Pa Ovi ("Place by the Spring where the Tall Reeds Grow"). Hopi scholar James notes that there are at least 57 spellings for the name of this village, one of three on Second Mesa (see also Shipaulovi and Mishongnovi). Shungopovi is located on the southwestern projection of the mesa.

Some Hopis consider the village to be the oldest Hopi settlement, but they are seemingly referring to Old Shungopovi, whose ruins are found on the hills below the present town. It is estimated to be about as old as still-occupied Oraibi, established during the fourteenth century according to tree-ring data.

The Mission of San Bartolome was established at Old Shungopovi in 1629. It has been estimated that at that time the population was two thousand persons. In the Pueblo Rebellion of 1680 the mission was destroyed and the friars killed. The remains of the mission still stand on the south side of the road leading up to Shungopovi.

According to the Shungopovi traditions, only seven village families escaped the reprisals of the Spaniards in the "peaceful" reconquest of 1692. They fled from Old Shungopovi to the site of their present village in 1629. In 1898, during a smallpox epidemic, military from Fort Wingate were obliged to arrest and remove Hopi priests, tear down houses, and vaccinate the villagers.

In 1941, the population was estimated at 353. Four traders (Peter Nuvamsa, Paul Saufkia, Sammy's Store, Archie Quamala) operated at that time. A day school (USIS) was opened on the lower bench of the mesa.

This village is often regarded as the most traditional (conservative) of all Hopi enclaves. In a bitter dispute between the "Conservatives" and the "Progressives" at Oraibi in 1906, a contingent from Shungopovi joined the conservative leader, Chief Youkeoma. They were evicted and went with Youkeoma to found Hotevilla. A couple of months later, however, cavalry troops visited Hotevilla and forced the Shungopovi residents to return home. (Youkeoma and 26 others were arrested and imprisoned at Fort Wingate.)

Shungopa Spring failed in 1870 when the slumping of the rim above created a minor earthquake. Masipa or Gray Spring, nearby, now supplies Shungopovi with water for drinking. Shungopovi hosts the Snake Dance in even years.

❖ Role in Hillerman Fiction:

Sacred Clowns: Deputy Sheriff Cowboy Dashee believes the clowns from Shungopovi, Hotevilla, and Walpi villages are "better" than those from Tano (chap. 1).

SICHOMOVI: (6200 ft) Navajo County, AZ. Also Sichomavi. Navajos refer to this Hopi First Mesa village as 'Ayahkin ("Underground House"). The Hopis call it Shichomovi ("Place of the Wild Currant Mound"). Also known as Middle Village, this community lies between Walpi and Hano villages.

Members of the Potki, Lizard, Wild Mustard, and Badger clans from Walpi built this village about 1750. Later, a Tanoan clan from the Rio Grande Valley is said to have joined the village after having been invited to help fight the Utes. (These are said to be the ancestors of the present Asa Clan).

This village is also reputed to have been a stopping place for certain Jemez groups fleeing the Rio Grande in the last decade of the seventeenth century. They later joined the Navajos in Canyon de Chelly and became affiliated with others to form the Navajo Mą'ii' Deeshgizhnii ("Coyote Pass People") clan.

The village was once decimated by smallpox, and the survivors fled to Tsegi Canyon, Monument Valley, and Zuni. They later returned and rebuilt the village. The population of Sichomovi in 1941 was 406. Traders at that time were Charley Naha and Robert Satala.

✤ **Role in Hillerman Fiction:**

The Dark Wind: Jim Chee and Deputy Sheriff Cowboy Dashee pass Sichomovi and Hano on their way to Piutki, where Chee learns who is vandalizing Windmill No. 6, and that there was a witness to Pauling's plane crash (chap. 21).

SIKYATKI: (approx. 6000 ft) Navajo County, AZ. Also spelled Sitkyatki. The Navajo name for this village is uncertain. Hopis call it Sikyatki ("Yellow House of the Firewood People," or, more likely, "Cut-Off/Divided Valley"). This ruin of a Hopi pueblo village sits at the eastern foot of First Mesa, two miles north of Polacca. It was destroyed by other Hopis in the fifteenth century.

The village's demise is attributed to inter-village strife between Sikyatki and Walpi, or between Sikyatki and a village known as Qöötsaptuvela. However, it is also said that Sikyatki met its end due to internal strife. In the latter version, two men vying for the love of a young maiden staged a foot race for the right to marry her. One resorted to witchcraft but still lost and was subsequently killed by the other. Bad blood led to growing animosities within the village, and its chief finally appealed to a neighboring chief to attack the village and destroy it. This was done, with nearly all the Sikyatki villagers killed, including the scheming chief. This nearly annihilated the Coyote Clan.

Pottery with a rich yellow slip and beautiful geometric and animorphic designs recovered during 1895 excavations inspired noted potter Nampeyo, the Hopi wife of one of the workmen, to use old techniques and designs.

Nampeyo became one of the premier pueblo potters, and her name has been for 80 years synonymous with First Mesa pottery. Her success started the Sikyatki Revival, the renaissance of First Mesa decorated pottery. Nampeyo lost her vision before her death, and her daughter, Fanny Polacca, carried on the tradition. Until recently, all decorated Hopi pottery has been made on First Mesa, with the other mesas manufacturing plainware for utilitarian purposes. Painted pottery has now spread beyond First Mesa.

✤ Role in Hillerman Fiction:

The Dark Wind: Burnt Water trader Jake West's deceased wife was from Sikyatki (chap. 26). Jim Chee visits here the night of the Washing of the Hair ceremony, during which he expects the person who stole the cargo from Pauling's crashed plane to sell it back to its owners (chap. 29).

SLEEPING UTE MOUNTAIN: (9977 ft) Montezuma County, CO. Also Ute Mountain. Navajos call this range Dził Naajiní ("Black Mountain Sloping Down"). These high, isolated mountains tower over the rolling plains and mesa country of the southwest corner of Colorado, immediately south of McElmo Creek and west of U.S. Highway 164. When viewed from the south, the range takes on the appearance of a person lying on his back with raised knees (8959-ft Hermano Peak) to the southwest, and his head (Ute Peak) to the north. The mountain has always been identified with the Utes, from the presence of the Moguache Utes, who lived along its eastern flanks at the time of European arrival in the vicinity.

According to Navajo medicine men, Ute Mountain is suspended from the sky by a cord of rain, and it is decorated with corn pollen, dark mist, and female (gentle) rain. It is said to be the home of Holy Boy and Holy Girl, who make rough jewels. The mountain is important in the Moving Upward Way, Enemyway, and Flintway rites. The mountain also plays a role in the Navajo Mountain Chant.

Medicine men who know the rite-myth of the Beadway Ceremony tell of a deep canyon called Tséyi' (the common Navajo descriptive term for a deep rock-walled canyon), which historian Van Valkenburgh believed was on Ute Mountain. In this canyon was a ruin called Tséyi' Kin (a house with one black wall, perched in a cave in the wall of the canyon). In this cliff dwelling the yé'ii (gods) found the white and yellow corn cobs used to create a pair of the Tséyi' Kiní. This canyon may be a branch of Mancos Canyon (called Tó Nts'ósíkooh, "Slim Water Canyon," by the Navajos), which passes south and east of Ute Mountain after exiting the Mesa Verde highlands. Mancos Canyon itself is important in Navajo rite-myth, including the Moving Upward Way, the Enemyway, and others.

Ute legend names this mountain as a deity who collected all rain clouds in anger. Storms come from clouds that happen to escape his pockets. Ute tradition says he will awaken some day and fight their enemies.

Early Spanish maps of the area labeled these mountains Sierra del Datil, commonly translated as "Date Mountains," as in the fruit of the palm. However, cultural historian David Brugge notes that in the southwestern United States, datil can also refer to the fruit of the yucca.

Some Navajos joined the Utes in the vicinity of Ute Mountain in 1834, due to miliary pressure from the Mexicans.

✤ **Role in Hillerman Fiction:**

Skinwalkers: A vast rain drenched the landscape from Ute Mountain south all the way to the Painted Desert (chap. 22).

Coyote Waits: Visible to the northwest, snow-capped Ute Mountain is overshadowed by thunderheads at sunset as Jim Chee and Janet Pete approach Red Rock in New Mexico (chap. 6). According to the late 1800s Blanding newspaper article discovered by Dr. Tagert, the two escaping train robbers were trailed south and west of this mountain before they disappeared (chap. 9). Ashie Pinto's grandfather told him of a group of Yucca Fruit People traveling here to retrieve horses stolen by Utes (chap. 14). (These Navajos also chased and killed two White men in the vicinity of Beautiful Mountain.)

The Fallen Man: From partway up Shiprock Pinnacle, Elisa Breedlove could see Ute Mountain, Casa del Eco Mesa, the Carrizo Mountains, and Mount Taylor (chap. 5). These mountains could be seen from the Sam home between Little Shiprock and Red Washes (chap. 11).

The First Eagle: Lying in the Northern Arizona Medical Center, the sheet-covered corpse of Anderson Nez reminds Shirley Ahkeah of this distinctive mountain (chap. 1).

Hunting Badger: Late rising moon can cause Ute Mountain to glow at any given time of night (chap. 1).

SOUTHERN UTE RESERVATION: (6100–8541 ft) La Plata and Archuleta Counties, CO. The Navajo name is uncertain, though Ignacio, the Southern Ute capital, is called Bíina, derived from the Spanish "pino," meaning "pine tree." This reservation is 70 miles long (east-west) and 15 miles wide, with the southern boundary resting on the Colorado–New Mexico state line.

Of particular significance to the Navajos is the valley of the Rio Los Pinos (also called Los Pinos River). Ignacio, capital of the Southern Ute Reservation, is located on Colorado Highway 172, in the valley of the Rio Los Pinos, approximately 15 miles southwest of Durango and some 10 miles north of the New Mexico state line. The name honors the famous subchief under Chief Ouray of the Tabeguache Band Utes. He was considered head of the Consolidated Utes after the death of Ouray in 1880, and was designated head chief of the Utes by Congress in 1895. Today's village is actually a merger of a smaller Ute village with an older Hispanic agricultural community.

The Southern Ute Boarding School was founded in 1902, serving Ute and Navajo children previously sent to Fort Lewis School. The Ute agency and school were eventually placed at Ignacio because of the concentration of Utes on allotted lands along the Rio Los Pinos.

The valley of the Rio Los Pinos is a fertile agricultural area and is well known to sportsmen for excellent trout fishing and views of the scenic San Juan Mountains that rise to the north.

The juncture of the Rio Los Pinos and the San Juan River (beyond the reservation boundary in New Mexico) is a sacred place to the Navajos, called Tó Hahadleeh ("Water Well"). It is likely the location of the "Shining Sands" where Navajo medicine men would read the "Page of Prophecy" in 1850, 1868, and 1929. This point is now under the waters of Navajo Lake.

✤ Role in Hillerman Fiction:

Hunting Badger: Hillerman places the fictitious Ute Casino on this reservation. The casino is where a robbery and the murder of a guard set the action in motion (chap. 1).

SPIDER ROCK: (approx. 8000 ft) Apache County, AZ. Also Spider Woman Rock and The Monument. Navajos call this spire Tsé Na'ashjé'ii, "Spider Rock." Located in Canyon de Chelly, at the mouth of Monument Canyon (some eight miles upstream from White House Ruin). This sheer sandstone pillar is 800 ft high.

Spider Rock is sacred to the Navajos as the home of Spider Woman, an important figure in Navajo legends who taught the Navajos the art of weaving, and who is said to have once woven her web over the rock.

Modern tales relate that she still lives there, coming down at night to steal away unruly children, whose names are told her by Face Rock. She devours

Figure 42. Spider Rock is one of the most photographed features in Navajo country, yet no photo can compare with seeing the grandeur of this gigantic monolith with one's own eyes.

them, and their bones litter the top of the spire. Geographer Steven Jett identifies Spider Rock and Face Rock as two monuments that were known as "The Captains" or "The Monuments" during the nineteenth century, and one of his informants identified Spider Rock and White House Ruin as the two most sacred features in the entire canyon complex.

Spider Rock can be readily viewed from the last vista point on the south rim of the canyon.

❖ Role in Hillerman Fiction:

Listening Woman: A Yeibeichai ceremonial was held at Spider Rock the day after the armored truck robbery in Santa Fe (chap. 3).

STANDING ROCK: (6300 ft) McKinley County, NM. Navajos call this feature Tsé Íi'áhí, meaning "Standing Rock" (literally, "Rock Extending [or Pointing] Up"). The name applies to a sandstone spire in a shallow basin on Navajo Route 9 at Standing Rock Wash, some 14 miles west of Crownpoint— and to a small community that has grown around the trading post that opened in 1925. (It later closed but reopened in 1975.) Besides the post, the community consists of a boarding school, a chapter house, and a number of homes scattered in the vicinity.

In the 1850s, this region was under the leadership of the elder Dilwoshí ("Shouter"). The location is mentioned in the Navajo Mountain Chant as Tsé Ceza ("Rock Standing Up"), but is also known as Tsé Deez'á, "Rock Point." The southeastern corner of the Navajo Reservation as defined in 1939 lies five miles south of Standing Rock, though the Navajo Tribe and individual Navajos own much of the land to the south and east of this feature in the region known as the Checkerboard Area.

❖ Role in Hillerman Fiction:

People of Darkness: Jim Chee determines that Roscoe Sam (survivor of the oil rig explosion) lived either here at Standing Rock or at Ojo Encino (chap. 22).

Sacred Clowns: Leaphorn and FBI Agent Dilly Streib drive past Nazhoni Trading Post, Coyote Wash, Standing Rock, and Nahodshosh Chapter on their way to Crownpoint to meet with Lieutenant Ed Toddy concerning the murder of Thoreau teacher Eric Dorsey (chap. 4). Jim Chee and BIA Police Sergeant Harold Blizzard check up on people here in their search for Delmar Kanitewa (chap. 11).

SWEETWATER and **SWEETWATER TRADING POST:** (6400 ft) Apache County, AZ. Also Sweetwater and Tolacon. Navajos call this location Tó Łikan, meaning "Sweet Water." This very small community is located on Kit Sili (Keet Seel) Wash, a mile upstream (northeast) of that channel's confluence with Sweetwater Wash, and about five miles south of Toh Atin Mesa. The trading post was opened between 1911 and 1915. Leroy Foutz was once a partner here. The community is home to the Sweetwater Chapter House.

❖ Role in Hillerman Fiction:

Coyote Waits: Navajos living near here were often attacked by Utes traveling from the Ladron Butte region, who crossed the San Juan near Montezuma Creek and traveled down Tsitah Wash to the Sweetwater skirt east of Toh Atin Mesa (chap. 7).

The Fallen Man: Hal Breedlove's Land Rover was found near here off of U.S. Highway 191 a week after Breedlove disappeared from Canyon de Chelly (chap. 3).

TABLE MESA: (5859 ft) San Juan County, NM. Navajos refer to this feature as Bis Dah Azká ("Adobe Mesa" or "Clay Mesa"). This imposing landform, which is really three separate mesas in very close proximity, lies west of and adjacent to U.S. Highway 666, some 15 miles south of Shiprock.

This may be the area in which Navajos first used coal as a fuel, in the 1890s. The discovery of oil here in the 1920s led to black-topping of the road between Shiprock and Gallup (later to become U.S. Highway 666), with the oil company providing the materials and the U.S. government providing the labor.

Figure 43. Table Mesa as seen from U.S. Highway 666, a couple miles south of the mesa. Although the mesa looks like a single feature from this angle, it is actually three close—but separate—mesas separated by deep, steep erosion vectors.

❖ Role in Hillerman Fiction:

Coyote Waits: Table Mesa is easily visible along U.S. Highway 666 as Janet Pete and Jim Chee drive to the Red Rock vicinity (chap. 6).

The Fallen Man: The road to Maryboy's hogan leads Jim Chee toward Rol Hai Rock and Table Mesa (chap. 19).

The First Eagle: Newly graduated officer Joe Leaphorn had driven from Shiprock to investigate skinwalkers near Rol Hai Rock and Table Mesa (chap. 6).

TAH CHEE WASH: (7200–6600 ft) Apache County, AZ. This wash rises on Rain Mountain, a feature atop the southeast margin of Black Mesa, and flows slightly north of east for about three miles before cutting abruptly to the south. It flows another four miles before merging with Polacca Wash.

✤ Role in Hillerman Fiction:

The Ghostway: After failing to reach Frank Sam Nakai's winter place via Greasewood Flats, Jim Chee circles back and drives through Round Rock, Many Farms, and Chinle, to the south side of Black Mesa, past Cottonwood and Blue Gap, before attempting to mount Carson Mesa again from the south to reach Tah Chee Wash (chap. 24).

TALL POLES BUTTE: Fictional location in the vicinity of Cove, AZ.

✤ Role in Hillerman Fiction:

The Blessing Way: Luis Horseman knows that the moving dust plume in the distance means that a truck or Jeep is on the dirt track leading to Horse Fell Canyon and Many Ruins Canyon, and ultimately to Tall Poles Butte, the site of the Army radar station (chap. 1).

TANO PUEBLO: A fictional place, the exact location of which is kept deliberately vague.

✤ Role in Hillerman Fiction:

Sacred Clowns: This fictional pueblo is the scene of much of the action throughout this novel.

TEASTAH WASH: (6200–6400 ft) Navajo County, AZ. Also Teas Toh Wash or Tees Toh Wash. Navajos call this 18-mile-long wash T'iis Tó, meaning "Cottonwood Water." It heads in the mesas east of the small trading and chapter community of Tees Toh that sits three miles east of Arizona Highway 87, 22 miles south of that road's junction with Arizona Highway 264. It flows south and southwest through Tees Toh and Seba Dalkai before joining Jadito Wash in an area of sand dunes, seven miles west of Seba Dalkai.

✤ Role in Hillerman Fiction:

The Blessing Way: Joseph Begay, on his way to pick up his daughter at the bus stop in Ganado, finds the body of Luis Horseman lying in the road at this wash (chap. 5).

TEEC NOS POS: (5450 ft) (Population: 317). Apache County, AZ. Also Tisnasbas. To the Navajos, this community is T'iis Názbas, meaning "Cottonwoods in a Circle." This small trading, chapter, and school community at the junction of U.S. Highways 160 and 64 was originally situated several miles south of U.S. Highway 64, where the BIA school now sits. The population has gradually migrated northward to the highway junction, which is mainly a commercial center.

Teec Nos Pos Trading Post was established in 1905 by Hamblin Bridger Noel (from Essex County, Virginia), who succeeded where others had failed before him. According to legend, Noel calmly demonstrated his proficiency with a high-powered Remington rifle to the local inhabitants, then mounted the rifle above his counter. The Navajos, under the leadership of Black Horse, held a day-long council before voting to let him stay.

In the fall of 1907, Noel believed this post was threatened with destruction by the Navajo participants in the Ba'álílii incident at Aneth, Utah, but Ba'álílii was quickly arrested and detained, and no trouble approached Teec Nos Pos.

Bert Dunstin and Al Foutz purchased the post in 1913. Ray Burnham was the manager in 1927, and purchased the post in 1945. In 1959 the post burned down and was rebuilt a few miles to the north at its present location at the intersection of U.S. Highways 64 and 160, where it serves as a "Gateway to the Four Corners Monument."

❖ Role in Hillerman Fiction:

The Blessing Way: In years past, an old singer was beaten to death near Teec Nos Pos as a witch (chap. 8).

Listening Woman: According to trader "Old Man" McGinnis, Hosteen Tso's son Ford married a girl from Teec Nos Pos (chap. 5).

The Dark Wind: Joseph Musket had been educated at the boarding school at Teec Nos Pos, before transferring to the school at Cottonwood (chap. 19). Teec Nos Pos is the home of Edna Nezzie, the girl who pawned at Mexican Water the necklace that Jake West identified as stolen from Burnt Water Trading Post by Joseph Musket (chap. 24).

The Ghostway: Joseph Joe knows Albert Gorman, leaving the shooting in the Shiprock Economy Wash-O-Matic, must turn either west and toward Teec Nos Pos, or south toward Gallup (chap. 1). Captain Largo later determines that he does not go toward Teec Nos Pos or west of Little Water (chap. 2). Jim Chee drives 70 miles over snowpacked highways, passing through Teec Nos Pos, Red Mesa, Mexican Water, and Dinnehotso, on his way to Frank Sam Nakai's winter place (chap. 24).

Skinwalkers: As a boy, Jim Chee first tasted cold pop at the trading post at Teec Nos Pos, when the bus driver bought enough for the entire baseball team (chap. 3). Someone is knifed at a wedding here while Jim Chee is on his way to Badwater Trading Post (chap. 6).

A Thief of Time: Jim Chee spends an afternoon at Teec Nos Pos searching in vain for a man who had broken his brother-in-law's leg (chap. 5).

The Fallen Man: Navajo Tribal Police Officer Teddy Begayaye lives at Teec Nos Pos (chap. 13).

The First Eagle: Shirley Ahkeah's aunt's hogan, from which she used to view Sleeping Ute Mountain, was located at Teec Nos Pos (chap. 1).

TESIHIM BUTTE: (6450 ft) Navajo County, AZ. Also (erroneously) Teshim Butte. The Navajo etymology is unknown. This broad, 400-ft-high mesa immediately west of Arizona Highway 77 is five miles south of White Cone.

✤ Role in Hillerman Fiction:

Talking God: The road to Agnes Tsosie's place passes the backside of Tesihim Butte (chap. 3).

TES NEZ IHA: (4800 ft) Apache County, AZ. Navajos call this place T'iis'-Nééz Íí'á ("Tall Cottonwood Stands"). This small community on U.S. Highway 160 is situated on the west bank of Chinle Wash, about five miles west of Mexican Water. A trading post was established here in the early 1970s.

✤ Role in Hillerman Fiction:

A Thief of Time: Jimmy Etcitty lives between Tes Nez Iha and Dinnehotso (chap. 8).

TESUQUE PUEBLO: (5700 ft) (Population: 1,498) Santa Fe County, NM. The Navajo name for this Tewa pueblo is Tł'oh Łikizhí ("Spotted Grass"). The Tewa name is Tesuge, meaning "Structure at a Narrow Place." This Tewa village is related linguistically to Nambé, San Ildefonso, Santa Clara, San Juan, and Pojoaque.

Tesuque is located seven miles north of Santa Fe on U.S. Highway 285. It has been occupied since 1694, after the original village (location uncertain) was abandoned shortly after the Pueblo Revolt of 1680.

The long-range prehistory of the pueblo likely parallels that of its sister villages, with the ancestral populace arriving in the region about A.D. 1300.

The Spaniards established the Mission of San Lorenzo here, which was destroyed (and the priest, Fray Juan Bautista Pio, killed) during the Pueblo Revolt of 1680. Two Tesuqueans, Nicolas Catua and Pedro Omtua, were runners sent to alert other pueblo leaders of the schedule of the revolt. When they were betrayed and captured by the Spanish, the Tesuque leadership moved the revolt up by several days, and it seems likely that the first bloodshed was at Tesuque.

The people gradually accepted Catholicism after de Vargas's reconquest of 1692, as the church relaxed its opposition to indigenous religious practices.

The Tesuqueans and Navajos have generally had very little contact with one another, except that the Tesuqueans served as auxiliaries in military raids against the Navajos.

✤ Role in Hillerman Fiction:

Sacred Clowns: Santa Fe gallery owner Desmond Clark tells Joe Leaphorn that Tesuque, Pojoaque, and Picuris Pueblos may have lost their Lincoln Canes during troubled times (chap. 22).

THIEVING ROCK: (6302 ft) San Juan County, NM. The Navajo name is uncertain. This outcrop of sandstone stands atop a westward projecting peninsula of the southern periphery of Mesa Verde, high above the floor of Salt Creek Canyon. It is roughly 15 miles northeast of the community of Shiprock.

✤ Role in Hillerman Fiction:

Coyote Waits: One of Dr. Tagert's transcriptions of Ashie Pinto's story had old-time Utes passing here to raid Navajos near Teec Nos Pos (chap. 11).

THIRD MESA: (6000–6450 ft) Navajo and Coconino Counties, AZ. The Navajo name is uncertain. This is the westernmost of three "fingerlike" peninsulas projecting southwest from the southern edge of Black Mesa. Collectively, they are known as the Hopi Mesas.

Third Mesa is 15 miles long (northeast to southwest) and varies from a half-mile to five miles across. On it are situated the Hopi villages of Hotevilla and Bacavi; Oraibi sits on the eastern flank. It is bounded on the west by Dinnebito Wash and on the east by Oraibi Wash.

✤ Role in Hillerman Fiction:

The Dark Wind: Hopi Albert Lomatewa had to walk 30 miles to cross Wepo Wash and climb the cliffs of Third Mesa after discovering the body of "John Doe" with fingers, palms, toes, and soles skinned off (chap. 3).

THOREAU: (7172 ft) McKinley County, NM. The Navajo name is Dłǫ́'áyázhí, "Little Prairie Dogs." This substantially Mormon village sits on the north side of the Burlington Northern Santa Fe Railroad and Interstate 40, 32 miles east of Gallup.

Old maps show the location immediately east of Thoreau as "Navajo" and "Campbell's Pass." The site of the town was laid out soon after the arrival of the Atlantic and Pacific Railroad in 1881. A sawmill was built the same year, and the village was known as "Mitchell," after the sawmill's owners, Austin and William Mitchell (who hailed from Cadillac, Michigan). They purchased 314,668 acres for the townsite from the Atlantic and Pacific Railroad at $2 per acre.

According to historian Richard Van Valkenburgh, the Mitchells sold the site to the Hyde brothers (financiers of the Hyde Exploring Expeditions to Chaco Canyon) during the 1890s, after the sawmill had ceased operations. They renamed the village for the naturalist author Henry David Thoreau, and used it as a freight point for Navajo art and crafts and for the plunder taken from the Indian ruins they were excavating in Chaco Canyon.

Around 1900, Herman Switzer encouraged a Thoreau trader to produce enough Navajo silver jewelry for commercial distribution by the Fred Harvey Company on trains and in the ubiquitous Harvey Houses along the tracks. Largo, a student of the well-known Naakaii Dáádiil ("Thick Lipped Mexican," also called "Big Lips"), was the leading smith during this period. Trading posts here have included Thoreau Mercantile (founded in the early 1880s and surviving until about 1970), Red Arrow Trading Post (opened just prior to 1900), and Lewis Trading (opened in the late 1940s).

When U.S. Highway 66 was rerouted a mile south of Thoreau in 1937, the town lost much of its livelihood. Navajo trading and stock shipping kept the village alive during the 1940s. An El Paso Natural Gas pumping station was constructed here, and mining—especially of uranium—was the mainstay of the community, until the early 1980s.

Today the community seems to exist almost exclusively for the schools situated there: Gallup-McKinley County Schools (Thoreau Elementary, Middle, and High Schools), Dló'áyázhí, a BIA Boarding School, and St. Bonaventure Catholic Mission School.

✤ Role in Hillerman Fiction:

People of Darkness: Captain Leaphorn asks Chee to check with a family at Thoreau concerning a man killed in a pedestrian hit-and-run accident (chap. 6). The sister of Windy Tsossie (a survivor of the oil rig explosion) lives between Thoreau and Crownpoint (chap. 28).

Sacred Clowns: Delmar Kanitewa was attending school in Thoreau, but left abruptly upon the murder of Eric Dorsey, the shop teacher (chap. 1). Murder suspect Eugene Ahkeah lives at Thoreau (chap. 5). Delmar Kanitewa's best friend Felix Bluehorse goes to school in Thoreau, even though he lives with his mother in Crownpoint (chap. 9). Delmar Kanitewa's dad had been driving to Gallup with Kanitewa, but dropped Kanitewa in Thoreau to pick up his friend's class project (a silver bracelet) from Eric Dorsey the afternoon of Dorsey's murder (chap. 9). From his home in Window Rock, Joe Leaphorn calls the police substation at Crownpoint, leaving a message for Lieutenant Ed Toddy to meet him at St. Bonaventure Mission in Thoreau (chap. 21). After dropping Eugene Ahkeah at his home in Thoreau, Jim Chee and Janet Pete drive in silence through "heavy traffic" between Thoreau and Farmington: a car and two pickup trucks in nearly 80 miles (chap. 26).

THREE TURKEY RUIN: (6400 ft) Apache County, AZ. Also Three Turkey House. Navajos call this ruin Chíiłigai ("White Ochre"), Tséníí' Kiní ("Rock Niche House"), and Tsązhii Bikin ("Turkey's House"). This Anasazi ruin sits at the headwaters of Three Turkey Canyon, six miles south of Canyon de Chelly. (The canyon is also known as Whitish Red Ochre Canyon.)

This 19-room cliff-dwelling dates to A.D. 1266–76, and was visited by Sam and Charley Day in 1900 under the guidance of Hataałiinééz. It is one of the best preserved cliff dwellings in Navajo country. Three red and white figures identified as turkeys, handprints, or gourds are visible on the plaster of one room. A small permanent stream trickles down the canyon, which also contains many old Navajo hogan sites predating the Long Walk of 1864. At the head of the canyon is an old deposit of ochre, which Navajos use in making the pigments used in sandpaintings.

✤ Role in Hillerman Fiction:

Skinwalkers: Three Turkey Ruin is marked on Leaphorn's map with a "q," meaning "quicksand" in Tse Des Zygee Wash (chap. 2).

TOADLENA: (7172 ft) San Juan County, NM. Navajos call this place Tó Háálį́, meaning "Water Flows Up." Located in the vicinity of numerous springs on the eastern slopes of the Chuska Mountains, this trading post and BIA school community sits 13 miles west of U.S. Highway 666, 60 miles north of Gallup.

Though the Navajos had settled here many years earlier, the post office came in 1917. A Mrs. Cole, a missionary at Toadlena around the turn of the century, served as a doctor to the traders and the Navajos along the eastern slope of the Chuskas. In the 1930s, there was a USIS hospital here.

The boarding school, the seventh on the reservation, was established in 1913 under the supervision of Agent W. T. Shelton, on land purchased for $600 from a Navajo known as "One Eyed Medicine Man."

Nearby was a Navajo dam and canal predating 1880. The Wetherill brothers rebuilt it in 1904 and called it Wetherill Canal. It did not meet their needs and was abandoned shortly thereafter. However, Navajos repaired it and it was still in use in 1941.

Toadlena Trading Post was built in 1909 by Merritt and Bob Smith. Shortly thereafter it was bought by George Bloomfield. In 1926, Smith purchased Aneth Trading Post in Utah from Dick Simpson. George Bloomfield and the Toadlena Post, along with Ed Davies and the Two Grey Hills Trading Post, played a role in the development of the Two Grey Hills–style Navajo rug.

✤ Role in Hillerman Fiction:

Listening Woman: Leaphorn's maternal grandmother was a renowned hand-trembler at Toadlena and Beautiful Mountain (chap. 18).

Figure 44. Historic Toadlena Trading post—still operating today, and now housing a spectacular museum of the Two Grey Hills Navajo rug and its weavers.

The Ghostway: A young boy getting off the bus from Toadlena school tells the police he saw a green sedan on the road from Two Grey Hills (Hillerman spells it Gray) toward Owl Spring (chap. 2). Leaving the Chuskas in the snowstorm, Chee had to drive three hours to get to the graded road leading toward the Toadlena Boarding School (chap. 23).

Skinwalkers: A girl from the boarding school at Toadlena was en route home when she saw an old Navajo man sitting in a pickup truck roughly at the point from which the shots were fired that killed Irma Onesalt (chap. 2).

Sacred Clowns: KNDN radio news transcripts from three days prior to Jim Chee's Crownpoint meeting with BIA Police Sergeant Harold Blizzard listed the replacement of the Toadlena school principal, who was retiring (chap. 8). Jim Chee drives past Toadlena on his way to see Frank Sam Nakai, his mentor singer (chap. 12).

Hunting Badger: Joe Leaphorn tells Professor Louisa Bourebonette that he used to live between Two Grey Hills and Toadlena as a boy (chap. 24).

TOHATCHI: (6300 ft) (Population: 661) McKinley County, NM. The Navajo name is Tó Haach'i, "Water is Dug Out with One's Hand." Linguist/historian Robert Young notes that though the wash here may look dry in summer, it used to be that one could scoop out sand by hand and quickly find the hole filled with water.

Starting as a trading post in 1890, this chapter settlement is located at the mouth of Tohatchi Canyon, at the foot of Deza Bluffs and Chuska Peak, and 24 miles north of Gallup on U.S. Highway 666. An Indian Service day school was opened in 1895, and was converted to a boarding school five years later. The community today includes public schools, a few businesses, quite a few homes, and BIA Chuska Boarding School. An El Paso Natural Gas pumping station was built across the highway from the village. The village's first English name was Little Water.

The community hosted a USIS hospital, Catholic and Christian Reformed churches, and a trading post run in 1941 by Albert Arnold. Chuska Trading Post opened in the mid-1960s. The boarding school, called Little Water, was only the second operated on the Navajo Reservation. A number of Anasazi pithouses are known in the vicinity of the community.

The southwest extension of the Chuska Valley, beginning at Tohatchi and extending south to Tohlakai, is commonly referred to as Tohatchi Flats. Navajos call this region Bis Niiyah, "Clay (or adobe) Storage Pit."

Tohatchi Trading Post was opened by George Washington Sampson, whom the Navajos called Hastiin Báí ("Gray Man"), in 1890. Sampson's first post had been at Sanders, Arizona, seven years earlier. In 1887 he operated a post at Rock Springs north of Gallup. He sold Tohatchi in 1892 to Percy A. Craig. (Later posts operated by Sampson included Tolakai and Coyote Canyon in New Mexico, and Lukachukai and Chilchinbito in Arizona.)

✤ Role in Hillerman Fiction:

Sacred Clowns: Jim Chee drives past Tohatchi on his way to see Frank Sam Nakai, his mentor singer (chap. 12).

TOH CHIN LINI BUTTE: (6400 ft) Apache County, AZ. Also Toh Chin Lini Mesa. The Navajo name for this mesa is uncertain, but it is named for Toh Chin Lini Canyon (Tó Ch'ínlíní, meaning "Water Flowing Out") at its base. The mesa is located on the western slope of the Carrizo Mountains, immediately south of Black Rock Point.

✤ Role in Hillerman Fiction:

The Blessing Way: Joe Leaphorn rode Sam George Takes's horse to Toh Chin Lini Butte in his search of Ceniza Mesa (chap. 15).

TORREON: (6370 ft) Sandoval County, NM. Also Dolion. Navajo: Ya'ni-ilzhiin, "Black (Dark) Pinnacle Above the Horizon." Also Na'neelzhiin ("Black Spots Extend Across"), referring to a line of old boundary markers. This small chapter community centers around a school on New Mexico Highway 197, 25 miles southeast of Pueblo Pintado, at the mouth of Piñon Canyon (Vicente Arroyo). The name Torreon is Spanish for a fortified tower, and is often applied to a combined tower and dwelling. It is an apparent reference to one or more of the numerous "fortified" Navajo sites in the region, which archaeologist Alfred Kidder asserted were occupied prior to 1800.

Local Navajos say that the Navajo name is derived from the view of Cabezon Peak some 20 miles to the southeast. The day school here, while it was run by the BIA Navajo Service, was the easternmost school in the system, being 100 miles east of Window Rock, Arizona. The school is now a Sandoval County school.

Colonel (Governor) Jose Antonio Vizcarra passed through this vicinity in 1823, and the most reliable all-season road to Chaco Canyon used to pass through Torreon.

Navajos in the Torreon area farm and raise livestock. The most common language in the area is Spanish, but most Navajos here speak this as well as their own language. A trading post was established here prior to 1920.

✤ **Role in Hillerman Fiction:**

Sacred Clowns: Jim Chee and BIA Police Sergeant Harold Blizzard search for Delmar Kanitewa at his mother's place near Torreon (chap. 10).

TOWOAC: (5800 ft) Montezuma County, CO. The Navajo name is uncertain. This community is the capital of the Ute Mountain Ute Reservation. The original village sits in the eastern foothills of Sleeping Ute Mountain, about two miles east of U.S. Highway 666. However, more recently, the Ute Mountain Casino, situated right on the highway, is also considered to be in Towoac.

The village houses tribal offices and BIA offices, as well as a small Indian Health Service facility.

✤ **Role in Hillerman Fiction:**

Hunting Badger: Professor Louisa Bourebonette needs to talk to anthropological informants at the Red Mesa Chapter House and Towoac (chap. 6).

TSAYA (TRADING POST): (5900 ft) San Juan County, NM. Navajos call this area Tséyaa, meaning "Under the Rocks." Located on New Mexico Highway 371, 10 miles north of Crownpoint, this trading post is on the north bank of the Chaco River at the mouth of Tsaya Canyon. (Historian Richard Van Valkenburgh described the location as 12 miles northwest of Pueblo Bonito in Chaco Canyon—either an error, or an indication that the post changed locations.)

The trading post was most likely built by H. L. Haines around 1887. It was run by Harvey Sawyer from 1906 until it was sold to the Blake brothers in 1910. Roy Burnham purchased it from the Blake brothers in 1918 (actually a rebuilt post).

Be'ek'id Łizhiní ("Black Lake"), situated one mile south of the store, has been identified by some Navajo medicine men as one of the stopping places in the wanderings of the early Navajo clans. Old (eighteenth- and nineteenth-century) Navajo campsites are found in the area, and numerous paleontological specimens are found in the sandstones and shales, which are of the Eocene geological period.

✤ Role in Hillerman Fiction:

A Thief of Time: At Coyote Canyon, Darcy Ozzie (of Old Lady Daisy Manygoats's outfit) tells Jim Chee that Slick Nakai had headed to a place between White Rock and Tsaya, before heading to Lower Greasewood (chap. 17).

TSAY BEGI: (5300 ft) Navajo County, UT. The Navajo name is Tsé Biyi, meaning "Rock Canyon." This broad, flat plain within Monument Valley lies east of Wetherill Mesa and southeast of Mitchell Butte.

✤ Role in Hillerman Fiction:

The Blessing Way: The clan of Luis Horseman's in-laws lives at Tsay Begi (chap. 1).

TSE A'DIGASH: Fictional location.

✤ Role in Hillerman Fiction:

Coyote Waits: According to Hillerman, the Navajo name means "Witchery Rock." This is very close to where Officer Delbert Nez is killed (chap. 10); it turns out to be the rock painted by the mysterious painter sought by Nez the night he is killed (chap. 22).

TSÉ BONITO (PARK): (6700 ft) McKinley County, NM. Navajos call this place Tsé Biníí'tóhí ("Spring Midway up the Rock") or Tsé Bííni'Tó ("Spring on the Face of the Rock"). The Anglicized "Tsé Bonito" is often misinterpreted as "Pretty Rocks," a mixture of Navajo (Tsé, meaning "rocks") and Spanish (Bonito, meaning "pretty").

This commercial suburb of Window Rock, Arizona, straddles the New Mexico–Arizona state line on Arizona and New Mexico Highways 264. Included are several chain fast-food restaurants, gas stations, a bank and a credit union, a motel, the Navajo Nation Museum and Navajo Nation Zoo, Navajo Arts and Crafts Enterprise, and a shopping center that once boasted a movie theater.

Tsé Bonito Trading Post was built by Lewis Sabin in 1932. He sold it to missionary Rev. Howard Clark in 1957, and it is operated today by the Griswold family, who formerly traded at Navajo, New Mexico (some 25 miles to the north).

✤ Role in Hillerman Fiction:

Sacred Clowns: From his Window Rock office, Jim Chee sees yellow trees and purple asters at Tsé Bonito Park.

TSE CHIZZI WASH: (6600–6100 ft) Navajo County, AZ. The Navajo name is Tséch'ízhí ("Rough Rock"). This 10-mile-long creek heads at Tse Chizzi Spring on Balakai Mesa, three miles southeast of Low Mountain. It flows north, then west, joining Polacca Wash some three miles west of Low Mountain.

✤ **Role in Hillerman Fiction:**

The Dark Wind: Pauling banks his plane to follow the course of this arroyo to avoid waking sleepers on the ground (chap. 2).

Sacred Clowns: Jim Chee can see autumn's yellow trees along Tse Chizzi Wash from his Window Rock office window (chap. 8).

TSITAH WASH: (5400–550 ft) San Juan County, UT, and Apache County, AZ. Navajos call this channel Tsiitah, translated as "Among the Hair." This dry wash east of White Mesa south of the San Juan River intersects the San Juan circa five miles upstream from Aneth.

✤ **Role in Hillerman Fiction:**

Coyote Waits: In the old days, Utes would travel down Tsitah Wash from Ladron Butte to raid on the Navajos near Red Mesa (chap. 7).

TUBA CITY: (4950 ft) (Population: 7,327). Coconino County, AZ. To the Navajos, this is Tó Naneesdizí ("Place of Water Rivulets"), a historic name referring to the irrigation ditches with which the Mormons irrigated their Moenkopi Wash fields. Older Navajo names include Sei Ha'a'eeł ("[Water] Washing Out Sand"), and Nahodits'ǫ ("Bog Hole"), referring to Charley Day Spring.

Tuba City is one of the largest communities on the Navajo Reservation. It is located at the foot of the southern escarpment of the Kaibito Plateau, at the junction of U.S. Highway 160 and Arizona Highway 264. It is a chapter seat, hosts several chain fast-food restaurants and a motel, and for decades had the only auto dealership (Chevrolet) on the reservation.

The name "Tuba" is from "Tuvi" or "Tuve," a Hopi chief who became a strong friend of the early Mormon settlers of this region in the 1870s. (He even accompanied Jacob Hamblin to Salt Lake City.)

Father Garcés reported an agricultural settlement of 50 "Mahave Apaches" here in 1776, along with Hopis cultivating their fields near a fourteenth-century pueblo ruin at the nearby site of Moenkopi.

Mormon missionary and pathfinder Jacob Hamblin passed through the vicinity on numerous trips to the Hopi villages during the 1850s and 1860s. In 1873, Horton D. Haight led a colony of Mormons to northern Arizona. They stayed at the site of Tuba City (then just Navajo cornfields) for some time, but moved on south to the Little Colorado River in the vicinity of present Holbrook. In 1875 another party of Mormons, under James S. Brown, arrived at

Figure 45. The Navajo Nation Police Headquarters at Tuba City, where Jim Chee is stationed in several of the Hillerman novels.

the Tuba City location and three years later Erastus Snow (later co-founder of Snowflake, Arizona) laid out the townsite.

While Mormon-Navajo relations were at first friendly, in 1894 the strife led to the killing of Mormon Lot Smith by a Navajo, and the tensions increased until federal intervention. In 1900, the Moenkopi Ward (of which Tuba City was a part) numbered 150 Mormons. In 1903, however, the Navajo Reservation was expanded to its present western boundary, and the non-Indian Mormons were forced to vacate the vicinity. They sold their property and improvements to the U.S. Indian Service for $45,000, and today the only evidence of the Mormon community at Moenkopi is the old cemetery at the Hopi village of Moenkopi.

In 1896, some of the first evangelistic missionary efforts on the reservation were initiated at Tuba City by the Gospel Union. In 1901, Blue Canyon School (the second boarding school built on the reservation, 18 miles to the east) was closed, and a boarding school for Hopi and Navajo students was opened at Tuba City a year later. The Western Navajo Agency developed from this school, eventually holding dominion over the entire western half of the reservation. In 1936, these regional jurisdictions were abolished in favor of the Central Navajo Agency at Window Rock.

There are at least two known sets of dinosaur tracks near Tuba City, and other geological features in the vicinity include the Stone Pumpkin Patch on U.S. Highway 89 (toward Cameron) and the Elephant's Feet, on U.S. Highway 160 (toward Kayenta).

Uranium mining took place in the Tuba City vicinity during the 1950s, and an old uranium mill is situated about six miles northeast of the community on U.S. Highway 160.

Figure 46. The famed Tuba Trading Post today is one of the main tourist attractions in the Tuba City region.

Tuba Trading Company was opened by C. H. Algert and was later owned by the Babbitt Brothers. The Babbitts conducted extensive remodeling in 1986. Another post in Tuba City was Navajo Trails, opened in the late 1950s.

❖ Role in Hillerman Fiction:

The Blessing Way: Murder victim Luis Horseman had a history of arrests here, as well as in Farmington and Gallup (chap. 10).

Listening Woman: Joe Leaphorn is stationed at Tuba City in this novel.

The Dark Wind: Jim Chee has been transferred to this subagency of the Navajo Tribal Police from Shiprock only a few months earlier (chap. 3). DEA agent Johnson (and later two unidentified men) ambush Jim Chee at his trailer house in Tuba City (chaps. 11, 25).

The Ghostway: Upon leaving Flagstaff, Jim Chee drives to Shiprock via Gray Mountain and Tuba City. Chee had memorized this part of the reservation when he was stationed at the Tuba City substation of the Navajo Police Department (chap. 22).

Skinwalkers: Joe Leaphorn sees "Tuba City Navajo" features in Jim Chee: tall, long torso, narrow pelvis (chap. 5).

Coyote Waits: According to Mary Keeyani, people would come from as far as Tuba City to have Pinto perform crystal gazing for them (chap. 3).

Sacred Clowns: A KNDN radio news transcript from three nights prior to Chee's Crownpoint meeting with BIA Police Sergeant Harold Blizzard listed a rodeo schedule change here (chap. 8). As in Window Rock, no one locks doors in the Tuba City police station (chap. 9). Jim Chee's supervisor, when he was stationed at Tuba City, told him of Joe Leaphorn's eccentricities as an investigator (chap. 9). When Jim Chee was stationed in Tuba City, Captain Largo often complained that he wouldn't follow regulations (chap. 20).

The Fallen Man: Jim Chee considers transferring Officer Bernadette Manuelito from Shiprock to Tuba City (chap. 9).

The First Eagle: Acting Lieutenant Jim Chee and Officer Benny Kinsman are stationed at the Tuba City Navajo Tribal Police substation (chap. 2). The missing Catherine Ann Pollard worked at the "little lab" in Tuba City (chap. 3). Victor Hammar, who had reportedly been stalking Pollard in Flagstaff, followed her to Tuba City (chap. 3). Pollard was last seen leaving Tuba City for work in the field (chap. 5). The deceased Anderson Nez had been spending most of his time in the region between Page and Tuba City when he contracted the plague (chap. 9). A lonely Joe Leaphorn calls Louisa Bourebonette in Flagstaff from Tuba City to tell her about Hammar stalking the missing Catherine Ann Pollard (chap. 10). Louisa accompanies Leaphorn back to Tuba City after his visit with her in Flagstaff (chap. 11). Jim Chee transferred from Shiprock to Tuba City after problems with Janet Pete, and after Officer Bernadette Manuelito asked for a similar transfer when she thought Chee was going to marry Pete (chap. 14). The missing Catherine Ann Pollard had been staying in a motel in Tuba City (chap. 15). A television station from Flagstaff is received in Tuba City (chap. 22). Janet Pete drives from Phoenix to Tuba City to discuss with Chee what they have in common and what they don't, and the future of their relationship (chap. 28).

Hunting Badger: Jim Chee has transferred from Tuba City back to his old home territory of Shiprock (chap. 2), as has Officer Bernadette Manuelito (chap. 2). Jim Chee remembers that he has banged up a couple of Navajo Tribal vehicles in his time (chap. 4). Horsekeeper's daughter Madeleine Horsekeeper, found at Red Mesa Chapter, teaches at Grey Hills High in Tuba City (chap. 6).

TWENTYNINE MILE CANYON and **WASH:** (5400–4000 ft) Coconino County, AZ. The Navajo name is uncertain. This deep, steep-walled channel comprises the last five miles of Shinumo Wash, as it empties into Marble Canyon of the Colorado River. The canyon is approximately 29 miles upstream from the juncture of the Colorado and Little Colorado Rivers—the source of the English name.

✤ Role in Hillerman Fiction:

The Dark Wind: Jim Chee visits Mary Joe Natonabah about someone trespassing on her grazing rights along this channel (chap. 18).

Coyote Waits: Mary Keeyani's youngest daughter saw a dust trail from a car (apparently carrying Pinto) traveling the road that went toward Twenty-nine Mile Canyon before it connects with the road to Cedar Ridge Trading Post (chap. 3).

TWO GREY HILLS: (5900 ft) San Juan County, NM. Also Crozier. Navajos call this location Bis Dah Łitso ("Yellow Clay at an Elevation"), referring to two Mesa Verde sandstone crags nearby. One of the most famous of the Navajo trading centers, Two Gey Hills is noted for its distinctive natural-hued Navajo rugs. The chapter house and trading post are located on the Toadlena road, 11 miles east of Newcomb. Early maps (prior to 1900) show the location as "Crozier."

Many prehistoric Anasazi and early historic Navajo sites are found on the mesas in this vicinity, many of which were discovered by Charles Bernheimer and Earl Morris in the 1930s. One mesa, lying east of Two Grey Hills and west of Newcomb, was named Cemetery Ridge because of the large number of burials uncovered.

Two Grey Hills Trading Post was founded near the old Dutch Reformed Church mission. The history of this post is among the best documented. Joe Wilkin (at Crystal only a year earlier) and brothers Frank and Henry Noel established this post in 1897. Frank sold out to another brother, H. B. Noel, in 1900. Win Wetherill purchased the post in 1902, and sold it to Joe Reitz (a former partner of Wilkin) two years later. An Englishman by the name of Ed Davies purchased a share of the post and later bought Reitz out. Vic Walker owned the structures in 1938, taking Walter Scribner as a partner in 1941. Willard and Marie Leighton purchased it in 1948. Derold Stock became a partner in 1972, but sold his interest back to Marie Leighton in 1981. Les Wilson purchased the post in 1987.

The Noels were instrumental in originating the Two Grey Hills style of rug, showing the Navajo weavers pictures of Persian rugs and publishing brochures and small catalogs to push the resulting rugs back east. This is now one of the most famous and best recognized styles of rugs exemplifying the Navajo weavings.

❖ Role in Hillerman Fiction:

Listening Woman: Trader "Old Man" McGinnis remembers that Leaphorn's mother, Anna Gorman, was from here (chap. 5).

The Dark Wind: A young Jim Chee received the worst whipping of his life in the boarding school at Two Grey Hills—at the hands of a maternal cousin (chap. 3).

The Ghostway: A young boy getting off the bus from Toadlena school tells the police he saw a green sedan on the road from Two Grey Hills (Hillerman spells it Gray) toward Owl Spring (chap. 2). Jim Chee learns at Two Grey Hills Trading Post that Ashie Begay is a traditional Navajo, so he notes certain behavioral oddities at Begay's hogan in the Chuska Mountains (chap. 2). Begay has lived in the Chuska Mountains above Two Grey Hills as long as any-

Figure 47. Two Grey Hills Trading Post as it appeared in the fall of 2000. The photo was taken on a Sunday afternoon, when the post was closed.

one can remember (chap. 5). Twelve days after the shooting at the Shiprock Economy Wash-O-Mat, Hosteen Begay shows up at the Two Grey Hills Trading Post looking for medicine for a friend who is injured and in great pain (chap. 5). Jim Chee handled the case of a pinto mare stolen from the Trading Post (chap. 6). Chee remembers lonely winters spent at the boarding school at Two Grey Hills (chap. 7). [*Author's note:* This boarding school is fictitious.] Jim Chee calls the trading posts at Newcomb, Sheep Springs, and Two Grey Hills in search of the 17-year-old runaway, Margaret Billy Sosi (granddaughter of the missing Ashie Begay) (chap. 11).

Skinwalkers: Joe Leaphorn grew up in the Two Grey Hills region (chap. 15).

Sacred Clowns: Jim Chee drives past Two Grey Hills on his way to see Frank Sam Nakai, his mentor singer (chap. 12). Jim Chee and Frank Sam Nakai travel to Two Grey Hills seeking Hosteen Barbone, the hataali who knows enough about older clan relationships to tell Chee if can marry Janet Pete (chap. 24). Joe Leaphorn had watched his mother's flocks here as a child (chap. 27).

The Fallen Man: Adolph Deer, who jumped bond after a robbery conviction, is sought by Officer Manuelito at the Two Grey Hills Trading Post, as he has been frequently seen here (chap. 24).

Hunting Badger: Joe Leaphorn tells Professor Louisa Bourebonette that he used to live between Two Grey Hills and Toadlena as a boy (chap. 24). They drive through Two Grey Hills (chap. 24). Leaphorn calls Jim Chee from Two Grey Hills and finds out about the mine Chee has discovered in Gothic Creek Canyon, and wonders how thoroughly the FBI could have searched it; he decides to meet Chee for further exploration (chap. 25).

TWO STORY TRADING POST: (7100 ft) Apache County, AZ. In Navajo, this is Ts'íhootso, "Yellow Meadow" (the name for St. Michaels, the mission community just a couple miles east of the trading post).

The trading post is located on Arizona Highway 264 on the eastern slope of the Defiance Plateau. Sam Day, Sr. (who had previously left nearby St. Michaels after selling his property to the Franciscan Friars for a mission school in 1901), opened the post in the early 1900s with his son Charles Day. Sam first opened a post at Chinle after leaving St. Michaels. He sold that post to John Weidemeyer (son of the Fort Defiance trader Charles F. Weidemeyer) in 1905, moving first to Navajo, then to Two Story Trading Post. Charles Day took J. P. Peterson as a partner in 1915.

✤ Role in Hillerman Fiction:

The Ghostway: The blizzard that caught Chee in the Chuska Moutains looking for Ashie Begay had closed Navajo Route 3 from Two Story to Keams Canyon (chap. 23). Jim Chee and Frank Sam Nakai search the archives at the Navajo Community College in Ganado, and find a medicine man at Two Story, over by Window Rock, who can conduct the five-day Ghostway (chap. 24).

TYENDE CREEK: (6000–900 ft) Apache and Navajo Counties, AZ. Also Tyenda Creek. To the Navajos, it is Téé'ndééh, meaning "Things Fall into Deeper Water." Rising on the northeast slope of Black Mesa, near a feature known as "The Fingers," this normally dry wash flows northeast some 20 miles to merge with Chinle Wash 10 miles downstream from Rock Point Trading Post, and 10 miles east of Dinnehotso (on U.S. Highway 160).

✤ Role in Hillerman Fiction:

The Ghostway: Jim Chee tries to approach Frank Sam Nakai's winter place by driving across Greasewood Flats, Tyende Creek Canyon, and Carson Mesa in the deep snow, before turning back to Dinnehotso to try another approach (chap. 24).

Skinwalkers: Wilson Sam's dog watched over his dead body in a dry tributary of Tyende Creek (chap. 5).

UPPER GREASEWOOD (TRADING POST): (7200 ft) Apache County, AZ. The Navajo name is Díwózhíí Bíí'tó ("Water in the Greasewood"). This post, opened about 1900 (Kelley 1977, 252), was four miles south of Lukachukai on Navajo Route 12. It no longer exists. It has also been called Greasewood Springs.

✤ Role in Hillerman Fiction:

Skinwalkers: Irma Onesalt was killed between Upper Greasewood and Lukachukai (chap. 2).

Figure 48. In winter, Wheatfields Lake freezes solidly enough to be a favorite ice-fishing location among Navajos and non-Indians alike.

UPPER WHEATFIELDS: (6300 ft) Apache County, AZ. Also simply Wheatfields. Navajos call this region Tó Dzís'á ("Strip of Water Extending Away into the Distance"), referring to a series of small lakes. Early Spanish intruders named the region Canyon de Trigo ("Wheatfield Canyon") for the fields of Navajo wheat found growing here, and the U.S. Army used the area (then called Cienega Juanico) for growing grain for Fort Defiance.

Situated 30 miles north of Fort Defiance, this community sits where Route 12 crosses Wheatfields Creek. (This stream, after passing through farming country, joins Whiskey Creek to form the headwaters of Canyon de Chelly.)

After traveling westward through Narbona (formerly Washington) Pass, Colonel John M. Washington traversed this vicinity in the summer of 1849. Lieutenant James Simpson reported that a great number of Navajo wheat fields were destroyed here. In 1864, Captain Albert Pfeiffer and his command "rounded up" the Navajos of this vicinity while making a circular approach to Canyon de Chelly.

A government irrigation project had been approved by the Commissioner of Indian Affairs in 1886, and work was begun by Agent Samuel Patterson in 1887. In 1892 Lieutenant W. C. Brown recorded the water resources of the vicinity, including the excellent flows of water from Wheatfields and Whiskey Creeks. Today, a modern diversion dam irrigates hundreds of acres of Navajo farm land.

A small lava hill southeast of the lake is known to the Navajos as Beexh Wahaaldaas ("Falling Flints"), and figures prominently in the Navajo hunter tradition.

❖ Role in Hillerman Fiction:

The Fallen Man: The Navajo Ranger investigating the "poacher" reported above the Nez home goes through Upper Wheatfields in a futile effort to reach the area where the poacher was seen (chap. 12). Navajo Route 12 is closed here by the snowstorm hitting Jim Chee and Officer Bernadette Manuelito between Cortez and Mancos in Colorado (chap. 26).

UTE CASINO: This a fictitious establishment on the Southern Ute Reservation (*not to be confused* with the Ute Mountain Casino, at Towoac, on the Ute Mountain Ute Reservation).

✦ **Role in Hillerman Fiction:**
Hunting Badger: This fictitious gambling establishment is the scene of a robbery in which a guard is murdered (chap. 1).

VAQUEROS WASH: (7800–6600 ft) Rio Arriba County, NM. Also Vaqueros Canyon. The Navajo name is uncertain. This tributary to La Jara Wash heads a mile or so east of the juncture of U.S. Highway 64 and New Mexico Highway 537, about 10 miles south of Dulce. The stream's course is paralleled by U.S. Highway 64 to La Jara Canyon.

✦ **Role in Hillerman Fiction:**
A Thief of Time: Vaqueros Wash is scouted by Jim Chee in his search for Joe B. Nails, whom he believes to be the Backhoe Bandit (chap. 5).

WALPI: (6225 ft) Navajo County, AZ. To the Navajos this village is Deez'áají' ("Up to the Point [of the Mesa]"), and Niiyahkinii ("People of the Kiva," or, more literally, "Underground Houses"). The Hopi name, Walpi, means "Place of the Gap," a reference to a "notch" in the mesa north of the village. This stone pueblo is located at the extremely rocky southernmost tip of First Mesa on the Hopi Reservation, where its nearest neighbors are Sichomovi and Hano (Tewa).

Walpi was constructed about A.D. 1700. Its protective location across "the Gap" from the other First Mesa villages may have offered protection to it from the reconquering Spaniards following the Pueblo Revolt of 1680, as well as from Ute and Navajo raiders. Tully Rock, on the trail up the south side of the mesa, is engraved with the record of Navajos, Apaches, and Utes killed by residents of First Mesa.

Because of Hopi conservatism concerning archaeologists and anthropologists, the exact beginning of human occupation of First Mesa remains uncertain. Pithouses on the slopes of the mesa date to about the time of Christ, and shortly after A.D. 1300, the Anasazi ancestors of the Hopis built a pueblo called Walpi below the present village, on a ledge called Quchaptuvela ("Gray Slope").

The first documented European contact with Walpi appears to have been the arrival of Espejo in 1583. In 1629, when the first Franciscan missionaries established themselves in Hopi territory, Walpi was not important enough to house a mission, though a visita was constructed on the ledge at the tip of the mesa. Many Hopis from Quchaptuvela settled around the visita, bringing with them the name Walpi. After the Pueblo Revolt of 1680, the population moved from the ledge to the top of the mesa. Thereafter, the site they abandoned on the ledge was called Kiisa'ovi ("Ladder House").

Modern Walpi can be reached by a paved road from Polacca, on the desert floor, though as late as the 1950s the road was unpaved, more winding, and far more precarious. Walpi used to host the Hopi Snake Dance in odd years, during which time the road was closed and visitors had to hike to the top of the mesa.

✤ Role in Hillerman Fiction:

The Dark Wind: Jim Chee thinks the stone walls of Walpi give this First Mesa village the appearance of an extension of the stone cliff it sits upon, as he and Deputy Sheriff Cowboy Dashee drive toward the mesa to visit the village of Piutki (chap. 21).

Sacred Clowns: Deputy Sheriff Cowboy Dashee believes the clowns from Shongopovi, Hotevilla, and Walpi villages are "better" than those from Tano (chap. 1).

WASATCH MOUNTAINS: (11,877 ft) Juab, Utah, Wasatch, Salt Lake, Summit, Davis, Morgan, and Cache Counties, UT. The Navajo name is uncertain. This extensive mountain range begins near the center of the state and runs north, nearly to the Idaho state line. Contained within the range are Naomi Peak (9980 ft), Heber Peak (10,274 ft), Currant Peak (10,584 ft), and Mt. Nebo (11,877 ft), near the southern terminus.

The original spelling was Wahsatch, for the Shoshone chief Wasatch, who was friendly with the Whites and became a Mormon convert. These mountains lay well to the north of what is generally considered Navajo territory.

✤ Role in Hillerman Fiction:

The Fallen Man: This range is generally buried under three feet of snow before winter hits the Four Corners in December (chap. 16).

WASHINGTON PASS: See Narbona Pass.

WATERSPRINKLER CANYON: Fictitious. See Many Ruins Canyon for discussion of this canyon in *A Thief of Time.*

WEPO WASH: (7700–5590 ft) Navajo County, AZ. The Navajo name is uncertain. This 35-mile-long tributary of Polacca Wash heads near the northeast escarpment of Black Mesa and flows southwest, through Piñon (20 miles downstream), and passes under Arizona Highway 264 midway between Polacca and Shimolovi. It merges with Polacca Wash a mile south of the highway.

It was along this wash that Tewas, seeking the right to settle at Hopi following the Spanish Reconquest of 1692, pursued a band of Utes that killed eight Hopis in an attack on Oraibi. The Tewas caught the Utes and killed all but one, who was sent home to warn the Utes that Tewa warriors were now living with the peaceful Hopis.

This channel was explored by Colonel (Governor) Jose Antonio Vizcarra's 1823 expedition.

✤ Role in Hillerman Fiction:

The Dark Wind: Albert Lomatewa, the Messenger, had to walk 30 miles to cross this wash and climb the cliffs of Third Mesa (chap. 1). The repeatedly vandalized Windmill No. 6 (erected to provide water for Hopis resettling in this area) is located near this wash; Jim Chee is keeping the windmill under surveillance the night Pauling's plane crashes in the wash (chap. 3). Chee repeatedly searches the wash for the crashed plane's cargo, and for signs of the car or truck he heard in the wash the night of the plane crash (chap. 8).

WHEATFIELDS: See Upper Wheatfields.

WHIPPOORWILL (SPRING): (5200 ft) Coconino County, AZ. Also called Whippoorwill. Shown on most maps as Sand Springs. In Navajo, this place is Sáí Biis Tóhí, meaning "Spring in the Sand." This tiny community on Dinnebito Wash, in the barren flats of the Painted Desert of the Hopi Reservation, is 15 miles west of Navajo Route 2 and 20 miles south of Coal Mine Mesa.

A trading post was opened here prior to 1910, and closed before 1925. It was a business outpost of Lorenzo Hubbell, Jr., operated by a Navajo manager. Carl F. Steckel also traded here.

✤ Role in Hillerman Fiction:

Skinwalkers: Joe Leaphorn races past the turnoff to Whippoorwill on his way to join the wounded Jim Chee at Badwater Clinic (chap. 22).

Talking God: Officer Chee and Mary Landon had attended the final night of an Enemy Way at Whippoorwill the night Chee decided to ask Mary to marry him (chap. 7).

WHITE CONE: (6420 ft) Navajo County, AZ. Navajo: Hak'eelt'izh, "Head of One's Penis," a descriptive name. This peak sits atop the broad, irregular butte that lies adjacent to Arizona Highway 77, about four miles north of Deshgish Butte. This promontory, along with nearby Indian Wells and Sunrise Springs, is home to various Ant People and figures in the hero's search for his family in the Rounded Man Red Antway Myth.

The name also applies to a small trading community that sits a couple miles north of the geological feature. A possible Navajo name for this village is Baa'oogeedí ("Where It Was Dug Into"). This small chapter community is located west of Beshbito Wash, some 12 miles north of Indian Wells, on Arizona Highway 77. The community boasts a new "subdivision" of modern housing about two miles south of the ruins of an older, smaller community. Don Pedro de Tovar of the Coronado Expedition of 1542 passed by this White Cone on the old Hopi-Zuni trail on his way to Awatovi and the Hopi towns.

White Cone Trading Post was established here between 1916 and 1920.

There are at least two other White Cones on the reservation, and it is important not to confuse them with one another. Séí Heets'ósí Ba'áád ("Conical Sands Female") is a high cone of whitish, friable Chuska sandstone located west of the main scarp of the Tunicha Mountains, and about a mile and a half southeast of Wheatfields Lake. Séí Heets'ósí Biką' ("Conical Sand's Male"), sits on the south bank of Whiskey Creek about a mile east of Navajo Route 12, and approximately 10 miles northwest of Crystal, New Mexico. Both are considered ceremonial in nature, and are visited by medicine men in curative ceremonies.

✤ Role in Hillerman Fiction:

Talking God: Lieutenant Leaphorn travels toward this location from Bita Hochee on his way to see Agnes Tsosie (chap. 3).

WHITE HORSE (LAKE): (7000 ft) McKinley County, NM. Also White Horse Lake. Navajos call this vicinity Tó Hwiiłhíní ("Where the Water Killed One"), or Łíí Łigaii Bito' ("White Horse Spring").

This community is situated at the junction of New Mexico Highway 509 and Navajo Route 9, 12 miles southwest of Pueblo Pintado. It is home to Whitehorse Lake Chapter House. Two trading posts have operated here: Buck (established between 1916 and 1920) and Rangel (opened in the early 1940s).

✤ Role in Hillerman Fiction:

A Thief of Time: This region is scouted by Jim Chee in his search for Joe B. Nails, whom he believes to be the Backhoe Bandit (chap. 5).

The Fallen Man: Abrasive New Mexico Brand Inspector Dick Finch trails a rustler who "picks up a load" in this vicinity every six months or so, using the same method as was used at Shiprock (chap. 13).

Figure 49. The upper stories of the ground-level roomblock at White House Ruin in Canyon de Chelly once provided access to the cliff dwelling above it.

WHITE HOUSE RUIN: Navajos call this ruin Kiníí' Na'ígai ("House with White Stripe Across," or "White Stripe Across its Middle"). This canyon-floor/cliff-dwelling ruin is two miles upstream from the juncture of Canyons de Chelly and del Muerto. The yellowish-white room perched in a niche 30 feet above the canyon floor gives rise to the English name.

White House is named in the Night Chant as a home to Navajo deities, and as late as the 1940s, only medicine men would enter the site.

White House was occupied by the Anasazi between A.D. 1060 and 1275, reaching its peak about 1200. The section on the canyon floor contained about 60 rooms and four kivas, and was multi-storied, the upper floors providing access to the 20-room complex in the cave above.

As many as 100 people lived here. The ruin was visited in 1849 by First Lieutenant James Simpson and sketched by Edward M. Kern, artist of Brevet Colonel Washington's expedition to Chinle. The first scientific excavations of the site were made in 1893 by Cosmos Mindeleff, archaeologist for the Smithsonian Institution, who called the ruin Casa Blanca (Spanish, meaning "White House") following Simpson's notes. Some 30 years later Earl Morris of the Carnegie Institute carried on additional excavations. The ruin contains "Chacoesque" core-and-veneer masonry and a possible tower kiva, though many archaeologists argue that such architecture might be an independent development and not necessarily indicative of Chacoan influence.

❖ Role in Hillerman Fiction:

A Thief of Time: Anthropologist Eleanor Friedman-Bernal had traced one of her potter's pots to this ruin in Canyon de Chelly (chap. 6).

The Fallen Man: The sniper shot and wounded Amos Nez from the overlook to White House Ruin (chap. 6).

WHITE MESA UTE RESERVATION: (4800 ft) San Juan County, UT. The Navajo name is uncertain. This small (approximately 25 square miles), isolated reservation is situated on U.S. Highway 191, approximately midway between Bluff and Blanding, Utah. The community of White Mesa is the only community on the reservation.

✤ **Role in Hillerman Fiction:**

Hunting Badger: Joe Leaphorn visits Oliver Potts at his ranch on Recapture Creek, five miles northwest of Bluff, Utah, one mile down a dirt road (which places it very close to this reservation) (chap. 7). Everett Jorie's computer file suggests looking for Ironhand and Baker near Recapture Creek, below the Bluff Bench and south of White Mesa Ute Reservation (chap. 9).

WHITE ROCK: (6000 ft) San Juan County, NM. Also called Stoney Butte, a name applied by oil men working in the area. Navajos call it Tsélgaii, meaning "White Rock." This small chapter community is five miles west of Tsaya on New Mexico Highway 371, approximately 20 miles north of Crownpoint.

White Rock used to be the terminus of the road north out of Crownpoint, but this road has long since been extended all the way to Farmington. The name apparently refers to a crumbling rocky mesa that dominates the rolling badlands south of the Chaco River in this region.

Currently this is the site of a day school and a chapter house. White Rock Trading Post was listed by Van Valkenburgh as being in service in 1941.

✤ **Role in Hillerman Fiction:**

A Thief of Time: At Coyote Canyon, Darcy Ozzie (of Old Lady Daisy Manygoats's outfit) tells Jim Chee that Slick Nakai had headed to a place between White Rock and Tsaya, and then was bound for Lower Greasewood (chap. 13). Jim Chee and Janet Pete drive through this location on their trip from Gallup to Aztec (chap. 19).

WIDE RUIN WASH: (7600–5000 ft) Navajo County, AZ. The Navajo name is uncertain. This 60-mile-long tributary of Leroux Wash heads near Highway 264, atop the Defiance Plateau, about seven miles west of St. Michaels. It flows south and westward, past Klagetoh and Wide Ruin, before meeting Leroux Wash and Sabito Wash in the flats of the Painted Desert, three miles northwest of the northwest corner of Petrified Forest National Park.

Chee Dodge, first chairman of the Navajo Tribal Council, once owned land along the wash, at a place shown on McComb's map of 1860 as Jara Spring, about eight miles upstream from the wash's confluence with Leroux Wash.

Wide Ruin Trading Post was located on Wide Ruin Wash, 17 miles north of Chambers. It was named for nearby Anasazi Indian ruins, which date to the late thirteenth century and contain Chacoan architecture. The post took on the Navajo name for the ruin, Kinteel ("Wide House"), though outer sections of the ruin were also called Tsin Naajinii ("Black Streak of Wood"). The Zunis called the ruin Heshota Pathlta, meaning "Butterfly Ruin," descriptive of the way the site covers two sand hills suggesting the wings of a butterfly. According to Zuni tradition, this ruin was home to their Le'atakwe People, who took part in a great northward migration of the Bear, Frog, Deer, Yellow Wood, and other ancestral clans long ago.

The Spanish called it Pueblo Grande ("Large Village"), the name used on McComb's map of 1860. It is possible that Tovar and Cardenas of Coronado's 1542 expedition stopped at Wide Ruin. American military parties did stop here, including Major Shepherd's command in 1859. A trade trail between Zuni and Chinle also passed the ruin, and it was on this trail that the great Navajo Peace Chief Zarcillos Largos was ambushed and killed by New Mexicans and Zunis in 1862. It is said that Zarcillos Largos killed three of his attackers before succumbing to his wounds.

Historian Van Valkenburgh described a pitched battle taking place a few miles south of Wide Ruin in 1805 between Spaniards (and their Zuni allies) and Navajos, following the slaughter of Navajos in Massacre Cave (in Canyon de Chelly). It is also included in Navajo rite-myths and is considered a stopping place in Navajo clan migrations. This region was not part of the Navajo Reservation until 1880.

The first trading post at Wide Ruin was fortresslike, built of sandstone slabs taken from the 12-ft-high walls of the Anasazi ruin, possibly by Sam Day, Sr., as early as 1895. A larger stone post was built across Wide Ruin Wash in 1902. It was later owned by Spencer Balcomb, Wallace Sanders, and Per Paquette. Walter and Sallie Lippencott purchased it in October 1938. They sold it to the Navajo Tribe in 1950, but the tribe sold it to Foutz and Sons, under the name of "Progressive Mercantile," a few years later. Jim Collyer—son of a Crystal trader—took over the location in 1957. He was joined by John Rieffer in 1964. Rieffer and his wife, Sharon, purchased it in 1973. The post no longer exists, having fallen into ruins by 1987. A chapter house is now the community center.

✤ Role in Hillerman Fiction:

Skinwalkers: Looking out his Window Rock office window, Joe Leaphorn knows it's raining near Wide Ruin while Chee is visiting the Dinnebito Wash country (chap. 19).

WIJIJI: (6400 ft) McKinley County, NM. Navajos call this ruin in Chaco Canyon Díwózhiishzhiin ("Black Greasewood," Sarcobatus vermiculatus); Kin Dootł'izhí ("Turquoise House" or "Blue House"); and Díwózhiikin ("Greasewood House").

The easternmost pueblo in Chaco Canyon, Wijiji is on the north bank, approximately four and one-half miles upstream of the mouth of Gallo Canyon. The site consists of at least 206 rectilinear rooms and two kivas, all built around A.D. 1110–15, using predominantly Chaco Masonry Types III and IV. Extensive stabilization work has been conducted by the National Park Service (1940, 1941, 1959, 1975, and 1978).

This ruin is important in Navajo mythology, and in his *Diné Bikeyah*, Van Valkenburgh recorded a legend concerning the origin of weaving:

> Jiní. They tell. Once there was a Pueblo woman who was a Navajo slave. She lived at Turquoise House. While wandering about searching for food, she saw smoke coming out of the ground. Looking down into the hole from where the smoke was coming, she saw an old woman spinning. This was Spider Woman, and when she saw the woman's shadow cast over her, invited her to come down into her house. She saw that Spider Woman was weaving the first blanket. It was a full black blanket. On the next day, Spider Woman started another blanket. She made this one square and it was just as long as from her shoulder to the tip of her middle finger. This was called "Pretty Designed Blanket." On the third day Spider Woman wove another blanket with black figures on a white field. On the fourth morning the Pueblo woman returned to Spider Woman's home and asked for yellow, black and white cotton. Her loom was not like that of the Spider Woman, but like those used by the Navajo women of today. She made two blankets. Pueblo men watched her and then went home and copied.
>
> After that, the Pueblo woman went back to Spider Woman and learned how to make water jars, carrying-baskets and other woven things. Then she returned to the Navajo camp and showed the Navajos how to weave these things.
>
> Spider Woman told her always to leave a hole in the center of a blanket like in a spider's web, for if this was not done, it would bring the weaver bad luck.
>
> All these things happened at Turquoise House in Chaco Canyon.

Wijiji also houses a feature of suspected archaeoastronomy (prehistoric astronomy). Behind the ruin, stairs in the cliff lead to a ledge on the canyon rim. A sunface is found on the cliff near the point where the winter solstice sun rises over a natural pillar of rock. Sunset some days sees the sun set in a natural cleft.

❖ Role in Hillerman Fiction:

A Thief of Time: Missing anthropologist Eleanor Friedman-Bernal had evidence connecting St. Johns Polychrome pottery from Chettro Ketl with pottery from Wijiji and Kin Nahasbas (chap. 10).

Figure 50. The Navajo Tribal Police Headquarters in Window Rock, where Joe Leaphorn is stationed throughout most of the Hillerman novels, and where Jim Chee temporarily occupies a second-story office. This photo was taken from the east.

WINDOW ROCK: (6755 ft) (Population: 3,306) Apache County, AZ. The Navajo name is Tséghahoodzání, meaning "Perforated Rock." At the time the Central Navajo Agency was established, Ni' Ałníí'gi, "Earth's Center," was proposed, but never used, because Navajos ridiculed it as Ni'ałníí'gó, "Your Middle."

Originally a couple of miles north of Arizona Highway 264, nestled at the foot of the sandstone formation that gave it its name, the capital of the Navajo Nation has now spread out to include the junction of Arizona Highway 264 and Navajo Route 7, virtually abutting the Arizona–New Mexico state line and the community of Tsé Bonito. Window Rock is the seat of the Navajo government, with many office buildings, including the Tribal Police Headquarters and the Tribal Council chambers. Also present are BIA regional offices and a growing business community.

Until 1936, Window Rock was simply the site of one of the major scenic wonders of Navajoland. That year Commissioner of Indian Affairs John Collier selected the site for the planned Navajo Central Agency, and the buildings were constructed of locally quarried rust-colored sandstone. White difficulties in pronouncing the original Navajo name, combined with traditional Navajo aversion to profane use of a sacred name, led to the community being officially named Window Rock.

Tséghahoodzání, the natural arch immediately north of the tribal administration complex, is important in Navajo ceremonialism and rite-myths of the Tohee (Waterway Ceremony). It was one of the four places Navajo medicine men went with their basketry water bottles seeking water for the prayer ceremony for abundant rain.

An interesting historical site in the Window Rock vicinity is "The

Figure 51. Window Rock, the feature for which the Navajo capital was named, is now a tribal park, situated across from the offices of the President of the Navajo Nation.

Haystacks," which the Navajos call Tséta' Ch'ééch'i ("Breezes Blow Out from Between the Rocks") or Tséyaatóhí ("Spring Under the Rock"). Located a mile south of the Window Rock, this small basin dotted with red sandstone monuments (the Haystacks) is now home to the Navajo Nation Zoo and new cultural center, museum, and library.

Tséyaatóhí was the first stopping place out of Fort Defiance when some 400 Navajos started their "Long Walk" to Fort Sumner in 1864.

A ten-room, thirteenth-century Anasazi site sits beneath the Window Rock itself.

✤ **Role in Hillerman Fiction:**

The Blessing Way: Location of Joe Leaphorn's office at the Navajo Tribal Police headquarters (chap. 2).

Listening Woman: The Tuba City substation of the Navajo Tribal Police receives instructions from the police headquarters here in Window Rock (chaps. 2, 3). Leaphorn used to work out of this office (chap. 3).

The Dark Wind: Chee's orders to stop the vandalism (presumably by an angry Navajo) at the Hopi Windmill No. 6 on Wepo Wash come from the Navajo Tribal Police Headquarters at Window Rock (chap. 3).

The Ghostway: Jim Chee and Frank Sam Nakai search the archives at the Navajo Community College in Ganado, and find a medicine man at Two Story, over by Window Rock, who can conduct the five-day Ghostway (chap. 24).

Skinwalkers: Three unsolved homicides marked on Joe Leaphorn's infamous map took place near Window Rock, along the Utah-Arizona state line,

and at Big Mountain (chap. 2). This is the main headquarters of the Navajo
Tribal Police Department, and Joe Leaphorn is stationed and lives here (chap.
10). Irma Onesalt worked in Window Rock prior to her murder (chap. 18).

A Thief of Time: Joe Leaphorn leaves here with Bureau of Land Management law enforcement officer L. D. Thatcher to drive to Chaco Canyon to
search for the missing Eleanor Friedman-Bernal (chap. 2). This being the
main headquarters of the Navajo Nation Police Department, reports from the
Shiprock office are sent here (chap. 3). Joe Leaphorn lives in Window Rock
(chap. 4).

Talking God: Lieutenant Joe Leaphorn's office is on the second floor of
the Navajo Tribal Police Building (chap. 3). Leaphorn learns that a Yeibeichai
ceremony will be performed at the Navajo Tribal Fair here, for a man named
Roanhorse (chap. 3).

> *Author's Note:* Actually, the Yeibeichai is commonly performed at the
> Northern Navajo Fair at Shiprock in October, but almost never at the
> Window Rock fair in September, because of the seasonality of the cere-
> mony.

Coyote Waits: Officer Delbert Nez was working out of the Window Rock
office of the Navajo Tribal Police at the time he was killed, and additional
officers are sent from here to the scene of Nez's death (chap. 2). Joe Leaphorn
is stationed at Window Rock (chap. 5).

Sacred Clowns: Janet Pete notes that one cannot blame tardiness on
traffic in Window Rock; this is where Roger Applebee is to lobby the Tribal
Council against the planned national garbage dump (chap. 6). Jim Chee is introduced to Roger Applebee here (chap. 6). BIA Police Sergeant Harold Blizzard is too tired to drive home to Albuquerque, so he ends up spending the
night at Chee's in Window Rock (chap. 10). Joe Leaphorn thought he and
Asher Davis may have crossed trails early on at the Navajo Nation Fair (in
Window Rock) (chap. 21). Jim Chee is late for his rendezvous with Joe Leaphorn in Thoreau because he had to detour to Window Rock to drop off lawyer
Janet Pete (chap. 27). The story's finale takes place here, where FBI Agent Dilly
Streib witnesses one prime murder suspect murder another shooting suspect
(chap. 28).

The Fallen Man: Jim Chee worked under Joe Leaphorn (now retired)
when both were stationed at Window Rock (chap. 3). Joe Leaphorn lives in
Window Rock; John McDermott and George Shaw meet with Leaphorn at the
Navajo Inn in Window Rock to discuss Leaphorn working for them (chap. 10).

The First Eagle: Retired Navajo Tribal Police Lieutenant Joe Leaphorn
still resides here (chap. 3). The Indian Health Service agency in Window Rock
first reported Catherine Ann Pollard's disappearance (chap. 5). At Yells Back

Butte, Leaphorn reminds Jim Chee and Louisa Bourebonette that they met previously in Window Rock (chap. 15). Leaphorn had built their home here with their bedroom facing the rising sun, because it pleased Emma; the house and sun now seem empty (chap. 20).

Hunting Badger: Retired Joe Leaphorn meets with rancher Ray Gershwin at the Motor Inn dining room in Window Rock, where Gershwin gives him information on the casino robbery (chap. 3).

WINSLOW: (4938 ft) (Population: a little over 11,000) Navajo County, AZ. Navajos call it Béésh Sinil ("Iron Lying Down"), referring to the stacks of rails stored here by the Atlantic and Pacific Railroad (later the Atchison, Topeka and Santa Fe and currently the Burlington Northern Santa Fe Railway).

This trading center and former sheep-shipping point is located on Interstate 40, some 56 miles east of Flagstaff. In the first half of this century, the town was home to the Navajo Service Tuberculosis Sanatorium.

The first settler in Winslow is thought to have been F. G. "Doc" Demerest, a hotel man who lived in (and did business from) a tent in 1880. Shortly thereafter, J. H. Breed, previously trading above Sunset (Leupp) on the Little Colorado River, moved in and constructed the first store building. After the Atlantic and Pacific Railroad arrived in 1882, the town began a rapid growth. A post office was sanctioned on January 10, 1882, with U. L. Taylor as postmaster. Fourteen miles north on Arizona Highway 87, Borderlands Trading Post was opened in the early 1960s.

The origin of the name Winslow is problematic. Some believe that it honors General Edward Winslow (president of the old St. Louis–San Francisco Railway, one of the companies that merged to form the Atlantic and Pacific), while others suggest that the town was named after Tom Winslow, an early prospector and inhabitant of the town.

❖ Role in Hillerman Fiction:

The Dark Wind: Jim Chee sees rain clouds between Hopi and Winslow as he visits Piutki (on Hopi First Mesa) with Deputy Sheriff Cowboy Dashee (chap. 21).

The First Eagle: A secretary with the Arizona Highway Patrol in Winslow claimed one of their officers had to break up a fight in Flagstaff over a woman, between Officer Benny Kinsman and a Northern Arizona University student (chap. 2).

YA TAH HEY: (6700 ft) McKinley County, NM. In Navajo, this is Yá'át'é'héi, meaning "Hello." According to linguist Alan Wilson, the vicinity is also called T'áá Bíích'íidii ("Devilish Person" or "Go-getter"), referring to erstwhile trader J. B. Tanner.

This trading post and bedroom community is eight miles north of Gallup at the junction of U.S. Highway 666 and New Mexico Highway 264. The renowned J. B. Tanner Trading Company closed here in 1990. T & R Market was established halfway between Ya Tah Hey and Gallup in the early 1970s, and thrives today. Wells from Ya Tah Hey provide nearly all of Gallup's water supply.

✦ Role in Hillerman Fiction:

A Thief of Time: Joe Leaphorn and Bureau of Land Management law enforcement officer L. D. Thatcher drive through Ya Tah Hey on their way from Window Rock to Chaco Canyon to investigate the disappearance of anthropologist Eleanor Friedman-Bernal (chap. 2).

Coyote Waits: Officer Delbert Nez's beat covered from Ya Tah Hey northward (chap. 1).

Sacred Clowns: Jim Chee and BIA Police Sergeant Harold Blizzard pass through Ya Tah Hey returning from their search for Delmar Kanitewa over near Torreon (chap. 11).

YAZZIE SPRINGS: Fictional location in the general vicinity of (equally fictional) Short Mountain Trading Post.

✦ Role in Hillerman Fiction:

Listening Woman: A Wind Way ceremony was performed for a young girl at Yazzie Springs the previous January by a singer from Many Farms (chap. 5).

YELLS BACK BUTTE: Fictional location created by Hillerman is an outcrop on the west face of Black Mesa, apparently in the vicinity of Blue Canyon, just a few miles east of Moenkopi.

✦ Role in Hillerman Fiction:

The First Eagle: Officer Benny Kinsman dies while trying to catch Robert Jano, the Hopi eagle poacher (chap. 2). Jim Chee retraces Robert Jano's footsteps from the eagle blind to the place Officer Benny Kinsman was killed (chap. 12); he encounters Al Woody and his mobile lab van and questions Woody about the missing Catherine Ann Pollard. Woody admits to having seen her in the area earlier, over at Red Lake (chap. 13). Chee tells Joe Leaphorn of the old trail coming up the other side of Yells Back Butte, possibly used by the old lady with the goats (chap. 15). Jim Chee goes hunting for Robert Jano's claimed "first eagle" (chap. 23). Leaphorn and Chee interview old Mrs. Notah at Yells Back Butte about what she saw the day Catherine Ann Pollard disappeared (chap. 26).

YON DOT MOUNTAINS: (6235 ft) Coconino County, AZ. (Called by Hillerman Yondots Mountains.) The Navajo name is Yaa Ndee'nil ("Series of Hills Going Down"). These are the low hills midway between Marble Canyon (on the west) and U.S. Highway 89, approximately three miles southwest of Bodaway Mesa.

✦ Role in Hillerman Fiction:

The Dark Wind: Largewhiskers Begay's camp was here; he was accused of trespassing on Mary Joe Natonabah's grazing rights near Twentynine Mile Wash (chap. 18).

Coyote Waits: Hosteen Pinto had lived "behind" these mountains (chap. 3).

ZUNI MESA: A fictional location in the vicinity of Fort Wingate, New Mexico.

✦ Role in Hillerman Fiction:

Talking God: A murder victim, apparently thrown from a passing train, is found north of this feature, east of Gallup (chap. 3).

ZUNI MOUNTAINS: (7800–9256 ft) McKinley and Cibola counties, NM. Navajos call this range Dził Łání, meaning "Many Mountains" (at the western end); and Shashkin, meaning "Bear's Home" (south of Thoreau). This broken highland region stretches from Gallup east to Grants, and from Interstate 40 south to New Mexico Highway 53.

Alcalde José Ortiz of Laguna Pueblo led an expedition of 12 men into these mountains against the Navajos in 1818. Lieutenant A. W. Whipple's command traversed the range in 1853, though they were then referred to as the Sierra Madre.

Mount Sedgewick, at 9256 ft, is the highest point in the Zuni Mountains. The origin of this name is problematic, though there is speculation that the peak was named after Civil War Major General John Sedgewick, commander of the Union VI Corps. Sedgewick was killed by a Confederate sniper on May 8, 1864, in the Wilderness Battle (a prelude to the Battle of Spotsylvania, Virginia). He is said to have just brushed off warnings from his troops, declaring that the snipers "couldn't hit an elephant at this distance," when a bullet to the brain knocked him off his horse. He had earlier proven himself at Antietam, Chancellorsville, Gettysburg, and Fredericksburg, and Ulysses S. Grant considered Sedgewick "worth a division" of troops.

✦ Role in Hillerman Fiction:

People of Darkness: The Zuni Mountains form the southern boundary of El Malpais (chap. 13).

Figure 52. Viewed from the vicinity of Interstate 40 at the village of Bluewater, New Mexico, the Zuni Mountains take on the appearance of a series of steep-walled mesas. The higher peaks are located farther to the south.

Skinwalkers: Joe Leaphorn can see strips of fog over the Zuni Mountains from the fifth-floor windows of the Public Health Service Hospital in Gallup (chap. 22).

Talking God: The Zuni Mountains are visible to the south from the location of the discovery of a murder victim's body along the railroad tracks (chap. 3).

Coyote Waits: From the overlook at Washington Pass, Joe Leaphorn can see the Zuni Mountains to the south, the Jemez Mountains to the east, and the San Juan Mountains (in Colorado) to the north (chap. 12). In studying rock formation photos in the darkroom of murdered Huan Ji, Joe Leaphorn and Louisa Bourebonette conjecture the formations photographed could be in several locations, including the Zuni Mountains (chap. 17).

ZUNI PUEBLO: (6575 ft) (Population: 5,857) McKinley County, NM. Navajos call Zuni Naasht'ézhí "Marked About with Charcoal," referring either to black paint around the eyes of Zuni warriors, or possibly to an old house at Zuni that may have had a black streak around it.

This village is located 43 miles south of Gallup, on New Mexico Highway 53, some 17 miles east of the Arizona state line. The pueblo had a population of 2,220 in 1940. The name Cuni (with the "C" pronounced as an "S"), which apparently derives from a Spanish corruption of the Keresan word "Su'nyitsa" (the meaning of which has been lost), was first used by Francisco Sanchez Chamuscado in 1580. Antonio de Espejo used the name Zuni in 1583.

Hunter-gatherer groups moved into the Zuni–El Morro region about 5000 B.C. With the introduction of farming about A.D. 400, the occupants began to settle into small, permanent villages, the dawn of the pueblo culture. Certain architectural features suggest contact with the people of Chaco Canyon about

A.D. 1000, when the region may have hosted as many as seven thousand people. At the time of earliest European contact in 1540, Zunis occupied six villages: Hawikku, Kechiba:wa, Kyaki:ma, Mats'a:kya, Kwa'kina, and Halona:wa (today's Zuni Pueblo).

Fray Marcos de Niza led a Spanish exploratory expedition into the region in 1539, in search of gold and silver. His Moorish slave, Estevanico, was the first European to lay eyes on the Zuni villages, sending de Niza a message suggesting unbelievable riches at Zuni. The Moor did not live to see his leader's disappointment, as he was killed by the Zunis at Hawikku, after making himself exceedingly unwelcome. De Niza, after seeing the villages only from a distance, carried Estevanico's lie back to Mexico City, claiming to have seen the Seven Cities of Cibola. The following year, Francisco Coronado led the largest army the New World had yet seen against the Zunis and defeated them. The Zunis retreated to the top of Dowa Yalani, their sacred mountain.

Following a half-century of peaceful privacy, the Zunis were again visited by Spaniards in 1598, with no apparent violence. Father Andres Corchado was sent that year to be Zuni's first missionary. In 1629, the Catholic Church built Franciscan missions at Halona:wa and Hawikku. These first attempts at "saving" the Zunis led to the death of Fray Letrado at Hawikku in 1632, and the missions were abandoned and not reestablished until 1640.

In the Pueblo Revolt of 1680, the churches at Halona:wa and Hawikku were destroyed and the priests killed by the Zunis, who then fled again to the top of Dowa Yalani. Zuni tradition holds that a missionary at Hawikku at the time of the Pueblo Revolt of 1680 escaped the martyrdom experienced by the priest at Halona:wa, and was adopted into the Zuni tribe. In any case, the mission was finally destroyed in the Revolt of 1680. In 1772, another friar at Hawikku was killed by raiding Apaches.

The present village was built atop Halona:wa in 1692, and things seem to have remained rather peaceful, except for a war with the Hopis between 1705 and 1715. Mormons sent missionaries to Zuni in 1875.

When Navajos appeared on the scene, they were known to the Zunis as "Apachu." They appear to have instantly become "traditional" enemies, even though a good deal of trade was carried on between the two tribes.

For the next two centuries, the Zunis allied themselves with anyone willing to fight the Navajos, and played a role in the 1805 Mexican massacre of Navajos in Canyon del Muerto. Many small-to-moderate skirmishes took place near the Zuni pueblos between the Zunis and Navajos, Zunis and Hopis, and Zunis and Apaches between 1703 and 1882. One of the more memorable took place in 1846, when Navajos attacked the Zuni farming village of Pescado. When warriors from Halona:wa rushed to the aid of Pescado, a larger force of Navajos lying in wait attacked Halona:wa. However, the Zuni women and

Figure 53. The heart of the old Zuni village is occupied by the historic mission church and cemetery. The church is in dire need of renovation and repair, and may not last much longer without an outside source of funding.

children successfully defended the village. A treaty between Zunis and Navajos was signed at the pueblo under American guard on November 26, 1846, but Navajo raids resumed in January 1850 and April 1851.

A smallpox epidemic struck the pueblo in the winter of 1854. Apaches raided in October 1856 and January 1857. This latter raid had a profound effect on the Navajos, because a victim of the raid was Navajo Agent Henry Dodge, a friend of the Navajos who had also married into the tribe.

Zunis proved highly valuable as guides in Colonel Kit Carson's final Navajo subjugation campaign in 1863–64.

When the Navajos returned to their homeland in 1868 after four years of exile at Fort Sumner, they resumed their harassment of the Zunis. In 1882, Frank Hamilton Cushing, an anthropologist who had become Priest of the Bow Warrior Society, led a punitive expedition of Zunis to kill Navajo stock for encroaching on Zuni land. (There is considerable speculation as to whether or not Cushing fulfilled the Zuni requirement of killing a Navajo in order to become a member of the Bow Warrior Society.)

Today the Zuni economy is based on agriculture, livestock, and arts and crafts, with a healthy infusion of U.S. government subsidy. The population is the largest of any pueblo.

Several trading concerns have been based at Zuni over the years. Graham Trading Post operated here in the early 1880s; C. G. Wallace Trading Post was open from the early 1880s until the mid-1960s; Vanderwagen operated a post here prior to 1900; and Sabin-R. Wallace ran a post from 1906 to 1910.

❖ Role in Hillerman Fiction:

Dance Hall of the Dead: This entire novel takes place on or near the Zuni Reservation, even though the main character is a Navajo policeman. Leaphorn confers here with Zuni policeman Ed Pasquaanti (chaps. 2, 10, 17) and with Father Ingles, Order of St. Francis (chap. 11). Leaphorn attends a Shalako ceremony here, during which George Bowlegs is attacked (chap. 19).

Sacred Clowns: Jim Chee once saw a funeral at Zuni (chap. 3).

ZUNI WASH or ZUNI RIVER: (6500–5367 ft) McKinley County, NM, and Apache County, AZ. Navajos possibly call this channel Abétó, meaning "Hidden Spring." This stream drains from Black Rock Reservoir, four miles southwest of the confluence of the Rio Pescado and the Rio Nutria. It is tributary to the Little Colorado River 70 miles downstream, 10 miles southeast of Petrified Forest National Park.

❖ Role in Hillerman Fiction:

Dance Hall of the Dead: The Folsom site being excavated by Ted Isaacs is near this watercourse. Kothluwala, a Zuni sacred site, is located near the confluence of this wash with the Little Colorado River (chap. 13).

A Short Bibliography

While this volume is far less academic than *Navajo Places: History, Legend, Landscape,* and contains no direct references, it stands to reason that many readers might enjoy furthering their knowledge of Navajo places, place names, and history. The following is a short list of sources I have found to be especially readable and/or informative.

Bailey, Garrick, and Roberta Glenn Bailey. 1986. *A History of the Navajos: the Reservation Years.* Santa Fe: School of American Research Press.

Iverson, Peter. 1981. *The Navajo Nation.* Albuquerque: University of New Mexico Press.

Julyan, Robert H. 1999. *Place Names of New Mexico.* Albuquerque: University of New Mexico Press.

Kelley, Klara Bonsack, and Harris Francis. 1994. *Navajo Sacred Places.* Bloomington and Indianapolis: Indiana University Press.

Linford, Laurance D. 2000. *Navajo Places: History, Legend, Landscape.* Salt Lake City: University of Utah Press.

McNitt, Frank. 1972. *Navajo Wars: Military Campaigns, Slave Raids & Reprisals.* Albuquerque: University of New Mexico Press.

Mcpherson, Robert S. 1992. *Sacred Land, Sacred View: Navajo Perspectives of the Four Corners Region.* Provo, UT: Charles Redd Center for Western Studies, Brigham Young University. Salt Lake City: Signature Books.

Pearce, T. M. 1965. *New Mexico Place Names: A Geographic Dictionary.* Albuquerque: University of New Mexico Press.

Van Cott, John W. 1990. *Utah Place Names.* Salt Lake City: University of Utah Press.

Van Valkenburgh, Richard F. *Diné Bikéyah (Navajo's Land)*. 1941. 197-page, mimeographed Office of Indian Affairs Document. Window Rock, AZ.

Wilson, Alan, with Gene Dennison, Navajo Consultant. 1995. *Navajo Place Names: An Observer's Guide*. Guilford, CT: Audio Forum, Jeffrey Norton Publishers.

And of course, the Joe Leaphorn and Jim Chee Novels of Tony Hillerman:

The Blessing Way (1970)
Dance Hall of the Dead (1973)
Listening Woman (1978)
People of Darkness (1980)
The Dark Wind (1982)
The Ghostway (1984)
Skinwalkers (1986)
A Thief of Time (1988)
Talking God (1989)
Coyote Waits (1990)
Sacred Clowns (1993)
The Fallen Man (1996)
The First Eagle (1998)
Hunting Badger (1999)

All are published by HarperCollins Publishers of New York, and all have been printed in hard cover and paperback editions. Mr. Hillerman is currently under contract to publish three more Joe Leaphorn and Jim Chee novels.

Navajo Pronunciation

This volume includes proper Navajo spellings for most place and proper names, with requisite phonetic diacritical marks to assist the novice in pronunciation. The guide below will give the reader an idea of what the words are supposed to sound like. Sound is critical in Navajo, as slight variations in pronunciation can significantly alter the meaning of a word.

This simplified pronunciation directory is derived from similar presentations in Richard Van Valkenburgh's 1941 *Diné Bikeyah,* and my own *Navajo Places* (2000).

Vowels

Letter	Navajo Example	English Sound Approximation
a	gad (juniper)	father
e	ké (shoe)	met
i	sis (belt)	sit
o	tó (water)	go

It is important to note that a pair of like vowels (such as "oo" or "ee") does not change the sound, but simply elongates or draws out the vowel's sound. Thus, "tooh" is not pronounced like the English "too," but as an elongated or slow motion "toe."

Vowels with a "hook" beneath the letter are nasalized, with some breath passing through the nose during pronunciation. All vowels following the letter "n" are nasalized, and are not marked.

Letter	Navajo Example	English Sound Approximation
ąą	tsinaabąąs (wagon)	No real equivalent
įį	sįįl (stream)	

Glottal Stops and Releases

Any letter followed immediately by an apostrophe (') will end abruptly as the throat above the vocal cords is "snapped" shut:

Letter	Navajo Example	English Sound Approximation
k'	k'ad (now)	No real equivalent
a'	annaa' (enemy, war)	

Likewise, any word preceded by an apostrophe will begin abruptly, as the throat is "snapped" open:

Letter	Navajo Example
'a	'azee' (medicine)

Tone

Tone refers to the ending of a vowel sound, which may end low (regular) or high (as with a question mark in English). Two words spelled the same can have entirely unrelated meanings depending on tone.

Letter	Navajo Example
ee	'azee' (medicine)
éé	'azéé' (mouth)

Diphthongs

There four diphthongs in the Navajo language:

Letter	Navajo Example	English Sound Approximation
ai	hai (winter)	aisle
ao	ao' (yes)	no real equivalent
ei	séí (sand)	weigh
oi	'ayoi (very)	Joey

The diphthong "oi," as in "Joey," will often be heard as "ui," as in the English word "dewy." All diphthongs can occur with and without glottal stops, and all can be subjected to tonal differences.

Consonants

Letter	Navajo Example	English Sound Approximation
b	bá (for him)	"p" as in papa
ch'	ch'osh (bug)	"ch'osen" ("chosen" with a glottal release)
d	díí (this)	"t" as in tie
dl	beeldléí (blanket)	badly
dz	dziil (mountain)	adze
g	gah (rabbit)	"k" as in keep
gh	hooghan (hogan)	no real equivalent; like "get" with a gargled "g"
h	háadi (where)	jailai (slightly fricative)
hw	hwaáh (whew!)	when
j	jádí (antelope)	jewel
k	ké (shoe)	kick
kw	kwe'é (here)	queen
k'	k'os (clouds)	"k'ick" ("kick" with a glottal release)
l	laanaa (would that)	let
ł	łid (smoke)	"tlid," sometimes interpreted as "klid"
m	mósí (cat)	man
n	naadą́ą́ (corn)	not
s	sis (belt)	sew
sh	shash (bear)	show
t	tó (water)	top
t'	t'iis (cottonwood)	"t'oo" ("too" with a glottal release)
tł	tła (grease)	rattling
tł'	tł'oh (grass)	"rattl'ing" ("rattling" with a glottal release)
w	'awéé' (baby)	wet
y	ya (sky)	you
z	zas (snow)	zoo
zh	'ázhi' (name)	azure

Index of Places by Hillerman Title

Little Water Wash, NM
Montezuma Creek, UT
Monument Valley, UT & AZ
Mount Taylor, NM
Nakaibito (Also Mexican Springs),
  NM
Narbona Pass, NM
Newcomb, NM
Red Lake, AZ
Red Mesa and Red Mesa Chapter, AZ
Red Rock and Red Rock Trading Post,
  AZ
Rol Hai Rock, NM
Sand Island, UT
San Juan Basin, NM
San Juan Mountains, CO
San Juan River, CO, NM, & UT
Sanostee, NM
Shiprock (Community), NM
Shiprock (Pinnacle), NM
Short Mountain Trading Post (ficti-
  tious location)
Sleeping Ute Mountain, CO
Sweetwater and Sweetwater Trading
  Post, AZ
Table Mesa, NM
Thieving Rock, NM
Tse A'digash (fictitious location)
Tsitah Wash, UT & AZ
Tuba City, AZ
Twentynine Mile Canyon and Wash,
  AZ
Window Rock, AZ
Ya Tah Hey, NM
Yon Dot Mountains, AZ
Zuni Mountains, NM

Dance Hall of the Dead

Corn Mountain, NM
Coyote Canyon and Coyote Wash,
  NM
Gallup, NM
Nutria Lake, NM
Ojo Caliente, NM
Ramah, NM
Shiprock (Community), NM
Zuni Pueblo, NM
Zuni Mesa (fictitious location)
Zuni Wash or Zuni River, NM & AZ

The Dark Wind

Albuquerque, NM
Bacavi, AZ
Balakai Mesa and Balakai Point, AZ
Big Mountain and Big Mountain Trad-
  ing Post, AZ
Black Mesa, AZ
Blue Hill, NM
Blue Point, AZ
Burnt Water, AZ
Cameron and Cameron Trading Post,
  AZ
Cedar Ridge Trading Post, AZ
Chuska Mountains, NM & AZ
Coconino Rim, AZ
Colorado River, CO, UT, & AZ
Cottonwood, AZ
Crownpoint, NM
Durango, CO
Dzilidushushznini Peaks, AZ
Farmington, NM
Flagstaff, AZ
Gallup, NM
Garces Mesa, AZ
Hano, AZ
Hopi Buttes, AZ
Hotevilla, AZ
Joint Use Reservation (Joint Use Area),
  AZ
Keams Canyon, AZ
Kisigi Spring (location withheld)
Little Black Spot Mountain, AZ
Low Mountain, AZ
Many Farms, AZ
Mexican Water (Trading Post), AZ
Mishongnovi, AZ
Moenkopi, AZ
Moenkopi Wash, AZ
Navajo Mountain, UT & AZ
Newberry Mesa, AZ
Oraibi, AZ
Oraibi Wash, AZ
Padilla Mesa, AZ
Painted Desert, AZ
Piutki (name of an ancient Hopi settle-
  ment)
Polacca Wash, AZ
San Francisco Peaks, AZ
Santa Fe, NM

Hopi Mesas (Hopi Reservation), AZ
Inscription House Trading Post, AZ
Kaibito, AZ
Kaibito Creek, AZ
Kayenta, AZ
Mishongnovi, AZ
Moenkopi, AZ
Moenkopi Plateau, AZ
Navajo Mission, AZ
Navajo Mountain, UT & AZ
Nazhoni Trading Post, NM
Page, AZ
Rainbow Plateau, AZ & UT
Red Lake Trading Post, AZ
Rol Hai Rock, NM
Santa Fe, NM
Second Mesa, AZ
Shiprock (Community), NM
Shonto, AZ
Short Mountain Trading Post (ficti-
tious location)
Sleeping Ute Mountain, CO
Table Mesa, NM
Teec Nos Pos, AZ
Tuba City, AZ
Window Rock, AZ
Winslow, AZ
Yells Back Butte (fictitious location)

The Ghostway

Acoma Pueblo, NM
Albuquerque, NM
Black Mesa, AZ
Blanca Peak, CO
Blue Gap, AZ
Borrego Pass (Trading Post), NM
Burnham, NM
Cañoncito, NM
Carrizo Mountains, AZ
Carson Mesa, AZ
Chinle, AZ
Chuska Mountains, NM & AZ
Cottonwood, AZ
Crownpoint, NM
Dinnebito Wash, AZ
Dinnehotso (Trading Post), AZ
Farmington, NM
Flagstaff, AZ
Gallup, NM
Ganado, AZ
Grants, NM

Gray Mountain, AZ
Greasewood Flats, AZ
Hesperus Peak, CO
Jemez (Pueblo), NM
Kayenta, AZ
Keams Canyon, AZ
Laguna Pueblo, NM
Little Pajarito Arroyo, NM
Little Water, NM
Lukachukai Mountains, AZ
Mancos Creek, CO & NM
Many Farms, AZ
Mesa Gigante, NM
Mexican Water, AZ
Moenkopi Plateau, AZ
Mount Hesperus, CO
Mount Taylor, NM
Navajo Mountain, UT & AZ
Newcomb, NM
Owl Spring, NM
Red Mesa and Red Mesa Chapter, AZ
Rio Puerco (of the East), NM
Round Rock, AZ
Salt Creek Wash, NM
Sandia Mountains, NM
San Francisco Peaks, AZ
Sangre de Cristo Mountains, CO &
NM
San Juan Basin, NM
San Juan River, CO, NM, & UT
Santa Fe, NM
Sheep Springs, NM
Shiprock (Community), NM
Shiprock (Pinnacle), NM
Tah Chee Wash, AZ
Teec Nos Pos, AZ
Toadlena, NM
Tuba City, AZ
Two Grey Hills, NM
Two Story Trading Post, AZ
Tyende Creek, AZ
Window Rock, AZ

Hunting Badger

Aneth, UT
Aztec, NM
Beclabito, NM
Black Creek Valley, AZ
Blanding, UT
Bluff, UT
Bluff Bench, UT

Aztec, NM
Beautiful Mountain, NM
Bisti (Badlands and Trading Post), NM
Bitani Tsosi Wash, NM
Bloomfield, NM
Borrego Pass (Trading Post), NM
Bosque Redondo, NM
Chaco Mesa, NM
Checkerboard Reservation, NM
Chico Arroyo, NM
Chinle, AZ
Chivato Mesa, NM
Chuska Mountains, NM & AZ
Coyote Canyon and Coyote Wash, NM
Coyote Pass Chapter (fictitious location)
Crownpoint, NM
Crystal, NM
De Na Zin Wilderness, NM
Escavada Wash, NM
Fajada Wash, NM
Farmington, NM
Flagstaff, AZ
Gallup, NM
Grants, NM
Greasy Water Trading Post (fictitious location)
Hopi Mesas (Hopi Reservation), AZ
Hotevilla, AZ
Iyanbito, NM
Jemez (Pueblo), NM
Kayenta, AZ
Kimbeto Wash, NM
Kirtland, NM
Lake Valley, NM
Mexican Water (Trading Post), AZ
Mishongnovi, AZ
Mount Taylor, NM
Nahodshosh Chapter (fictitious location)
Nakaibito (Also Mexican Springs), NM
Naschitti (Trading Post), NM
Navajo Agricultural Industries, NM
Nazhoni Trading Post, NM
Newcomb, NM
Picuris Pueblo, NM
Pojoaque Pueblo, NM
San Juan River, CO, NM, & UT
Santa Fe, NM
Sheep Springs, NM

Shiprock (Community), NM
Shungopovi, AZ
Standing Rock, NM
Tano Pueblo (fictitious location)
Tesuque Pueblo, NM
Thoreau, NM
Toadlena, NM
Tohatchi, NM
Torreon, NM
Tsé Bonito (Park), NM
Tse Chizzi Wash, AZ
Tuba City, AZ
Two Grey Hills, NM
Walpi, AZ
Window Rock, AZ
Ya Tah Hey, NM
Zuni Pueblo, NM

Skinwalkers

Badwater Clinic (fictitious location)
Beclabito, NM
Big Mountain and Big Mountain Trading Post, AZ
Black Mesa, AZ
Blue Gap, AZ
Borrego Pass (Trading Post), NM
Burnt Water, AZ
Cañoncito, NM
Carrizo Mountains, AZ
Casa Del Eco Mesa, UT
Checkerboard Reservation, NM
Chilchinbito Canyon, AZ
Chinle, AZ
Chinle Wash, AZ
Chuska Mountains, NM & AZ
Cross Canyon (Trading Post), AZ
Crownpoint, NM
Crystal, NM
Dinnebito Wash, AZ
Dinnehotso (Trading Post), AZ
Farmington, NM
Flagstaff, AZ
Forest Lake, AZ
Fort Sumner (Old), NM
Gallup, NM
Ganado, AZ
The Goosenecks, UT
Greasewood Flats, AZ
Hopi Mesas (Hopi Reservation), AZ

Canyon Where Watersprinkler Plays
His Flute (fictitious location)
Carrizo Mountains, AZ
Ceniza Mesa, AZ
Chaco Canyon, NM
Chaco Mesa, NM
Chaco Wash, NM
Checkerboard Reservation, NM
Chetro Ketl, NM
Chuska Mountains, NM & AZ
Chuska Valley, NM
Comb Creek, UT
Counselors, NM
Coyote Canyon and Coyote Wash, NM
Crownpoint, NM
Dinnehotso (Trading Post), AZ
Dulce, NM
Durango, CO
Dzil Na O Dith Hle School, NM
Escavada Wash, NM
Escrito and Escrito Spring, NM
Fajada Butte, NM
Farmington, NM
Gallup, NM
Ganado, AZ
Glen Canyon, AZ
Gobernador Canyon and Creek, NM
Gobernador Knob, NM
Gothic Creek and Gothic Creek
Canyon, UT
Hogback, NM
Huerfano Mesa, NM
Jicarilla Apache Reservation, NM
Kayenta, AZ
Kin Nasbas, NM
La Jara Wash (and Canyon), NM

La Plata Mountains, CO
Lower Greasewood, AZ
Many Farms, AZ
Many Ruins Canyon (fictitious location)
Mexican Hat, UT
Mexican Water (Trading Post), AZ
Montezuma Creek, UT
Monument Valley, UT & AZ
Mount Taylor, NM
Nageezi (Trading Post), NM
Navajo Lake, NM
Navajo Mountain, UT & AZ
Nokaito Bench, UT
Nokaito Mesa (fictitious? Nokai Mesa?)
Ojo Encino, NM
Red Rock and Red Rock Trading Post,
AZ
Rough Rock, AZ
Salmon Ruin, NM
Sand Island, UT
San Juan River, CO, NM, & UT
Shiprock (Community), NM
Shiprock (Pinnacle), NM
Teec Nos Pos, AZ
Tes Nez Iha, AZ
Tsaya (Trading Post), NM
Vaqueros Wash, NM
Watersprinkler Canyon (fictitious location)
White Horse (Lake), NM
White House Ruin, AZ
White Rock, NM
Wijiji, NM
Window Rock, AZ
Ya Tah Hey, NM

The Author

While still in high school in Santa Fe, New Mexico, Larry Linford took a summer job washing potsherds. This started a 16-year archaeological career, the last four years with the Navajo Nation. In 1982 he became the Executive Director of the Inter-Tribal Indian Ceremonial Association, honing a deep respect for the ceremonialism and arts of America's Indian tribes. Since 1995, responding to a growing concern for the education of his sons (Justin and Micah) and other children, he has worked as grant writer for the Gallup-McKinley County Schools.

He has earned degrees from the University of New Mexico, the University of Arizona, and Western New Mexico University. Larry and his wife, Karen, have lived in Gallup, New Mexico ("The Heart of Indian Country") since 1978.